P9-ARO-626
39011012871929

Moved by the State

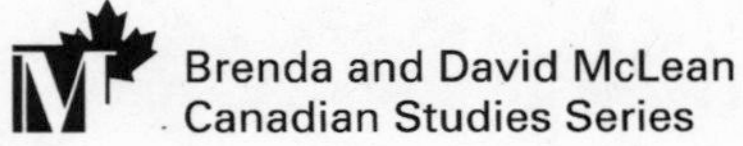

UBC Press is proud to publish the Brenda and David McLean Canadian Studies Series. Each volume is written by a distinguished Canadianist appointed as a McLean Fellow at the University of British Columbia, and reflects on an issue or theme of profound import to the study of Canada.

W.H. New, *Borderlands: How We Talk about Canada*

Alain C. Cairns, *Citizens Plus: Aboriginal Peoples and the Canadian State*

Cole Harris, *Making Native Space: Colonialism, Resistance, and Reserves in British Columbia*

John F. Helliwell, *Globalization and Well-Being*

Julie Cruikshank, *Do Glaciers Listen? Local Knowledge, Colonial Encounters, and Social Imagination*

Sherrill Grace, *On the Art of Being Canadian*

R. Kenneth Carty, *Big Tent Politics: The Liberal Party's Long Mastery of Canada's Public Life*

Tina Loo

Moved by the State

Forced Relocation and Making a Good Life in Postwar Canada

UBCPress · Vancouver · Toronto

© UBC Press 2019

All rights reserved. No part of this publication may be reproduced, stored in a retrieval system, or transmitted, in any form or by any means, without prior written permission of the publisher, or, in Canada, in the case of photocopying or other reprographic copying, a licence from Access Copyright, www.accesscopyright.ca.

28 27 26 25 24 23 22 21 20 19 5 4 3 2 1

Printed in Canada on FSC-certified ancient-forest-free paper (100% post-consumer recycled) that is processed chlorine- and acid-free.

ISBN 978-0-7748-6100-7 (hardcover)
ISBN 978-0-7748-6101-4 (softcover)
ISBN 978-0-7748-6102-1 (PDF)
ISBN 978-0-7748-6103-8 (EPUB)
ISBN 978-0-7748-6104-5 (Kindle)

Cataloguing-in-publication data for this book is available from Library and Archives Canada.

Canadä

UBC Press gratefully acknowledges the financial support for our publishing program of the Government of Canada (through the Canada Book Fund), the Canada Council for the Arts, and the British Columbia Arts Council.

This book has been published with the help of a grant from the Canadian Federation for the Humanities and Social Sciences, through the Awards to Scholarly Publications Program, using funds provided by the Social Sciences and Humanities Research Council of Canada, and with the help of the University of British Columbia through the K.D. Srivastava Fund.

Printed and bound in Canada by Friesens
Set in Garamond by Lime Design
Copy editor: Barbara Tessman
Proofreader: Lana Okerlund
Indexer: Marnie Lamb
Cartographer: Eric Leinberger
Cover designer: George Kirkpatrick
Cover images: *front,* photo by Bob Brooks, 1961, Library and Archives Canada, e010975945; *back,* photo by Bob Brooks, 1961, Library and Archives Canada, National Film Board fonds, e011177529

UBC Press
The University of British Columbia
2029 West Mall
Vancouver, BC V6T 1Z2
www.ubcpress.ca

In memory of Edwin Frederick Johnston

Contents

List of Figures and Tables / viii

Acknowledgments / x

Introduction / 3

1 "No More Canadians Will Starve!": Development, Discipline, and Decolonizing the North / 28

2 "The Governmentality Game": Problematizing, Resettling, and Democratizing Newfoundland / 56

3 "Artisans of Their Destiny": Participation, Power, and Place in Quebec's Backcountry / 91

4 "Deviating from the Strict Letter of the Law": Race, Poverty, and Planning in Postwar Halifax / 121

5 "A Fourth Level of Government"? Urban Renewal, State Power, and Democracy in Vancouver's East Side / 157

Conclusion / 197

Notes / 208

Bibliography / 247

Index / 265

Figures and Tables

Figures

I.1 Case study locations / 5
1.1 The Keewatin region / 29
1.2 "Near death," from Harrington's *The Face of the Arctic* (1952) / 31
1.3 From Rudnicki's "thematic apperception test," 1958 / 35
1.4 Workers in the shaft of a nickel mine, Rankin Inlet, 1961 / 39
1.5 Plan of mining buildings at Rankin Inlet, 1957 / 43
1.6 Artist working in clay at Rankin Inlet / 46
1.7 Pottery work area at Rankin Inlet / 46
1.8 Willie Adams adjusting the Comminterphone, 1972 / 52
2.1 House of Malcolm Rogers being towed by a boat, 1961 / 57
2.2 Newfoundland outports / 60
2.3 Robert Wells discussing resettlement with Dover residents, 1961 / 75
3.1 Eastern Quebec / 94
3.2 Map showing the location of protests associated with Opérations Dignité / 112
3.3 Demonstration in Esprit-Saint, 1971 / 112
3.4 Gathering to protest, Esprit-Saint, 1971 / 113

3.5 Inside the church at Esprit-Saint, 1971 / 115
4.1 Africville / 123
4.2 Gordon Stephenson's study area, 1957 / 131
4.3 Jacob Street, 1961 / 133
4.4 Areas targeted for redevelopment before Africville / 134
4.5 Building inspector John MacDonald working, 1961 / 135
4.6 "Boil water" warning sign in Africville, ca. 1965 / 138
4.7 Two Halifax officials outside an Africville house, ca. 1965 / 147
4.8 Africville resident orienting city officials, ca. 1965 / 149
5.1 The *Vancouver Redevelopment Study* area, 1957 / 161
5.2 The East End Survey Area, 1957 / 163
5.3 Dilapidated house in Strathcona / 164
5.4 Three phases of redevelopment in Strathcona / 165
5.5 Shirley Chan, Robert Andras, and the Chinese Benevolent Association, 1969 / 180
5.6 House under renovations in Strathcona, August 1973 / 188
5.7 Shirley Chan addresses a SPOTA community meeting, 1973 / 192

Tables

4.1 Settlements with Africville relocatees / 151
5.7 Settlements with non-relocatees / 152

Acknowledgments

THIS BOOK HAS BEEN a long time coming, thanks to vagaries of work and life. It would undoubtedly have taken much longer had I not had the honour of holding the Brenda and David McLean Chair in Canadian Studies at my home institution, the University of British Columbia. Chair holders have the privilege and the pressure of giving three lectures on their research to an audience consisting of members of the public, students, and faculty – which in my case included people who had taught me when I was an undergraduate biology major. Gulp. So my first debt is to the McLeans for their ongoing generosity in funding Canadian Studies and to Matthew Evenden, chair of the program at the time. You focused my mind. The three lectures I gave in 2015 are the foundation for this book. I wrote and delivered them while serving as department head. That I managed to do so was due largely to the administrative support provided by Jocelyn Smith, Janet Mui, Tuya Ochir, Jason Wu, Judy Levit, and Hart Caplan.

UBC's History Department is a stimulating place to work, because of the students in our classes and the colleagues in our corridors. I would like to acknowledge the graduate students and postdoctoral fellows I've been fortunate enough to work with over the course of writing *Moved by the State:* Tina Adcock, Adam Coombs, Brandon Davis, Henry John, Sean Kheraj, Nicholas May, Peter Robinson, Howard Stewart, Jocelyn Thorpe, Henry Trim, Philip Van Huizen, and Mark Werner, scholars whose work on topics sometimes far from my own pushed me to read and think about things I might not otherwise have considered. I continue to learn from my colleagues present and past, some of whom read parts of this manuscript: Michel Ducharme, Laura Ishiguro, Robert McDonald, Bradley Miller, Paige Raibmon, and Jessica Wang.

Parts of the research in this book have been presented to audiences at the Wilson Institute at McMaster University; the City Talks Series and the Landscapes of Injustice Spring Institute, both at the University of Victoria; the Seventeenth Annual Graduate History Conference at Dalhousie University; and the Rural History Roundtable at the University of Guelph. I thank them for their patience and their thoughtful questions, some of which I still have no answers to.

I've also benefited from discussions and feedback from many people, including Jerry Bannister, Stephen Bocking, Kevin Brushett, Emilie Cameron, Shirley Chan, Dan Coates, Julie Cruikshank, Peter Evans, the late Terry Fenge, Arn Keeling, Laura Madokoro, Suzanne Morton, Rosemary Ommer, John Sandlos, Andrew Stuhl, Frank Tester, Shirley Tillotson, Peter Usher, and Jeff Webb.

Chapter 1 appeared in slightly modified form in Stephen Bocking and Brad Martin, eds., *Ice Blink: Navigating Northern Environmental History* (Calgary: University of Calgary Press, 2017). Parts of Chapters 3 and 5 were published as "'We Was Drove!,'" in *Canada's History,* August/September 2013, 26–33 and "Africville: The Dynamics of State Power in Postwar Canada," *Acadiensis* 39, 2 (Summer/Fall 2010): 23–47.

A grant from the Social Sciences and Humanities Research Council allowed me to carry out much of the research in this book and to hire a series of crackerjack research assistants: Dane Allard, Brennan Dempsey, Giselle Giral, Connie Gunn, Scott Midgley, Elizabeth Paradis, Norman Potter, Amanda Ricci, Amanda Sauermann, and Kylea Thoms. Archivists Susan McLure (Halifax Municipal Archives), Melanie Tucker (The Rooms, Newfoundland), Robin Weber (Prince of Wales Northern Heritage Centre, Yellowknife), and Linda White (Memorial University) answered my many queries and made it possible for me to do research at a distance. Michel Ducharme and Stéphanie O'Neill helped with French translation.

Thank you to the two anonymous readers of the manuscript for their very helpful suggestions, to Eric Leinberger for the maps, and to Darcy Cullen and Ann Macklem at UBC Press for getting it over the finish line. Any errors are my own responsibility.

Not too long after I'd contemplated starting this project, I lost my partner to cancer. Many people helped get me back on track and keep me there.

For their friendship, support, enduring humour, and generosity, I am grateful to have these people in my life: Elizabeth Baverstock, Colleen Campbell, Janine Falck, Anne Gorsuch, Sarah Hechtenthal, Derek Loo, Eileen Mak, Robert McDonald, Suzanne Morton, Leslie Paris, Susan Scott, Meg Stanley, and John Stubbs.

Moved by the State

Introduction

IT WAS GOOD TO FINALLY BE STILL, and even better to be inside, sitting around the kitchen table. They'd spent the day with the men of Francois on Newfoundland's southwest coast, handlining for cod. It was as research for their book, published the next year as *This Rock within the Sea* (1968). Farley Mowat and John de Visser had intended the book as a celebration of a place and people they loved. But its purpose changed because of encounters like the one they had that evening. "It's been fine you come to visit us," said their host over tea. "But I'm wondering, could you, maybe, do one thing for we?"

> Could you, do you think, say how it was with us? We wouldn't want it thought, you understand, that we never tried the hardest as was in us to make a go of things. We'd like for everyone to know we never would have left the places we was reared but ... we ... was ... drove!"[1]

The vehicle driving them out was the Fisheries Household Resettlement Program, recently established and jointly funded by the government of Canada and the province of Newfoundland. Aimed at modernizing the fishery by consolidating its workforce, it offered residents of "outports" like Francois incentives to move to larger communities where better social services and economic opportunities were believed to lie.

Despite the fact that it was voluntary, Mowat considered resettlement nothing more than a "coastal clearance scheme." By the time the program came to an end, more than twenty thousand people had been displaced and hundreds of communities abandoned – largely for nothing. For many, the promise of a better life went unfulfilled. Instead, resettlement doomed outporters to become "rootless migrants" in "unlovely and unwished for industrial centres, there to lose themselves in the faceless jungles of mass-man."[2] As the scheme's effects became clearer, the tone of the book shifted from celebration to defiant lamentation: "We who had come to chronicle human life in its most admirable guise remained to record the passing of a people."[3] Resettlement had killed rural Newfoundland.

Outside of the context of war, outport resettlement is one of the better-known instances of forced relocation in Canada, thanks, in large part, to the work of writers and photographers such as Mowat and de Visser, as well as the painters, poets, and musicians who have rendered it into a defining moment in the island's history. Like the Grand Dérangement for the Acadians and internment for the Japanese, it forged a powerful collective identity centred on displacement and rooted in the island's imagined rural communities, ones peopled by small-scale producers. Poor, proud, and unpretentious, these folk also had little power. Many could only watch as their homes floated across the bay – destined, as they were, for an uncertain and often jarring landing. Embedded in the popular cultural representations of such uprooting was a critique of the urban and industrial, and of the modernization that underpinned the process and served as the rationale for the state-sponsored shifting of people from the places "they was reared."

A signal event in the history of the province, the Fisheries Household Resettlement Program as well as the censure it inspired weren't unique. From the 1950s to the 1970s, the Canadian state moved people, often against their wills, for what was believed to be their own good. In the chapters that follow, I examine five relocations that capture the geographic reach of the welfare state and the diversity of the people it moved. In addition to outport resettlement in Newfoundland, I look at the relocation of Inuit in the central Arctic, in what was then called the Keewatin District and is now the Kivalliq region of Nunavut; the closing of "marginal parishes" in the Lower St. Lawrence and Gaspé region of Quebec; the razing of Africville, a black neighbourhood in Halifax, Nova Scotia; and the partial destruction of Vancouver's East Side, a working-class and culturally diverse area with a sizable Chinese Canadian population (Figure I.1).

These relocations are well known in the regions where they occurred, if not far beyond them. Much of that knowledge comes from popular

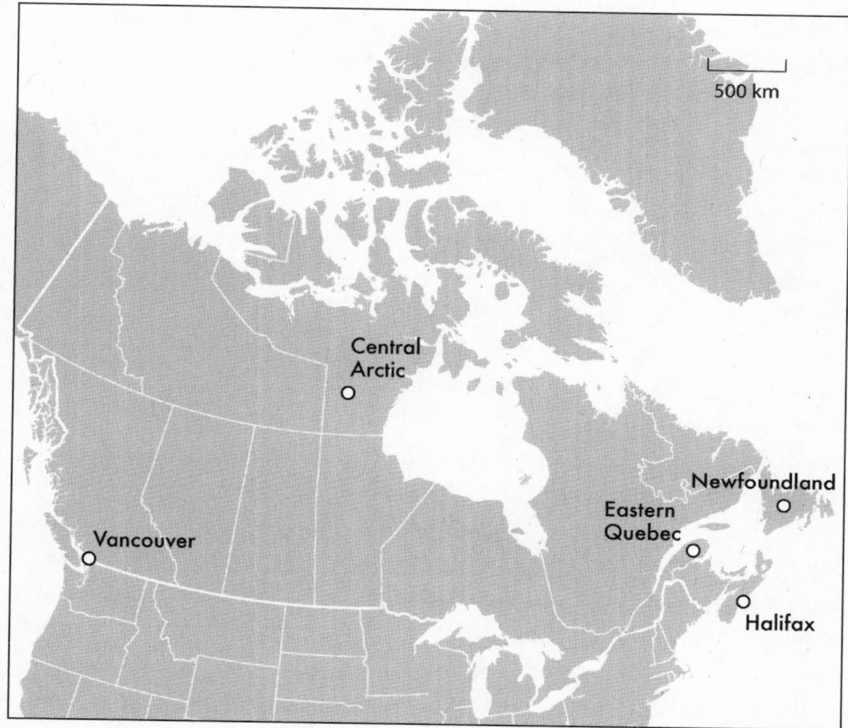

Figure I.1 Case study locations

historians and, as with Newfoundland, from novelists, poets, painters, playwrights, musicians, and filmmakers. Each of these relocations has also attracted the attention of scholars from different disciplines and to different degrees.[4] Together, this powerful work focuses on the experience of those who were displaced, on their trauma, their resentment, and, occasionally, their resistance.

In 2006, anthropologist Frédéric Laugrand and his colleagues interviewed some of the Keewatin Inuit who had been relocated in the 1950s. The violence of their removal remained with Job Muqyunniq more than fifty years later. He recalled the bulldozer driver telling his family to get out of their tent at Ennadai Lake, after which he drove over it, "back and forth," pulverizing their possessions. "This man had a stick … He directed us to the plane." Although the Inuit spoke no English, they understood his words: "He said we were garbage." Flown to Nueltin Lake in the spring of 1950 and left with no supplies, the group subsisted on fish and slowly began to make their way back to Ennadai by December. Not everyone survived. For Muqyunniq, it was "the saddest time of my life."[5]

Even when relocation was officially voluntary – approved by secret ballot rather than conducted at the sharp end of a stick – people often experienced it as coercion: many rural Newfoundlanders would have agreed with the fishermen of Francois who insisted they "was drove!" Confronted with the prospect of having to leave, some residents of Quebec's Gaspé region were equally clear: "I want to stay," said one. "Our home is our home," said another. The residents of the ironically named St-Octave-de-l'Avenir whom filmmaker Marcel Carrière interviewed were equally eloquent about the meaning of relocation. "I remember when I was young in school we learned 'never destroy a bird's nest – that will bring misfortune,'" recalled Aurèle Fraser. "It's not a bird's nest they're destroying, it's our families. I don't know if that will bring tragedy, but it's a bad omen."[6]

The better life that relocation promised – access to jobs and services, improved housing, and modern conveniences like sewers and safe water – looked appealing only if one ignored what really made for social security in places like Africville: a house that you could call your own, with neighbours you knew and trusted, people who were like you. "We all live in our own homes out here, detached homes, where our children can run around," explained Africville resident Leon Steed in 1963. "We couldn't go and live in no apartments [i.e., social housing in Halifax] today, segregated or not segregated, discriminated against as we are. Anything that happens, the first thing they're going to do is blame us: 'the Negroes is who done it!'"[7] Told that urban redevelopment would improve her life and that of her parents and neighbours on Vancouver's East Side, Shirley Chan challenged the picture government officials had of the "blighted" area she lived in: "I didn't know it was a slum until the city told me it was."[8]

It's impossible to ignore voices like these, ones that speak with such visceral force to the impacts of relocation. They resonate even as I take another approach, one that differs in three ways. First, I focus much more on the people who did the moving rather than those who were moved. In doing so, my aim is to attach faces and names to "the state," to render a picture of its agents that is as textured and empathetic as the one we have of the victims of relocation. In that sense, my purpose is broadly similar to E.P. Thompson's more than fifty years ago when he wrote *The Making of the English Working Class* – namely, to deliver a group of people from "the enormous condescension of posterity."[9] Despite the work that has been done on these relocations and the emphasis given to the power of "the state," we know little about the politicians, bureaucrats, university-based experts, and other professionals who designed and carried them out.

Their motives, rationales, and actions reveal a different aspect of the political culture of postwar Canada, an era we associate with affluence and anxiety, growth and containment. But as much as that was the case, the postwar period was also a time of hope. It was a time when people believed governments could and, more importantly, should intervene to improve the lives of citizens. It was a time when a belief that there was "a new world coming" inspired the work of those who laboured inside state and university bureaucracies as much as it did those who assailed them from the outside. As an exploration of the power of hope, *Moved by the State* takes seriously the sincerity and optimism that lay behind declarations that the government would "eliminate poverty" and build a "Just Society" with "citizen participation." It explores how people with some power tried to realize those hopes, all the while navigating a world of imperfect choices, where the boundary between benevolence and oppression was easily crossed. Understanding how they did so is crucial for anyone interested in the dynamics of "state power."

Second, I look at these instances of forced relocation together, rather than separately. Doing so reveals how pervasive it was as a strategy to make good on the state's promise of universality. Whether it was the departments of Northern Affairs, Fisheries, or Agriculture, or the Central Mortgage and Housing Corporation (CMHC), the welfare state saw social security as a question of spatial justice: it moved a diversity of people like the fishermen of Francois, Job Muqyunniq, Aurèle Fraser, Leon Steed, and Shirley Chan to places where more and better services and opportunities were thought to lie. Universality was inherent in the language of what T.H. Marshall called "social citizenship," the social responsibilities the state had to its citizens. Articulated most explicitly in the postwar period, they included everything from "the right to a modicum of economic welfare and security to the right to share to the full in the social heritage and to live the life of a civilized being according to the standards prevailing in society."[10]

The idea of social citizenship – that all citizens should share in the benefits of a common set of social welfare programs, have access to the same public services, and enjoy a certain reasonable standard of living – was visible in the creation of the Department of Northern Affairs and National Resources in 1953. According to its first minister, its purpose was "to give the Eskimos the same rights, privileges, opportunities, and responsibilities as all other

Canadians, in short to enable them to share fully in the national life of Canada."[11] Since being a Canadian precluded starvation, his department moved the Keewatin Inuit off the land and into permanent settlements.

Joey Smallwood, the man who would be his province's first premier, used the benefits of Canadian social citizenship to convince Newfoundlanders to say yes to Confederation.[12] For many, however, taking advantage of those benefits meant lifting "the curse of isolation" that bedevilled the island, something both his centralization program and its successor, the Fisheries Household Resettlement Program, aimed to do by consolidating the population.[13]

Similarly, razing Africville and relocating its residents was justified in the name of ending the segregation of this group of African Nova Scotians and giving them access to the basic municipal services like clean water and sewers that other Haligonians enjoyed. As town planner Gordon Stephenson noted in his redevelopment study of Halifax, "Africville stands as an indictment of society and not its inhabitants. They are old Canadians who never had the opportunities enjoyed by their more fortunate fellows."[14]

The state's pursuit of social security didn't end with forced relocation and the delivery of people to services and opportunities. The poor were rarely left to their own devices after being moved. Instead, they and the places they lived were the focus of "development" efforts aimed at extending social citizenship and upholding what Pierre Trudeau called the "right to a good life." For the Jesuit-educated justice minister, and later prime minister, "a good life" wasn't defined primarily in material terms. Instead, it was one in which people could achieve their full potential as individuals regardless of their location. As he put it, "Every Canadian has the right to a good life whatever the province or community he lives in."[15]

Examining forced relocations as part of a larger, more encompassing project of improvement rather than as ends in themselves is the third way my approach differs from existing work. *Moved by the State* explores how rural and urban poor from coast to coast to coast were relocated and remade into productive, self-sufficient citizens – or that was the goal. State-sponsored development aimed to "help people help themselves" by facilitating their participation in the fundamental decisions that shaped their collective futures. Doing so was the key to making a good life, to realizing their potential fully.

The state's efforts to improve the lives of Canadians were informed by concerns about regional inequality, the rediscovery of poverty, and international development, as well as by the ideas about universality and social citizenship I've noted. Canada is one of the most regionalized countries in the world and, early on, the federal government realized that its economic policies would have to deal with that challenge. Perhaps the best-known of these saw Ottawa provide subsidies to railway companies to lower their freight rates on goods moving into and out of the west and east. The Crow's Nest Pass Agreement (1897) facilitated the transportation of goods from the prairies to British Columbia and subsequently lowered the cost of shipping western grain to ports on the Great Lakes. Similarly, the Maritime Freight Rates Act (1927) allowed goods from Atlantic Canada to get to central Canadian markets at competitive rates. Ralph Krueger argues that, in addition to these transportation agreements, government subsidies to Canada's mining, fishing, forestry, and agricultural sectors to encourage production and modernization can also be considered efforts at reducing regional economic disparities. "Because the primary industries are for the most part located away from the heavily urbanized areas, the subsidies to these industries have helped buoy up the economy of these more peripheral areas, and thus have assisted to some degree in ameliorating the problem of regional disparities."[16]

While Ottawa's economic policies reflected the country's regionalized character fairly early on in Canada's history, it would not be until the 1930s and especially after the Second World War that its social policies did as well. In 1957, it introduced equalization payments, one of a number of measures that came out of the Great Depression and the Rowell-Sirois Report (1940). The events of the 1930s laid bare the differing abilities of the provinces to deal with mass poverty caused by the economic and environmental crises that defined the Great Depression.[17]

Equalization payments were meant to address these imbalances by ensuring the revenues poorer provinces accrued from personal and corporate income taxes and succession duties matched those of the wealthiest. By equalizing revenue, the federal government made it possible for all provinces to offer an adequate level of social services at comparable levels of taxation. As such, Penny Bryden considers equalization "a policy that enabled universality" as well as "a creature of the mid-century move towards universality" in welfare policy. While there were changes to the equalization formula over time, those details are less important for my purposes than the principle underlying the federal government's actions – namely, tackling poverty by reducing inequality among regions. Significantly, as Bryden points out, the principle of "regional universality" was entrenched in section 36 of Canada's Constitution Act (1982) "in a way that is not true for the universal programs in whose service equalization was established in the first place."[18]

In the 1960s and 1970s, concerns about income inequality led the state to intensify its efforts to reduce regional differences. Unlike Australia and the United States, where regional differences in per capita income decreased to the point of nearly disappearing after the Second World War, in Canada such differences persisted. Moreover, from the 1920s to at least the 1970s, the position of each region relative to the national average stayed the same, with individuals in British Columbia and Ontario earning the most, those in Atlantic Canada the least, and people in the Prairie provinces and Quebec consistently earning incomes in between them.[19] It was clear that the prosperity of the postwar years was unevenly distributed. Given this, the Economic Council of Canada, a federal Crown corporation that advised government, observed that "it would be hazardous to assume that rapid economic advance at the national level ... would be sufficient in itself to reduce income disparity significantly."[20] Reducing the economic and social disparities that came with growth would require programs tailored to the challenges of particular regions and locales.

To that end, the federal government introduced a number of national initiatives best known to Canadians through their acronyms: ARDA, FRED, and DREE, to name but three – the Agricultural Rehabilitation and Development Administration (1961), the Fund for Rural Economic Development (1966), and the Department of Regional Economic Expansion (1969). The government of Quebec took advantage of federal funding from ARDA to fund planning for the redevelopment of eastern Quebec, and DREE took over from the federal Department of Fisheries in funding and helping to administer resettlement in Newfoundland. All of these programs and departments aimed to modernize rural areas, something that usually involved spatial reorganization, including relocation, industrialization, and efforts to develop the human resources of the region.[21] Cities didn't escape notice: the federal state's efforts to tackle urban poverty emerged from a concern about the amount and quality of housing in the postwar years, something that led to the creation of the Central Mortgage and Housing Corporation (CMHC) in 1946. In 1956 the CMHC funded municipalities, including Halifax and Vancouver, to come up with comprehensive plans for their redevelopment. Restructuring city space through something called "urban renewal" would, it was believed, elevate the condition of all residents, particularly the poor, who would be delivered from the "slums" and rehoused in gleaming modern apartment buildings.

These programs, departments, and agencies speak to the growth of the Canadian state, especially during the *trente glorieuses,* the three decades after 1945, a period of economic growth and prosperity. Its interventions and expanding reach were justified in terms of the need to secure the welfare of all Canadians by countering the effects of the market. What one analyst identified as a key assumption underlying ARDA was true of the approach the state took to economic development and social security generally at the time. "The market alone is unable to guarantee the most efficient and desirable employment and the use of natural resources in every instance," observed James N. McCrorie. "Nor is it able to improve the standard of living of those ... who are under-employed, live and attempt to survive on marginal land or resources, or who are engaged in production of a commodity for which the demand in the foreseeable future is far less than the supply."[22] In short, the market alone couldn't assure a good life for everyone.

Given its shortcomings, bureaucrats and politicians from across the political spectrum believed they were right to use the power of the state to improve the lives of all Canadians, particularly those who were less fortunate. As we'll see, their interventions were shaped and propelled by a remarkable and widely shared confidence in the power of social scientific expertise to understand and transform the world, and especially its peoples, for the better. Dubbed "high modernism" by anthropologist James C. Scott, this belief was embraced by regimes from left to right and around the world. From the 1930s, and especially after 1945, their leaders turned to centralized, top-down, rational planning and scientifically informed management "to improve the human condition" – often with mixed and sometimes devastating effects.[23]

The efforts by Canada's politicians and bureaucrats to address spatial inequality were also shaped by the rediscovery of poverty in North America in the late 1950s and early 1960s. Just a little more than a decade after the end of the Second World War, unemployment became a concern for the first time since the 1930s. Like incomes and social services, it was also unevenly distributed. Residents of the Atlantic provinces and Quebec were afflicted by higher unemployment than the Canadian average, and many lived below the poverty line, commonly estimated at a yearly income in urban areas of $3,000 for a family of four and $1,500 for a single person. In rural areas, the rate was 80 percent of those figures. By this measure, estimates were that one in five, and perhaps as many as one in four, Canadians suffered from poverty in the mid-1960s.[24]

In addition to region, poverty levels differed by class, age, gender, and race. Income levels were lower in rural areas, among those with no formal education beyond elementary school, and where the head of the family was over the age of sixty-five or was a woman.[25] By Ottawa's own admission, the statistics for Indigenous peoples were "brutal": in 1965, an estimated 78.5 percent of Indigenous families had yearly incomes below $3,000. Indeed, over half had incomes of less than $2,000 per year, and over a quarter earned less than $1,000 per year.[26]

Statistics alone did not account entirely for Canadians' rediscovery of poverty. Michael Harrington's influential bestseller, *The Other America* (1962), called attention to the problem and shaped responses to it. The socialist and journalist argued that mass poverty existed amidst the general affluence of the United States. Numbering fifty million, the poor were nevertheless invisible, rendered so by the very growth that fuelled their country's wealth. Poverty had a rural face in an urban nation; it was, as Harrington put it, "off the beaten track." If city dwellers didn't see the immiseration that characterized parts of the countryside, neither did they come in contact with it closer to home. Over the twentieth century, urban space had become differentiated, and it was possible for people who worked, shopped, and otherwise conducted their business or pleasure in town to avoid seeing, much less coming into contact with, the inner-city poor. "The failures, the unskilled, the disabled, the aged, and the minorities are right there, across the tracks, where they have always been. But hardly anyone else is," Harrington observed. Urbanization had "removed poverty from the living, emotional experience of millions upon millions of middle-class Americans. Living out in the suburbs, it is easy to assume that ours is, indeed, an affluent society."[27]

Spurred by Harrington's book, Canadian journalists began to write about poverty above the forty-ninth parallel. *Maclean's* magazine ran an editorial praising US president Lyndon Johnson's "War on Poverty" in 1964, calling it "the most hopeful declaration of US policy since the salvage of Europe a generation ago." It regretted "the cramped spirit that has kept Canada's public men from initiating such an attempt," especially as this country was in a stronger economic position than its counterpart to the south. "We have never been better able to afford such a great idea and we have never needed one more," it concluded. Remarkably, from the perspective of the twenty-first century, Canadian business journals called for government intervention. As David Suderman put it in *Canadian Business,* the continued presence of the poor in Canadian society suggested that "the orthodox techniques of 'pump-priming' and economic management are no longer adequate – if they ever have been – to ensure that prosperity would be enjoyed by all."[28]

Sociologist John Porter's systematic, empirical study of class and power published in 1965 also shaped discussions of poverty. Rather than the egalitarian, diverse, middle-class society most in the country considered it to be, Canada, he argued, was best viewed as a "vertical mosaic," a place divided by ethnicity but more fundamentally by class. While the focus of Porter's book and the subsequent commentary was on the various elites that controlled Canada and the implications of that control for democracy, his message that the country was not the land of opportunity for all certainly resonated with those concerned with poverty.[29]

By the latter half of the 1960s, there was a sense among Canadian activists as well as its bureaucrats and politicians that things were not as they should be, that this was not the Canada they recognized or wished to live in. In the view of human rights lawyer Alan Borovoy, Canadians were reluctant to recognize the existence of inequality at home and he advocated that they think more and act on Porter's insights. R.A.J. Phillips was especially offended at the high rates of poverty among Indigenous peoples. As the director of the Special Planning Secretariat of the Privy Council told a Vancouver audience in 1966, "This is not some utterly forgotten, inaccessible, backward country we are talking about. It's Canada." The Economic Council of Canada was equally blunt. "Poverty in Canada is real. Its numbers are not in the thousands but the millions. There is more of it than our society can tolerate, more than our economy can afford, and far more than existing measures can cope with," it noted in 1968. "Its persistence, at a time when the bulk of Canadians enjoy one of the highest standards of living in the world, is a disgrace." For Liberal Justice Minister John Turner, dealing with poverty required structural changes. "We must disabuse ourselves of the myth that poverty is somehow caused by the poor," he told a gathering of North American judges in 1969. "We must recognize that the law often contributes to poverty. We must understand that, whereas the law for most of us is a source of rights, for the poor the law appears always to be taking something away. That we have to change."[30]

Following Johnson's initiatives in the United States and reflecting the optimism of the age, in 1965 the Liberal government of Lester B. Pearson announced it too would act by "developing a programme for the full utilisation of our human resources and the elimination of poverty among our people."[31] Canada's "war on poverty" was one conducted from within the walls of the Privy Council Office, through a Special Planning Secretariat (SPS). Because the provinces administered the majority of anti-poverty programs in Canada, it was impossible for the federal government to emulate the American model exactly and take the lead in forging new policy directions. The Special Planning Secretariat would not, as its director noted, administer new programs or embark on any "dramatic new budgetary excursions of its own."[32] Instead, its job was to coordinate existing initiatives across the country and raise awareness about poverty, to end the invisibility that Harrington argued was the chief obstacle to its elimination.[33]

Although the SPS was disbanded after just two years, its call for more social science research on poverty and its insistence, through its publications, that the poor be heard from directly and have a say in planning what was good for them continued to be articulated by the Special Senate Committee on Poverty (1968–71) and the Economic Council of Canada.[34] As will be discussed, these calls for greater citizen participation were heeded – albeit in different ways – in efforts to address poverty and immiseration in the North, Newfoundland, and eastern Quebec, as well as in Halifax and Vancouver.

If national efforts to deal with regional inequality and domestic poverty provide a context in which to understand the forced relocations examined in this volume, so too does international thinking. These removals reflected a particular moment in postwar history, one in which a "will to improve" informed the exercise of state power and pushed governments around the world to invest in "development" beyond their borders.[35] As other scholars have argued, that word naturalized a process that was anything but natural. Development – "growth with change," as the United Nations put it – was a normative concept. As such, some argue that, instead of asking what it is, it is more fruitful to ask what development was intended to do.[36]

To governments in the postwar West, development meant modernization, progressing through what the American economist Walt Whitman Rostow identified as universal "stages" of growth. Spurred by external demand for resources and new technologies, traditional societies would commercialize their economies and "take off." As they progressed to "maturity," defined as the "age of high mass consumption," they would acquire liberal democratic values and embrace individualism, private property, industrialization, and the free market. The job of governments and non-governmental organizations engaged in development was to overcome the innate conservatism of traditional societies, cultivating "individual initiative, risk taking, innovation, and freedom from kinship constraints and customary obligations" – in other words, the practices and values associated with liberal modernity and capitalism.[37]

As Michael Latham observes, modernization was both a theory and an instrument of global change, "a framework for objective social analysis and a powerful vehicle for social engineering."[38] During the Cold War, the government of the United States channelled money and experts to the "Third World," hoping to contain and stabilize the unpredictable and dangerous forces of decolonization and facilitate the transition to American modernity.

But even as the top-down Rostovian model of development was imposed around the world by foreign governments and the heads of newly independent states, there was resistance to it, both on the ground from those who were the objects of "improvement" and among intellectuals on the right and the left.[39] Modernization was never universally embraced, not even within the ranks of government. As Daniel Immerwahr argues, we shouldn't conflate development with modernization. During the 1960s, when Rostow's ideas reached the height of their influence, social scientists and policymakers also pursued "development without modernization." Community development initiatives aimed "to shore up small-scale solidarities, to encourage democratic deliberation and civic action on a local level, and to embed politics and economics within the life of the community."[40]

Regardless of whether Western governments thought big or small when it came to development, modernization was an ideological project that was premised on and generated new kinds of knowledge. Modernization theory linked the ivory tower to the corridors of power, bringing the social sciences to geopolitics. For instance, while he was director of MIT's Center for International Studies, Rostow advised US president Dwight Eisenhower on foreign and economic policy before being appointed to the Kennedy and Johnson administrations, eventually serving as national security adviser.[41] Anthropology was also deployed in the service of the state, particularly as the shortcomings of Rostovian modernization became apparent. Indeed, James Ferguson goes so far as to argue that development was anthropology's "evil twin." As experts on "traditional" societies and "primitive" peoples, anthropologists were well placed to do development work.[42] Ironically, their knowledge was deployed to transform the very societies they studied into ones that looked progressive, modern, and, as US senator Kenneth Wherry revealed, familiar. "We will lift Shanghai up and up, ever up," boasted the Nebraska politician in 1940, "until it is just like Kansas City."[43]

During the United Nations' "Development Decade" (1960–70), the Canadian state's energies of improvement were focused inward as well as outward, toward bettering the condition of those who lived in its underdeveloped regions and impoverished inner cities. Indeed, scholars of international development have challenged the distinction between "foreign" and "domestic" spheres, arguing that American perceptions of "others" at home shaped their approach to them abroad.[44] Taking up the insights of theorists such as Andre Gunder Frank and Immanuel Wallerstein that development was colonialism in another guise, they have called for work that assesses the connections between the American government's treatment of Indigenous peoples in the United States and its postwar modernization agendas in the Third World.[45]

International historian David Meren has begun to do that for Canada, exploring what he calls the "entangled history" of Canadian foreign aid and Aboriginal policy in the decades following the Second World War. Not only did the Canadian government's views and policies regarding Indigenous peoples influence its understanding of foreign aid, but Canada's experience in the global South also came to inform its relationship with Indigenous peoples.[46]

As with international development, making a good life in postwar Canada involved universities and social scientists as well as government departments and bureaucrats. They were all engaged in the task of assessing the material and human potential of Canada's poor rural regions and urban neighbourhoods. Doing so was just the beginning of their work: those tasked with development also believed that improving people's social condition was best guaranteed by cultivating community. But the kind of community they sought to build was not the insular, hide-bound, collectivity of an earlier era, the kind of traditional society Rostow and his followers criticized as an obstacle to modernization. Instead, the solidarities development workers aimed to foster were ones that encouraged people to come together in collectivities beyond the family, faith, and race to help themselves. Doing so required seeing community as a locality – a place – made up of people with a variety of views and to seeing strength and purpose in giving public voice to that diversity. Equally importantly, their initiatives were also designed to help people see their community (in all its diversity) in relationship to other scales of affiliation, including the region, province, and nation, and to parse their allegiances accordingly.

Creating the kind of community that could meet the demands of modernity often began with efforts to build the capacity of the poor to make decisions collectively, to participate in deciding the kind of future they wanted for their community and how they might achieve it. Those efforts reveal the influence of arguments about the "culture of poverty" prevalent at the time. First articulated by anthropologist Oscar Lewis in the late 1950s, this theory explained the persistence of poverty in terms of a set of attitudes and behaviours that had been inculcated in the poor by the material conditions in which they lived. The culture of poverty was characterized by "feelings of marginality, of helplessness, of dependence, and of inferiority." As well – and significantly, in terms of understanding the approach to development undertaken in the case studies I examine here – Lewis argued that two of its "crucial characteristics" were "a minimum level of organization beyond the level of the nuclear and extended family" and "the lack of effective participation and integration of the poor in the major institutions of the larger society."[47] In other words, the poor were not much part of civil society nor did they possess a civic culture. Echoing Lewis, the Economic Council of Canada argued that "to feel poverty is, among other things, to feel oneself an unwilling outsider – a virtual nonparticipant in the society in which one lives."[48]

Lewis's arguments were also evident in Maurice Sauvé's remarks about the role of government in addressing poverty. The member of Parliament for Îles-de-la-Madeleine in eastern Quebec and the minister of forestry considered it essential that the poor have a say in the policies undertaken to help them. Without such input, any state intervention was doomed to failure. But there was a problem: in his view, and that of others engaged in development, the poor lacked the ability to articulate their views and participate in such discussions. "Until the low-income groups are assisted in arriving at some consensus, and of more or less formalizing their demands, we can do little," he argued in 1965.[49]

The role of government was thus to help people articulate their demands, to introduce the poor to the institutions and practices of deliberative democracy. This was something best achieved through community development.[50] It would build the capacity to participate, to help people arrive at a consensus and formalize their demands. In explaining what community development was, Sauvé quoted directly from the United Nations' definition, underscoring the connection between international and domestic development thinking: "The term 'community development' has, in international usage, come to connote 'The processes by which efforts of the people themselves are united with those of governmental authorities to improve the economic, social, and cultural conditions of communities, to integrate these communities into the life of the nation, and to enable them to contribute fully to national progress.'" While these processes were complex, Sauvé contended that the "essential element" was "the participation of the people themselves, and the provision of services in ways which will encourage initiative, self help, and mutual help."[51]

Indeed, citizen participation was an important goal of development and not just a means to achieve it. Whether they were drawn from the ranks of government or the universities, those who were engaged in the project of improvement in Canada saw participation as a means of what we would now call "empowerment." Exploring how empowerment was elicited reveals the disciplinary aspects of making a good life, something hinted at by Sauvé's reference to "integrating communities into the life of the nation." It has been overshadowed by critics' narrow focus on relocation rather than the larger project of which it was a part. In postwar Canada, people weren't just moved by the state: they were also shaped by its subsequent efforts to craft a civic political culture; that is, they were subjected to sovereign as well as disciplinary power, to use Michel Foucault's terms. As political scientist Timothy Mitchell and anthropologist Tania Murray Li have argued for Egypt and Indonesia, "the rule of experts" and expertise in international development gave rise to different forms of power and domination that Foucault called "governmentality."[52] The term describes the techniques and rationalities used to produce citizens whose behaviours and ways of thinking made them governable. As we will see, addressing poverty in Canada through participatory community and regional development also involved creating particular kinds of political subjects and ultimately reconfiguring democracy.

I BEGIN MY EXPLORATION of forced relocation and development in the North, where the disciplinary aspects of improvement were apparent and where we can begin to appreciate the relationship between poverty, democracy, and a good life. In the postwar period, the federal government took a greater interest in the region thanks in large part to the Cold War, which highlighted its strategic importance, and an increasing appreciation of its economic potential. But as diplomat and commissioner of the Northwest Territories Hugh Keenleyside recalled, the country's postwar engagement with the North also stemmed from Canadians' expanded sense of community and responsibility. In his view, there was "a growing appreciation of the social responsibility of those living in a more favourable environment for the welfare of others of our common destiny who had been existing in half-forgotten isolation beyond the horizon of the north."[53]

Until the 1950s, Canada's northern affairs were largely left to the Hudson's Bay Company, the Royal Canadian Mounted Police, and Christian missionaries, all of whom believed the Indigenous population of the region was self-sufficient. The situation began to change when prices for Arctic fox declined and the caribou on which many Indigenous peoples depended became scarce. Inuit began spending more time in the region's settlements, hoping to find the support they needed. Confronted with the prospect of rising welfare costs, the federal government pushed people such as Job Muqyunniq back onto the land, believing it would provide for them as it always had. Not only would forced relocation prevent welfare dependency, but, in the view of Ottawa's bureaucrats, it would also preserve Inuit culture and, in the case of the High Arctic relocations, maintain Canadian sovereignty.[54]

When a number of Inuit starved to death in the central Arctic in the late 1950s, the federal government changed what Frances Abele called its "state of nature" policy.[55] Inuit would not be made to live on the land but instead would be encouraged and, indeed, coerced to settle in permanent communities. As "Arctic migrants" became "Arctic villagers," they were subjected to greater oversight and control, to power that has been described as "totalizing."[56] Once represented only by the RCMP, the state came to figure more prominently in the daily lives of northerners through its social welfare programs, first in the form of family allowance and old age pensions, then through its provisions for housing, education, and health care.

The extension of social welfare to the North was part of what John David Hamilton has called an "Arctic revolution."[57] In the postwar years, the federal government greatly expanded its presence in the region, reconfiguring its governance to build a "full-scale colonial administration" in less than a generation.[58] The scope of Ottawa's power was such that Alvin Hamilton considered that his appointment in 1957 as the federal minister responsible for the region made him "Czar of the North." More than ten years and a different government later, attitudes had not changed: named minister of Indian and northern affairs by Liberal Prime Minister Pierre Trudeau in 1968, Jean Chrétien referred to himself as "the last emperor in North America."[59]

New and different kinds of knowledge were brought to bear on Ottawa's northern realm. "We hired social workers, writers, and Inuktitut language teachers," recalled Bent Sivertz of the early days of the Arctic Division of the Department of Northern Affairs and National Resources.[60] In the central

Arctic, they were joined by people trained in anthropology, wildlife science, and resource economics, who all brought their expertise to bear on the task of giving the North a future, one that included its Indigenous peoples.

The cooperative was one of the development tools of choice for northern administrators. Co-ops would provide an institutional foundation for a local and regional economy and school its members in the workings of the market. Equally, if not more importantly, running a cooperative would teach Arctic villagers, many of whom were strangers to each other, how to make decisions publicly and collectively, something that would prepare them to govern their own affairs. In that way, helping Inuit establish cooperatives across the region would fulfil the mandate of Northern Affairs.

Cooperatives also figured in the Newfoundland story, as did some of the same government bureaucrats. But as Chapter 2 shows, the actors who featured most prominently were not just those drawn from the ranks of government. Instead, they also came from the university. Memorial University of Newfoundland's Institute of Social and Economic Research (ISER) and its Extension Department advised the federal and provincial governments about resettlement and were directly involved in the project of rural development.

The rule of experts this was not, however. Nor did the planning and implementation of resettlement bear anything more than the lightest imprint of high modernism. French economist François Perroux did provide the theory that informed it, observing that development was uneven, polarized around an industry or group of industries that drew people to them. His "growth pole" idea was one of development's "travelling rationalities," seized upon by modernizers around the world in the 1960s and 1970s, including those behind the Fisheries Household Resettlement Program.[61] They inverted Perroux's observation, reasoning that concentrating Newfoundland's population would spur economic development by providing industry with a supply of labour. But beyond designating a handful of communities as "growth centres" and setting out a process by which communities could apply to be resettled, there was no further planning or study of any kind, nothing like the area economic surveys undertaken in the North or the extensive, government-funded, multi-volume study of eastern Quebec's agricultural, fisheries, mining, and forestry sectors that was underway even as resettlement was being planned.

It was thus perhaps predictable that Newfoundland's Department of Community and Social Development, which oversaw resettlement, was unprepared for and completely overwhelmed by applications from people who seemed all too ready to sign up for the "shifting money" while it was on offer. In the bureaucratic chaos that ensued, rural Newfoundlanders subverted the purpose of the program to a surprising degree, moving not to designated growth centres but to communities closer to home, where the men could have access to their familiar fishing grounds. The economists and sociologists brought in to assess the program after its first few years of operation interviewed outport residents and identified points of friction and frustration. But far from challenging the necessity of relocation, they offered suggestions about how to improve its effectiveness and, in a sense, criticized it for not being sufficiently high modern.

Even as their ISER-based colleagues advised government about how to make resettlement work better, the staff at Memorial's Extension Department were collaborating with some of the same officials to strengthen rural Newfoundland. Here, as elsewhere, relocation and development went hand-in-hand. As in the North, development required transforming attitudes and behaviours – in this case, helping outporters shake off the heavy burden of tradition that shaped social relations to create a new kind of community, one with a modern civic political culture.

Working with the National Film Board of Canada (NFB), the Extension Department produced a series of films featuring individuals from different communities on Fogo Island speaking frankly about the problems and challenges of outport life, and in ways that they would not speak with their neighbours. A medium that is intimate yet distancing, film revealed islanders' differences as well as their shared interests in a way that allowed for discussion and the creation of new relationships, ones that helped the people of Fogo Island come together enough to forestall resettlement. The NFB called this "communication for social change," and the technique, which became known as "the Fogo Process," became a staple tool in community development work in Newfoundland and beyond.[62]

The story of how the people of Fogo Island managed to take charge of their future is usually presented as a story of resistance. Outporters drew on the very culture that government had denigrated to fight back against the assumption that they and their communities had "no great future," as Premier Joey Smallwood put it. But as much as Fogo's survival was a testament to islanders' strength, it also spoke to the effectiveness of the community development efforts undertaken by the Extension Department and the NFB. They managed to inculcate different scales of affect and affiliation among islanders, to create new political subjectivities that allowed them to avoid resettlement. In other words, Fogo Island's persistence can be read as a measure of the success of a particular technique of governmentality as well as of the agency of its residents.

Governmentality and high modernism found their fullest expression in the efforts to develop eastern Quebec, the subject of Chapter 3. Seized with the ambition to make Quebecers *maîtres chez nous,* the provincial government entered into an agreement with Ottawa to fund development planning for the Lower St. Lawrence, Gaspé, and Îles-de-la-Madeleine region in 1963. As was the case in Newfoundland, fighting poverty and developing eastern Quebec involved relocation – in this case, moving a projected 60,000 people in a population of 325,000, and closing eighty-five villages deemed to be "marginal."[63] Unlike what happened in Newfoundland, however, relocation and development were the subject of intensive planning carried out by the Bureau d'aménagement de l'Est du Québec (BAEQ; the Eastern Quebec Development Office), a non-governmental body that was funded by the federal and provincial governments through ARDA.

Based in Mont Joli, the BAEQ commanded a small army of researchers, many from Laval University, with expertise in the applied, natural, and social sciences. Conducted over three years, their work culminated in a ten-volume, two-thousand-page plan that called for the modernization of the region's main economic sectors, agriculture, forestry, mining, and fisheries. The overall objective was "to catch up with the Province of Quebec, and thus virtually to eliminate disparities in employment, productivity and income," something that would, in part, require improvements to the occupational and geographical mobility of the labour force and creating "regional enthusiasm" among its residents.[64]

But, as in Newfoundland, this was not the usual development-as-the-rule-of-experts story either. As much as the BAEQ relied on academics to draft a plan for eastern Quebec, it also turned to the people of the region for their input. Indeed, "participatory planning" and the citizen engagement it would cultivate were goals themselves, designed to further development by investing the people of eastern Quebec in the future of the region as a whole, and not just the particular community in which they lived.

To do so, the BAEQ's planners and development workers built an elaborate structure of participation, the foundation of which was something called "animation sociale" (social motivation or facilitation). This was a technique – a pedagogy – used by development workers both to understand the issues confronting poor communities from the bottom up and also to teach community members to define their interests and goals in relation to those of other communities and the region. By facilitating discussion, the BAEQ's *animateurs* hoped to forge a new civic political culture, one that consisted of the rules and practices of deliberative democracy and a particular way of seeing local interests in a larger context. In that sense, the planning process itself was a technique of government.

Just as Newfoundlanders engaged with their resettlement program, the people of eastern Quebec embraced the BAEQ's process – so much so that, when the plan they had played a role in drafting was largely shelved, they rose up in protest. Using the democratic language of *animation sociale,* which encouraged and empowered the poor to become "artisans of their destiny," they came together as Opérations Dignité. The resulting series of three protests between 1970 and 1972 were among the largest mass demonstrations in the history of rural Quebec. In making their demands, the protesters articulated a different relationship between the region and the province and a different sense of what it meant to be *maîtres chez nous*. Ultimately, the protests revealed the space between governmentality and local politics, a space in which other futures, other possibilities, could be expressed and realized.

Together, these three case studies reveal differences in the kind and degree of state coercion in both relocation and the expertise brought to bear on development. Despite these differences, what happened in the central Arctic, Newfoundland, and eastern Quebec shows the extent to which rural Canada was the object of state-sponsored improvement in the postwar years. In many ways, it is to the rural we must turn to understand the meanings and impacts of modernization. Doing so reveals the urban bias of relocation and development and, by extension, what the shape of "a good life" was, according to the state. In the North, Newfoundland, and eastern Quebec, the Canadian state tried to reduce poverty by centralizing rural populations, moving them to larger settlements that offered a concentration of services and, it was thought, better economic opportunities.

Of course, urban areas were not without their own pockets of poverty. These were also the targets of government-funded efforts that, like the ones already discussed, were informed by expertise and aimed at transforming people as much as places. In the postwar years, the federal government took a more activist role in shaping Canadian cities through housing policy and what was called "urban renewal." Aimed at overcoming the jumbled land-use patterns that were the result of the historical development of cities, urban renewal was meant to increase land values and hence tax revenues through clearing slums; separating residential, commercial, and industrial land use through zoning; and making better provision for traffic. Between 1948 and 1968, Ottawa, through the Central Mortgage and Housing Corporation, administered forty-eight major urban redevelopment projects that saw the demolition of thirteen thousand residential units and the construction of eighteen thousand new ones, mainly in the form of social housing.[65]

But urban renewal was also meant to improve the lives of the poor people who lived in the areas targeted for clearance. To urban reformers and planners, physical decay and moral decay went hand-in-hand. Fixing the former would also repair the latter: building better cities was a way to build better people. That connection was apparent in Leonard Marsh's 1950 report on slum clearance and urban rehabilitation in Vancouver's East Side. In it, the University of British Columbia professor and architect of Canada's welfare state argued that the danger posed by such areas was not limited to their impact on a city's tax base. Instead, "the biggest cost of the slum to society is apathetic, dreary living, which is a menace to every aspect of healthy citizenship."[66] Like those engaged in rural development, Marsh was also concerned with building a civic culture among the urban poor, in this case by structuring their built environment.[67]

Given the urban bias of development, one might expect that the state would devote as many, if not more, resources to alleviating urban poverty as it did to addressing it in rural Canada. That was not the case in the 1960s, and some politicians who represented urban ridings, like Phil Givens, resented it. "We seem to spend ninety per cent of our time talking about wet wheat, fish, and the Newfie Bullet," the member of Parliament for York West noted.[68] Ottawa was constitutionally constrained in what it could do, as matters urban fell under provincial jurisdiction. Yet housing policy was one way it could intervene, and throughout the 60s, it continued to try to expand its influence in this area. Those efforts culminated in 1971 with the creation of a short-lived Ministry of State for Urban Affairs.

Not only did the state devote fewer resources to urban development, but its efforts to improve the lives of the urban poor occurred in a much less consultative way. In contrast to the development efforts undertaken in rural Canada, urban renewal remained very much expert-driven, its technocratic character largely unleavened by citizen participation. For most of the decade, the people in areas slated for renewal were not invited to participate in any aspect of urban planning. That said, municipal authorities in Halifax and Vancouver were sufficiently conscious of the disruptive nature of relocation and redevelopment to think about how to treat those affected fairly. Their efforts are the subject of the next two chapters.

Both Africville, a neighbourhood at the north end of Halifax, and Strathcona, on Vancouver's East Side, were targets of urban renewal in the 1960s, and each has become emblematic in its own way. The destruction of Africville is a symbol of racism and the power of the state, while the survival of Strathcona has come to signify the reconfiguration and redistribution of that power, thanks to the successful efforts on the part of area residents to stop renewal and convince the government to fund the rehabilitation of their neighbourhood.

There are, however, other ways to see their significance. The way urban renewal unfolded in postwar Halifax reveals the power of race and rights to shape the city's ideas about how to minimize the disruption of urban renewal for Africville's residents. While the razing of Africville and the relocation of its residents certainly speaks to the systemic racism prevalent in Halifax, municipal authorities also recognized the role racism had played in creating the poor conditions in the neighbourhood in the first place. As I discuss in Chapter 4, although they weren't willing to undertake the kinds of improvements that would allow residents to continue to live in their homes, city bureaucrats were sensitive to the need to relocate them in a way that reflected the principles of "natural justice," as they put it. Doing so meant giving Africville residents more consideration than was extended to other poor Haligonians – both black and white – who lived in other areas of the city that were also slated for demolition and redevelopment.

While the city used the standard expropriation procedures to acquire properties in other areas targeted for urban renewal, it deviated from them in dealing with the residents of Africville. In an effort to avoid perpetuating the racism that characterized the city's treatment of the neighbourhood in the past, it negotiated with individual property owners, hiring a social worker to do so, and it also compensated those without property – that is, those who were tenants or who boarded or lived with relatives. In addition, to review compensation agreements, city council created a special subcommittee whose members included the community's advocates. Finally, the city agreed to help relocated residents find housing and jobs as well as get the education they needed to open up opportunities for them. Significant as they were, these efforts were also largely ineffective and reveal the limits of the prevailing understanding of justice. For the municipal state and for Africville's advocates, fairness focused on providing opportunities for individuals to help themselves, rather than addressing the structural barriers that prevented people from taking advantage of such opportunities.

Planning in Vancouver began on the same trajectory as Halifax, with a comprehensive, top-down, expert report that identified areas of the city's East Side for redevelopment and estimated that doing so would necessitate the relocation of approximately 6,000 poor and working-class people, 30 percent of whom were Chinese Canadian. But, as Chapter 5 shows, rather than depart from the usual expropriation process as Halifax did, the city of Vancouver tried to mitigate the disruption of urban renewal by making two different provisions for citizen input. Both the Mayor's Redevelopment Consultative Committee and the Strathcona Rehabilitation Committee reveal how participation could be a technique of government. The Mayor's Redevelopment Consultative Committee consisted of individuals who, though they were not residents of redevelopment areas, were deemed to have the standing and networks that would allow them to give advice about the impact of urban renewal. Its actions revealed the city understood citizen participation as a communications strategy and a means of managing risk rather than a way to decentralize decision making and share power.

By the time the most disruptive phase of redevelopment was scheduled to start in the Strathcona neighbourhood in 1969, civic officials found their views of urban renewal and citizen participation out of step with those of their federal counterparts. Enough doubts had been raised about the effectiveness of urban renewal, its costs, and the wisdom of excluding those who would be affected from the planning process, that Ottawa – which provided half the funding – was prepared to call a halt to it. Thus, when activists and grassroots organizations like the Strathcona Property Owners and Tenants Association (SPOTA) demanded to be included in the decisions that affected their neighbourhoods, they found federal officials to be receptive.

The Trudeau government had just been elected on a platform of participatory democracy, and the interventions of its ministers were key in diverting funds earmarked for demolishing Strathcona to rehabilitating it. In addition, both federal and provincial officials supported SPOTA's demand for citizen participation; specifically, that it be given an equal role along with representatives from all three levels of government in first designing and then implementing a rehabilitation program. But as SPOTA's experience on the

Strathcona Rehabilitation Committee revealed, the state could share power in ways that reinforced its own. The ways the state elicited citizen participation in Vancouver over the 1960s and 1970s reveals the complicated relationship between participation, empowerment, and democracy.

In making these arguments linking forced relocation, development, and governmentality, *Moved by the State* engages with the provocative and ambitious framework Ian McKay offers for rethinking Canada's history, and more particularly for getting beyond the two solitudes – of social and cultural history on one hand and national and political history on the other – that have long characterized academic writing in the field. McKay argues that we should understand Canada "simultaneously as an *extensive* projection of liberal rule across a large territory and an *intensive* process of subjectification, whereby liberal assumptions are internalized and normalized within the dominion's subjects."[69] In other words, the story of Canada's making is a story of how the state extended its power over ever more peoples and places. An inherently violent process, it was also a matter of formal politics. But governing Canada also depended on people within its borders adopting a set of liberal democratic values about individuals and their relationship to the market and the state, as well as about the role of the state, among others. The internalization and normalization of these values – whether in school, church, the factory, or the playground – meant people regulated themselves. Self-discipline of this kind was the key to the liberal project of rule.

While the instances of forced relocation and development discussed in the following chapters are examples of the increasing scope and intensity of the liberal state's power in the postwar period, they also nuance McKay's argument in important ways. The development efforts I discuss certainly disciplined the poor even as they empowered them. But this didn't mean that state power was such that it determined outcomes. As we will see, the kind of empowerment facilitated by development invited the poor to challenge the very authority that disciplined them.

1

"No More Canadians Will Starve!"

Development, Discipline, and Decolonizing the North

In the early months of 1950, documentary photographer Richard Harrington set off on his third trip to the Canadian Arctic in as many years.[1] This time his destination was Churchill, the starting point for a journey along the west coast of Hudson Bay and into the Keewatin (now Kivalliq) region, or the "Barrenlands" (Figure 1.1). By the time he returned, he could no longer take pictures – his fingers had been frozen one too many times.[2] But Harrington was lucky: he would recover. Long before he got home, many of the people he had met were dead. His photographs had become a collective obituary.

More than records of the passing of a way of life, Harrington's images were meant to provoke a complacent public. Confronted with starvation among the Padleimiut, a group of Caribou, or inland Inuit, Harrington could do no more than bear witness to a tragedy. When death came, tea and tobacco were all he had to greet it.

> February 11 [1950]: For the first time I realize how serious it is when caribou don't come ... Dogs are dying everywhere. Remaining dogs: skin & bones, shivering, listless. Since Eskimos must travel to obtain food & furs, it means they cannot move around anymore ... By & by, no more tea, coal-oil, matches. Real hardships begin ...

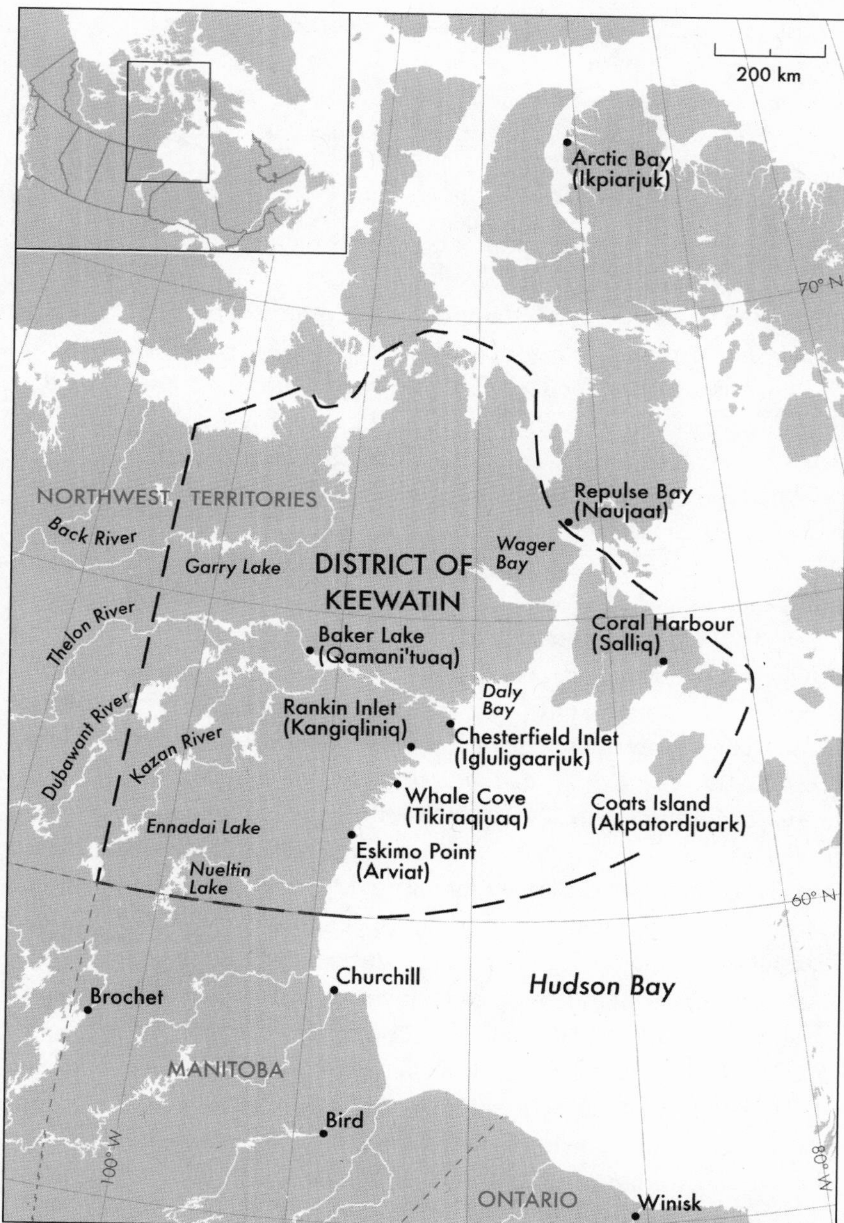

Figure 1.1 The Keewatin region

February 25: Left alone in a cold, iced-over igloo, Arnalukjuak sat hunched over, in threadbare clothing, her hair frosted over, saying nothing. I put some tobacco in her soapstone pipe, but she was too weak to suck on it. By next morning, she had died of cold & hunger. Her relatives sealed off the igloo.[3]

Two years later, when his photographs were published as *The Face of the Arctic,* Harrington gave public voice to what he had seen. Arnalukjuak was not named in his "portrait of famine," but is identified only as a "starving Padleimiut." Another of his subjects did not merit even this designation. The cold and lack of food had reduced her identity to a state of being. Beyond anonymity, she was neither Alaq, the name he recorded in his diary, nor a Padleimiut. Instead, she was "near death." The next sentence turned that description into an indictment, aesthetics into politics: "Near death. Note Government identification tag" (Figure 1.2).[4]

As other scholars have argued, knowledge is the key to statecraft, especially in the modern period.[5] People have to be visible, or "legible," to the state in order to be subject to its power. In Canada, the census and system of social insurance numbers are two commonplace techniques of tracking and control, and so too were the government tags Harrington referred to. With no standardized spellings of Inuit names and in the absence of surnames, authorities found it difficult to keep accurate trade accounts and police records. Implemented in 1941, the E-number (E for "Eskimo") identification system was meant to distinguish Inuit by issuing each a unique number worn on a tag around the neck. It became especially important for the delivery of family allowances, the first of Canada's universal social programs, established in 1944.[6] But as Richard Harrington made clear, legibility was no guarantee of social security.

Whereas Harrington chose to be a witness, his contemporary, writer Farley Mowat, assumed the job of prosecutor in the court of public opinion. The same year the public was shown *The Face of the Arctic,* Mowat published his first book. Also set in the Keewatin, *People of the Deer* (1952) was an explicit condemnation of the Canadian government's deadly neglect of a group of inland Inuit Mowat called the "Ihalmiut" (Ahiarmiut).[7] Exploited and rendered dependent by the Hudson's Bay Company (HBC), many of them starved to death when the barren-ground caribou that sustained them failed to arrive in sufficient numbers and, Mowat charged, the government authorities responsible for their welfare took no action. These were serious accusations that elicited criticism and debate, including

Figure 1.2 Richard Harrington featured this photograph in *The Face of the Arctic* (1952) with the caption "Near death. Note Government identification tag." His diary identified her as Alaq. Through Project Naming, she has subsequently been identified as Alariak, more commonly known as Alanaaq. | Richard Harrington, Library and Archives Canada, PA-114716

in the House of Commons. Despite questions about the book's accuracy, some considered *People of the Deer* "a strong indictment of the handling of Eskimo affairs."[8]

The work of both Harrington and Mowat came at a time when Canadians and their government were taking a more active interest in the North and the welfare of northerners. In part, that interest was forced by the Second World War, which brought an influx of outsiders to the area. As R. Quinn Duffy points out, the American military personnel and civilians sent north to build and operate strategic air bases were shocked at the conditions Inuit lived in and were critical of Canada's failure to provide them with adequate housing, medical care, and education. Although territorial officials and the HBC dismissed their concerns as groundless, "malicious tattle by over-zealous, uninformed humanitarians who did not appreciate the harsh reality of life in the Arctic," the federal government nevertheless began to address the issue of northern welfare through the universal family allowance program, inaugurated in 1944.[9]

But it was really not until after the war that Ottawa's commitment to social security and the greater intervention into the lives of all Canadians – including northerners – gained full expression. In addition to housing, hospitalization, unemployment, and care for the elderly in the form of universal old age pensions, the government also interpolated itself into areas as fundamental as people's diets.[10] Yet, despite the lofty promises of the Atlantic Charter and the subsequent growth of the welfare state, Ottawa's safety net did not adequately protect the Indigenous peoples of the region.[11]

To repair the holes, in the 1950s the government turned to the airplane, using it to fly food into remote locations and, when that was deemed ineffective, to arrange for "Eskimos [to] fly to new hunting grounds."[12] In other words, relocation was a welfare measure. The state moved Inuit like Job Muqyunniq and other Ahiarmiut to areas where game was believed to be more plentiful and where they could not rely on morally corrupting "handouts" from traders, missionaries, or military personnel. Even when they walked hundreds of kilometres from Nueltin and Henik Lake in order to return home to Ennadai Lake in the 1950s, officials with Northern Affairs insisted that they had agreed to be moved.[13] But when thirty-three Inuit died around Henik and Garry Lakes as a result of starvation in the Keewatin over the winter of 1957–58, the government was forced to change its "state of nature" policy.[14] Famines did not happen in Canada, and people were certainly not supposed to die from a lack of food.

Death by starvation was not the kind of publicity the recently established Department of Northern Affairs and National Resources had in mind for the region it had charge of, especially since its objective was, in the words of Minister Jean Lesage, "to give the Eskimos the same rights, privileges, opportunities, and responsibilities as all other Canadians, in short to enable them to share fully in the national life of Canada."[15] Scandalized by what happened in the Keewatin, Prime Minister John Diefenbaker echoed the mandate of Northern Affairs in directing the civil service to act so that "no more Canadians will starve!"[16]

Once a predictable, if tragic, end for "primitive" peoples, death from hunger, by the late 1950s, was no longer tolerable for any of Canada's citizens. However, the change in the semantics of starvation didn't mean the government abandoned relocation as a technology of welfare. Instead of dispersing people on the land, it was used to centralize the population, turning "Arctic migrants" into "Arctic villagers."[17] In the Keewatin, over a hundred starvation survivors were flown to communities on the west coast of Hudson Bay where a new future awaited them.[18]

Establishing Inuit in permanent settlements was only the start of government efforts to address poverty and immiseration in the North. The region posed a fundamental challenge to the liberal welfare state's aspirations of universality. Meeting that challenge required more than just moving people around: it also required developing the region in a way that would make it self-sustaining – not just socially and economically, but politically as well. As the deputy minister of Northern Affairs and National Resources, Gordon Robertson, put it, "Our Department is aiming at building up a region where race lines are unknown and where the North will be run by its own people standing on their own feet and doing the job better than we from the South could do it."[19]

For Robertson, there were clear parallels between what was happening in the global South and in Canada's North. Unfortunately, in his view, Canadians "have never thought of themselves as being a 'colonial power' with dependent regions to administer and develop." But they needed to, for "the problems of administration in the Canadian north are basically problems of the colonial power in bringing subject peoples and subject lands to a state of maturity, prosperity, and political equality."[20]

In undertaking this program of modernization, Ottawa adopted what P. Whitney Lackenbauer and Daniel Heidt call a "whole of government approach," a new way of thinking about northern development. Bringing together the ministers and senior bureaucrats of all federal departments with an interest in the region, the Advisory Committee on Northern

Development addressed questions of sovereignty, scientific research, governance, and social and economic development in a coordinated way.[21] Established in 1948, its deliberations speak to the belief that prosperity for the North and, by extension, for Canada, depended on exploiting the region's non-renewable resources, namely, its precious and base metals as well as its oil and gas. This "Northern Vision," as Conservative leader John Diefenbaker later dubbed it, could be realized only by building the necessary infrastructure – "roads to resources" – and, more fundamentally, by bringing new kinds of knowledge to bear on the question of development.

Giving the North and its citizens a future would depend on understanding and exploiting the region's capacity, both material and human. In the central Arctic, mining seemed to be the answer, then as now. Inuit were brought in or came to work as wage labourers at the North Rankin Nickel Mine, then the most northerly hardrock operation in the world.[22] When it closed in the early 1960s, Ottawa widened its focus to include renewable resources to sustain the region.

Social work and anthropology in particular were important in realizing these initiatives, but wildlife management and resource economics, as well as the techniques and technologies of regional and community development, were also deployed to define and solve the "problem" of the central Arctic. Important as these approaches were, development was not simply a technocratic issue, a matter of applying expertise. As will be discussed, ensuring the social security of northerners was also a matter of exercising disciplinary power to create self-governing and ultimately self-sustaining subjects.

In the aftermath of the killing winter of 1957–58, the Department of Northern Affairs and National Resources sent Walter Rudnicki to interview the starvation survivors at Eskimo Point (Arviat). It was a telling choice. He was not the usual northern hand, a man with connections to the Hudson's Bay Company, the RCMP, or Christian churches. Instead, he was a psychiatric social worker with a degree from the University of British Columbia and experience working with recent immigrants in Vancouver. At Eskimo Point, Rudnicki put his professional training to work, administering the "thematic apperception test" to the survivors. One of the most commonly used psychological diagnostics, it involves showing participants a series of provocative yet ambiguous drawings about which they are asked to tell a story. Psychologists believe that the stories participants tell reflect their state of mind, their sense of self and the world.

Figure 1.3 Walter Rudnicki created his own drawings and used them in the "thematic apperception test" he administered to the relocated starvation survivors at Eskimo Point in 1958. | Walter Rudnicki, University of Manitoba Archives and Special Collections, Walter Rudnicki fonds, MSS 331, box 81, file 1

Instead of using the usual set of standardized pictures, Rudnicki, a talented sketch artist, created his own, depicting some of the events leading to the starvation (Figure 1.3). Following the tests, he reported that there was no evidence of "mental pathology," and that, insofar as he had reason for concern, it lay in the attitudes the survivors had toward non-Inuit. In pictures where only Inuit were present, the starvation survivors perceived the people to be happy and helping each other. But when white men were depicted, the response was different: "The general reaction seemed to be that the Eskimos were unhappy, sad, or frightened ... White men were not differentiated, that is, police, northern service officer, etc. All were regarded as 'big bosses' and seemed to be equally viewed with fear and suspicion."[23]

What Rudnicki identified was a psychology of colonialism created by regular interactions with Hudson's Bay Company traders, missionaries, and members of the Royal Canadian Mounted Police at small and scattered settlements across the North. After the war, those interactions had increased for certain groups and individuals who were drawn into construction work along the Distant Early Warning (DEW) Line. In Rudnicki's opinion, overcoming the fears borne of their encounters with colonial power would be the key to rehabilitating the survivors.

That process began at Itivia, a community established just outside Rankin Inlet to deal with the Henik and Garry Lake people. Having been moved two, and perhaps three, times in short order before getting there, the starvation survivors found themselves subjected to a regime that was meant to do more than restore their physical health. "Rehabilitation" meant cultural transformation. As the supervisor of the department's largest rehabilitation centre in Frobisher Bay (Iqaluit) described it, the process entailed "deliberately breaking down an old pattern of life and ... help[ing] the individual and the group work out the resulting conflicts and to build positive new patterns that will take the place of what we have broken down."[24] For instance, Inuit like "Charlie and Lydia" arrived at the rehabilitation centre in poor health and unable to support themselves on the land. "The couple were introduced to work routines and taught how to live in a house, to manage income, to prepare white man's food. There was also an assessment made of Charlie's skills and potential. Around six months later, he was placed in a job in a community."[25] The same philosophy of rehabilitation – if not the extensive infrastructure that existed at Frobisher – was in evidence at Itivia.

In Keewatin, the rehabilitation process came to encompass all Inuit, not just the starvation survivors. In Rudnicki's view, starvation was just a symptom of the larger problems that afflicted the entire region. Dependent on caribou, inland people may have been the first to be affected by the loss of their subsistence and the decline of the fur trade, but they were not the only ones facing an uncertain future. The situation on the coast was also precarious. At Eskimo Point, for instance, Rudnicki reported that people were "ill clothed, demoralized and living chiefly on flour." Even at Rankin Inlet, where the mine provided some wage employment for Inuit (discussed below), prospects were dimming because of a decline in commodity prices.[26]

Under the circumstances, Rudnicki argued that what was required was a comprehensive development plan that would "preserve the basic fabric of Eskimo culture and, at the same time, create an enlightened Eskimo population in Keewatin which could take advantage of the employment opportunities of the future."[27] While trained social workers like him were crucial, creating such hybrid northern citizens required other kinds of experts, people who knew something about Inuit. As the deputy minister of Northern Affairs and National Resources observed, "One of the greatest difficulties facing those responsible for the health, welfare, and education of the natives of northern Canada is a lack of basic information on their social and cultural patterns."[28] Thus, in Canada, as in other parts of the world at the time, anthropology as well as social work came to be implicated in development, influencing the design of initiatives in the North and shaping the state's understanding of what development was.[29] While anthropology wielded its influence through the Northern Coordination and Research Centre (NCRC), established by Northern Affairs in 1954 to support and coordinate scholarly research about the North, in Keewatin it also made an impact through the more informal interventions of Ottawa's agent in the field.[30]

In the Barrenlands, Northern Affairs' man on the ground was an amateur anthropologist. Almost immediately after Rudnicki visited Eskimo Point in 1958, the department appointed a new welfare officer to the region whose responsibilities included overseeing the rehabilitation of the starvation survivors at Itivia and attending to the welfare needs of the growing Inuit population of Rankin Inlet, where he was based. Staffordshire-born Robert G. Williamson arrived in the Keewatin community just as the ink had finished drying on his undergraduate anthropology degree.[31]

Although his diploma was new, Williamson was not – to fieldwork or the Canadian North. He had immigrated to Canada as a young man and made his way to the western Arctic, working on the Mackenzie River barges. While wintering at Fort Simpson, he recorded Dene folklore and later published his findings in the scholarly journal *Anthropologica*. After a year-and-a-half in the western Arctic, he moved to take a job with the Eastern Arctic Patrol. He became fluent in Inuktitut and continued his ethnological investigations around Pangnirtung (Panniqutuuq) and Cumberland Sound. In 1954 he moved to Ottawa and, while working there, enrolled at Carleton University, where he earned an undergraduate degree in 1957. He later went on to earn a doctorate in anthropology at Uppsala, Sweden, in 1974, and to have an academic career at the University of Saskatchewan – after having done a great many other things, including a stint in the civil service with Northern Affairs.[32]

Looking back, Williamson considered himself both an exemplar and a proponent of applied anthropology, a sub-discipline committed to applying the methods of anthropology in order to solve practical problems. His undergraduate education coincided with the field's emergence in the postwar years, when hope reigned supreme about the prospects for a new world order in which all nations would enjoy the benefits of democracy and modernity. Anthropologists, no less than economists, became implicated in this global project of transformative change.[33] Funding and positions opened up in government and non-governmental organizations for anthropologists willing to use their skills in the service of what became known simply as "development."

Williamson's early career with Northern Affairs provided him with the opportunity not just to see social change, but also to intervene in it as a welfare officer, using some of the tools of anthropology. What he saw and did would form the basis of his doctoral dissertation, a study of socio-cultural change in the Keewatin.[34] As a field of study and a form of practice, applied anthropology was controversial, particularly by the time Williamson undertook his graduate studies. Its detractors considered it "second rate, both intellectually and morally" – a form of neo-colonialism. Its practitioners shot back that their critics were "irrelevant, both theoretically and politically."[35] If Williamson were aware of these debates, he likely would have dismissed them: for him, there was no contradiction between intellectual rigour and political engagement. After his undergraduate degree, he leapt at the chance to leave "the quiet contemplative corridors of the National Museum" for a post with the federal government in the North. "There was so much to be done that one could not sit, eyes cast to the ceiling, fingertips together, thinking only abstractly," he recalled. "One had to respond to one's responsibility to make use of one's knowledge."[36]

Once on the ground, the amateur anthropologist got to work. Although part of his time was spent at Itivia with the starvation survivors, he devoted a good portion of his energies to helping manage the Inuit working at the North Rankin Nickel Mine, which started underground operations in 1953 (Figure 1.4). Like the starvation survivors, the Inuit miners and their families were also relocatees, drawn from the Keewatin's coastal communities by the company and the federal government as a labour force.[37] Their mobility was not unusual. Throughout this period, the Department of Northern Affairs and National Resources facilitated the movement of Inuit men and women from different parts of the Arctic within the region and beyond for training and work. The DEW Line provided jobs for many, but it was not the only employer. After leaving his community near Aklavik to take training as a commercial wireless operator, Alex Illasiak got a job at one of the Department of Transportation's stations in the North. Nora Noru and Celine Mandeville of Fort Resolution were sent to Edmonton for a course in clinical laboratory work and X-rays with the hope they could find work in a northern hospital.

Figure 1.4 Thomas Legjuk and other workers in the shaft of the North Rankin Nickel Mine, 1961. | Kryn Taconis, Library and Archives Canada, PA-175654

In 1957, thirty Inuit went south to Edmonton as part of a new government vocational training program to teach them how to operate and maintain heavy equipment.[38]

Having recruited and trained Inuit, the operators of North Rankin's mine were flummoxed when some employees withdrew after three or four days, or dropped their pickaxes, picked up their rifles, and headed off to sea or to the floe edge when a whale or a group of seals was sighted.[39] Without enough shift workers, operations ground to an expensive and annoying halt. Despite "their natural quickness to learn" the technical aspects of the work, the Inuit persisted in this seemingly undisciplined behaviour.[40] Ultimately, it was the company that changed its practices, and, according to Williamson, it did so on his advice.[41] For Williamson, the key to solving North Rankin's labour problem lay in re-creating the pattern of "cultural commuting" he had first seen in the western Arctic. The Indigenous people of the Mackenzie River and Delta seemed to experience the least social disruption when they were able to shuttle back and forth between life on the land and life in trading posts, between their old lives and their new ones.[42] Although the physical distance between social worlds had collapsed in Rankin, he still hoped to create a space that would act in the same way, as a buffer. He did so not by physically removing Inuit from the settlement, but by suggesting how the work regime at the mine might be reconfigured. Specifically, Williamson convinced management to train more men than they would employ at any one time and to redefine what a "shift" was. Indeed, doing the first allowed for the second. Instead of particular individuals, a shift came to consist simply of a certain number of people. An Inuit "straw boss" would have the responsibility of ensuring there was the necessary number of men to fill each one.

In essence, Williamson convinced the mine to work with cultural difference and to treat Inuit labour as a collective endeavour. While his innovation did not win him many friends in North Rankin's accounting department, his proposed restructuring freed individual Inuit to hunt or mine as they wished and could negotiate with their fellow workers. Modified for an industrial setting, Williamson's cultural commuting was a structure of practice that combined the new time-work discipline, governed by the clock, with an older pattern of work, one that was sensitive to and shaped by environment and opportunity. This mutual adaptation was what made the North Rankin experiment stand out to the producers of a National Film Board of Canada documentary on the mine and miners. Focused on "Kusserktok," a hunter turned miner, *People of the Rock* (1961) made the point that "he is not the only one adapting. Kusserktok's [white] foreman had many years of mine experience before he came to the sub-arctic. But at this mine he has had to accept new standards of work discipline."[43]

Despite the apparently successful adaptation on the part of both the Inuit and North Rankin's management to mining in the Canadian North, operations wound down in 1962, the victim of falling commodity prices and a decision by the US government not to continue stockpiling strategic minerals.[44] The news, when it came, was not a surprise; the threat of closure seemed to hang over its operations almost as soon as they started.[45] With 520 people, or about 30 percent of Keewatin's population, dependent on the mine, its shutdown provoked Northern Affairs to declare a "state of emergency."[46]

Again the anthropological ambulance responded to the call, with Robert Williamson at the wheel. Just as he had helped facilitate the transition to industrial employment in Rankin, he intervened again to ease the disruption associated with its end. The year before the mine closed, Williamson conducted a survey of fifty-nine men who worked in the mine to ascertain what they wanted to do. Some told Williamson they would happily go back to hunting. But most, he reported, wanted to pursue wage work, concerned about whether the hunt could reliably sustain their families. That said, they were quite specific about the conditions under which they would labour: for at least one man, "work in white man's land [was] not a happy thought." Another told Williamson he "would go elsewhere in Esk[imo] country to work, but not to the white man's land." A third made a distinction between the kinds of mining work he wanted to do, noting "outside work happiest. Underground work worst, especially as no extra pay. V. frightening."[47] In sum, most wanted to continue to work for wages, in Rankin if possible, or at other mines in the North. Only a few wished to go back to their home communities or to other ones where they could hunt and fish.[48]

To meet the wishes of those who wanted to work for wages, as well as to capitalize on a trained labour force and diminish a potentially crippling welfare bill, Williamson made the case with his superiors for relocating Rankin's Inuit – but he did so with an anthropologist's sensitivity to context. Only those most likely to succeed in their new jobs would be moved, and then only to other mines in the North. To identify the most promising candidates, Williamson assessed each family's "adaptation potential": he constructed genealogies, believing that relocation would be successful only if a miner's family went with him to a new job, and he noted whether husbands and wives were competent in English. While facility in English contributed greatly to an Inuit family's potential to adapt, Williamson also recorded whether they possessed things like stoves, fridges, washing machines, radios, and record players. For the anthropologist, these consumer goods were another indicator of a family's acculturation.[49]

With Williamson's recommendations in mind, Northern Affairs worked with various companies through the 1960s to send Rankin miners and their families to Tungsten and Yellowknife in the Northwest Territories, to Lynn Lake in Manitoba, and to Asbestos Hill in arctic Quebec. While the numbers of Inuit relocated were never large – three to twelve families – the level of attention directed at them was great, speaking perhaps to the importance the department attached to their success or failure and to the reach of the state.[50] Williamson's insights about the need to take culture seriously in crafting employment policy and practice circulated well beyond the central Arctic. The department repeated them in advising companies thinking of operating in the North, particularly as resource extraction sped up in the 1970s.[51]

But at the same time that Williamson was using his anthropological training to help relocate Rankin's miners, professional anthropologists funded by the federal government were raising serious questions about whether industrial wage work alone was all that was required to develop the North. In their report for the NCRC, Robert and Lois Dailey argued that just because the Inuit at Rankin had been integrated into the wage economy did not mean they were treated fairly. Far from it: they were paid less than white men for similar work, and they were subjected to blatant discrimination. In 1958, Rankin was a segregated community, with Inuit and Qallunaat (Inuktitut for "non-Inuit") sleeping and eating in different facilities and using the one rec room on different days (Figure 1.5). To the Daileys, each Inuk on the mine's payroll was being "trained to be a labourer – not a citizen."[52] What had been achieved at Rankin was the creation of a workforce, not a community. It was, argued the Daileys, no model for the future.

Four years later, things had not improved. Like the Daileys, Jean Malaurie, whose work was also supported by the NCRC, worried about the corrosive effects of industrialization. The ethnohistorian and geographer's views were shaped by his relationship with an Igloolik (Iglulik) man who worked as a labourer in the North Rankin Nickel Mine and, unusually, kept a diary. While, for Malaurie, the mere act of keeping a diary was a sign of the Inuk's distress, he found its contents even more disturbing. As the hunter became an alienated wage labourer, there was a slow but inevitable closing of his "diaphragm of expression" until "the man of before is replaced not by a new man but by a void pure and simple." Suffocation and annihilation was the effect of "deculturation."[53]

Charged by the NCRC with understanding why the government's selective, anthropologically informed relocation of Inuit for industrial employment had such variable success, David Stevenson argued it had little to do with workers' technical skills. Although there was rarely a problem with the work the miners did, there were signs of "mal-adjustment," including absenteeism, drunkenness, and a high turnover of labourers, all familiar problems in resource-extractive workplaces. As well, he noted that alcohol abuse among Inuit women, neglect of children, and an indifference to maintaining functional households were, to different degrees, common among the relocatees. Moreover, insufficient housing, a lack of familiarity with managing daily expenses, and an inability to comprehend the informal social rules governing white society made adjustment all the more difficult. For many Inuit, relocation was a fundamentally isolating experience.

When people talked about their alienation, they made no distinction between the social and the environmental. Yellowknife felt more "remote" than Rankin when distance was measured in terms of exotic presences and

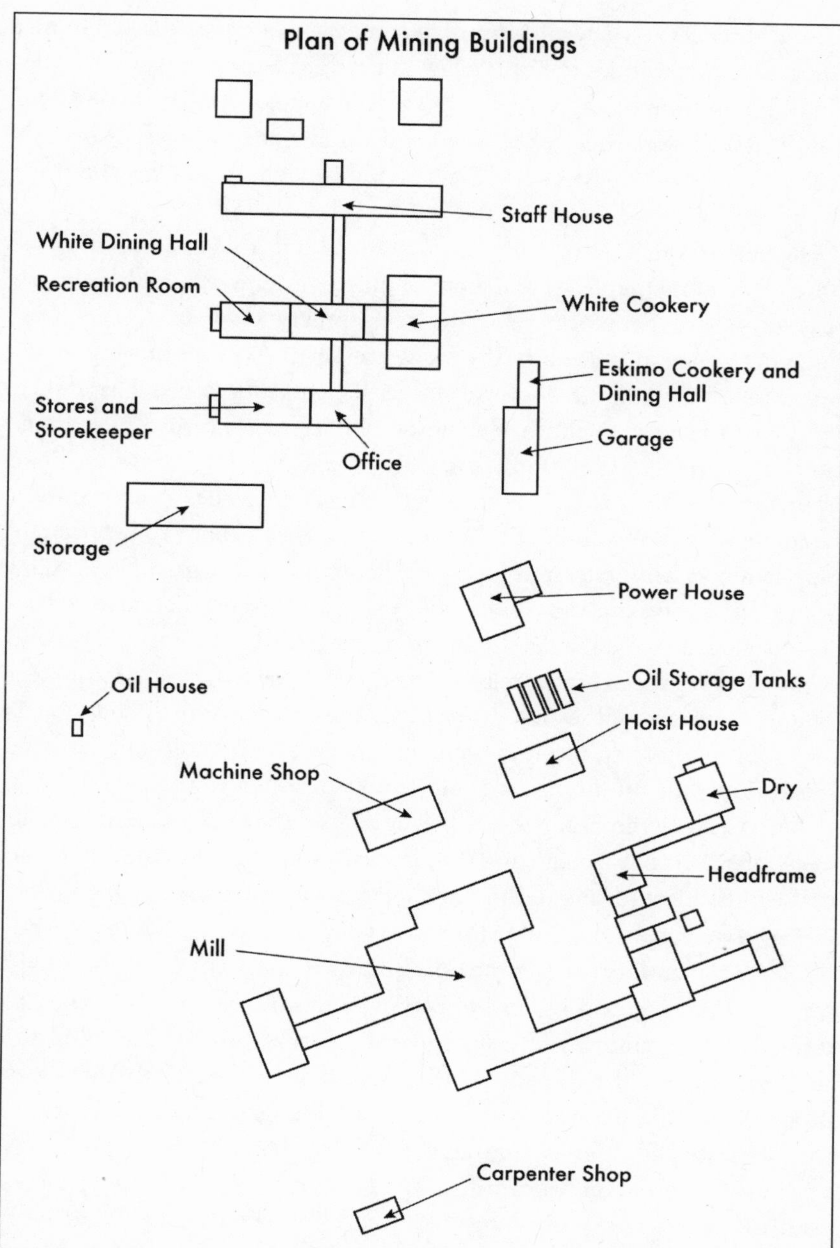

Figure 1.5 Plan of the mining buildings at Rankin Inlet, adapted from Robert C. Dailey and Lois A. Dailey, *The Eskimo of Rankin Inlet: A Preliminary Study* (1961)

gaping absences – when spiders and heat replaced family and kin. For one Rankin man, the trees around Yellowknife signalled his separation, preventing him from seeing very far. "It's just like looking at the floor under you."[54] Asked why they repeatedly went on alcoholic binges, two Inuit women living in Hay River told Stevenson it was "'because I have no place in this land.'"[55]

As much as they were critiques of wage labour, these anthropologists' observations also pointed to the shortcomings of the government's approach to development. For Northern Affairs, development was a matter of addressing a deficiency in the Inuit. The focus was squarely on improving them, rather than changing the workplaces or settlements they joined. For all their sensitivity to culture, neither Williamson nor Stevenson turned their attention to ascertaining the kinds of social settings that might best facilitate improvement. Their concern was almost exclusively on the capacity of Inuit to adapt, not on the ability of the workplace or settlement to incorporate new members. Yes, better housing would help, and yes, the negative attitudes of the business people and landlords in Yellowknife were an obstacle to successful relocation and the development of a mobile labour force. But beyond acknowledging the existence of racism and its corrosive effects on the project of improvement, neither the experts engaged by Northern Affairs nor its own officers chose to tackle it, perhaps recognizing it could not easily be addressed, while Inuit capacity could – or so they thought.

Nevertheless, the department did modify its approach to development in significant ways, recognizing that mining would not sustain the region in the immediate future. Rather than focus on training and placing people in waged work, development plans had to be tailored to exploit the potential of the region and its peoples more fully. Northern Affairs needed to build capacity from the existing foundation of Inuit culture, even as it tried to dismantle that culture and reconfigure it. To that end, beginning in the early 1960s, after the Rankin mine closed, the department initiated two programs for the Keewatin Inuit, both of which sought to capitalize on their identity and skills as hunting peoples.

The first centred on handicrafts. Borne of a belief that engaging people's creativity would have positive psychological effects, arts and crafts had been a part of the rehabilitation program for the starvation survivors from Itivia's beginnings. With the closure of the mine, however, the scope and intensity of artistic production increased as the broader Inuit community of Rankin Inlet was brought into the enterprise. Northern Affairs believed "the potential for the development of arts and crafts was great" – both to build confidence in the producers and to inject some much-needed revenue into their communities.[56] Certainly that had been the case in international development contexts, and it had also worked closer to home, at Cape Dorset in the eastern Arctic, where, in the late 1950s, Northern Service Officer James Houston had helped the Inuit launch a successful printmaking venture, which continues to this day.[57]

According to the head of Northern Affairs' Industrial Division, in a world where "very little work was getting done by skilled craftsmen," the kind of authenticity represented by Indigenous art was increasingly desirable. "People employed in the industrial complex were very anxious to obtain hand-made crafts. As a result ... the market for Eskimo arts and crafts would grow rather than decrease."[58] To take advantage of that market, in 1963 Northern Affairs hired Claude Grenier, a unilingual francophone from Chicoutimi, to oversee an arts and crafts program based in Rankin Inlet. Trained at the École des Beaux-Arts de Québec, the artist and teacher worked with Inuit men who turned soapstone, ivory, and antler – familiar materials – into sculptures depicting the hunt or stories from their past. Cécile Grenier, his wife, worked with Inuit women, teaching them to deploy their traditional sewing skills on wool and duffle to make parkas, mittens, and dolls for a southern market.[59]

Northern Affairs' concern with authenticity and marketability was at odds with Grenier's artistic sensibilities and pedagogy, as well as one of the aims of rehabilitation, which was to encourage free expression, something that had been suppressed by colonization. As art historian Stacey Neale argues, carvings made of traditional materials were immediately recognizable as "Eskimo" and found a ready market as such, but Grenier, a ceramist, wanted to see what Inuit could do with his chosen medium, clay, which was foreign to them. By all accounts, they excelled: the malleable quality of clay made it easier to work with than stone, and they used it to produce large sculptural forms and bowls depicting a mix of human and animal heads or hunting and fishing scenes (Figure 1.6). The Arts Centre became a magnet for artists from across the community – eighty of them in 1964 – who drew inspiration from each other (Figure 1.7).[60] "I think back to the big crafts studio where the artists sang softly as they worked, where everyone stopped at midday for a bite of whale muktuk and a good hot cup of tea," Grenier recalled. "During those exciting years the community seemed to come alive."[61]

Figure 1.6 An unknown artist working in clay at Rankin Inlet, n.d. | University of Saskatchewan Libraries, University Archives and Special Collections, RG2100, Institute for Northern Studies fonds, INS-152

Figure 1.7 Pottery work area at Rankin Inlet, n.d. | University of Saskatchewan Libraries, University Archives and Special Collections, RG2100, Institute for Northern Studies fonds, RG2100-INS-S2-3709

Northern Affairs didn't share Grenier's enthusiasm for ceramics or that of the artists working under his direction. When the first work arrived in Ottawa for inspection in early 1964, it was greeted with bemusement: the bureaucrats thought they were getting stoneware, serving bowls "with Eskimo motifs" that people might use in their kitchens and dining rooms. What they got was art, an expression of Inuit creativity. "I teach the technique only but the design never," insisted Grenier. "I say nothing about that because the Eskimo knows. He is filled with art." But whether that art would sell was doubtful – at least to Northern Affairs. Even after examples of the work were displayed to critical acclaim at Expo 67, the World's Fair held in Montreal during Canada's centennial year, doubts remained about whether ceramics were "a truly Eskimo art form."[62] While the ceramics project continued for another decade with government support, Neale argues it never achieved the momentum and impact it might have, largely because of these misgivings about authenticity.[63] Ironically, Northern Affairs could celebrate the capacity of Inuit to adapt to wage labour and work underground, but when some of those hunters-turned-miners then became ceramic artists, it could not bring itself to do the same. Inuit adaptation in one context was the key to developing the Keewatin, but not in another.

The second development program initiated by Northern Affairs in the wake of the closure of the North Rankin mine aimed to exploit the Keewatin's renewable resources more effectively for both a regional and a southern market. Like the arts and crafts program, it too was rooted in an understanding of Inuit as a hunting people but it built more directly on their existing skills. It also had a more explicitly disciplinary function that sheds light on how relocation and development were part of a larger project of rule. If the North were to have a future, the capacity of its residents for collective action would have to be cultivated. The purpose of the "organized resource harvesting" and marketing program was to teach Inuit who were strangers to each other to work together and govern their own affairs.

In thinking about how to exploit the region's renewable resources more effectively, Ottawa drew on wildlife management, resource economics, and international development. The man responsible for pulling these various strands together into a concrete plan for the North in general and the Keewatin particularly was Donald Snowden, head of Northern Affairs' Industrial Division. He entered the civil service with Northern Affairs about the same time as his colleague Walter Rudnicki did. Trained as a journalist, Snowden put those skills to work in the publicity department of Northern

Affairs, where he was employed for a short time before being appointed to the Industrial Division as its director, beating out some three hundred other applicants for the challenging task of tackling the region's economic development. "His particular genius for taking a mix of familiar ideas and weaving them into a new pattern" and "his driving energy and single-minded approach" would serve him well.[64]

Starting in the 1950s, government wildlife biologists conducted the first systematic population surveys of barren-ground caribou. These showed a significant decline in their numbers, especially among the animals the Inuit in the Keewatin depended on, the Beverly and Qamanirjuaq herds. The Canadian Wildlife Service imposed severe limits on hunting and in some cases insisted on overseeing the hunt itself. To prevent what it considered waste and overhunting, it provided communities with freezers and produced educational materials – a filmstrip, comics, and storybook – designed to teach Inuit about the importance of conserving caribou. Beyond this, the Wildlife Service also encouraged Inuit to get their protein from other sources, providing them with fishing nets.[65]

If the region's future depended on exploiting renewable resources as Snowden and his colleagues believed, then caribou could not be among them. To determine what might, Snowden commissioned a series of area surveys by resource economists to learn what renewables northerners could depend on and where they could be found. Having ascertained that, the authors of the *Keewatin Mainland Economic Survey* (1963) then compared the distribution of people and food, identifying which communities were overpopulated or underpopulated or had the "optimum" number of humans. Putting the Keewatin on a stable footing would require policymakers to pay attention to its carrying capacity – that is, to balance resources with a "theoretical" population number that was derived from the food value of "expectable yields" of various species of wildlife and the calorie requirements of a family of five.[66]

Achieving that balance meant moving people from overpopulated to underpopulated communities within the region. But while relocation continued to be a government strategy to deliver social security in the North, in the 1960s it was used in combination with efforts at building capacity. Deemed the most overpopulated settlement in the region, Rankin Inlet was a prime example of this "new" old strategy.[67] Identified as one of the communities with more people than resources, it became the site of what one civil servant jokingly called the department's "Back to the Land with Joy" program.[68] In 1964, Northern Affairs engineered the removal of fifty-four Inuit, approximately 10 percent of Rankin's population, sending them to Daly Bay, more than 150 kilometres north.[69] Making their case for relocation, the survey's authors argued that, unless Inuit moved to other "areas of opportunity" in Keewatin, many of them would have "no hope at all for social and economic advancement."[70]

But unlike the relocations that occurred the decade before, the Inuit were not left at Daly Bay to subsist from the land as they always had. Instead, Northern Affairs moved them so they could participate in an "organized" char fishery and work in the cannery it had built. What made the resource harvesting conducted there, and at other Keewatin communities, "organized" was the scale at which it occurred and the "efficiency" with which it was carried out.[71] Under the direction of the department's field officers, Inuit were taught to hunt and fish more intensively, producing enough to feed not just themselves but other communities in the region, as well as to supply commercial markets.[72] Relocation was thus a strategy of development, not an end itself.

The federal government believed that canned char, whale, and seal might, if properly processed, packaged, and promoted, find a lucrative market outside the region. With that in mind, when the Inuit working with Northern Affairs officer Max Budgell caught a hundred whales off Eskimo Point in 1961, the department sent its specialty foods officer to investigate what might be done with them. A German who had spent some time in a Canadian internment camp during the Second World War, Erich Hofmann had "a positively wild interest in preserving food," to the extent that his colleagues believed that "no living thing is safe from him."[73] With his experience processing traditional, or "country," foods in Wood Buffalo National Park and the Mackenzie delta, Hofmann went to the Keewatin in 1962, working with Inuit women at Whale Cove to make muktuk sausage.

By the next year, Hofmann was convinced that his program "could not only help the Eskimo achieve a degree of self-sufficiency through preservation of foods for local use, but in areas of surplus could also generate income by means of export to southern markets." He set about proving it at Daly Bay and Rankin Inlet. By 1965, flash-frozen, smoked, and canned char and herring were making their way south, some of them ending up as samples in Donald Snowden's briefcase. As writer Edith Iglauer recalls, the head of the Industrial Division was so committed to the project that he went from restaurant to restaurant in Montreal flogging "his" canned goods.[74] When the decade closed, more than one hundred thousand tins of seven different kinds of country food were being produced yearly. Inuit consumed half of this, and Canadian Arctic Producers, a non-profit marketing company, distributed the other half.[75]

As important as acknowledging carrying capacity and harvesting and marketing renewable resources in a new way were, making the region "self-generating" required more – specifically, transforming the attitudes and behaviours of northerners. The department drew on the technologies and strategies common to development work, and, specifically, community development work, elsewhere. According to Welfare Division chief F.J. Neville, the 1964 "War on Poverty" waged by the government of the United States and the initiatives undertaken in the global South by a number of industrialized nations of the world inspired Northern Affairs.[76] Indeed, the language of the department's policy directive on community development was taken from a 1957 United Nations report discussing its work in underdeveloped countries.[77] But the books and reports in the Northern Affairs library suggest the intellectual genealogy of its community development initiatives stretched back further and was entangled with empire: in addition to a variety of studies by the United Nations, there were works dealing with community development in Fiji, Ghana, Jamaica, and South and Southeast Asia carried out by governmental and non-governmental organizations, including the British Colonial Office and Christian missions.[78]

As a strategy, community development relocated change. Rather than being animated by outside investment or connections to markets, it proceeded on the assumption that changing the lives of the poor had to begin from the inside out – that is, it had to be grounded in the human resources in each of its settlements. The job of community development workers was to help people identify their collective wants and the means to achieve them. Stated simply, community development was "the process of helping people to help themselves."[79]

The existing literature taught the bureaucrats and fieldworkers in Northern Affairs that the success of any development initiative among Inuit depended on a sense of shared purpose and a shared future that went beyond their extended families. As one of the department's economists put it, "the Eskimo must begin to think outside his tent."[80] The development literature also gave them the tools to do so – namely, the radio and the cooperative. Both would address what planners considered a major obstacle to development: the absence of a collective sense of belonging within the North's new communities and the region as a whole. Inuit had never lived in large, multicultural, and permanent communities before, and they would need to learn how. "The people of Keewatin today can be described aptly as 'different-place-miut,'" observed planner D.M. Brack in 1962. "Adjacent houses for example in Rankin are occupied by families who may not know each other's names, and in other parts of Keewatin there are many instances of group cohesion inhibiting full community action and consciousness ... If regional planning is to be really effective as a medium of social development then the people themselves must become region conscious."[81]

Through its use of communications technology, and particularly the radio, Northern Affairs tried to facilitate a sense of cohesion among the Inuit of Keewatin, one that would overcome the fragmentation caused by starvation, relocation, distance, and linguistic and cultural difference. Radio could connect people and communities, especially when broadcasts were in Inuktitut. Relatively inexpensive, it had the potential to engage people in discussion about common issues, build consensus, and help them come to collective decisions.[82]

Again, Robert Williamson played a role: having pushed Northern Affairs to publish a magazine wholly in Inuktitut in 1959, he remained committed to the idea that language played a central role in creating community cohesion. As a private citizen living and working in Rankin Inlet, he wrote and produced two Inuktitut-language programs that ran weekly on CBC North from 1962 to 1964.[83] Equally important, Williamson supported Rankin Inlet as the site of the Department of Communications Northern Pilot Project, which would test the "comminterphone" (Figure 1.8). Developed by Bell Northern Research Laboratories, the "community interaction telephone" was its answer to "a growing concern for the communications needs of the social, cultural, and political groupings which characterize Northern Canada." It combined the features of a party line with those of radio: by dialing in, up to four callers could participate in a conversation with a radio host that was broadcast over a low-power AM transmitter over a five-mile radius.[84]

Comminterphone service was initiated in 1971 and within a year had become a popular source of local information. Although it did not become a vehicle for discussing community issues or for consensus building, both communications researcher Gordon Wensley and Robert Williamson argued that it had created "a sense of involvement in what is going on around the settlement, an association – even if passive – with the events and feelings

Figure 1.8 Rankin Inlet resident Willie Adams makes adjustments to the relays of the comminterphone conference unit, 1972. | University of Saskatchewan Libraries, University Archives and Special Collections, Institute for Northern Studies fonds, INS 808

of the day." They believed that, over time, "living in an atmosphere of overheard activity would appear to add to the ambiance of community feeling amongst a collection of migrants heretofore somewhat fragmented and semi-isolated."[85]

In part, the mixed results of the comminterphone experiment spoke to the internal dynamics of the settlements in Keewatin, which D.M. Brack had hinted at. Fostering public conversation and debate about community issues among "different-place-miut" required building their capacity to do so. To this end, Northern Affairs turned to the cooperative. As institutions organized for the mutual benefit of their members, cooperatives have roots going back to medieval Europe. But the cooperative movement is of more recent vintage. Originating in mid-nineteenth-century England and Europe, it was a reaction to industrialization and the economic hardships it visited on urban workers and small farmers. The cooperative movement came to Canada in the early twentieth century as part of the broad culture of reform initiated in part by the middle-class members of its Christian churches.[86] As locally owned businesses, cooperatives kept capital in communities through profit sharing with their members, took direction from their membership in how business was conducted, and ensured fair prices.

In establishing cooperatives in the North, Industrial Division chief Donald Snowden drew from international examples, but also on the work of Fathers Moses Coady and Jimmy Tompkins and the Antigonish Movement in Nova Scotia to alleviate rural poverty in the 1930s and 1940s.[87] Taken up globally, the program of social reform, centred on adult education oriented toward cooperative action, drew from the ideas of liberal Catholicism, as well as papal encyclicals dating to the late nineteenth century, and enjoyed broad support from clergy of all denominations.[88] For one development officer in the Northwest Territories, the philosophy of cooperation was "simple and easy to understand. It is found in the Sermon on the Mount and in the Golden Rule."[89]

To their promoters, co-ops were instruments of social, as well as economic, development. In the North, they built capacity by schooling Inuit in the processes of formal democracy and self-government, as well as the workings of the market, teaching them about "interest on loans and amortization of capital" as well as secret ballots and voting.[90] As Northern Affairs' supervisor of cooperatives put it in 1960, "The practice of democracy in the economic sphere ... set an example for democracy in the larger sphere."[91] Gordon Robertson agreed. The deputy minister considered co-ops to be an "incubator from which political leaders emerged"; during his time in office, he observed how Inuit men moved from being directors of their community's cooperative to the most prominent members of its "Eskimo Council."[92] Indeed, sociologist Marybelle Mitchell argues that Arctic cooperatives played an important role in forging an Inuit nationalism that ultimately contributed to the creation of Nunavut.[93]

In essence, using cooperatives to develop northern communities was a political project. It involved nothing less than creating a civic political culture from the ground up, helping Inuit to govern their own lives and convincing them "that their world does not begin and end with Government action or its lack."[94] They might make mistakes, but, as Snowden noted, "Wasn't that just part of the whole process of learning how to make their own decisions and carry their new responsibilities?"[95] To Northern Affairs, "community development and self-determination are inseparable."[96]

From their start in arctic Quebec in 1959, co-ops sprang up quickly. Just five years later, nearly 20 percent of Canada's Inuit were members of one of nineteen such institutions across the North.[97] By 1970, northern co-ops handled over $2.5 million in sales of goods and services yearly, returning close to $1.25 million to members in the form of salaries, purchases from members, and patronage dividends.[98] Ten years later, in 1980, sales amounted to an astonishing $27 million, with payouts of $9.1 million.[99]

While it might be easy to see co-ops simply as instruments of assimilation, the intentions of Northern Affairs in promoting them as part of community development in the North were more complex. Co-ops were a kind of "intermediate technology" of development, a way to build on the perceived communalism of Inuit culture and introduce Inuit to the market.[100] They were vehicles for capital accumulation *and* redistribution; they were meant to discipline the Inuit to Western forms of democracy *and* to teach them how to subvert power. For Alexander Laidlaw, Coady's colleague at St. Francis Xavier University and head of the Co-operative Union of Canada, the latter aspect of cooperatives was especially significant, given how large the state had come to loom in people's lives by the mid-twentieth century. "Welfare measures are being pushed farther and faster all the time in all parts of the world – and rightly so," he wrote in *North* magazine in 1963. "But in order to prevent domination by government bodies and the official mind, citizens must be strongly organized to do things for themselves ... Cooperatives are proving to be one of the most effective agencies in this role."[101]

Those working in Northern Affairs shared Laidlaw's concerns about the need to counter domination by government bodies. Not only were Inuit unfamiliar with formal participatory democracy, but cross-cultural differences regarding communication and the impact of colonialism left them unlikely to challenge authority. There was no better example of the disastrous consequences of such miscommunication than what happened in the winter of 1957–58. Misunderstanding over whether the Ahiarmiut had agreed to be resettled to Henik Lake and their knowledge of the resources of the area had contributed to the deaths of eight of them that winter. Privately, senior bureaucrats in Northern Affairs felt that "their decision to move ... was probably because they regarded it as a command of the white man."[102]

Although officials could exercise more care in interpreting Inuit responses, the long-term solution was to end Inuit diffidence. That was why co-ops were so valuable: as Donald Snowden told Edith Iglauer of the *New Yorker*, "I don't believe that the government is infallible, and the co-ops make it possible for the Eskimos to give us hell."[103] Asked later about what he thought he had accomplished at Northern Affairs, Snowden singled out cooperatives, institutions that allowed people to live in the region and govern their own lives in a changing world. "[They] now know they can continue to live where home is for them and that they can do this through their own efforts. They know THEY can make decisions."[104] The Inuit interviewed about their participation agreed, arguing that co-ops gave them "a way to regain some of the control [over our lives] we previously had." Others went further, pointing out co-ops' long-term political consequences: according to former Inuit politician Thomas Suluk, co-ops were "underground governments" that provided the foundation for a "pan Inuit solidarity that had no historic precedent."[105]

Snowden's and Suluk's statements point to the broader meaning and contradictory purpose of development. Poverty and a lack of social security were entry points for the Canadian state to pursue its larger disciplinary project of rule. Social work, anthropology, wildlife conservation, resource economics, and international development shaped how bureaucrats and fieldworkers understood the North. As much as improving life in the region was about the application of new kinds of knowledge, it was also about transforming its peoples, making them capable of governing themselves collectively. Cooperatives schooled Inuit in the institutions and practices of the market and participatory democratic governance, cultivating the basis of a civic political culture for the North in the process. In that sense, development was colonialism in another guise – in this case, the northward extension of the liberal order. But it was also imagined as a way to facilitate independence and, ultimately, decolonization, by putting the region on a sustainable footing and teaching Inuit to give the bureaucrats and experts hell, to place limits on the very power that disciplined them.

2

"The Governmentality Game"

Problematizing, Resettling, and Democratizing Newfoundland

Come all you young fellows and list' while I tell,
Of the terrible misfortune that upon me befell;
Centralization they say was the name,
But me, I just calls it the government game.

– Al Pittman and Pat Byrne,
"The Government Game"

In the late 1960s, Fred Earle witnessed the damage caused by the latest version of "the government game." There had been earlier efforts to centralize Newfoundland's population, but nothing matched the joint federal-provincial Fisheries Household Resettlement Program, which moved more than twenty thousand people in the ten years it was in operation, all in the name of improving their lives.[1]

"We read of human rights," Earle, a community development worker, wrote in his diary:

> Yet, on November 8, 1969, men and women and children were resettled from Batteau [Labrador] during darkness, wind and snow flurries. The open skiff made three trips from their homes two miles away before all persons and belongings were on the Coastal boat. A lady of 72 (who was making her first trip on a steamer) was in tears and so was a younger lady

Figure 2.1 The house of Mr. Malcolm Rogers being towed by a 40-horsepower motor boat during relocation from Fox Island to Flat Island, August 1961. | Bob Brooks, Library and Archives Canada, National Film Board fonds, e011177529

> who remarked – "They made us leave our Island. When I locked my door it was the hardest thing I did in my life to turn my back on my home."[2]

Some never did turn their backs, preferring to hang on as long as they could. Partially deaf and blind, an eighty-three-year-old accordion player whom Earle met on a separate trip to the community of Exploits was its only resident; indeed, he was the only person living on Burnt Island. Everyone else had been resettled. "I asked him if he ever gets lonely," Earle wrote. "He said a man only gets lonely when he leaves the place he likes. He would be lonely if he went to a City and there was nothing to do but look through a window. He mentioned several old fishermen who left their native homes to live with sons and daughters in places like Toronto – they soon died."[3]

Others hung on in different ways. Some brought their houses with them (Figure 2.1). Those who went to Arnold's Cove on Placentia Bay left their imprint on the land in another way. Some of its streets bear the names of the communities whose people resettled there: there's Woody Island Drive, Port Anne Heights, Spencer's Cove Road, Kingwell Crescent, Merasheen Crescent, and Harbour Buffett Road. "But," resident Randy Boucher added in 1970, "we are all Arnold's Cove people now. Although when we moved we naturally stuck with our neighbours, the people we knew, there is no keeping apart, we all mix together."[4]

Resettlement was a defining moment in Newfoundland's history, one that fuelled an explosion of literature, art, and music in the 1970s and 1980s celebrating pre-Confederation outport life, from journalist Ray Guy's acerbic stories revealing the homespun wit and wisdom of the bayman, to Al Pittman's elegiac poetry, printmaker David Blackwood's lonely renderings of moving, and Farley Mowat's furiously romantic ones, among others. As much as it looked back with laughter, tears, and anger, however, this renaissance also created an identity that allowed Newfoundlanders to look forward with neo-nationalist pride to what the island and its people were and could be. The "Newfcult phenomenon," as journalist Sandra Gwyn dubbed it, gave Newfoundlanders roots and wings.[5]

But the story of resettlement is more complicated than what memory and politics sometimes allow. If Newfoundlanders were pawns in a government game, their moves shaped how it was played. Short of refusing to go, those who participated did so in such numbers that they subverted the purpose of resettlement, sometimes working the program to their advantage. In the process, they revealed the gaps between policy, implementation, and outcomes, ones that those who describe resettlement as "high modern" and "rational" might do well to recognize.[6]

Because the story of resettlement is focused on the traumatic aspects of uprooting and the rural world that was lost, the larger context and purpose it served has been somewhat overshadowed. As Miriam Wright and Raymond Blake argue, resettlement was one aspect of a larger government policy to modernize Newfoundland's fisheries and, I would argue, to develop the province and uplift its residents. Modernization may have been premised on centralizing the population, but the project of improvement didn't end there. Instead, as in the North, developing Newfoundland also entailed transforming Newfoundlanders, building their collective capacity to govern themselves democratically.

In that sense, resettlement was part of a governmentality game, one in which people like Fred Earle played a significant role. Earle worked for Donald Snowden, who was introduced in the preceding chapter. But he wasn't a government agent. Instead, both he and Snowden were employed by the Extension Department (Extension) at Memorial University of Newfoundland, Earle as a fieldworker and Snowden as its director, thanks in no small part to the latter's success establishing Arctic cooperatives. Important in understanding the story of resettlement and development in Newfoundland, the work of Extension, along with Memorial's Institute of Social and Economic Research (ISER), also reveals that the project of improvement in postwar Canada was one that enrolled non-governmental institutions and agents to its cause, universities and their faculty, staff, and students being among the most important. As will be discussed, expertise from economics, anthropology, sociology, and community development informed resettlement and the subsequent development of the province.

But before Newfoundlanders could be moved and the province improved, the place they lived had to be invented – as a problem.

Discussions of resettlement in Newfoundland in the 1960s and 1970s almost always begin by linking the province's settlement pattern to its social and economic woes. Carl Goldenberg, counsel for the province, told the Royal Commission on Canada's Economic Prospects (the Gordon Commission) in 1955 that "the small, sparsely populated and poor settlements scattered along 6000 miles of coast could not afford to pay for even the minimum public services required by modern communities."[7] Provincial economist Robert Wells agreed and went further, arguing in 1960 "that social and economic development in Newfoundland has been retarded because our population is scattered around 6000 miles of coastline in some 1144 settlements"[8] (Figure 2.2). Explaining his government's resettlement program to a national audience of Liberal Party members, Minister of Community and Social Development William Rowe argued that Newfoundland's problem was "demographic": its "population of less than one-half million [was] scattered among thirteen hundred settlements." While this dispersal reflected the region's historical reliance on the inshore fishery, such a settlement pattern was as "obsolete" as that fishery was. In the mid-twentieth century, "the plain ecological fact is that coastal Newfoundland is over-populated in relation to the inshore, midshore or offshore fishing employment opportunities ... There is no need to understand why the average income of inshore fishermen ... has been eight hundred dollars annually."[9]

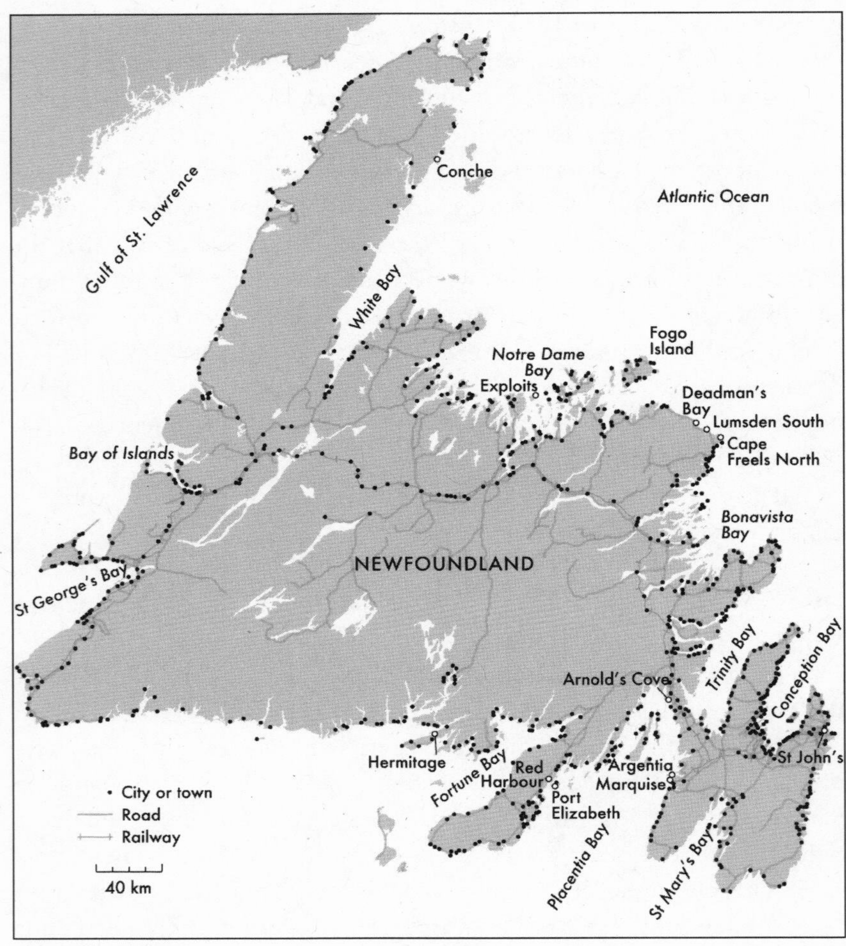

Figure 2.2 In the 1960s, there were literally thousands of settlements (outports) along Newfoundland's coast.

The image Goldenberg, Wells, and Rowe invoked, of a small, needy population scattered along the edges of a large island and dependent on a declining fishery, captured the problem confronting Newfoundland. It did not simply reflect the partisan view of a government bureaucrat and minister but was widely shared, reiterated in the assessments of the government's resettlement program made by scholars in the 1960s and 1970s. Although they found its policy wanting in different ways, these experts did not take issue with the government's fundamental evaluation of Newfoundland's predicament: the province's future would lie in overcoming its impoverishing combination of history, geography, and demography.

In their 1968 study, sociologists Noel Iverson and D. Ralph Matthews linked Newfoundland's low standard of living and inadequate social services to its settlement pattern. "From the beginning the population of Newfoundland was dispersed around its coastline and, as a consequence, there exists today some 1,100 separate communities, many with a population of less than 200 people," they observed. "One of the major problems facing the Newfoundland Government is the difficulty in providing modern services to these people. The cost ... is extremely high because of the inaccessibility of these tiny communities and, in the case of those who live on off-shore islands, it is often simply impossible."[10]

The province's settlement pattern reflected its economic history: dependent on the international salt-fish trade, the Europeans who colonized Newfoundland had faced the sea since the seventeenth century, eking out what economist Parzival Copes called a "primitive self-sufficiency" in scattered coastal settlements.[11] There was little connection among outports or their people. In that respect, Newfoundland was similar to other staples-based colonies of British North America. But, unlike them, it retained this settlement pattern well into the twentieth century. While the population of other colonies and provinces had centralized and urbanized, Newfoundland's had not: in the postwar period, it appeared to Copes like a place out of time.

Having escaped urbanization, the colony and then province had also escaped prosperity. As Copes showed in his 1972 study, although forestry, mining, and construction drew Newfoundlanders away from the fishery during the Second World War and in the years immediately after their joining Confederation in 1949, the province's economic boom was short-lived. No significant permanent urbanization or industrialization occurred, and, in fact, by the second half of the 1950s, Newfoundland experienced a severe economic downturn: unemployment was 24 percent in 1961, with peak winter levels reaching 31 percent.[12] Unlike farmers who often sold their land when they migrated to the cities for better opportunities, fishermen could always go back to the sea – and many did. Indeed, in the 1960s Newfoundland saw an increase in the number of people fishing while all other Canadian provinces experienced a decline in this sector.[13] With more people pursuing a diminishing resource, the livelihood it provided fell well short of the national average.[14] From 1949 to 1970, the personal income of

Newfoundlanders was just 55 percent of the average Canadian.[15] Among inshore fishermen, the situation was more dismal: taking into account their large families, one political scientist estimated their incomes were one-sixth the national poverty level.[16]

Like their settlement pattern, Newfoundlanders' family size was interpreted as a symptom of backwardness. When Newfoundland joined Canada in 1949, it did so as the country's most fecund province.[17] In 1969, its birthrate was 25.3 per 1,000, more than the Canadian average of 17.6 and higher than that of the "more developed" regions of the world.[18] While Premier Joey Smallwood saw his province's birthrate as another sign of its potential, the economist Copes read it differently.[19] To him, Newfoundland's high birth rate was due to the province's "failure to complete the process of industrialization."[20] The "largely pre-industrial society of the outport" had resisted "the trend toward smaller families that is so evident in advanced urban economies."[21]

Implicit in these analyses is the idea that, in becoming modern, societies took on a particular spatial form and demographic and economic profile: populations of urban people with small families and full-time jobs in the industrial or service sector characterized modernity. In that regard, Newfoundland was an "anomaly," an anachronism whose days were numbered – or should have been. In Copes's view, the persistence of its premodern character was due, paradoxically, to the modern welfare state. Federal transfer payments in the form of family allowances, old age pensions, and unemployment insurance buffered people against the "natural" rationalizing forces of the market and the environment, allowing them to continue to live where and how they otherwise could not and should not have.[22] With a regular source of cash income, people could get by in the outports when, in the economist's view, they would have been better off leaving. For the province's minister of Community and Social Development, the immobility of outport Newfoundlanders was a sign of their poverty; it denied them choice and prevented them from realizing their potential.[23]

In fact, census figures suggest that outmigration continued after Confederation, despite the introduction of federal transfers. Indeed, after the mid-1950s, it increased.[24] As elsewhere in the world, those who were able to move to improve their circumstances did. When economists and politicians spoke of the immobility of outport people, then, they were referring specifically to school-age children, the elderly, and adults whose economic prospects were limited by a variety of factors, mainly education: in the late 1960s, the federal government assessed "the average adult household level of education" in Newfoundland's isolated outports to be less than a Grade 4, or mid–primary school, level.[25]

If the modern welfare state had slowed Newfoundland's transition to modernity by immobilizing a sector of its population, then it had to intervene again to deal with those unintended consequences by shifting its people – through space and, with it, time. Indeed, Newfoundlanders' evolution was contingent on their physical movement. As Iverson and Matthews pointed out, resettlement was meant to transform "a peasant subsistence-level society into a market-oriented industrial one."[26]

Despite the seeming clarity of these arguments about modernity, they were based on at least two misunderstandings. The first concerned the nature of the outport economy. As Rosemary Ommer and Nancy Turner argue, outport residents were enmeshed in an informal economy that not only gave people a living but also contributed to the social cohesion and health of the communities they lived in. From the beginnings of permanent European occupation in Newfoundland, settler families sustained themselves through a combination of work in the seasonal fishery, subsistence production, and cooperation among kin and neighbours. Firewood might be traded for potatoes, moose meat for help repairing gear. The dynamics of the informal economy were such that they kept "people working productively even when they were not employed."[27] Indeed, Ommer contends that the informal economy remains crucial to the rural economy and culture: "Fishers in Newfoundland were and, I would suggest some still are, non-industrial in culture, outlook and attitude."[28] While she warns against romanticizing the quality of life that was sustained, it was certainly the case that the social security provided by the informal economy was not something that was legible to governments for whom industrial development was normative and who understood poverty and justified welfare and economic policies – including resettlement – in light of statistics on annual income and unemployment.

If policymakers overlooked the significance of the informal economy in providing rural Newfoundlanders with social security, they also misunderstood the relationship between the province's settlement pattern and its economic development. One needed to look no further for proof than the countries of Scandinavia, as Norwegian sociologist Ottar Brox pointed out to his Newfoundland colleagues at the time. In the mid-1960s, places like England and Norway were similarly well off in terms of their per capita gross national product, but their degree of urbanization differed greatly: it was 80 percent for England and 32 percent for Norway. Iceland also provided a useful point of comparison. Like Newfoundland, its largely rural population was also scattered in small settlements, but Icelanders enjoyed a high standard of living.[29]

Although these Nordic examples suggested that economic development was the outcome of political choices rather than geography, the connection between Newfoundland's settlement pattern and its poverty remained, and invoking it became the customary way to begin discussions of the province's development. As political scientist Timothy Mitchell observes, "Fields of analysis often develop a convention for introducing their object."[30] The simple and powerfully evocative image of a province defined by its geography and demography conjured by Rowe, and repeated by both the supporters and critics of his government's program, invented Newfoundland as a development problem, inviting certain kinds of intervention and foreclosing others.

Even after the resettlement program ended, the image persisted in the textbook histories and academic analyses of the province.[31] It endures still: when one of the *St. John's Telegram*'s journalists announced he was leaving the province in November 2017, he gave his readers this advice: "Here's the honest truth: It's in the economic self-interest of every man, woman and child in this province to do the same thing I'm doing: pack up and move literally anywhere else. The province has a demographic problem and a geographic problem. There are too many old people."[32]

In presenting Newfoundland as a place constrained by its geography and demography, these assessments of the province's history reiterated the logic of resettlement. Indeed, as historian David Alexander wryly observed, "The burden which Newfoundland has carried is to justify that it should have any people."[33]

In a sense, resettling was nothing unusual for Newfoundlanders: movement had characterized outport life since there were outports. People supplemented their incomes from the traditional inshore fishery by leaving to go sealing, or to take up wage work in construction, forestry, mining, and the pulp and paper industry. Nor was government involvement in resettlement novel: in an effort to diversify the colony's economy, the Commission of Government that ran Newfoundland from 1934 to 1949 instituted a land settlement scheme in the 1930s aimed at moving people from the outports to model agricultural communities where they could farm full time.[34] A decade later, as a result of the Leased Bases Agreement between Britain and the United States, 750 residents of Argentia and Marquise on Placentia Bay were relocated to make way for the construction of a massive naval air station and army base, home to over 12,000 American military personnel.[35]

What was new about the program undertaken by the Smallwood government was its scale, how directive the state was, and its disciplinary intent. Although people complained about the first iteration of resettlement in the post-Confederation period, Smallwood's Centralization Program involved a minimum of bureaucracy and interference – and gave people a minimum level of support in return: $150 per family when the program started in 1954, rising to $600 per family when it ended in 1965. Aimed at encouraging the wholesale abandonment of communities, it was administered by the provincial Department of Welfare, which provided financial assistance to individuals only if everyone in a given settlement agreed to move.[36] In all, 110 communities were shut down and approximately eight thousand people moved in the eleven years the program was in operation.[37]

Committed to centralizing its population, the province was also keen to divest itself of the financial burden of doing so – modest though the level of assistance it provided was. Adept at squeezing money from "Uncle Ottawa," Smallwood asked the federal government to help, calling for a national fisheries development program that paralleled the one for agriculture under the Agricultural Rehabilitation and Development Administration. As Raymond Blake discusses, Ottawa eventually agreed, in 1965. Like the province, the federal government saw centralization as the key to industrializing the fishery, improving Newfoundland's economic prospects, and reducing the burden of supporting a poor population and unproductive inshore sector.[38]

In return for assuming the majority of the costs (70 percent), the federal government restructured centralization, giving those who administered it a much more activist role in shaping the movement of Newfoundlanders. Governed by two successive federal-provincial agreements (1965–70 and 1970–75), the Joint Fisheries Household Resettlement Program was voluntary: it paid eligible households to move, and paid them more generously than in the past: $1,000 per household and an additional $200 per member in the first phase, and somewhat more in the second. In return, the program directed their movements to particular places – namely, to "growth poles" or "growth centres," so called because they were considered bases for the offshore fishery and processing industry.[39]

While Smallwood is often singled out as the architect of modernization in Newfoundland, the "growth pole" or "growth centre" idea that underpinned the resettlement program was imported, not homegrown. Indeed, according to political scientists Bernard Higgins and Donald Savoie, in the 1960s and 1970s "there was scarcely a developed or developing country in the world that did not make use of the concept in formulating its development policy."[40] Among the governments that embraced this "travelling rationality" of development, however, Smallwood's stood out. As geographer Michael Staveley observed, "Rarely in North America was there such an overt confluence of academic analysis and applied public policy as in the Canadian province of Newfoundland," whose resettlement program was premised on growth pole theory.[41]

In offering this theory in the 1950s, French economist François Perroux challenged existing understandings of development. In contrast to neoclassical economists who argued that the market would spread growth evenly through space, Perroux insisted that development was always uneven, concentrated around "poles" or "centres" of economic activity. Rather than evolving toward some sort of spatial balance, growth would always be polarized, with certain centres dominating their regions. (Perroux never distinguished between "growth poles" and "growth centres.") Investing in growth poles or centres directly or indirectly, by attracting "propulsive industries" to them, would have "spread effects": not only would the pole or centre draw more investment and people, but it would also diffuse innovation and prosperity outward, enriching its periphery. In short, Perroux's growth pole theory was a way of seeing how uneven economic growth could work to reduce disparities among regions.

Or so it appeared. According to Higgins and Savoie, in the 1960s and 1970s growth pole theory was especially appealing to regional planners because it offered a seemingly easy solution to a complex problem, and one that was not contingent on social or political context but could work anywhere. Simply attract industries to an underdeveloped area and wait for the spread effects to work their magic, making regional economic disparities disappear.[42] In the view of government bureaucrats, one way to attract industries to Newfoundland was to provide them with a labour force by concentrating the population in particular areas.

Unfortunately, Perroux never meant for his ideas to be applied like this (or perhaps at all), insisting that it was "untenable to reduce the theory of development poles to a mere instrument of regional planning."[43] His high modernist theory of economic growth was not based on what he called "banal space," in other words, on conventional, bounded, contiguous, territorial space – what most people would consider "real" space. Instead, his theories dealt with "economic space," with markets and flows that cut across international boundaries. Because of its transnational and often global character, economic space was not amenable to planning by government authorities whose power was limited to the boundaries of the nation-state.[44] Its dangerous combination of intuitive appeal and utter impracticality meant that "of all the concepts utilized since World War II in the formulation of regional development plans, none generated so rapid a rise in popularity, nor so early and so complete disillusionment, as 'growth poles.'"[45]

Because Perroux was a theorist, it was left to federal and provincial officials to turn his high modernist ideas into administrative practice. Their struggles to do so reveal the spaces between Perroux's idea, resettlement policy, and implementation, ones created by the illegibility of Newfoundland and the material and political contexts in which authorities worked. Within these spaces, Newfoundlanders were able to shape resettlement, often to their own purposes. They may not have wanted to go for the ride, but, as backseat drivers, they were able to wield some influence over where the vehicle of modernization took them, even if Smallwood and his bureaucrats remained firmly at the wheel.

Neither the members of the Resettlement Committee, who oversaw the day-to-day administration of the program, nor the members of the Joint Planning Committee, who met quarterly to discuss questions of policy and provide direction, ever came to a conclusive answer about where Newfoundlanders should be moved. When resettlement got underway in 1965, there did not seem to be a list of growth poles. Instead, there was a list of thirty-two "reception points." Soon after, however, committee members were using an elaborate typology consisting of ten different categories of receiving communities. The connection between resettlement and industrializing the fishery was particularly apparent in the first agreement. Not only were there "designated major fishery growth centres," but there were also "other portions of major fishery growth centres," "suitable communities within commuting distance of a major fishery growth centre," and "other fishery growth centres."

The typology didn't end there. Recognizing more jobs were needed than the offshore fishery could provide, Ottawa and St. John's agreed the resettlement program would fund moves to "other growth points," "approved organized reception centres," locations that were "being organized," "other advantageous locations involving additional land costs," "approved reception locations," and "any area with improved circumstances for widows, retired and incapacitated persons." The actual number of settlements included in these categories changed over the life of the program, increasing in number and encompassing places that ranged in size from less than a thousand people to tens of thousands.[46]

When the Department of Regional Economic Expansion (DREE) took over the federal government's responsibility to oversee resettlement from the Department of Fisheries in 1970, the movement away from its strictly fisheries focus continued: it identified eight "special areas" to which Newfoundlanders might be assisted to move. They and the designated receiving communities within them were defined by their potential for growth in other economic sectors as well as the fishery.[47]

The shifting typology of receiving communities and the fluidity of the number of places it encompassed reflected the problems the federal and provincial government encountered in translating economic theory into public policy. Bureaucrats were hobbled by a lack of information. As anthropologist Ian Whitaker, the co-director of ISER, noted in 1961, Newfoundland was distinguished by the absence of "vital social statistics which for other provinces of Canada may already be available to the public in predigested format."[48] The fishery had been the subject of much study, often by formal commissions of inquiry, but there had been no in-depth description or analysis of Newfoundland's communities before bureaucrats began making decisions about where people should be sent from and go to. While the 1967 Pushie Commission on the Economic Prospects of Newfoundland and Labrador agreed that resettlement would help with "an orderly transition from the traditional, semi-subsistence way of life to a modern, monetary economy," its benefits could not be fully realized because of "a lack of an overall development plan for the Province," something that depended on having basic demographic and economic information.[49]

The confusion surrounding the identification and categorization of communities was also rooted in the context in which resettlement was administered. Responsibility for operating the program fell to one division of one provincial government department. Possessed of a small budget and staff, the Resettlement Division of the Department of Fisheries and then the Department of Community and Social Development must have been as surprised as it was unprepared to deal with the overwhelming response to it. Very quickly, hundreds of applications involving thousands of people poured in from all parts of the province – so many that, six months into the fiscal year of 1967, the division's Resettlement Committee found itself having to approve applications conditionally because it was close to outrunning the program's annual budget.[50] It was a situation that would be repeated, for the five-year period from 1966 to 1971 accounted for 85 percent of those who were resettled, some 17,584 people.[51]

Whereas in rural Newfoundland "moving fever" manifested itself in the form of applications for resettlement, among the staff of the Resettlement Division in St. John's it presented itself as stress. Confronted with a rush of paper, they found themselves in a reactive position, having to decide – quickly – if the places Newfoundlanders proposed to move to were appropriate. Did Conche have enough jobs to absorb resettlers? Were there enough serviced lots at Arnold's Cove for people who wanted to build houses?

In an effort to collect more information on which to make decisions, the provincial departments that oversaw resettlement dispatched fieldworkers to interview the individual householders who had applied for assistance.[52] At the same time, federal planners tried to systematize the criteria for receiving communities by developing a scoring system they hoped would eliminate the "ad hoc" decision making that had characterized the operation of the first federal-provincial agreement.[53] In the process, bureaucrats spent a great deal of time debating and refining the criteria and whether specific places fit them. In part, their difficulties were due to the illegibility of rural Newfoundland: planners and policymakers simply lacked adequate demographic and economic information and struggled to identify the best sources.[54] It was not until August 1968 that federal government planners, working with the Dominion Bureau of Statistics, managed to ascertain the precise number of unincorporated communities in the province, and hence those "that could be theoretically considered with reference to the Newfoundland Centralization Programme."[55] In other words, not until mid-way into the first resettlement agreement did the governments of Canada and Newfoundland actually know its scope.

Finding out how many of those communities were "isolated" and hence candidates for resettlement was the next step. As W.P. Rossiter, the technical adviser to the assistant deputy minister overseeing the "Isolation Criteria Program," noted in 1970, at the end of the first federal-provincial resettlement agreement, no one could agree on "the actual number of communities in comparative isolation, with estimates varying between 700 and 1200 communities." By weighting three variables – educational (50 percent), medical (25 percent), and communications (25 percent) facilities – DREE's analysts came up with a numerical scale to measure "major," "intermediate," and "minor" isolation for the province's ten census divisions. While information on seven census districts was compiled, the project does not appear to have ever been completed.[56]

To complicate matters, designating receiving communities was also politically fraught. Applicants to the program sometimes wrote directly to Smallwood for information and to make their case for why they should be funded, often reminding the premier that they were good Liberals and paid-up members of the party. Such letters invariably made their way to the Resettlement Committee – as a matter of routine administrative practice but perhaps also because Smallwood was well aware how important the "fishermen's vote" had been – and was – to his electoral success.[57] In addition to individuals, local development associations and provincial and federal politicians also lobbied the Resettlement and Joint Planning Committees, keen to make their cases about why particular places ought to be designated receiving communities.[58]

More often than not, the Resettlement Committee approved the applications it got, in part because of what might be called administrative momentum. Having invested themselves in a high profile and contentious policy like resettlement, and having got Newfoundlanders to apply – to actually volunteer to relocate – bureaucrats were under some pressure to follow through – that is, to process the applications they received and get people moved.

From a distance, in Ottawa, it seemed means were rapidly becoming ends; federal and provincial civil servants in St. John's were losing sight of the purpose of the program amidst the flurry of applications, moving people almost for the sake of moving them.[59] Mobility replaced modernization as the purpose of resettlement. In 1970, for instance, the Resettlement Committee made Lumsden South a receiving community, despite the fact that it had no water or sewer system, because it was the only place where people from Cape Freels North and Deadman's Bay would resettle. Similarly, it designated Hermitage because it was the only place that appealed to elderly people and fishermen as a destination.[60] The force of administrative momentum is indicated by the extent to which the mere existence of the resettlement policy became its rationale. As applications began to decline toward the end of the second agreement, in 1972 the members of the

Resettlement Committee decided to revisit the files it had rejected earlier, convinced that thousands more people could be relocated if only the criteria for receiving communities were expanded.[61]

Decisions like these were rooted in the sometimes conflicting aims of resettlement as well as the immediate pressures of administration. The program was supposed to improve the social security of Newfoundlanders and modernize the province's economy. But one didn't inevitably follow from the other. What should take precedence, needs or opportunities? As a welfare measure, the aims of resettlement were met if people were moved to places with better social services than existed where they lived before. But these communities were not necessarily the ones with the best prospects for industrialization. If economic development were the goal, people had to be sent to a handful of larger centres.

As important as the circumstances in which resettlement was administered and its dual purposes are to understanding the difficulties the state encountered implementing it, the larger political context in which modernization occurred also limited what bureaucrats could do. Despite complaints about "King Joey" being "the sole fountainhead for most, if not all, major and minor decisions concerning Newfoundland," the province was a liberal democracy and it was difficult, if not impossible, to force people to move – especially to realize their potential as individuals.[62] Over and over again, both the federal and provincial governments reminded Newfoundlanders the program was voluntary. The state could offer incentives to resettle and exert all sorts of indirect pressure to achieve the outcomes it wanted, but in the end it was politically unpalatable to compel Canadians to move, much less to move them to specific places.

Given all of this, Newfoundlanders found themselves with a surprising degree of latitude to move to places of their choosing and to get government funding to do so. And they used it. Although more than 20,000 people moved under the auspices of the federal-provincial resettlement program, only a third of them went to growth centres under the first agreement. Instead, the majority found their way to approved reception centres or non-designated relocation communities.[63] The program was more successful in directing people in its second iteration, moving 47 percent of them to the designated "special areas," but it was still the case that the majority of households that received resettlement assistance went to places other than those designated as optimal.[64] Despite the efforts to develop criteria for identifying receiving communities and the federal government's desire to restrict their number, over the decade it operated, the resettlement program funded moves to 332 different places across the province, many of them just "a few miles down the road" from where the resettlers had lived.[65]

If the state had limited success in moving Newfoundlanders to particular places, it also found it difficult to move them entirely from others. Under both resettlement agreements, all householders could qualify for assistance to move if 90 percent of the population in their community signed a petition indicating their willingness to move (lowered to 80 percent in 1966) – in other words, if they agreed to dissolve their community.[66]

What is less well known is that people from these "designated outports" were not the only ones the resettlement program funded to move. It also helped widows, the handicapped, and the incapacitated to move to places that were better serviced. As well, recognizing that jobs in some fish-processing plants and on offshore trawlers were going unfilled, federal and provincial officials agreed that an individual household could qualify for "the shifting money" even if the community it was part of did not, but only if the householder were moving to a job in a fisheries growth centre.[67]

Over time, this provision of the resettlement agreement was modified further – "watered down," according to one frustrated federal bureaucrat – to facilitate movement, first, to a job in any growth centre; then from a recognized "sending community" (a place where "a substantial proportion of the inhabitants" had indicated their "wish to move") to a recognized "receiving community"; and finally from any place that was not a receiving community.[68] The result of all these changes was to shift the purpose of the program. Resettlement would focus on enabling "individual moves to places where opportunities are better, rather than on the closure of communities."[69] As Tom Kent, the deputy minister of the Department of Regional Economic Expansion, grumbled, the government had ended up funding a program in which "anyone could apply [for assistance to move] from anywhere in the province."[70]

In all, the Resettlement Committee received applications from 582 different places. Of these, 148 were totally evacuated, and the rest – three-quarters – were not.[71] While we tend to conflate resettlement with community abandonment, individual moves accounted for 43 percent of the people who were relocated, more than the one-third the federal government deemed ideal.[72]

The pattern of mobility under resettlement as well as the number of outports that were shut down belie conventional views of the program. It was not a "coastal clearance scheme," as Farley Mowat charged. Nor was it wholly "high modern," firmly rooted in expert planning and exemplary of the "rationality policy model," in which there is "an orderly and incremental path from problem to solution," and "outcomes are purposefully chosen because they are the best alternatives."[73]

Instead, resettlement spoke to the limits of state power, ones that were imposed in part by the actions of ordinary Newfoundlanders. Their use of the resettlement program was consistent with how they had engaged with prior and subsequent initiatives aimed at improving their condition over the twentieth century. As Rosemary Ommer observes, whether these programs were proposed by the government or by a non-government organization like the Fishermen's Protective Union, Newfoundlanders bent them to their purposes as much as they could in order to "preserve a way of life." Welfare and unemployment insurance payments served as "start-up capital" in the same way merchant credit had in the past; that is, it allowed fishers to set themselves up for another and, they hoped, better season. Introduced in 1992 in the wake of the moratorium on fishing, the Northern Cod Adjustment and Rehabilitation Program was one of a number of financial aid programs meant to help fishers retrain for other jobs or ease them into retirement. But some used "the package," as it came to be known, for other purposes, like buying all terrain vehicles. While their critics considered spending on "recreation" to be foolish, for fishers such a purchase was strategic, a way to buttress the informal economy and ensure their social security: an ATV allowed them to hunt and supply themselves with country food more efficiently.[74]

Perhaps the most revealing example of how limited state power could be when it came to resettlement comes from Placentia Bay. As George Withers details, in 1969, forty-five families from Port Elizabeth on Davis Island agreed to be relocated, but only to the previously abandoned community of Red Harbour, just five kilometres away on the Newfoundland "mainland." These families represented a group of older fishers, men whose investments in the inshore fishery in the form of gear and infrastructure amounted to more than half a million dollars. From Red Harbour, they could continue fishing their grounds and maintain their independence, independence they believed they would lose by moving to Marystown or Burin and participating in the offshore industrial fishery. Equally importantly, moving as a group would allow them to sustain their sense of community, the connections between place, faith, and kin. With the support of the local merchant, who agreed to move with them, the clergy, their member of the House of Assembly, and their member of Parliament, they convinced the Resettlement Committee to let them do so – in contravention of the law, which forbade the permanent reoccupation of officially abandoned outports. In December 1969, just four years after Red Harbour had been abandoned, it was designated a reception centre, and Port Elizabeth officially closed.[75]

By proposing to go to places other than those designated by the state and by exploiting the opportunity provided by the provision to resettle individual households rather than entire communities, Newfoundlanders made different futures for themselves, albeit not under conditions of their own making. Their actions forced bureaucrats to refine and modify the resettlement program to accommodate their wishes and, in the process, fundamentally shifted its purpose from evacuating communities to moving individuals. Indeed, the extent to which rural Newfoundlanders succeeded in fundamentally changing resettlement is suggested by the fact that the provincial Conservatives, who had campaigned against it, chose not to cancel the program when they took power in 1972 but to continue it for another five years. They did so perhaps because resettlement in 1972 was not what it had been in 1965: the program had changed from one aimed at urbanizing the province's population to one that consolidated its rural population in rural centres. Doing so was consistent with the new government's emphasis on rural development.[76]

The limits to state power and the ability of Newfoundlanders to influence the program and exploit it to their ends did not in any way diminish their sense of being coerced. In part, this was because of the way the program was administered. From the beginning, the Resettlement Committee limited the amount of information it circulated about its workings for fear of adverse publicity. Not only did it get such publicity anyway, but the committee also managed to generate a good deal of anxiety among Newfoundlanders in the process. Rumours circulated about how the government would cut off services to force resettlement, and of the existence of a government "black list," communities that the Resettlement Committee wanted to shut down. While such a list did not exist per se, politicians and bureaucrats did refer to "sending communities" and worked on identifying "potential sending communities," which seemed close enough.[77]

While the secrecy that enveloped the workings of the Resettlement Committee created uncertainty among Newfoundlanders, the coerciveness of resettlement lay largely in how the program was initially structured: it

Figure 2.3 Robert Wells, Department of the Attorney General, discussing resettlement with Dover residents, August 1961. | Bob Brooks, Library and Archives Canada, National Film Board fonds, e011177532

targeted communities and generated, and perhaps even relied on, informal pressure to work. Despite the other ways in which to qualify for resettlement assistance, the initial information provided to prospective resettlers focused entirely on the process by which communities could be abandoned. People who wanted to relocate were advised to discuss the matter with their neighbours and, if there was sufficient interest, to contact the provincial Resettlement Division in St. John's for the necessary forms. Sometimes the forms arrived along with government agents who helpfully explained the process. Their presence may have taken some in the community aback, making the prospect of resettlement seem more real (Figure 2.3). Regardless, when the paperwork arrived, those interested in moving had to call a public meeting to discuss resettlement further and to elect a chairman, secretary, and one other person to a committee which was responsible for circulating a petition for resettlement among householders, securing the required number of signatures, and acting on behalf of the community in its dealings with St. John's.[78]

The emphasis on moving communities rather than individuals had the effect of pitting neighbour against neighbour, one generation against another. Those who wanted to avail themselves of resettlement assistance tended to be younger and often had children at home; they were people who would benefit from the opportunities and services in larger communities. Those who wanted to stay were often older people whose limited education and finances made moving more of a risk. But staying was also a risk: as people drifted away, services eroded. In some cases, the resettlement program created the very kind of isolation it was supposed to alleviate.

Perhaps because it was alive to the controversial nature of the program, Ottawa was eager to monitor its implementation, enlisting the assistance of the new provincial university, itself a symbol of the modernity Newfoundlanders were meant to embrace. In particular, it drew on the expertise of Memorial University's Institute of Social and Economic Research, which had been established in 1961 with the explicit purpose of helping the province deal with the challenges of modernization. According to its directors, the rapid transformation experienced by Newfoundland's isolated, pre-industrial, "peasant" communities made it an ideal place to study social change – and to help direct it. Doing so would require basic research: as Jeff Webb notes, "the plain fact was that there was little known of the 1300 communities along 6000 miles of coastline, and without a description of the society the university would be unable to describe social change, let alone intervene in it." As well, ISER was keen to take advantage of the opportunities for applied research, making its members available for contract work from the federal government.[79]

With funding from the federal Department of Fisheries, in 1966 the institute engaged sociologists Noel Iverson and Ralph Matthews to investigate the attitudes of people who had been relocated and to provide an evaluation of the federal-provincial resettlement program with an eye to improving it.[80] Like the anthropologists who evaluated the effects of wage labour on Inuit, they were highly critical of this attempt at redevelopment. Based on interviews with 120 householders and published in 1968, their report took particular issue with how the joint program was administered. While they and the people they spoke to agreed that resettlement was crucial to the economic development of the province, they took issue with how it was carried out. In particular, Iverson and Matthews decried "the almost total lack of preparation, on the part of government, industry, and reception communities to receive the migrants and to assist them in adjusting to their new surroundings and help them find work."[81] Sympathetic to the difficulties encountered by the people they interviewed, Iverson and Matthews suggested ways to make the resettlement program run more efficiently.[82]

Concerned by the sociologists' criticisms, Ottawa immediately funded another ISER-led investigation of the resettlement program. Based on data gathered from 362 households, some 40 percent of those moved between 1965 and 1967, economists A. Leslie Robb and Roberta Edgecombe Robb provided a favourable cost-benefit analysis of the program in 1969.[83] Of those surveyed, nearly two-thirds (64 percent) said they were "generally satisfied" with their move. Of these, a majority thought they were better off. The 23 percent who were "dissatisfied" with moving felt that way because they had been unable to find work.[84]

The Robbs' study provided economist and former director of ISER, Parzival Copes, with a key piece of evidence with which to build his critique of the resettlement program: the problem was the lack of jobs, not the process of moving people. Funded by the Department of Regional Economic Expansion, which took over responsibility for resettlement on behalf of the federal government, his 1972 study argued that the resettlement program did not deal with the basic problem confronting Newfoundland's economic development, namely, its surplus population. Echoing the area economic survey done for the Keewatin, Copes argued that the province had more people than jobs that could support them. Moving people to growth centres would go some distance to alleviating their circumstances, but, if Newfoundland was to prosper, the provincial government needed to help people leave the province entirely. (The federal government already provided this kind of assistance through the Canada Manpower Mobility Program, established in 1967.)[85] Unfortunately, "consideration of sponsored population movement to the Canadian mainland was barred on political grounds," he wrote. "The challenge now is [to] break the political taboo against sponsored extra-provincial migration. When this is achieved ... its people may then be rescued from the socially debilitating environment of a permanent welfare colony."[86]

Despite their differences, none of these authors took issue with modernization and its assumptions about the inherent value and inevitability of an urban industrial future. Iverson and Matthews argued "resettlement is an absolute necessity if future generations of Newfoundlanders are to keep pace with the challenging employment requirements of the province," and Copes called for the state to divest Newfoundland of its population surplus. If anything, their critiques reinforced the state's project of improvement and the extension of its power: Iverson and Matthews concluded their report by noting that the problem with the resettlement program was "that government does not take a strong enough role."[87]

Not only did these social scientists see resettlement and the modernization project of which it was a part as legitimate exercises of state power, but they also left unchallenged one of the central procedures through which Newfoundlanders were made to decide if they would move. By requiring public meetings, elected committees, and signatures on formal petitions, the federal and provincial governments hoped to ensure that community resettlement was voluntary and that the process was transparent and people openly accountable.

The problem was that these conventions for collective decision making were largely alien to the political culture of rural Newfoundland, something anthropologists funded by ISER were in the midst of documenting.[88] Their ethnographies revealed outports to be small, egalitarian places made livable by a set of social rules that minimized open disagreement and confrontation. On Fogo Island, for instance, Cato Wadel reported that "one does not talk publicly about controversial topics; every man has a right to an opinion, and one man's opinion is as good as another's; one does not give advice to one's neighbour; to do so can be regarded as questioning a man's ability to think for himself."[89] James C. Faris and Melvin M. Firestone made similar observations of other outports, noting that people preferred to withdraw in the face of potential conflict and adopt a relatively permissive attitude to behaviour.

Most rural Newfoundlanders had very little, if any, experience with municipal government or public meetings; indeed, many settlements would not have had a community hall in which to hold a large meeting. There were churches, but sectarian divisions sometimes meant they were not neutral spaces. Insofar as outports had public places, they took the form of the merchant's premises, where men spoke to each other informally and in small groups. Eventually, after a variety of opinions had circulated through such conversations and key people, "community feeling" emerged. Thus, a very different form of politics and decision making was at work in the outports, one that the bureaucrats in Ottawa and St. John's might not have recognized.[90]

By requiring that Newfoundlanders abide by the standard forms and processes of participatory democracy, the resettlement program, like cooperatives in the North, imposed a discipline on the individuals and communities it touched, schooling them in the conventions of modern politics and decision making. But resettlement merely hinted at the pedagogy of modernization: the community development initiatives that were undertaken simultaneously in rural Newfoundland gave full expression to it, exemplifying the disciplinary effects of state-sanctioned development.

COMMUNITY DEVELOPMENT might seem to be a contradictory proposition in the context of a modernization agenda premised on centralization. It was certainly positioned that way by the provincial Progressive Conservatives, who contrasted the governing Liberal Party's agenda with their own. Whereas Smallwood's Liberal government had given up on outport Newfoundland, pursuing a policy of resettlement, the Conservatives would "offer a dynamic program of rural development" signifying their faith in its future.[91]

The Extension Service of Memorial University of Newfoundland reinforced the oppositional quality of community development. Having established itself as a key institution of adult education in the province, the Extension Service had its mandate reconfigured in the mid-1960s by its second director.[92] Under Donald Snowden, Extension tried to instigate social change through a variety of initiatives aimed at empowering rural Newfoundlanders to take charge of their own futures rather than letting others decide it for them. Snowden called their collective efforts "community development." In framing development in this way, Snowden took his lead from the United Nations and the larger critique of top-down development planning that began to emerge in the late 1950s as part of the reaction against the international efforts at modernization undertaken by the nation-states of the global North in the global South.[93]

Looking back on Extension's work in Newfoundland in the 1960s and 1970s, Snowden's colleague and successor as director, Tony Williamson, considered it a contribution to building an alternative kind of development. It was not just about growth or meeting the material needs of the poor but also about cultivating knowledge and political expression. Fundamentally, development was about facilitating citizen participation. "Just as men have a right to food, they also have a right to speak, to know, to understand the meaning of their work, to take part in public affairs and to defend their beliefs," Williamson argued, quoting a 1975 Dag Hammarskjöld Foundation report to describe Extension's rationale.[94]

Although Extension insisted that it was politically neutral, some of the province's politicians and bureaucrats disagreed, especially after it expanded its mandate under Snowden. For instance, while Don Jamieson, the Liberal member of Parliament for Burin-Burgeo (and later federal minister of Regional Economic Expansion), praised Extension's educational efforts, he wondered whether it was working at cross-purposes with the government. Extension seemed to be "strengthening rural life in areas where, in fact, there is very little hope for any strong future." In doing so, it was "contributing to a romantic idealism that hurts rather than helps people."[95]

Despite such claims, community development and resettlement were not policies at odds with each other. Like ISER, Extension had ties to both the federal and provincial government and hosted a training conference for fieldworkers from government departments and non-governmental organizations, devoting two days of the week-long meeting to resettlement.[96] Snowden attended the meetings of the Joint Planning Committee that oversaw resettlement, arguing in 1966 that the program needed to devote more of its resources to community development to prepare people to move. Someone needed to "be responsible for creating a receptive atmosphere to the centralization programme through the various media – public meetings, radio, television, etc., to explain what resettlement is all about, so as to educate people to move."[97]

Even Smallwood saw no contradiction between pursuing a policy of centralization alongside community development. In 1966, his government created a new ministry to implement resettlement along with other programs arising from the federal government's War on Poverty that were aimed at strengthening local communities.[98] At the regular meetings of the section heads of the Department of Community and Social Development, the director of resettlement, Kenneth Harnum, presented his report in concert with those of his colleagues, men charged with implementing leadership training and local initiatives programs, with no sense of inconsistency.[99]

If the provincial government saw no incongruity between resettlement and community development, neither did Ottawa. In a position paper for Fisheries written in 1966 and circulated to a number of departments, Robert Hart argued that resettlement should be given "high priority" as part of the federal government's community development activities.[100] Another federal bureaucrat considered community development vital to the success of the resettlement program. "Nobody on the [Resettlement] Committee seems to be aware of such a thing as community development work to convince people to move out," wrote Guy Lemieux. "And they require an 80% approval by people to close down a community. With proper community action and adequate financial incentives, there should be no trouble."[101]

Lemieux's comments along with Snowden's speak to the multivalent character of community development: building capacity could be used to sustain communities or destroy them. It certainly was not inconsistent with the larger modernization agenda pursued by Ottawa and St. John's. Nor was modernization at odds with what Extension was trying to do. Indeed, the development it pursued was centrally concerned with reconstituting community by cultivating citizen participation through the institutions and practices of participatory democracy. In doing so, the university both spread and challenged the state's project of modernization and its power.

While Extension used several different tools to empower rural Newfoundlanders, all of them were aimed at addressing what Donald Snowden believed to be the root of poverty, namely, a lack of information. To rectify that situation, Extension carried out its work through a field staff that lived in the areas they served and could make people aware of the government programs and services that were available to them. Fieldworkers also organized workshops and conferences, bringing outsiders in to talk about topics of interest to local people, like fish processing or starting a cooperative, and to facilitate music, drama, and sporting events.[102]

But their most innovative and well-known tool for community development was film and, later, videotape. Established in 1961, Extension's Media Unit began producing *Decks Awash,* a television program dealing with issues of interest to fishermen, making copies available for broadcast in remote communities. Just as Extension's work in television built on earlier efforts by the Broadcasting Corporation of Newfoundland to use radio to encourage adult education and cooperatives in the 1930s and 1940s, the National Film Board of Canada (NFB) benefited from Extension's experience when it came looking for a partner to produce films on poverty in the mid-1960s as part of Canada's War on Poverty.[103]

Working with Extension, the NFB pioneered the use of film as a medium for social change. Both Donald Snowden and filmmaker Colin Low wanted to challenge conventional views of poverty held by Canadians and their governments. Equally importantly, they hoped to show "the poor" to themselves. By documenting people's hopes, fears, and frustrations, film could capture a community's capacity and reflect it back to its members, helping them to "discover their own needs and ways of dealing with these needs."[104] By acting as a "mirror," film had the ability to break down the barriers to collective action, showing people their common ground.[105]

This experiment in "communication for social change" began on Fogo Island. Shot over a five-week period in the summer of 1967 with the assistance of Fred Earle, the twenty-eight films that constituted the "Newfoundland Film Project" featured islanders being interviewed about a variety of issues confronting them. The footage was shown at community meetings and, eventually, to members of the provincial government. An exercise in participatory filmmaking and the first project in what would become the NFB's Challenge for Change program, it was an attempt to forge community and collective action in a troubled place. When the film crew arrived on Fogo, about 60 percent of its population of nearly five thousand was on welfare, the island's merchants had shut down operations, and some people were considering taking advantage of the government's resettlement program or leaving Newfoundland altogether. Despite repeated attempts, the most recent earlier that year, efforts to establish a cooperative on the island had failed.[106] Fogo Island was at a crossroads, and islanders had three choices, according to Premier Joey Smallwood: they could "drift and perish," resettle, or develop the island so they could stay.[107] The filming would help residents decide which path they would take.

Together, the Fogo films revealed a remarkable consensus among islanders. They agreed that the problems confronting them were related to the decline of the inshore fishery and their own lack of unity. For Snowden and Low, exposing this consensus was exactly what made the films so effective. In their wake, islanders established a shipbuilding and producers' cooperative as well as a non-sectarian school board. In the mythology that has grown up around the films, the "Fogo Process," as this technique of community development came to be known, saved the island from resettlement. In contrast, both Low and Snowden insisted that Fogo Islanders were the ones who deserved the credit – not them, and not the films: after all, film did not do anything: people did.

While the islanders were certainly instrumental in saving Fogo, the roles played by Low, Snowden, and Earle were equally significant. If film was a "mirror," it was one that had their fingerprints all over it. Like resettlement, both the Fogo films and the program of community development of which they were a part were acts of social engineering undertaken by Extension to transform traditional outport society. The consensus featured in the films was created through a selective focus on particular individuals and values, and through the screening process. But community development was not just about authorizing particular values; it was also centrally concerned with creating modern political subjects.

Despite the fact that the Fogo films had their genesis in a desire on the part of both Snowden and the NFB to make films about poverty that would change attitudes about what it was and who the poor were, no one from the "fifty to seventy per cent" of the island on welfare was featured, nor was the island's welfare officer. Instead of "giving voice to the silent," the films amplified the opinions of the already articulate.[108] Fully one-third of the films featured members of the Fogo Island Improvement Committee, a self-appointed group of influential islanders that aimed "to make Fogo viable in the twentieth century" through "'self-help' or cooperative projects." In other words, the committee was dedicated to community development, just as Extension was. Indeed, the members of the Improvement Committee had had dealings with Extension before: a fieldworker had helped revive it when interest flagged and had then helped it to organize a conference on cooperatives.[109]

An economically and socially powerful minority, the Improvement Committee had existed in one form or another since 1963 but had been unable to achieve much in the way of results.[110] Thanks in large part to Fred Earle, its views were literally broadcast throughout Fogo, solidifying its leadership position. Born into one of its merchant families, Earle grew up on Fogo Island and worked as an office boy and accountant for Earle Sons and Company. Before joining Extension in 1964, he had a varied career with the Bank of Nova Scotia and the Finance Department of the provincial government, and as the manager of a wholesale company in Lewisporte.[111] In his capacity as a fieldworker, he acted as a liaison between islanders, the university, and the NFB, helping to identify individuals who would be filmed, suggesting topics, and in many cases doing the interviewing himself.[112]

Coming from away, Colin Low depended on Earle to secure the participation of Fogo's residents in the film project. The fieldworker's local knowledge, family connections, and work history positioned him in a way that likely shaped who participated in the films and how they did so. Given this, it is perhaps not surprising that the members of the Improvement Committee figured as prominently as they did in the Fogo films: they would have been comfortable with someone like Earle, and he with them. As an Extension worker, Earle would have supported the Improvement Committee's agenda, for it represented the kind of local initiative that Extension was eager to facilitate.

Even when the members of the Improvement Committee were not featured directly, the values they professed – ones we might label modern, middle class, and entrepreneurial – were evident in the discussions about education, the economy, and welfare. Among those who were filmed, there was a sense that traditional sectarian divisions and petty jealousies were keeping the island back, particularly because of their impact on education.[113] At the time of the filming, there were six different school boards on the island. The settlement of Seldom alone had four two-room schools, each serving a different religious group.[114] Inefficient and uneconomical, they persisted despite the fact that conditions prevented these school boards from recruiting good teachers.

Indeed, in the opinion of Andrew Brett, the poor education Fogoites received as a result of their sectarianism was why they were so resistant to change in the first place. A lack of education had made people "afraid," and fear was perhaps behind the tendency of people to "be contrary to one another."[115] One of the teachers on the island argued that Fogo's failure to support a cooperative was due to people's ignorance: in his view, young people needed to be given scholarships to St. Francis Xavier University in Nova Scotia to be educated in the cooperative movement.[116] But, as shown in one of the films, Betty was ready to throw out denominational education altogether. The wife of a former schoolteacher and member of the school board in Joe Batt's Arm, she had no time for divisiveness, whatever its roots: "Denominational education is the ruination of Fogo Island ... We have to be over all this. We have to be over all these things!"[117]

The fishery was the focus of discussion in many of the films, and, while no one made the case for factory trawlers and an industrialized fishery, the islanders interviewed threw their support behind an intermediate technology, the longliner. These larger boats could go farther and get more fish. More technologically and capital-intensive than the trap fishery practised by many islanders, fishing with a longliner was portrayed as progressive and modern, as were the men who pursued it.[118] But, like the Arctic cooperatives, the longliner was meant to bridge cultures, in this case work cultures. It allowed its captains and crews to maintain their independence as producers while still intensifying their production. Dismissing the argument that cost was what kept fishermen from longlining, Dan Roberts argued it was timidity: Fogo's fishermen had to learn to take risks with the money they had and "go along with the times" – just as he did.[119]

The film on Jim Decker and that on the *Up Top* reinforced risk taking as a positive value but also celebrated the traditions of self-help and trust on the island, as well as the skill possessed by islanders. Not able to get a loan to buy a boat, Decker was nevertheless determined to build a longliner from local materials, using his own labour and that of his neighbours. At the launch of the *Atlantic Queen II,* Eric Jones, the local member of the House of Assembly, declared "Jim and his crew have proved it's still possible to do things here on Fogo Island!"[120] Similarly, *The Story of the Up Top* related how one fishing family salvaged an old passenger boat that had been sunk for four years and converted into an operating fishing vessel, with "no encouragement at all" from the government. As the skipper told Fred Earle, "It can be done, sir!"[121]

The importance of initiative was reinforced in the discussions of welfare, in which the island's more articulate and powerful citizens condemned its "demoralizing" influence. Merchant Brian Earle argued that welfare had made Fogo Islanders less inclined to work – perhaps, he noted ruefully, because they were good capitalists, always looking "to get the most for the least." What would have happened if the government had sunk the money it devoted to welfare into promoting industry on the island? he wondered.[122] Other islanders mused about diverting welfare money into funding for longliners.[123] Certainly, had that happened, Billy Crane would have stayed instead of choosing to move his family to Toronto. For Crane, going down the road was far better than going on welfare.[124] Betty might have agreed: while welfare was necessary, "the welfare state" had "squelched the spirit" of the people, and, unless that changed, bringing industry to the island would make no difference to its prospects. Perhaps hinting at what she thought might revive that squelched initiative, she observed, "Nothing brings out the best in people like hard times."[125]

Making these films was just the first step in community development; the real changes would grow out of the conversations that ensued about them – conversations that were explicitly designed to elicit and contain debate through the screening process. Snowden and Low were keenly aware of the importance of showing their films in a particular order. "It would be possible to have such a soporific effect that nobody would be thinking or talking," Snowden recalled. "So we worked out systems of using material that would provoke thought and discussion but you could interject film to cool things down and leave people at the end of a meeting with a good feeling." It was especially important not just to present problems, or people would walk away: "They could lose interest, they can become overwhelmed and say this is too much trouble, it's too bothersome, it causes friction and controversy."[126]

Colin Low's notebook of audience reactions reveals the limits of the consensus he and Snowden tried to build. The films did cause "friction and controversy," despite the care Low had taken in screening them. As he and his colleague Bill Nemtin noted, "Between a dynamic and fruitful exchange and fist fights there is a delicate line."[127] For instance, he recorded "stone silence and [a] walkout" of a hundred people at Seldom after the screening of *Brian Earle on Merchants and Welfare.*[128] As noted, the anthropologists who studied Newfoundland in the 1960s argued that withdrawing – in this case, by walking out – was a common response to controversy in the outports. It was a way of preserving order in small-scale, face-to-face societies where there was a social premium on avoiding direct confrontation.

But walking out was not the reaction that Low or Snowden wanted. Instead, they hoped to transform the traditional rules and practices of social discourse in the outports and cultivate a different culture of engagement, one that would allow for public discussion about difficult issues. In their view, individuals had to be able to confront each other with different opinions and work through those differences directly and openly if they were to make their own futures together, as a community. The "cool medium" of film gave the people of Fogo the space to do that, detaching the opinions from the individuals who held them. Although things might have gotten a little too hot at Seldom, the films fulfilled their role in eliciting engagement in other places. A few days after the screening at Seldom, there was what Low called "the first real discussion" in the town of Fogo after he showed the film dealing with Dan Roberts: "First indication of resentment of the wealthy and Improvement Committee. No fishermen on it."[129]

In all, over 4,500 people attended the screenings, which were held from November 1967 to the end of January 1968. While Low was confident that the films "aroused community discussion on a very large scale," he admitted "it is difficult to assess what effects the films had on a number of events." He noted that, in the midst of the screenings, some residents called a meeting to form an island-wide shipbuilding and producers' cooperative. The gathering was announced at one of the film screenings and held the next day, with 150 men attending. They asked that Low film the proceedings. He witnessed the formation of the co-op and its initial 125 members vote for a board of directors. "It is significant that the two leading directors elected to the board were Dan Roberts and Jim Decker, two men featured in the films," he noted.[130]

In the end, Low argued that the impact of the Fogo films was to create "a consensus for action. The films seemed to cause a certain tension or impatience to do something."[131] When an opportunity arose, as it did with the meeting to establish a cooperative, local people were only too happy to lend their support. Despite the different individuals and values they gave voice to, the Fogo films nevertheless seemed to break down the existing barriers to social engagement within settlements and among them – at least enough to establish a cooperative and an amalgamated school board. And that's all community developers needed to do. Assessing the impact of the films in 1969, Cato Wadel concluded that "the major change that has occurred on Fogo Island would seem to be that *some* people from *all* the settlements are committed to an island-wide community. Together, these individuals form a sizable group although they are a minority."[132]

Creating islanders did not begin to exhaust the transformative potential of film, nor did it complete the job of community development. In the wake of the Newfoundland Film Project, Extension used its Film Unit to forge connections among more far-flung settlements.[133] It edited some of the Fogo films and showed them on *Decks Awash*.[134] It also lent the films out to interested groups. As well, it travelled to Tignish, Prince Edward Island, and Prince Rupert, British Columbia, to film the efforts of fishermen there to set up cooperatives. The circulation of these films resulted in relationships being formed among these communities and the Fogo cooperative, resulting in the exchange of both information and expertise.[135] Writing in 1970, Tony Williamson, Extension's fieldworker in Labrador, reported that some people there compared their situation to what they had seen of Fogo Island's from the films, even quoting Andrew Brett.[136] According to Donald Snowden, the Fogo films "helped residents of rural Labrador develop a greater awareness of their individual roles, their need for organization and collective action, and a new confidence in their ability to participate in taking steps to improve conditions – controlling their lives."[137]

Not only did Extension use film to facilitate connections among rural communities, but it also deployed it to build relationships between those communities and the provincial and federal government. While Fogoites would never express their frustrations directly, especially to government officials, they were not shy about being filmed doing so. When members of Smallwood's cabinet saw the films, they were favourably impressed, so much so that Aidan Maloney, the provincial minister of Fisheries, agreed to be filmed responding to the concerns that Fogo's residents had articulated. The provincial government's acknowledgment of local views turned into action at Port aux Choix on Newfoundland's Northern Peninsula, where the Fogo Process was repeated. When officials saw a film showing locals criticizing the location of the community's new breakwater, they reversed their decision.[138]

In Labrador, Extension pushed the Fogo Process further, developing what it called a "video 'White Paper.'"[139] Concerned about a recent decision by Ottawa to cut radiophone service, the residents of coastal Labrador agreed to have Extension film them discussing its impacts. Tony Williamson showed the videotape to an audience that included Eric Kierans, the federal minister responsible, as well as a vice-president of Bell Canada, and a number of bureaucrats. The next day, he interviewed Kierans, recording his response on videotape and screening it for Labradorians when he returned. Asked for his reaction to the film, Kierans reflected on how it had challenged the perspective from which he usually made decisions, replacing his schematic vision of the coast with a feeling for it: "For me, normally, to look at a map and to see that the coast is about 800 miles long (or the part that concerns us here) and you look at it and that's it, that's the sum total of your reaction," he admitted. "But yesterday, looking at the video-tape – looking at you, Tony, talking to Mr. Lewis, Uncle John Campbell, to others there, you got a much better feel ... You began to feel it."[140] Like the provincial officials who heard the concerns of the residents of Port aux Choix, Kierans reversed his decision.

By facilitating discussions within and across Newfoundland's communities and between their residents and the people who governed them in St. John's and Ottawa, Extension sought to develop a civic political culture in a province whose rural residents had little direct experience with formal government.[141] Newfoundlanders had just over a century of experience electing a legislative assembly before the British Colonial Office suspended representative institutions in 1934. An appointed Commission of Government then oversaw their affairs for fifteen years, until Confederation. Nor did local government provide an opportunity for people to participate in formal politics. In 1949, St. John's, the capital, was the new province's only incorporated municipality. Indeed, what experience most Newfoundlanders had with participatory democracy in the mid-twentieth century was recent and disagreeable, coming in the form of the two successive and deeply divisive referenda that resulted in the decision to join Canada.

Developing a culture of participatory democracy in the 1960s meant overcoming this history and helping Newfoundlanders act together, to see beyond the boundaries of sect and settlement and to identify more broadly. With echoes of Northern Affairs' economist R.D. Currie's comment that the "Eskimo must begin to think outside his tent," Tony Williamson observed that outport Newfoundlanders "have a very great difficulty in seeing beyond their own community, their own harbour, their own bay." Extension's task was "to help people assess their situation, not only in terms of their community, but in terms of the region, of the province and the country as a whole," and to act.[142] In other words, community development was aimed at encouraging multiple scales of political affiliation and action.

But action was a matter of organization as well as affect. It was one thing for rural Newfoundlanders to feel they were members of a more encompassing body politic, and quite another to translate that sense of connection into concrete action. Participatory democracy was thus about institutions and behaviours as well as attitudes. Recognizing this, Extension also worked to encourage rural Newfoundlanders to form cooperatives, community councils, and local development associations, all of which gave structural form to public opinion, transforming individual views into formal deliberations and enforceable decisions.

The structure imposed by the explicit rules governing these organizations lent to public discussions a formality that had the same effect as the "coolness" of film: it facilitated the decision-making process by depersonalizing it, so much so that sociologist J.D. House considered local development associations responsible for "democratizing rural Newfoundland."[143]

Community development empowered individuals to determine their own futures collectively, sometimes in opposition to decisions made in St. John's and Ottawa. But cultivating the institutions and practices of participatory democracy also extended the reach of the state over rural Newfoundland by formalizing and institutionalizing outport politics and decision making in representative bodies. In fact, Williamson and Snowden were quite explicit about Extension's role in making rural Newfoundland legible to St. John's: writing in 1967, they argued that the work it did "could be of benefit to government" by "assisting in the formation of responsible local and regional agencies and associations which can give government the information and logistic links they need."[144] Assessing its accomplishments in 1975, Snowden noted that not only had Extension helped institutionalize rural Newfoundland, but it had also helped create a body politic, responsible citizens able to govern themselves and to lead. Without its efforts, "there would be substantially fewer incorporated communities and those who filled elected and appointed positions in them would do so with considerably less knowledge of how to perform their work." In fact, many people who ran for office would never have done so without the leadership training Extension Service provided.[145]

By teaching people to run their own affairs, Extension's community development activities were thus a form of liberal democratic "government" in Foucault's sense, cultivating particular subjectivities and shaping relationships among people and between people and the state in a way that allowed it to rule at a distance.[146]

Resettlement and community development in Newfoundland were forms of disciplinary power. They entailed the imposition of the spatial and economic forms of modernity and the creation of an engaged citizen, a particular kind of political subject. Both initiatives were part of a larger state-sponsored project of improvement that enlisted a variety of non-state agents and institutions, particularly academics and the university, to its cause. Along with government officials, sociologists, economists, anthropologists, and adult educators working through Memorial University all contributed to making Newfoundland modern.

The project of improvement in Newfoundland, like those undertaken elsewhere, was not entirely successful – in no small part because of the actions of ordinary Newfoundlanders who managed to make their own modernity under conditions they had little control in shaping. Whether by resettling where they wanted or by recording a video White Paper, they influenced the trajectory of development on a local scale.

As will be discussed in the next chapter, when the disciplinary power of state development was greater, people's impact on development was too: paradoxically, eastern Quebecers became "artisans of their destiny" under the auspices of what was the most high modern of the projects I examine.

3

"Artisans of Their Destiny"

Participation, Power, and Place in Quebec's Backcountry

Confronted with the news that the government was planning to shut down his hometown of Saint-Paulin-Dalibaire in 1970, young Réjean Cardinal decided he wanted no part of it. One day, while shooting old tin cans, he accidentally hit one of the government agents overseeing the closure. Convinced he'd be arrested, he and his pal Ti-Pierre Drouin hid in an abandoned house, helped by Réjean's girlfriend and Ti-Pierre's sister, Ginette, who supplied them with food and some other necessaries. They provided for themselves through a series of small thefts until the police spotted them one day and gave chase. The boys escaped, but Ginette was shot; she died in the emergency room in Matane. The whole village turned out for her funeral and heard the priest give an impassioned eulogy, about Ginette but also about the doomed village in which they lived: "faut pas lâcher" – "don't give up."[1]

This scene, from Jean-Claude Labrecque's 1972 film *Les smattes,* was a fictionalized account of a real event: Saint-Paulin-Dalibaire was one of a number of communities in eastern Quebec targeted for closure by the provincial government in the late 1960s as part of an overall plan set out by the Bureau d'aménagement de l'Est du Québec (the Eastern Quebec Development Office; BAEQ) to address rural poverty by modernizing the countryside.[2] It captures the lack of opportunities for young men in rural Quebec, the trauma of dislocation, and the disillusionment that characterized many Quebecers' view of the state in the 1970s. Bureaucrats – "les smattes," or the wise guys – may have had school smarts, but they were short-sighted technocrats who had little empathy for the villagers or their attachment to place.

What happened in eastern Quebec was not unique. As in the North and Newfoundland, state-sponsored relocation was part of a larger plan to address poverty through "development." The initiatives that fell under this rubric were aimed at rationalizing and capitalizing on the region's resources, particularly its human ones. Doing so required expertise drawn from government and especially universities, much of which was directed, in eastern Quebec, at cultivating a civic political culture so that the people of the Lower St. Lawrence, Gaspé, and Îles-de-la-Madeleine could become "artisans of their destiny."[3]

What made this project of improvement different and significant was the involvement of the people of eastern Quebec in creating the development plan for their region. In the North and Newfoundland, planning was the purview of government bureaucrats, who, if they tried at all, manufactured consent after the fact. In contrast, in eastern Quebec, the purported beneficiaries of planning – local people – were brought into the process from the start. That said, "participatory planning," like cooperatives in the North and Newfoundland, was nevertheless meant to discipline the residents to set their priorities together and to imagine their futures in relation to those of other communities and the region as a whole. In addition, the structure of consultation that planners created to encourage different scales of political affiliation was also meant to serve as the foundation for a new level of government, a regional one.

Emblematic of the combination of technocratic and democratic impulses that characterized Quiet Revolution Quebec, development planning in the Lower St. Lawrence, Gaspé, and Îles-de-la-Madeleine is also the most thorough, richly funded, expertly driven, and high modern of the initiatives I examine. In the 1970s and 1980s, it captured the interest of sociologists and political scientists, who were largely critical of the enterprise.[4] In summarizing this literature, Jean-François Simard notes that it portrays the BAEQ's plan as "the most resounding failure of the Quiet Revolution, the prototype of technocratic drift, an illustration of the collapse of centralized planning, [and] the incarnation of the coldness of the state in the face of citizen demands."[5] In contrast, Simard and others offer a different interpretation, focusing on the positive legacy of the BAEQ. For these scholars, the BAEQ's efforts, along with those of the Tennessee Valley Authority, stand as two of the "most prominent regional development initiatives in North America." According to both

Simard and Lawrence Desrosiers, not only did BAEQ shape subsequent regional and local development in the province, but it also decentralized political power and services in meaningful ways and professionalized the public service.[6] Indeed, for Hugues Dionne, what was attempted in eastern Quebec "remains an extremely important foundational act of democratic and regional planning, a highlight of the Quiet Revolution not to be forgotten."[7]

Rather than assess the BAEQ's success or failure or the ways in which development initiatives in eastern Quebec encapsulated the political culture of the Quiet Revolution, this chapter explores the ideological and political work done by participatory planning. Eastern Quebec's planners were highly effective in soliciting citizen involvement and thus engaging ordinary people in their own development and that of their region. This effectiveness was why, paradoxically, their efforts also manifested themselves in the greatest expression of resistance rural Quebec had ever seen when the government failed to follow through on the plan it had so painstakingly encouraged people to make their own.

The three separate rural protests in the early 1970s, known as Opérations Dignité, delineated a different kind of development, one that was more attentive to the needs of communities in the region and, ultimately, one that local people believed was more democratic. What planners attempted in eastern Quebec, and the reaction it elicited, sheds light on the complex relationship between participation, empowerment, and democracy that lay at the root of understandings of development – then and now.

The problem of poverty and underdevelopment in postwar Quebec was cast by government officials, planners, and academics in terms similar to those used in Newfoundland. Like the outports, the eastern Quebec "backcountry" ("l'arrière-pays") had seemingly been left behind by history (Figure 3.1). Although it was the site of Jacques Cartier's 1534 landing and the location of some of the first seigneuries outside the Quebec, Montreal, and Trois-Rivières area in the 1630s, the Lower St. Lawrence and Gaspé region was not occupied by Europeans in any great number until the mid-nineteenth century. It received the bulk of its settlers in the 1930s, when both church and state turned to agricultural colonization – what geographer Serge Courville termed the "forced humanization of remote areas" – as an answer to the upheavals of the Great Depression.[8]

For Georges-Henri Dubé, the head of the BAEQ, that is when the story of eastern Quebec's marginality started.[9] Despite the influx of people,

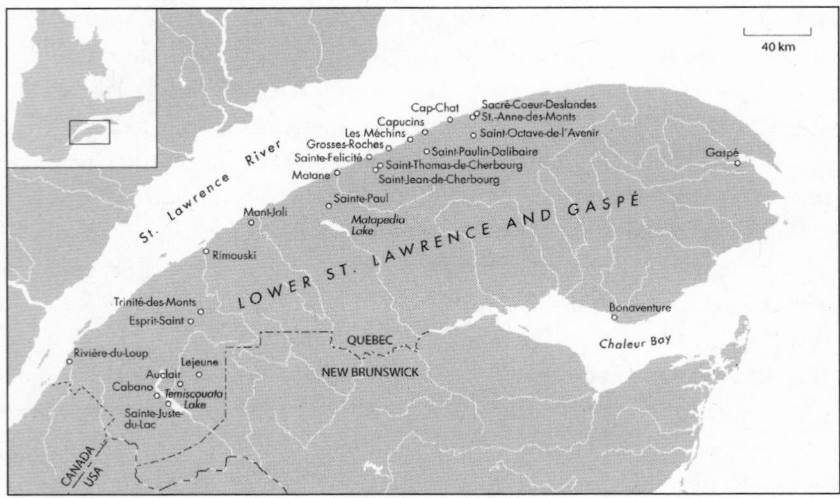

Figure 3.1 Eastern Quebec

settlement remained dispersed, an obstacle to the kinds of efficient industrial economies of scale that postwar governments believed were the basis of prosperity. People in the Lower St. Lawrence, Gaspé, and Îles-de-la-Madeleine made a bare-to-modest living from small farms, combining mixed agriculture with logging, or they worked in the inshore fishery. In the early 1960s, the region was the poorest in the province. Its residents earned just half the provincial average, 28 percent of which came from government transfers.[10] Seasonal unemployment was high – some 35 percent – and levels of education low.

While planners and politicians felt that the region possessed a great deal of potential, both material and human, they also believed that a kind of culture of poverty prevented it from being realized fully. In addition to their settlement pattern, eastern Quebecers were apparently burdened by the past in another way: "A difficult legacy of dogmatism and authoritarianism" meant they were used to being told what to do – whether by the clergy or the government.[11] That deference, along with the parochialism of rural life, had left them at a disadvantage as Quebec entered the 1960s. They were neither used to making collective decisions on matters concerning their own lives, nor were they inclined to think regionally, much less in terms of the province.

"Development" would change all that. Defined by the planners as "the rational organization of the resources of a given territory for the improved well-being of the population living there," it was premised on "changes in economic, administrative, political, social and psychological structures, which in time enable growth to appear and to continue." In short, development was an encompassing project of economic, social, and political transformation that was achieved through a series of planned interventions designed and guided by experts to facilitate sustained growth.[12] To that end, the government of Premier Jean Lesage took advantage of federal funding through the Agricultural Rehabilitation and Development Administration (ARDA) to fund the Bureau d'aménagement de l'Est du Québec in 1963. An amalgamation of two development organizations in the region, it was a private, non-profit, non-governmental agency charged with the task of coming up with a comprehensive development plan for the Lower St. Lawrence, Gaspé, and Îles-de-la-Madeleine. In the absence of adequate statistical information on the region's resources, population, and socio-economic situation, the BAEQ assembled a team of 150, including 75 researchers. Many were from Laval University and represented a variety of disciplines, including the social sciences.[13]

With a budget of nearly $4 million over three years, the BAEQ was, at the time, the largest planning initiative in the history of both Quebec and Canada, emblematic of the postwar interventionist state and the technocratic and high modernist character not only of development but also of the Quiet Revolution. With over a third of its budget going to research, the BAEQ produced a two-thousand-page, ten-volume study of the region in 1966, enumerating its resources and their potential for development and making some 231 recommendations.[14] Its job done, the BAEQ dissolved itself. The implementation of its plan was the subject of a federal-provincial agreement, which had funding of $411 million over eight years.[15]

For the BAEQ's planners, the key to developing the backcountry lay in centralizing its population of 325,000 and rationalizing the region's economy. The planners' purpose, framed in nationalist terms, was nothing less than to close the gap in incomes and standard of living between the province's poorest citizens and their wealthier counterparts and, by doing so, to strengthen Quebec.[16] As economist and BAEQ secretary Jean-Claude Lebel put it, "the BAEQ's plan is a catch-up plan."[17] To that end, eastern Quebec's small mixed farms and woodlots would be consolidated, and its inshore fishery reorganized to focus only on the most profitable species. Doing so would "free" labour to work full time in the pulp and paper industry, larger dairying operations, the offshore fishery, and the "dynamic, new activities" that government would promote for the region in mining and tourism.[18]

As in Newfoundland, French economist François Perroux's growth pole theory informed the BAEQ's plan for the development, albeit in a much more substantial way. Planners called for the consolidation of the region's more than two hundred municipalities into twenty-five administrative units and identified places that could act as "growth poles." The latter task was a challenge, as no such centres were obvious. The BAEQ's planners nevertheless called for reconfiguring the Lower St. Lawrence and Gaspé administratively around three sub-regions, each with its own centre. Rimouski would serve as the centre for one sub-region, and Rivière-du-Loup for another. The third sub-region, situated at the end of the Gaspé peninsula, lacked any such centre.

This administrative reorganization necessitated the "rationalization of human occupation." In contrast to what happened in Newfoundland, planners developed criteria for categorizing places as marginal in advance of any relocation. The criteria were based on an assessment of soil quality, the size and profitability of farms, and the standard of living of residents. In its final report, the BAEQ made two recommendations that called for the progressive closure of areas that lacked the resources to sustain a population and the communities that had been established there.[19] In its view, Saint-Jean-de-Cherbourg, Saint-Paulin-Dalibaire, Saint-Thomas-de-Cherbourg, Saint-Octave-de-l'Avenir, and Sacré-Coeur-Deslandes were places where "the state of resources does not indicate any possibility for these populations to satisfy their aspirations according to criteria considered normal in a modern society."[20]

The 1968 federal-provincial agreement to implement a development plan for eastern Quebec included both these recommendations, and the question of "marginality" was studied further. In addition to the criteria developed by BAEQ planners, the regional branch of the provincial Department of Municipal Affairs also came up with its own measure of marginality, basing it on population size and its rate of growth or decline, the community's accessibility by road or rail, the total municipal tax valuation, and annual municipal expenses.[21] Guided by these indices, in August 1969 the provincial government identified an additional five settlements that could be closed. They were located in the easterly reaches of the region, in the counties of Matane, Gaspé-Nord, Gaspé-Sud, and Bonaventure.[22] In these communities, only 17 percent of those of working age were earning a living, mainly as loggers. According to Metra, the consulting firm hired by the government to assess its relocation program in 1970, the situation was "economically catastrophic."[23] Given this statistic and others suggesting that people were already leaving the region's marginal areas at the rate of 370 households a year, the consultants argued that the question for the state wasn't if such communities should be abandoned, but how it could intervene to ease the transition. "It's clear that the question 'Should we close marginal localities?' makes no sense. They're closing on their own," they observed. Instead, the question was "Can the state intervene to eliminate this economically irrational situation and ease as much as possible the painful transformation felt by the residents of these marginal localities?"[24] In that sense, the state was just rationalizing what was an already-occurring natural process of out-migration.

State intervention took the form of setting out a clear process for relocation and letting people decide for themselves what to do. As in Newfoundland, Quebec's government officials underscored the fact that relocation was voluntary and that the process was distinct from expropriation. The program's purpose was to move people from places without futures to ones that were "in sync with society's evolution."[25] Communities as a whole decided whether to avail themselves of the assistance to leave. To indicate their willingness to relocate, communities had to follow two steps. First, half the population had to indicate their agreement to hold a vote on relocation by signing a petition circulated by a recognized local authority. If, in that vote, 80 percent of the population voted "yes," then all residents would be eligible for relocation assistance, and the process of negotiating compensation for their properties could begin. The government envisaged that the entire process, from the vote of approval to the closure of the community, would unfold over thirty months, after which any remaining residents would be eligible for neither assistance nor compensation, nor would they have any guarantee that public services would be maintained. A later order-in-council modified the process somewhat to make the consequences of inaction less dire, albeit more directly coercive: eighteen months after a positive vote, residents who had not initiated compensation proceedings would have their property expropriated, thus giving them at least some financial return on their holdings.[26]

Given how the process was structured, not everyone experienced it as "voluntary" – particularly those who didn't sign the petition or who voted against leaving. Although relocation carried the day in nine of the ten communities identified by the province in 1969 as marginal, in all but one of them there were people who did not want to leave.[27] Taking note of this, and cognizant of the social and psychological dynamics at play, the government's consultant wondered if state-sponsored relocation could ever really be completely voluntary or a free choice. Perhaps the only thing people in designated communities were at liberty to decide was when they left. Nevertheless, Metra estimated that eighty-five "marginal localities" in eastern Quebec could be closed, necessitating the relocation of some sixty thousand people.[28]

Although it did not entirely eliminate its coercive dynamics, the government took steps to ensure that people were engaged in the relocation process as much as possible and in that way gave them a modicum of control over it. It structured opportunities for them to participate by holding public meetings where they could ask questions, weigh their options, and express their points of view.

In their recollections, the people involved in planning and implementing the closure of marginal parishes stress that no one was forced to leave, and that, in many cases, relocation was pursued at the instigation of local people. Even Pierre De Bané, the member of Parliament for Matane and someone who championed the cause of his constituents, took issue with the impression left by the media that communities were closed at the whim of anonymous bureaucrats who made the decision hastily. "It was the opposite," he insisted. In his view, the subject had been studied thoroughly, and the possibility of closure and relocation arrived at after long discussions with the leaders of the regions and the people of different parishes "who saw things as they were."[29] Underscoring this point, former relocation agent Robin d'Anjou remembered that the chairman of the citizens' committee in Saint-Thomas-de-Cherbourg told him how the BAEQ had helped residents see that relocation was their only realistic option. Having come to this conclusion, they then wanted the government to act quickly to allow them to leave. "You showed us we were naked. Get us out!" Given this, he believed that "history has left us with a distorted image."[30] While d'Anjou was taking issue with the idea that government agents forced the closure of eastern Quebec's marginal parishes, I would argue that there is a different kind of distortion at play: the focus on closure and relocation, which has been the subject of films and music, has overshadowed the earlier planning process undertaken by the BAEQ, something that sheds light on the nature of state power and the disciplinary aspects of participation.[31]

Beyond its role in relocation, the BAEQ considered citizen participation crucial to development planning generally. Indeed, the agency was distinguished by its methodology of public participation. "Development is something recent, something new," observed the BAEQ's research director, Gérald Fortin. But, he added, "There is perhaps something that's even newer than planning and development, and that's planning and development done with the participation of the population." Beyond its novelty, citizen participation in development was an indicator of progressive change, "an example of democratization that maybe is being tried for the first time."[32] What was happening in eastern Quebec was so unusual that it drew development tourists, representatives of other government and non-governmental agencies from around the world, to see the BAEQ's experiment in action.[33]

For the BAEQ, participation was both a means and an end with respect to development. It was a way to set priorities and ensure development goals matched the needs and desires of the residents of eastern Quebec, hence the name given to its methodology: *l'enquête-participation* (participatory inquiry). But an *enquête-participation* was also a way in which people could relieve themselves of the weight of the past. For planners, citizen participation would help forge a new political culture and subjectivity of self-determination that was as crucial to modernizing the region as was the rationalization of its settlement pattern and the industrialization of its economy.

As one BAEQ official noted, the success of any development plan depended on engaging – and implicating – people in the process and the results. The government could have imposed its program on people, forcing them to act, but doing so would have been neither humane nor effective. Instead, "it seemed to us that the most humane, effective, and rational way was to involve the population itself in the change that was to occur, so that the economic situation in the region would improve."[34]

Meaningful participation didn't just happen; it had to be elicited. To that end, the BAEQ used *animation sociale,* which, in this instance, was not just a technique but an entire regime designed not just to prompt people's involvement but also to shape and contain it. The job of the *animateur* or facilitator was to "harness the creativity of a group, to transform it into usable energy, to make it productive."[35]

The model of participation used by the bureau, as well as its understanding of the purpose of regional planning, had its origins in the 1930s and Louis-Joseph Lebret's work with the fishermen of St. Malo, France. A Dominican priest, Lebret developed his model of *enquête-participation* in the course of helping the men establish a union. Through that work, which highlighted the expertise ordinary people brought to solving the problems that confronted them, Lebret came to appreciate the need for a "human-centred economy." In 1941 he founded the économie et humanisme movement, whose governing idea was that the economy should be at the service of people, not profit. According to Lebret, "Economic effort must focus on the possibility for all men to have what's necessary ... Any economic regime that does not do so must be considered inhuman and any policy that does not is misguided." In his view, development could not be narrowly construed as growth or limited to matters of economy. So radical were Lebret's views that he was called "the Karl Marx of Christianity."[36]

With François Perroux – of growth-pole fame – he introduced the idea of territorial planning, a technique aimed at establishing an economy that would develop the whole person. As his collaboration with Perroux suggests, Lebret believed planning could be both human-centred and high modern. To overgeneralize, Lebret's approach to development was bottom-up, emphasizing the knowledge of those who were the objects of development. His alliance with Perroux, who was the proponent of a kind of top-down development planning based on mathematical abstractions, suggests that he thought the two approaches were consistent, or could be made so. The BAEQ's planners shared this conviction. As Gérald Fortin noted, "Father Lebret was the fundamental influence" on the organization.[37]

The key to *animation sociale* was its non-directive character: the facilitator was "un homme sans projet," a person with no agenda or vested interest in particular outcomes.[38] According to André Tétrault, deputy director of the Institut canadien d'éducation des adultes, *animation sociale* was a distinct kind of pedagogy; it aimed to get people to act, but not by telling them what to do or explaining why they should do it. Instead, what made the pedagogy practised by facilitators distinct and potentially revolutionary was its emphasis on helping people to discover their own capacity by asking questions and getting them to do the same. The assumption was that, once convinced that they possessed the proficiency to act, people would be more inclined to do so. Expertise was its own motivation.[39]

At the same time that Tétrault and others underscored the non-directive character of *animation sociale,* however, they also argued that the job of the facilitator was to give people new ways of thinking and new habits. For instance, in Tétrault's view, agricultural development was not just a matter of enlarging farms and equipping them with modern technology. Instead, facilitators would "have to think about the training of men who will have to acquire new ways of thinking and new habits to carry out this plan."[40] The authors of the introduction to the BAEQ's final report echoed these sentiments, noting that it had used *animation sociale* to render the local population "disposed to certain major changes."[41]

Animation sociale may thus have been less directive than other pedagogies and approaches to development planning, but it was still an attempt to influence outcomes. *L'homme sans projet* was not *l'homme sans pouvoir*. BAEQ planners and the proponents of *animation sociale* spoke to the influence exercised by facilitators when they referred to them as "agents of change" who "harnessed" a group's creativity and instilled new ways of thinking.[42] Jean-Jacques Simard later described them as "technocrates cybernétistes" to convey their froideur – and probably their hauteur.[43] The social distance separating BAEQ researchers and facilitators from the population they studied and worked with only accentuated the differences in power. Most were young – their average age was twenty-eight – and urban and had little work experience. Eastern Quebec was "another world" for them.[44] Looking back on his time as a researcher with the BAEQ, Jacques Godbout recalled the clash of cultures "between these young academics full of development theories they had come to apply in the region, and this population that needed concrete projects immediately."[45]

Some *animateurs,* such as Roger Guy, were deeply uncomfortable with the power they were expected to wield. Guy worked for the BAEQ as a facilitator between 1963 and 1965, while he was earning his master's degree in social work at Laval.[46] He observed a tension in participatory development between what he identified as the two grand dreams of Quebecers: the "technocratic dream," and the dream of autonomy and self-determination, what he termed "self-management." For the technocrats, *animation sociale* was a way to overcome resistance to change; the experts studied the mentality of rural society to change it or to get around it in order to put their expert plans for development in place. In Guy's view, this was unethical. Facilitators like him, who were more influenced by the dream of self-determination, believed that development should be shaped by and reflect the aspirations of ordinary Quebecers. *Animation sociale* was supposed to be a tool to help them articulate their ambitions so they could be taken into account in planning.[47] Guy quit when it became apparent to him that the technocratic logic prevailed and the development plan would be shaped by BAEQ experts and not by the people whose interests it was supposed to serve. "The project was carried out according to technocratic logic and we ended up with a plan designed by researchers as opposed to the participation of those involved ... I left the BAEQ deeply disappointed."[48]

If the people of the Lower St. Lawrence and Gaspé participated in planning, then, they did not do so as equals. Nor, as it turns out, did they do so under conditions of their own making. *Animation sociale* and the participation it was designed to elicit constituted a bureaucratic structure as much as a process, one that was meant to support specific outcomes – namely, the emergence of a leadership group and a regional awareness. As well, it was also meant to put a permanent structure of consultation in place as part of an overall effort on the part of the province to decentralize political power to the regions.

The importance the BAEQ gave to *animation sociale* was reflected in the portion of its budget devoted to it, some 26.7 percent, an amount second only to what it spent on research. Part of this went to salaries for the seventeen facilitators it employed.[49] They lived in one of the eight administrative zones created by the bureau in eastern Quebec. Each was responsible for helping to organize local development committees in the parishes under their charge and, in the first stages of facilitation, to raise awareness about the problems confronting the region, disseminate information about development, and generally popularize the BAEQ's mission and make it that of the population. As facilitation proceeded to the second, third, fourth, and fifth stages, the job of the *animateurs* was to expedite the emergence of a leadership group and a regional consciousness, as well as to provoke a change in mentality among the people they dealt with. When the bureau released its draft plan in April 1965, the goal was to elicit, build, and strengthen a consensus about its broad orientation. Having done all this, its final task was to render the institutional framework of participation and consultation it had helped put in place more autonomous.[50]

That framework rested on the local development committee. Established shortly after the BAEQ's creation, its members discussed the objectives and means of development among themselves and in public meetings they convened. In doing so, they used the local resource inventories they had compiled: putting those together was meant to prepare committee members for a future that would see residents take control of their own development. But the BAEQ's attempts to structure participation did not end there. To model the kind of discussion it felt was useful, the bureau provided local development committees with discussion guides. If that were not enough, using a set of four pointed questions, it also dispensed advice to committee members about how to behave in a way that would achieve equitable and representative participation:

Have you tried to involve people other than yourselves in your committee's work?

If a young person came to a meeting, did you give him or her an opportunity to put their ideas forward?

Is your committee a private club for a small group?

Do some committee members prefer to do all the work alone rather than divide responsibilities?

If committee members answered "yes" to the last two questions and "no" to the others, it was because they had the wrong attitude and their motivations were suspect: "In the end, you only trust yourselves and may be protecting your own personal prestige."[51]

The local development committees were the foundation of a much larger bureaucracy of participation. Starting in the winter of 1964 and continuing until the planning process was formally completed, the BAEQ facilitated broader discussions aimed at elaborating the structure of consultation. It divided the region into eight zones, convening meetings of the localities in each. The zone committees discussed the reports and recommendations that each local committee had prepared about its own situation and compiled a comprehensive report, which they sent on to one of the three larger sectorial committees, each of which was charged with coming up with recommendations for the development of a particular resource. These sectorial committees produced their own synthetic reports and sent them to the BAEQ itself, which used them to produce a comprehensive draft plan – which was then sent back to all committees for discussion.

As much as this iterative process was aimed at producing the best possible development plan for the region, it was also meant to create new local leaders with different ways of seeing. The BAEQ considered the existing traditional patterns of rural authority and social relations "dysfunctional." Social power and political influence resided in the priest, powerful businessmen, professionals, and politicians, and worked through the church and political parties. Apathy was the result: with access to political office in the hands of a powerful few who were invested in the status quo, not many people were engaged with local politics.[52]

Beyond its self-interested character, however, the problem with local politics as it was traditionally configured was its parochialism, something that BAEQ researchers argued was rooted in how agriculture was organized. In a sociological study of agriculture in the region, Gilles Picard and Albert Juneau argued there was a relationship between production methods, social organization, and values. Agriculture in eastern Quebec was family based and relied on techniques that hadn't changed much since the Middle Ages. Rural communities tended toward "stability" and "security," embracing "conservatism" rather than "innovation." Social participation was almost entirely confined to the family. In the view of Picard and Juneau, while people were members of a parish, parish life was not enough to create a sense of community. Indeed, insofar as any solidarity was forged through the parish, it was mobilized against other ones. Such parochialism only divided eastern Quebecers, preventing the emergence of any regional consciousness.[53]

By creating a structure of consultation in which local committees met with their counterparts from other areas of eastern Quebec, the BAEQ hoped to teach local people not just to take control over the development of their own community but also to see and analyze its development at different scales, in the context of the area in which they lived, the region as a whole, and ultimately the province. Indeed, the BAEQ designed this structure of participation with an eye to the future, seeing it as the basis for what would eventually be an entirely new level of government between the municipal and the provincial ones. Creating a new regional government was a continuation of the policy of "deconcentration" that characterized the BAEQ's efforts to solicit and structure local participation.[54]

Of course, only a minority of people attended development committee meetings of any kind, whether local, zonal, or sectorial. To cultivate a regional consciousness among the population more generally, the BAEQ's social animation department undertook an information campaign using newspapers, radio, television, and film to raise and craft awareness. *L'aménagement* was a free, four-page weekly newspaper with a print run of more than twelve thousand. Started in June 1964, it aimed at informing people of the development activities that were occurring in the region.[55]

Les Jaseries du Père Clophas (Father Clophas's Conversations) was the most popular of the radio shows that the BAEQ produced; it aired daily on the region's stations until it was pulled after seventy-five episodes because of the language its main character used. Like Frère Untel (Brother

Anonymous), upon whom he may have been modelled, Clophas was critical of the status quo. He made the case for planned development, castigating those who preferred the traditional ways of carrying on, like patronage, petty politics, and parochialism.[56]

But perhaps the most telling efforts the BAEQ's Information Division undertook to raise and create a consciousness about the need for development involved television and film. As in Newfoundland, both initiatives revealed the values that underlay the project of improvement. In 1965, the BAEQ produced eighteen television shows dealing with problems confronting the region. They were broadcast weekly on the five stations in the region under the general title *Télé-Club*. People discussed what they had seen in one of 324 Télé-Clubs organized by the local development committees. Each brought about a dozen people together to talk about the shows using discussion guides the BAEQ sent out each week in advance of the broadcast to ensure a productive exchange of views. As the Information Division observed, "There are those who discuss things informally, others who do so systematically using the discussion guide provided by the Development Office." Afterwards, the Télé-Club members recorded the content of their discussions in the guides they had been sent and returned them to the bureau. There, its information officers selected extracts that were published in *L'aménagement*.[57]

The Télé-Club broadcasts signalled BAEQ goals and celebrated expertise as the key to a better life in eastern Quebec. For instance, in late February 1965, the bureau aired a segment dealing with forestry, the sector many in the region depended on for their livelihoods. After discussing the importance of the resource, its maintenance, and the need to develop pulp, paper, and furniture industries, the specialist who was featured came to the point, asking "How many people could live off the forest?"[58] The implication was, of course, that, while consolidating and industrializing resource exploitation would ensure greater prosperity for the region, it might not lessen the need to move. Labour mobility was a valued characteristic for populations to possess. Similarly, another Télé-Club discussed how rural families might budget more effectively. Like the broadcast dealing with forestry, this one featured an expert – in this case, an economist – who enlightened audiences on the best practices.[59] Beyond their specific subject matter, the Télé-Clubs reiterated the importance of participation, encouraging people to engage their friends, neighbours, and colleagues in discussions about development and to organize more groups to do so.

Harnessing the power of film to elicit group discussion was also an integral part of the BAEQ's partnership with the National Film Board of Canada (NFB). Like initiatives in Newfoundland, the bureau used documentary film to raise awareness and instigate social change. As well as producing its own documentaries, it commissioned NFB directors Raymond Garceau and Pierre Lemelin in 1964 to produce twenty-six films funded by ARDA about the challenges confronting eastern Quebec.[60] The key to the films' effectiveness was that they were shot on site, using local people. Documentaries produced outside the region, featuring individuals unknown to audiences in eastern Quebec, could be easily dismissed as entertaining diversions. The familiar would have shock value.[61] "I made films about the different problems of the area by going to see people, putting them on the screen, and confronting them with each other and the situation," recalled Garceau in 1969. "There are people there who had never talked about their lives before. They revealed their problems for the first time."[62] Confronting Gaspesians with each other and "the raw truth" would, it was hoped, bring a "healthy clarity."[63]

It turned out that the truth was more cooked than raw. As with the Fogo films, those of Garceau and Lemelin did not so much document a diversity of views as they presented a selection of them. These were used to build a case for development of the kind the BAEQ wished to pursue – namely, modernizing the region with the involvement of local people and for their benefit. The filmmakers portrayed life in eastern Quebec as having always been difficult.[64] To the extent settlers had been able to overcome the adversity of isolation and environment, it was because of their self-reliance and initiative: they worked hard and together to make lives for themselves. But the challenges confronting people in 1965 were different than they had been in 1925, and locals would be hard-pressed to meet them. That was because the region had not entirely been left behind by history. According to Garceau, modernity had come to the Gaspé, but in a way that saw people experience its worst effects while reaping few of its benefits. The culture of mass consumption had made inroads where few real roads existed: the residents of eastern Quebec wanted all the modern conveniences even if they could not really afford them.[65] Their desire to live beyond their means was facilitated by the welfare state, whose programs supported people just enough for them to get by while eroding the very qualities that had allowed previous generations of Gaspesians to live well – namely, their autonomy and inventiveness.

If eastern Quebec were to be developed in the way the BAEQ envisaged, its residents would not only have to draw on the values of previous generations, but also have to adapt their institutions and themselves to the economic realities of modern life. Specifically, they would have to cooperate and participate. While, for instance, cooperatives had long been the salvation of many a small rural community, providing them with an important source of income, it was unlikely they could continue to do so given the growth and integration of the economy. This did not mean that the idea of mutual assistance that informed their creation and operation was outdated, however. Instead, the traditional patterns of collective action merely had to be reconfigured, made modern: the hundreds of cooperatives with thousands of members in the region needed to consolidate. Larger numbers would mean better prices for both producers and consumers. "The population realizes that the small parish cooperative can't return a profit anymore," intoned the narrator of one of Garceau's films. "Cooperatives can no longer be rooted in local communities. If co-op members think such an association is still well-suited to defend their interests, they must act accordingly. Cooperatives with greater social and economic power might better reflect the dynamism of the region's population."[66]

If cooperatives could be scaled up and adapted to big business, then so too could people's attitudes.[67] As the narrator of *Le milieu* put it, "Maintaining a standard of living requires money, and to have money you have to produce. If production depends on the abundance of natural resources, doesn't it also depend on the attitude of the population?"[68] For the planners at the BAEQ, changing political attitudes and practices was as important to development as adapting economic ones. People had to come together, not just in cooperatives, but also at public meetings and in Télé-Clubs, film screenings, and local development committees to air their views and hear those of others. It was only in these ways that they would learn to run their own affairs, or, as one of BAEQ's meeting facilitators put it, "take responsibility for parish development."

Garceau's films showed them doing so enthusiastically, even if participation could be an initially sobering, even shocking, experience. With the BAEQ's help, residents of eastern Quebec were able to appreciate the extent of the challenges confronting them, to compare, for instance, the yields they got from their forests with those of other regions. The gap surprised them – "many were scandalized" – and they realized their methods of cutting and conservation were outdated. When farmers did the same thing, they could conclude only that "traditional agriculture was no longer enough to feed a landholding family."[69] With continued participation, however, shock gave way to a more constructive response, and ultimately an empowering one: the people of the Lower St. Lawrence and Gaspé realized that solutions to their problems would come from where they always had – themselves – but only if they were armed with more education and worked together in groups that extended beyond their local communities. As important as their consolidated and collective efforts were to development, so too was the new "regional climate" that emerged from the meetings.[70]

But the films did not simply make the argument that people needed to lift themselves out of poverty; they also underscored the state's responsibility to intervene in significant ways to make a better future for its citizens. Government could gather the expertise necessary to help guide development and democracy, as it had through the BAEQ, but it also had to provide electricity, water, and roads, and, ultimately, it had to reorganize the market. It was the only institution powerful enough to do so.

The emphasis on the need for an activist state was characteristic of the political culture of Quiet Revolution Quebec. The Lesage government came to power on a promise to re-establish the province's economic advisory council. First created during the Second World War, it was eliminated by the Duplessis government in 1944 and then restored by Lesage in 1961. In addition to providing advice, the Conseil d'orientation économique du Québec (COEQ) was also charged with the responsibility of preparing an overall development plan for the province.[71] In Lesage's view, an activist state, dedicated to planning and working through organizations like COEQ, was crucial to Quebecers' collective survival. "The only powerful means we have is the Quebec state," he told a Saint-Jean-Baptiste Society gathering in 1961. "If we refuse to use our state, out of fear or prejudice, then we would deprive ourselves of what may be the only recourse we have left to survive as a minority."[72]

In eastern Quebec in the 1960s, the activist state was a technocratic one, and perhaps one that, if the BAEQ is any indication, was not entirely democratic. Jacques Godbout argued that its vision of planning evolved from an emphasis on the total participation of the population to limited consultation – and that consultation being with elites.[73] But development planning did more than reinforce existing social divisions; it also aimed to remake the political sphere, using *animation sociale* to produce particular subjectivities.

We can think of the BAEQ as an exercise in "guided" or "managed democracy," terms that come from the political histories of Indonesia and Russia; but perhaps an equally useful way to look at development is in terms of a concept the bureau's planners used – *encadrement.* They used it in reference to creating an institutional framework *(cadre)* to guide participation for the purposes of planning and to decentralize provincial political power, but that framework was also meant to shape and contain discussion and shape the discussants into a *cadre,* or leadership group.

Regardless of whether participation and participants were guided or managed, the bureau seemed quite successful in generating interest in development planning. The residents of eastern Quebec formed 200 local development committees that held at least 3,000 meetings over the three years the BAEQ existed. Some 6,000 adults participated in the adult education program it offered in 1964, and another 400 enrolled in its Centre d'étude en développement régional, which offered training to members of local development committees.[74]

Despite the fact that the BAEQ completed its much-anticipated plan in 1966, the province took no real action to implement it until 1968, when, as noted earlier, it struck an agreement with Ottawa for funds to do so. The delay didn't sit well with many in eastern Quebec: supported by the government, the BAEQ had worked for three years to convince them of the need to modernize, and now the same government seemed to be dragging its feet. Worse, the only concrete step toward redeveloping the region it did take was to implement its relocation program. In the absence of any more positive and popular initiatives – like improving the road system, for example – the government's intentions seemed even more suspect, a "betrayal" of the BAEQ's ten-volume vision for a better future.[75]

If the government wasn't going to act, residents would: they would take charge of their own development just as they had been encouraged to do. As the residents of Esprit-Saint put it, "au lieu de déménager, on va aménager!" – instead of moving, we'll develop! Between 1970 and 1973, eastern Quebecers articulated a different kind of development, one that would sustain them economically and socially in the place they called home.

As Premier Robert Bourassa made plans to travel to the region in August 1970 to close St-Thomas-de-Cherbourg and Saint-Paulin-Dalibaire, people in Sainte-Paule were also planning – a demonstration. On 22 September, the sixty-five families who lived there were joined by many others in the vicinity. In all, some 3,000 people gathered to express their opposition to the government's relocation policy and, more importantly, to lend their support to a long-standing forestry proposal their local development committee had crafted, one that would allow them to maintain themselves and their communities.[76]

An example of what we would now call sustainable development or community forestry, the proposal called on the province to improve the road system to make the region's forests more accessible, and to create five forestry farms *(fermes forestières)* of 600 to 800 acres each and place them under private local control. Their owners would manage them in accordance with a plan they and forestry experts from Laval University crafted. By implementing a rotation system of cutting and reforestation, the Comité d'aménagement de Sainte-Paule believed the farms would return a profit in a few years and eventually become self-sustaining. In part, their profitability was ensured through an agreement with the Compagnie internationale de papier (CIP) at Matane to buy forest waste from areas that had been logged.[77]

According to Léonard Otis, the head of the local Union des cultivateurs catholiques and one of the drafters of the plan, private local ownership ensured better management over the long term. Owners were invested in managing the resource sustainably because they knew it was crucial to the ongoing viability of their communities. Employees of big forestry companies tended to cut and run. As Otis put it, "They aren't people tied to the land." In contrast, forestry farm owners took a different, and more sustainable, approach. "Yes, we will want to exploit the forest to earn a salary. But this forest is also an asset that we want to exploit in a way that creates surplus value."[78] Indeed, Otis was so convinced of the potential of the region's forests that he argued that people could abandon agriculture completely and make a living through the committee's model of forestry.[79]

While it was not quite as enthusiastic as Otis was, the provincial government, through its Office de développement de l'Est du Québec, was convinced enough to provide funding for the *fermes forestières* project in Sainte-Paule in 1968.[80] Despite the initial support, the project did not proceed. But the government's plans for relocation did. By September 1970 and the protest at Sainte-Paule, then, frustrations were high.

Interestingly, sustainable regional development through *fermes forestières* did not preclude the kind of centralization and relocation envisaged by BAEQ planners. Despite the fact that the Comité d'aménagement de Sainte-

Paule was committed to fostering local potential and keeping it in place, it also called for amalgamating the population around Sainte-Paule to create a *village forestier*, or forest town. In a secret vote held in that community and in Trinité-des-Monts, the other proposed site of the *fermes forestières* in the Rimouski-Témiscouata area, 90 percent of the population voted in favour of moving.[81]

For the members of Sainte-Paule's Comité d'aménagement, local support for the *fermes forestières* and amalgamation spoke to the determination of a population that wanted to be helped to make an honest living where they were rather than have to move and receive charity.[82] Indeed, for Léonard Otis, the *fermes forestières* – and the sustainable development they represented – were as much about cultivating self-respect as trees. "There's great pride in working for a living. The pride and joy are doubly great for someone who through his or her work has helped create jobs so that others can earn a living," he observed. "But there are no words for the pride and joy of someone who, through his or her work, has helped develop his or her part of the country. You have to experience it."[83]

These sentiments were encapsulated in the name the protesters in Sainte-Paule chose for their movement: l'Opération Dignité. According to its president, Charles Banville, its purpose was to allow the region's population to fashion its own future and thereby restore its dignity. As with the BAEQ, local participation was crucial to the kind of development the demonstrators envisaged. "The ultimate objective of Opération Dignité is to uplift a population that's often considered marginal, through the discovery that its dignity lies in taking control of its future and the exploitation of its resources – among other things, its forest."[84] In addition to choosing what they would call themselves, the group created a formal committee structure consisting of representatives from fourteen different parishes in the Matane-Matapédia area and an executive. Representation later expanded to include people from twenty-seven different communities. Despite fighting a series of battles with the province over the course of the next year, the group remained committed to local participation, holding regular meetings, attendance at which never fell below fifty people.[85]

Other communities in eastern Quebec took their lead from what those in the Matane-Matépedia region accomplished: protests in Esprit-Saint and Les Méchins in 1971 and 1972 led to the formation of Opérations Dignité II and III, both of which were animated by the same desire on the part of local people to govern their development (Figures 3.2, 3.3, and 3.4).

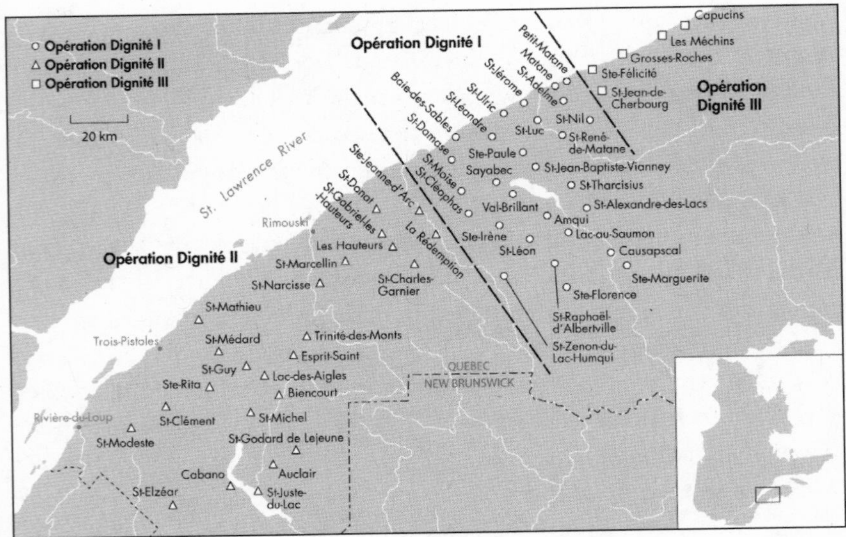

Figure 3.2 Where Opérations Dignité were active, adapted from Charles Banville, *Les Opérations Dignité* (1977)

Figure 3.3 "We will live again with dignity!" Demonstration at Esprit-Saint, Quebec, August 1971. | Centre de mise en valeur des Opérations Dignité, photo OD-95

Figure 3.4 People gathering to protest at Esprit-Saint, Quebec, August 1971. | Centre de mise en valeur des Opérations Dignité, photo OD-99

Opération Dignité II was centred in the Rimouski-Témiscouata area. While their neighbours to the east were gathering at Sainte-Paule, many of the residents in this area were engaged in a battle over the construction of a factory at Cabano, one that likely taught them about the importance of controlling their own forests. Owned by New Brunswick magnate K.C. Irving, D'Auteuil Lumber Company had received a large concession from the Quebec government in return for promising to build a wallboard factory, something that would alleviate the high unemployment in the area. When D'Auteuil reneged, the Cabanois took to the streets, vandalizing company property in August 1970. Many threatened to burn their forests rather than let the Irving-owned company profit from them, attracting the support of the Front de libération du Québec, which offered to supply them with bombs, Molotov cocktails, and personnel. The protest ended when the Minister of Lands and Forests cancelled D'Auteuil's cutting rights.[86]

Given this context, it's not surprising that the idea of locally owned *fermes forestières* was appealing to people in the Rimouski-Témiscouata area. After seeking advice from the Sainte-Paule Opération Dignité executive about how to proceed, individuals from three different towns organized their own committee and called a public meeting at Esprit-Saint for 15 August 1971, where they launched Opération Dignité II. The twenty-seven parishes it represented worked to develop and manage their forestry resources – again through the *ferme forestière* model and drawing on the expertise at Laval University. As well, it kept an eye on developments at Cabano, where local initiative eventually resulted in government funding and the establishment of a citizens' pulp and paper mill in 1972.[87]

Local participation and control over resource development was also at the heart of the protests that led to the formation of the third manifestation of Opération Dignité. Instead of forestry resources, the people of Les Méchins, a coastal settlement approximately fifty kilometres to the east of Matane, wanted to develop the inshore fishery, an industry that the BAEQ had, in its report, deemed largely unprofitable. In 1967 they established an association of independent fishermen, hoping to convince the federal government to make their community a fish-landing centre. However, the returns – fourteen thousand pounds of fish, worth $980 in 1969 – were too limited to make the investment worthwhile.[88] Buoyed by what had been accomplished in Sainte-Paule, in the summer of 1971 a group of "engaged citizens" from Matane came together to study what could be done for Les Méchins; in November, the community itself formed a citizens' committee and began working over the winter to convince people along the coast of the need to join forces. Opération Dignité III was born. Its facilitators were slowed by the independence of the population, their days filled with efforts "to correct a tendency towards individualism among the fishermen of the region." While the fishermen of Les Méchins and Les Capucins did come together to form a cooperative in 1972, their attempts to extend it to include people from Grosses-Roches, Sainte-Felicité, and Cap-Chat were ultimately thwarted by mutual suspicion.[89]

Notably, Catholic clergy led all three Opérations Dignité (Figure 3.5). Fathers Charles Banville (OD I), Jean-Marc Gendron (OD II), and Gilles Roy (OD III) were referred to as "the Three Wise Men," eastern Quebec's version of the "brain trust" that was said to run Ottawa at the time: Pierre Trudeau, Jean Marchand, and Gérard Pelletier.[90] The principles underlying the church's support for what the people of eastern Quebec were trying to accomplish were articulated more explicitly and at greater length in a statement circulated among rural communities in the counties of Matane and Matapédia in the immediate wake of the Sainte-Paule demonstration. Released by the Diocese of Rimouski, the "manifeste des curés en colère" (the manifesto of the angry priests) reflected the leadership role the church and its clergy took in the Quebec of the 1960s.

Figure 3.5 The leaders of Opérations Dignité were priests, and local churches, like this one in Esprit-Saint in August 1971, often served as places of protest. | Centre de mise en valeur des Opérations Dignité, photo OD-97

Declaring the actions and demands of the first Opération Dignité to be realistic and justified, the Diocese of Rimouski backed its parishioners, "our eternal slaves," who wanted the government to invest in silviculture rather than social assistance. Given the administrative sluggishness that followed the release of the BAEQ plan, it was no surprise that the people of eastern Quebec had lost confidence in their political leaders. Evoking Pierre Trudeau's promises, the *curés en colère* asked if the "Just Society" would become more than a dream. "It's in the name of truth, justice, and human dignity that we sound our cry of liberation. In the spirit of the Encyclical *Populorum Progressio* and the message of the Canadian bishops ... Let the deaf hear us!"[91]

As the diocesean statement suggested, in lending its support and moral authority to the cause of Opérations Dignité, the clergy were guided by Catholic social teaching. In his encyclical *Populorum Progressio* (1967), Pope Paul VI expressed his concerns about growing global inequality, warning against the excesses of laissez-faire capitalism and industrial development undertaken without regard to its social impacts. Development was not just about economic growth but also had to concern itself with securing workers' rights and eradicating hunger, poverty, and disease. Failing to do so would only widen the gap between rich and poor and lead to more conflict. In the pope's view "development [was] the new name for peace."[92] In many ways, he was arguing for a "human-centred economy" – not surprisingly, given that Louis-Joseph Lebret, one of the originators of *animation sociale* and *l'enquête-participation,* was "one of the principal instigators" of his encyclical.[93]

The pope's emphasis on "concerted planning" and the necessity for development that allowed people to become "artisans of their destiny" was of particular importance in understanding the motives of eastern Quebec's priests and the movements they led.[94] While the pope recognized that "goals must be defined, methods and means must be chosen, and the work of select men must be coordinated," he also insisted that "such planned programs do more than promote economic and social progress." They also had to "enhance man's dignity and his capabilities."[95] To that end, Paul VI hoped the disadvantaged would "discover the road to cultural and social progress ... while remaining faithful to the native genius of their land" – that they would be able to collaborate with development experts in a meaningful way, "to take part in the construction of a better world."[96]

This balance between people relying on outside expertise and taking their future into their own hands was particularly apparent in the first two iterations of Opération Dignité. The people of Sainte-Paule had relied on forestry engineer Louis-Jean Lussier to help draft their development initiative, and he in turn recommended that they avail themselves of the expertise of foresters at Laval University, drawing on those associated with the Fonds de recherches forestières de l'Université Laval (FRUL; the Laval University Forestry Research Fund). While the FRUL worked with communities in the regions from which Opérations Dignité I and II drew their support, those communities took pains to ensure their point of view was central to any development plan the university foresters came up with. As Charles Banville recalled, in 1970–71, the FRUL collaborated closely with the local population, with "no decision being taken without its consultation." Indeed, it was legally obligated to engage in such consultation, as its contract with the Quebec government specified that the FRUL "will have to work in constant collaboration with Opération Dignité. It must hold at least one monthly meeting with that organization."[97]

That the government of Quebec would legally require the experts it hired to consult with the local population in developing a forestry-management plan suggests the impact that rural protest had. Opérations Dignité I, II, and III reshaped government policy as well as the form and trajectory of regional development in the province. Most immediately, the government reconfigured its relocation program, ending its focus on closing communities. Instead, from 1972 on, it would simply provide financial support for families and individuals from designated places to move.[98] In all, the relocation program had closed ten communities and displaced just over two thousand people – a significant number, but only a small proportion of what the province had envisaged when it implemented the policy.[99]

In concert with changing its relocation policy, the provincial government also altered its approach to forestry management in eastern Quebec. Building on the *fermes forestières* model, and acting on the advice of the FRUL, the Minister of Lands and Forests divided the region into thirteen private forestry-management units *(groupements forestières)* in 1972, assigning them to syndicates of local users who administered their development through different *sociétés d'exploitation des ressources* (SERs; resource-development corporations) or through producers' cooperatives.

The most ambitious of the SERs was the Société d'exploitation des ressources de la Vallée (SERV), which covered the territory that had been politicized by Opération Dignité I. Created in 1974, it had five major objectives: to battle against the closure of parishes, to develop all the resources of the area, to assure the participation of the local population, to create employment, and to stimulate the local economy. Of these, according to political scientist Alain-G. Gagnon, creating employment was SERV's central preoccupation. In addition to various forestry projects, SERV spearheaded ventures into agriculture, fisheries, tourism, and financial investment.[100] People in the territory covered by Opération Dignité II took a slightly different approach to local development, establishing JAL, a producers' cooperative in 1973 (the acronym derived from the three communities that formed its membership, Saint-Juste-du-Lac, Auclair, and Lejeune). Like SERV, it had its basis in forestry but quickly diversified its economic activities, establishing itself as the prime contractor for development in the area. Where it differed from SERV was in its practice of making the new enterprises it established independent companies, with itself acting as the parent organization.

As these experiments in forestry management and development proceeded, the government revisited its relocation policy once more in 1974, this time to bring a formal end to provincial support for migration altogether.[101] The language it used in its order-in-council speaks again to the impact of rural protest. Once considered natural and indispensable to development, relocation was suspended because it potentially compromised the government's plans to pursue "integrated development of backcountry resources."[102] The emphasis on integrated resource development marked a significant shift away from the sectorial approach that the BAEQ had outlined and that the province had tried to implement up to that point, one that focused on exploiting a single resource. Instead, integrated resource development considered how all of a region's resources could be utilized in a way that would sustain a population in place. It was what the leadership and supporters of Opérations Dignité, the SERs, and JAL wanted and exemplified, and it appears to have won the day, even if it was achieved by bureaucratizing the countryside, as Gagnon notes.[103]

If the BAEQ's development plan exemplified the confidence of the Quiet Revolution and the faith evinced by Quebecers in the technocratic state as a tool to improve their status, for some scholars it also represented its biggest failure, marking a shift from the optimism of the 1960s to the disillusionment of the 1970s.[104] To become masters of their own house – *maîtres chez nous* – the provincial government resorted to dispossessing some of its poorest citizens of theirs and worked at transforming them into new political subjects.

The government often presented opposition to relocation as well as the rural protests that gave full voice to alternative kinds of development as stemming from the conservatism of the countryside: they were impractical and romantic reactions motivated by sentimentality rather than a hard-headed realism. In his initial consideration of the *fermes forestières,* for instance, the Minister of Lands and Forests rejected Sainte-Paule's plans as being too small-scale and lacking in impact and its backers as short-sighted and limited in ambition. "Quebec can no longer develop with an artisanal economic policy," Kevin Drummond insisted in October 1970. To ensure that people understood his government's perspective on both the protesters and their plan, he added, "Let's stop being small-minded and finally understand that we need to unite to build [the province]."[105]

But the conservatism – if it was that – of eastern Quebecers' response to relocation should not blind us to the fundamental challenge they posed to the prevailing assumptions about development. The idea of integrated resource development, whether through *fermes forestières, sociétés d'exploitation des ressources,* or producers' cooperatives like JAL, exposed the urban bias of development and social security. Planners and politicians in Quebec and Newfoundland believed modern economies necessitated a certain spatial organization, one that was urban. The idea that modernity could take another form, one characterized by a dispersed settlement pattern and low population densities, was beyond their imaginations.

Given the urban bias of development, it seems somewhat paradoxical that planners focused on empowering rural communities to achieve their ends. As in the North and Newfoundland, the focus of development in eastern Quebec was on building people's capacity. Through cooperatives and social animation, they would learn to govern their futures, to become "artisans of their destiny." But, as I have argued, capacity building through the disciplinary processes of participatory democracy was intended to transform even as it built, to create different scales of affiliation and affect, and ultimately to subsume the local to the regional and the provincial. The latter agenda was made explicit in a report issued by the federal Department of Regional Economic Expansion in 1970. The authors, Benjamin Higgins, Fernand Martin, and André Raynauld, argued that regions were to serve the interests of growth poles. Insofar as eastern Quebec would benefit, it was through the loss of its unemployed people, its "excess" labour, to Montreal: "There is nothing wrong with eliminating poverty and unemployment in an underdeveloped region by attracting it to a dynamic city."[106]

Once empowered to express themselves, however, many people in the targeted regions formulated a different idea of development. Sainte-Paule's local development committee committed itself to "keep the current human potential in place and, if possible, increase it."[107] For them, regional development had to serve the interests of the region and the people in it first.

Beyond articulating a different spatial configuration of what a modern economy would look like and a different understanding of whose interests it should serve, eastern Quebecers also did something that, in the opinion of Gilles Roy, was even more innovative. As coordinator of *animation sociale* for JAL, the former president of Opération Dignité III argued that they had transformed democracy. The BAEQ's "bureaucratic democracy, centralized and paternalistic, [was abandoned] in favour of a grassroots democracy built on genuine participation, self-management, and control of the common good by all citizens."[108]

As philosopher Jay Drydyk points out, the relationship between participation, empowerment, and democracy is complex: one does not necessarily lead to another.[109] In eastern Quebec, rural residents participated in creating a development plan for the region that the government then chose not to implement. And while planners were presented with the perspectives of ordinary people, the planning process was not a democratic one. Facilitators guided participation toward particular goals and did so within a structure of consultation that subsumed local needs to those of the region and the province. Insofar as participatory development empowered and democratized, it did so almost inadvertently. When people such as Léonard Otis were denied, they heeded the lessons they were taught. The alternative development they envisaged and forced the government to implement was one that had their needs at the centre.

The issues relocation and development in Newfoundland and Quebec raised about democracy and the spatial organization of modern society were not limited to rural areas. In the 1960s, the state also addressed urban poverty in Canada as a problem of spatial justice. As we'll see, "chez nous, c'est chez nous" was a sentiment the residents of the neighbourhoods of Africville in Halifax and Strathcona in Vancouver shared when confronted with slum clearance.[110]

4

"Deviating from the Strict Letter of the Law"

Race, Poverty, and Planning in Postwar Halifax

Our living conditions are abominable. We're third class citizens. All we want is what our White neighbours have. We don't want their money, we just want the essential things of life. We ain't living now. We're just existing.

– Leon Steed, Africville resident, 1962

Can a modern urban metropolis tolerate within its midst a community or grouping of dwellings that are physically and socially inadequate, not served with pure water and sewage disposal facilities? Can a minority group be permitted to reconstitute itself as a segregated community at a time in our history, at a time in the social history of western industrialized urban nations, when segregation either de jure (in law) or de facto (in fact) is almost everywhere condemned?

– Albert Rose, professor of social work,
"Report of a Visit to Halifax with Particular
Respect to Africville," 1963

There was a decidedly urban bias to regional and rural development projects in Canada. In the North, Newfoundland, and eastern Quebec, the Canadian state tried to reduce poverty by centralizing rural populations, relocating them to places that offered a concentration of services and more and better social and economic opportunities. But as both Leon Steed and Albert Rose could attest, population density was no protection against privation. In the postwar period, the three levels of government in Canada combined to confront urban poverty in ways that were broadly similar to those discussed in the preceding chapters – that is, through state-funded development efforts that were informed by expertise and animated by a commitment to "a good life."

In Halifax, as elsewhere, planners were central to the project of building better cities. After a number of attempts to initiate redevelopment, in 1956 Halifax took advantage of federal funds from the Central Mortgage and Housing Corporation (CMHC) for slum clearance, or "urban renewal," as it was called, and engaged Gordon Stephenson, an internationally recognized British architect and urban designer to come up with a plan. Released the following year, his report identified twelve sites for redevelopment, including the predominantly black neighbourhood of Africville on Bedford Basin, at the city's far north end (Figure 4.1). Settled for more than a century, Africville was serviced neither by paved roads nor piped water and sewers, a situation that provoked critical commentary and, up to that point, no remedial action. In addition to Stephenson, other university experts, such as public housing specialist Albert Rose, as well as human rights advocates and professionals, such as social worker Peter MacDonald, all intervened in the early 1960s to shape the acquisition of Africville lands and the relocation of its residents.[1]

The literature on Africville focuses on the racism and tragic consequences of urban renewal but does not put the razing of the neighbourhood and the displacement of its residents in the context of efforts made by the state to combat poverty across the country through relocation and redevelopment. Jennifer J. Nelson's article comes closest to doing so: it focuses on the discourses of poverty, criminality, and race that ran through planning documents like the Stephenson report and academic studies of the situation of black Nova Scotians in the city and province. These discourses, she argues, constructed Africville as a problem whose solution lay in slum clearance.[2]

Important in itself, Africville's fate also sheds light on the divergent approaches taken by the Canadian state to combat poverty. In contrast to what happened in rural Canada in the 1950s and 1960s, urban redevelopment

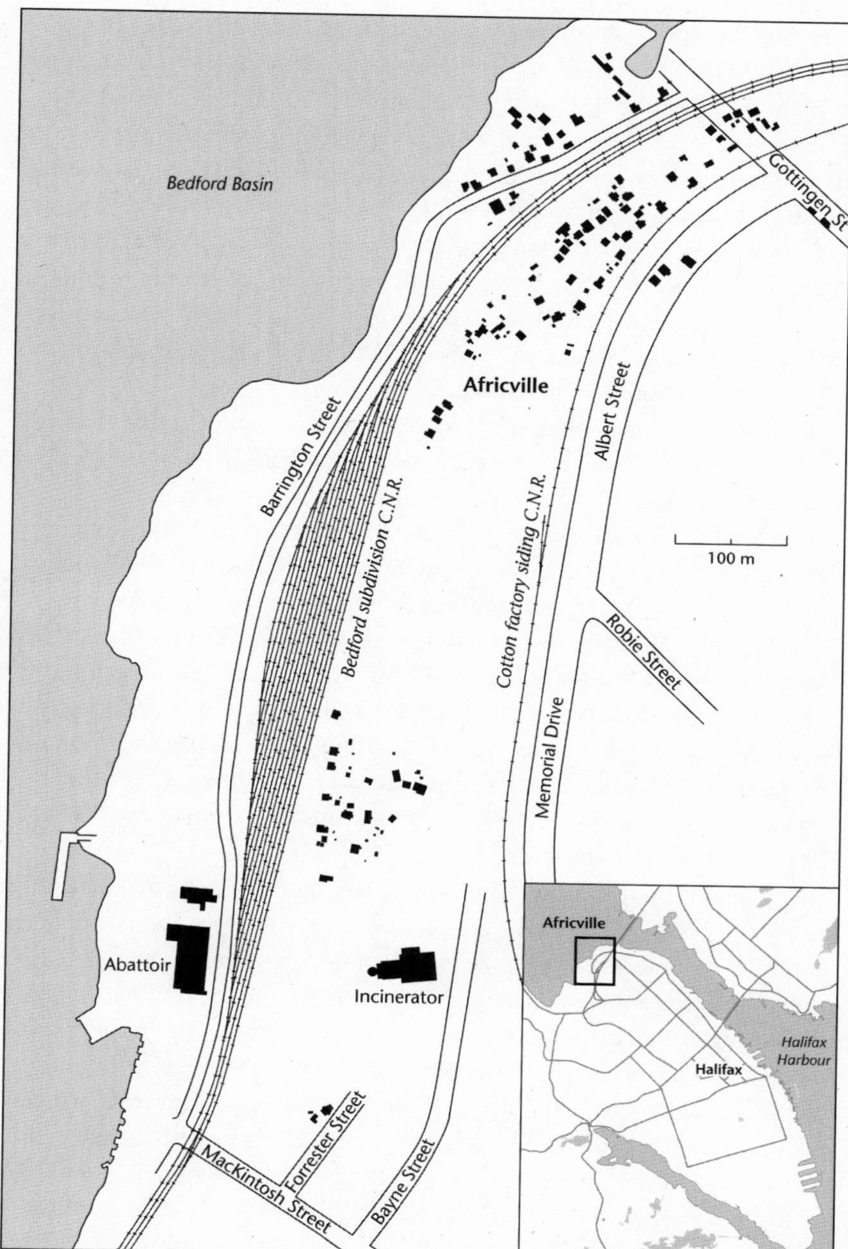

Figure 4.1 Located at the far north end of the city, on Bedford Basin, Africville was geographically and socially segregated.

planning was done on the cheap and implemented without consulting those who would be directly affected by it and, moreover, without soliciting their consent to relocation and their active participation in planning, unlike in eastern Quebec. While there were attempts to improve opportunities for Africville's residents by providing them with a chance to upgrade their education, nothing like the community development initiatives of the sort discussed in previous chapters were put in place or even considered. Urban renewal remained a largely top-down affair, dictated by people who were, in the context of Africville, outsiders by virtue of their class, race, and education, or some combination of those factors. Nevertheless, the process created engaged citizens in Halifax, albeit inadvertently.

Perhaps more surprising, much of the literature on Africville does not place it in the context of urban redevelopment in Halifax. Geographer Ted Rutland's book is an exception. By far the most theoretically informed work dealing with Africville and urban renewal, Rutland argues that black lives didn't matter to planners. Like Nelson, he contends that planning's project of improving people's lives was profoundly shaped by race. Blackness defined the limits of humanity, and planning both reflected and enforced those limits. As he puts it, "Anti-blackness structures planning's conception of human life ... [;] it brings into being the always-already pathological spectrum into which various individuals and populations can be slotted." Ultimately, he argues, "Displacing blackness from the field of planning's concerns and (sometimes) from the physical terrain itself is thus the opening and continually repeated move of modern planning."[3]

Rutland's is a powerful and provocative argument, but one that overlooks how the city realized its plans – that is, how it actually went about acquiring properties in its redevelopment areas. Examining that process reveals some telling differences in how the city implemented urban renewal in areas outside Africville compared to how it proceeded there. Those differences speak to how, beyond relocating people and subjecting them to "development," the state extended "social citizenship," the core idea of the liberal welfare state. According to T.H. Marshall, the sociologist who came up with the concept, "social citizenship" was "the right to a modicum of economic welfare and security and the right to share to the full in the social heritage." But it was also the right "to live the life of a civilized being according to the standards prevailing in society."[4] For Pierre Trudeau, social citizenship was simply "the right to a good life."[5]

As we have seen, in the North, Newfoundland, and eastern Quebec, granting social citizenship led the state to move people against their wills so they could fulfil their potential as individuals. In each of these cases, the state tried to ease that contradiction by manufacturing consent, or at least its appearance, by asking people if they wanted to move or by helping them to make collective decisions about their future.

Not so in Halifax. Because they considered slum clearance an act of spatial justice, part of the process of integrating a racially segregated city, municipal authorities not only insisted residents leave – as they did in all urban redevelopment areas – but they also wouldn't countenance moving them to a location where they could live together. To do so would be to undermine their social citizenship; it would contravene the right of Africville residents to "live the life of ... civilized being[s]." The standards of the time deemed that living in ethnic or race-based enclaves amounted to segregation, something that was unacceptable. Segregation amounted to isolation, and, as was the case in Newfoundland and Quebec, isolation – whatever its source – eroded the ability of individuals to realize their potential.

That said, acquiring land and buildings in Africville and relocating its residents did force the city to grapple with questions of process, to consider how to do right by Africvillers in a way it did not for people – both black and white – who lived in other areas that were cleared. If it was going to move Africville residents against their will – forcibly include them in Halifax society – then it had to do so in a way that was fair.

Fairness required "deviating from the strict letter of the law."[6] Specifically, it meant that, rather than follow the usual process of expropriation, the city assigned a social worker to untangle the complexities of land ownership in the neighbourhood and negotiate compensation; it recognized residents' ownership of lands and buildings in the absence of any legal record; it compensated the propertyless; it established a special subcommittee of the city council to review compensation agreements; and, in a gesture toward helping people help themselves, it committed to helping residents after they were relocated to find employment and improve their education and hence their opportunities. While Rutland contends that "it is difficult to identify a single example in which planning sought to understand, sustain, or improve the specific circumstances of Black people," the case of Africville, surprisingly, appears to be one.[7]

The majority of Haligonians, both black and white, who were displaced as a result of the Stephenson redevelopment plan did not get this kind of consideration. But receiving it was no guarantee of better results, of actually securing social citizenship for this group of poor African Nova Scotians. The shortcomings of urban renewal in Africville speak to the limits of postwar liberality – specifically to the idea of fairness that shaped how the city and the community's advocates dealt with residents and the limits of a particular rights-based approach to address the systemic causes of poverty.

Broadly conceived, urban planning is a way to control land use to create an environment that meets the needs and works for the collective benefit of a community over the long term. Because not everyone necessarily agrees on what a community's needs are or which should get priority, urban planning was, and is, inherently political. It is also political because it involves the allocation of a scarce resource: land. In that sense, planning is a kind of conservation: it is concerned with wise use and management. Reflecting this point of view, the federal government's Commission of Conservation (1909–21) appointed prominent British town planner Thomas Adams one of its advisers in 1914. Concerned about the consequences of the unregulated growth of cities, particularly the immiseration of the poor, the commission promoted comprehensive scientific planning to create economically and socially productive cities.[8]

From his position in Ottawa, Adams hoped to establish planning as a profession in Canada and embed it in government through a comprehensive framework of laws and institutions that regulated development but stopped short of direct government involvement. While he managed to do the former, establishing the Town Planning Institute of Canada (now the Canadian Institute of Planners) in 1919, he fell short of the latter, largely because of the exigencies of war and a Conservative government that was less than enthusiastic about expanding the role of the state, even to the limited degree Adams proposed. While the Great Depression and Second World War pushed Adams's ideas further to the margins in the short term, both events also provided the context that helped establish urban planning and the provision of decent housing as functions of government in the postwar period.[9]

If the economic crisis of the 1930s highlighted the need for an activist state, mobilizing for war also proved how effective government intervention and coordinated planning could be. As a result of the Great Depression and the Second World War, "social planning" emerged and gained fuller expression in the 1950s and 1960s, eventually taking institutional form in municipal departments of social planning across the country. Articulated by the League for Social Reconstruction, a group of left-wing intellectuals who came together in response to the Great Depression, social planning brought the humanitarian aspects of the enterprise to the fore: it was planning that "put the interests of the mass of the population first," particularly the need for housing.[10]

In critiquing capitalism, the league argued that town planning in particular was crucial to addressing the social costs of industrialization: in Canada as elsewhere, as cities grew, their functions encroached on each other: industrial areas pushed into commercial ones, commercial into residential, and residential into the green space around cities. The result was a jumble of uses and inner-city "blight." This vague and encompassing term described the physical condition of buildings and the process of decline and its spread. The outcome of unregulated growth, blight was the dilapidation and disrepair that often infected the urban core and spread like a disease. Not only did it have negative economic effects, driving down land values and hence municipal tax revenues, but it also had social consequences for the poor and working class who lived in the inner city. Unable to afford to move to the green and growing suburbs, they were subjected to increasingly crowded, polluted, unsanitary conditions. As well, because of the assumed link between physical decay and moral decay, inner-city residents were also deemed in danger of falling victim to vice and crime as well as being corrupted themselves.[11]

For the league, "organized planning [was] the answer to this chaos of irresponsibility and waste." Going beyond Adams, it argued for direct government intervention: town planning had to "be made a specific government responsibility in every large city, coordinated and encouraged through the Federal Housing (and Town Planning) Authority which would be set up in Ottawa." Still, the job of planners remained the same: they were to consider each part of the city in relation to the whole by conducting scientific surveys, mapping the location of industry, commerce, retail businesses, and residential areas, noting where blight existed, as well as taking into account the physical geography of the city. With "the defects of urban composition" cartographically exposed, "the town planner with the cooperation of the sociologist and economist is able to decide which are the areas most appropriate for housing schemes."[12]

The Second World War only underscored the need for a coordinated, comprehensive, expert response by the state to industrialization and deepened the connection between urban planning and the provision of decent housing. Historically, urban growth had been unplanned, and the war just made things worse. With the onset of global conflict, people flocked in great numbers to Canada's cities for jobs in the country's newly established wartime industries, putting pressure on what in many cases was a limited supply of housing.[13] With little residential construction during the 1930s and resources diverted to the war effort, what accommodation existed was often in poor condition. In Halifax, a key location of wartime industries and military personnel, the number of workers more than doubled between 1939 and 1942, and many found themselves living in overcrowded, poorly ventilated, and unsanitary rental accommodation.[14]

In planning for peace, the federal government's Advisory Committee on Reconstruction realized that many if not most of these industrial workers were in Canada's cities to stay, and their needs would have to be met. In the Final Report of the Advisory Committee on Reconstruction's Subcommittee on Housing and Community Planning, authors C.A. Curtis and Leonard Marsh estimated that between 37,500 and 57,000 housing units would have to be built every year to meet Canada's needs, a significant increase over the 24,000 that had been built in 1941 and the 18,000 in 1942.[15] The scale of the task led them to the sobering conclusion that "among the many problems confronting the cities and towns of Canada today and in the postwar period, none looms greater and with more far-reaching implications than the planning and regulation of land and building development."[16]

Meeting the challenge required a coordinated approach to town planning and the provision of housing, one that was led by the federal government but also involved the provinces and municipalities. In 1944, Ottawa amended the National Housing Act, committing the federal government to build new housing and rehabilitate and modernize existing stock. Two years later, it created the Central Mortgage and Housing Corporation, an agency that was charged with implementing Ottawa's national housing policy and, for the first time, planning for the country's housing needs. Through the CMHC, the federal government played a significant and sometimes controversial role in shaping urban life and addressing urban poverty in the second half of the twentieth century.[17]

One of the most important ways it did so was by encouraging "urban renewal." A program of redevelopment aimed at putting city lands to more productive use, it would also increase the tax revenue accruing to municipalities. Although "urban renewal" is an American term, governments in North America and Europe embraced this kind of land redevelopment from the mid-nineteenth century on, and particularly from 1949 to 1974.[18] Not coincidentally, the height of urban renewal overlapped with the "golden age" of planning, said to be the twenty or twenty-five years after the Second World War.[19]

Thanks to amendments to the National Housing Act in 1954 and 1956, not only would the federal government pay part of the cost of a preliminary survey to identify areas in need of renewal and articulate a plan for such renewal, but it would also contribute up to 50 percent of the cost of acquiring and clearing an area and rehousing the people who were displaced. Perhaps more importantly, the 1956 amendment also dispensed with the requirement that the land targeted for clearance be substantially residential and redeveloped for the same purposes. Instead, it allowed formerly residential lands to be cleared and redeveloped for their "highest and best use," whether that was residential, commercial, or industrial, a change that allowed municipalities to plan comprehensively. And many did: from 1948 to 1968, the CMHC approved and oversaw a total of forty-eight major inner-city redevelopment projects.[20]

Having lobbied for these amendments, Halifax was one of the first places to take advantage of these federal funds.[21] In 1956, the CMHC recommended that the city retain Gordon Stephenson, then a professor of planning at the University of Toronto, to undertake a survey of housing conditions, identify areas in need of development and redevelopment, provide advice on the best ways to rehouse people who would be displaced, and recommend the best uses of land slated for redevelopment.[22] After more than a decade of intermittent discussion about the need for slum clearance, the mayor and council agreed with the CMHC recommendation and requested $12,000 from the federal government to retain Stephenson.[23]

Born to a working-class family in Liverpool, Gordon Stephenson (1908–97) was educated as an architect and city planner and worked in Paris as an assistant to the noted Swiss-French architect and exemplar of high modernism Le Corbusier in the 1930s. After graduate work in the United States and a stint with the British civil service rebuilding bombed-out cities, he went on to academic positions in Australia and Canada. His time in Paris confirmed what would be a lifelong commitment to modernism and socialist politics.[24]

Echoing and elaborating on Thomas Adams, Stephenson believed in the power of architecture and planning to improve lives. "Every family has a right to a decent home," he argued, and "those in the greatest need should come first." In short, good planning "begins and ends with people."[25] While he was working on the Halifax redevelopment plan, he told a national conference in Vancouver that designing great cities required planners to be "talking of children instead of cars, the good life rather than dollars, of the city as a symbol of our civilization."[26] Yet Stephenson's working-class roots and his commitment to "compassionate town planning" and working "on a human scale" did not democratize his view of expertise. Indeed, architecture and design could uplift only if the authority of the planner was respected. He agreed with Le Corbusier that "authority must step in, patriarchal authority, the authority of a father concerned for his children."[27]

The Halifax commission offered Stephenson the opportunity to exercise that authority on a city Mayor Leonard Kitz described as "worn thin" by "two centuries of living."[28] Building on a survey done the previous year, the planner focused his attention on a 119-block study area surrounding the downtown core (Figure 4.2), believing that "in all cities decay takes place most rapidly on the fringe of the centre. Halifax is no exception." On the western and northern edges of the city there was visible "deterioration and overcrowding of worn-out houses ... interspersed with small businesses and industries, and unkempt vacant lots." Streets in the area beyond the southern edge also had "houses in various stages of obsolescence, some of them in a very bad state."[29]

Donning his "scientific cloak," Stephenson compiled information from a wide range of sources that he believed would help him pinpoint the areas in need of redevelopment. In addition to assessments of the physical state of each building in each block of the study area, he brought to bear on his task everything from statistics on the incidence of crime, fire, welfare, and tuberculosis to the presence of hot and cold running water, average incomes, rents, and taxes. As planners Jill L. Grant and Marcus Paterson discuss, the results were displayed in a series of fourteen maps that made a powerful visual case for redevelopment and confirmed that the blocks most in need of redevelopment were the city's poorest in terms of residents' income, infrastructure, and amenities.[30]

On the basis of his analysis, Stephenson outlined twelve redevelopment schemes, seven of which encompassed lands in his study area. The remaining five, which included Africville, did not. Taken together, these schemes

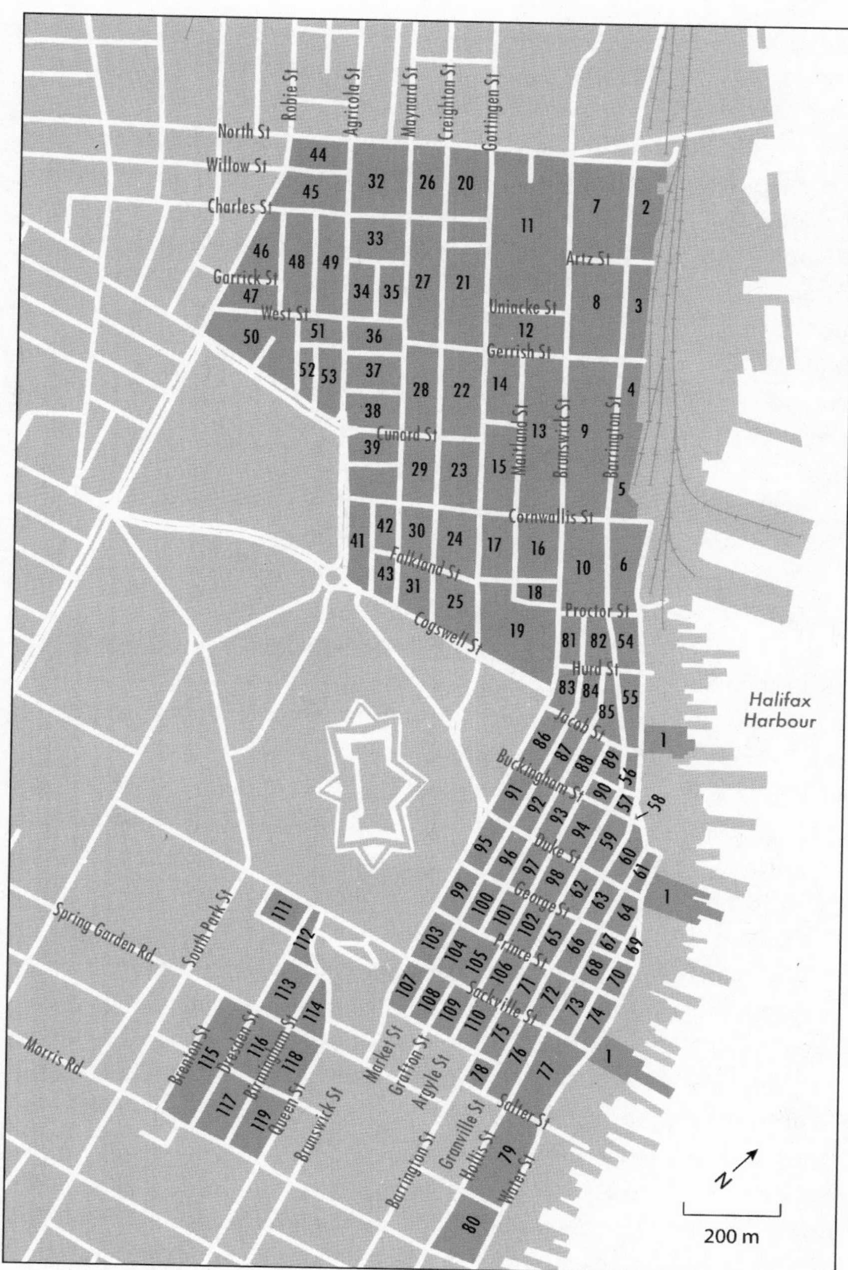

Figure 4.2 Planner Gordon Stephenson's study area. Map adapted from Stephenson's *Redevelopment Study of Halifax, 1957*.

reflected many of the assumptions of the time about how to build a better and modern city: they proposed to clear slums, differentiate and separate land use through zoning, make better provision for traffic, and build housing outside the central core of the city. Most of the nearly 6,500 people Stephenson estimated would be uprooted by his plan were tenants. Indeed, he noted that just 10 percent of the dwellings in the study area were owner-occupied and that the proportion would be even lower were it not for the African–Nova Scotian population. Poor though that population was, the need for security in the face of discrimination made acquiring a house – even one that was small and perhaps run down – of paramount importance. For reasons of racism and household finances, it would be hard for them and their tenant neighbours to buy or rent elsewhere. Recognizing this, Stephenson cautioned the city not to proceed with redevelopment until adequate public housing was in place, and he identified lands in the city's North End as a possible location.[31]

Of the twelve schemes, Stephenson recommended starting with a nine-acre site between city hall and Jacob Street that was home to 1,620 people. Today it is the location of a multilevel highway, the Cogswell Interchange, and Scotia Square, a complex consisting of a shopping mall, office towers, apartment buildings, and a hotel. But in 1957, Stephenson considered it the "worst part of the central area," with dilapidated tenements, "dirty cinder sidewalks," and "patches of cleared land littered with rubbish" (Figure 4.3). Because of its location, he imagined it would be well suited for both commercial development and a highway that would connect Cogswell Street to the proposed Harbour Drive, another freeway that would facilitate traffic flow.[32]

The mayor and city council as well as the Halifax press greeted the release of Stephenson's plan in August 1957 with great enthusiasm, with one alderman calling it "the civic Bible for future development."[33] The first demolitions in the Jacob Street Redevelopment Area (later called the Central Redevelopment Area) started six months later, in February 1958.[34] By 1962, before it turned its attention to Africville, the city had acquired and cleared just over seventeen acres in the downtown area (not the nine Stephenson had recommended), demolishing 908 dwelling units and displacing approximately 3,000 people in the process.[35] Fully materializing Stephenson's vision proved to be a more protracted process. Construction on Scotia Square didn't begin until 1967. When the complex opened in 1969, construction on the Cogswell interchange started. As Christopher Parsons notes,

Figure 4.3 Planner Gordon Stephenson considered the Jacob Street neighbourhood one of the worst areas in Halifax and advised the city to target it first. This is Jacob Street, looking north, between Starr Street and Poplar Grove, 1961. | Halifax Municipal Archives, 102-39-1-716.5

"A half decade after his recommendations were made public the downtown of Halifax resembled the bombed out English cities where Stephenson first plied his trade."[36]

Even as the city proceeded with acquiring and clearing properties in the Jacob Street area, it also initiated four other redevelopment projects – all before turning its attention to Africville (Figure 4.4).[37] The process the city followed in implementing Stephenson's plan in Africville differed – purposefully – from the one it used in other redevelopment areas. The differences are evidence not only of the pressure the community's advocates were able to exert on the city, but also of an awareness on the part of municipal authorities of the need to take the legacy of racism into account in dealing

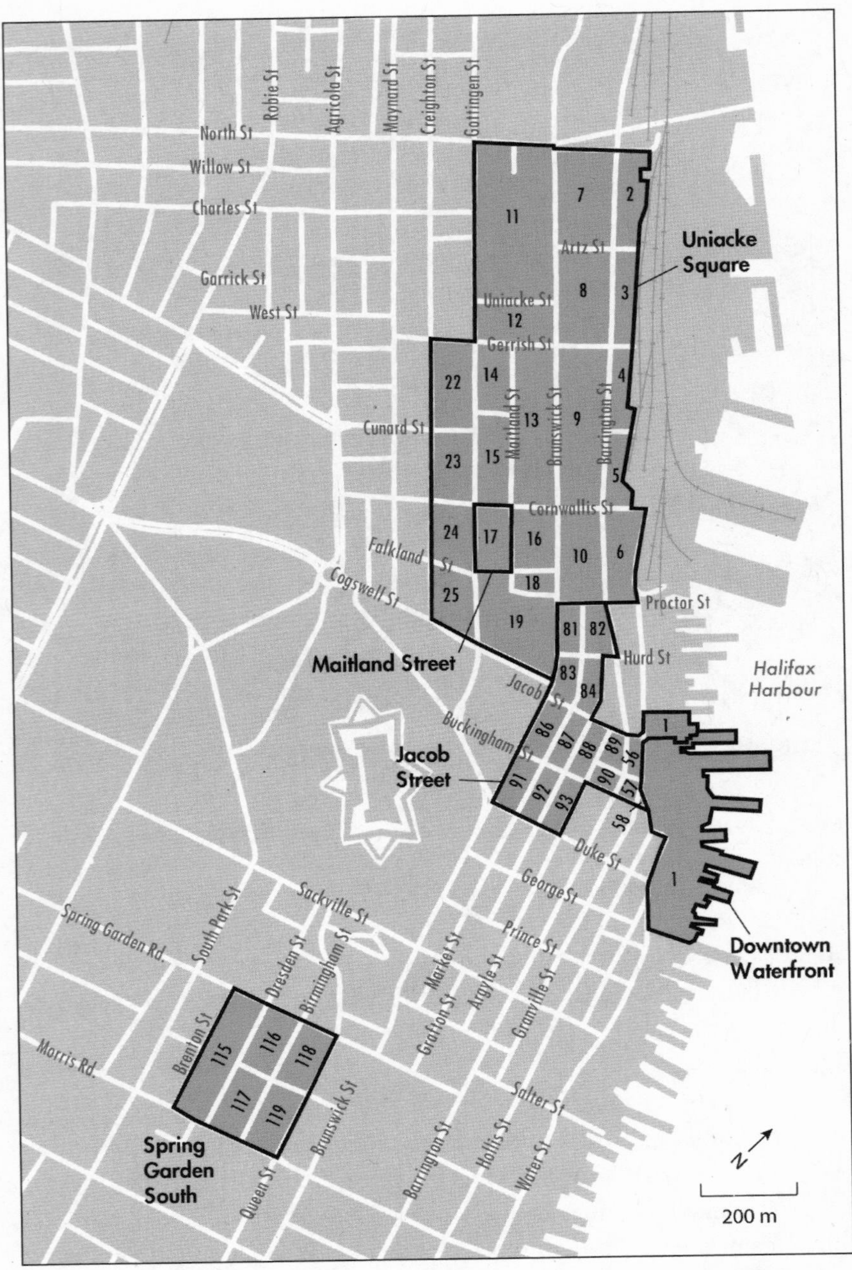

Figure 4.4 Areas targeted for redevelopment before Africville were Jacob Street, Maitland Street, Spring Garden South, the Downtown Waterfront, and Uniacke Square.

Figure 4.5 Building inspector John MacDonald inspects 385 Gottingen Street, 1961. | Halifax Municipal Archives, 102-39-1-912.8

with Africville. In their struggles to define and then do the right thing for its residents, activists, experts, and municipal officials revealed the meanings of progressive politics and the limits of the liberal welfare state to extend social citizenship.

With the exception of Africville, building inspectors working for the city's Department of Works set the wrecking ball of redevelopment in motion. As Stephenson recommended, they began enforcing Ordinance No. 50 as well as sections of the city charter, examining buildings for violations of the minimum standards for housing accommodation and health and safety, respectively[38] (Figure 4.5). The Committee on Works reviewed their reports and the photographs they took documenting the condition of the buildings in question, and then held a public hearing to determine the fate of the property. In most cases, the committee ordered the buildings demolished at the owner's expense.[39]

The municipal Development Department dealt with the lands on which the buildings stood, initiating a process of expropriation. While the city compensated owners at market value, the tenants who lost their housing to redevelopment received nothing. Because Mulgrave Park, the 349-unit public housing project built as part of the redevelopment process, did not open until 1961, three years after the demolitions started, many tenants were forced to move from one condemned tenement in the Jacob Street area to another as they waited to be permanently rehoused. In any case, the number of people in need of housing was far in excess of what Mulgrave Park could accommodate. Just two months after the Jacob Street demolitions started, the rate of evictions rapidly outstripped the city's ability to rehouse people. In April 1958, the city manager reported that between 500 and 600 people had lost their housing, and 110 had been "put on the streets" in a single night.[40]

Because redevelopment decreased the supply of housing, tenants often found themselves having to pay more in rent as well; sometimes much more. In the winter of 1959–60, for instance, average rent for a two-bedroom apartment on Jacob Street was $7.50 per week. By January 1961 it was double that, $15 per week.[41] The lack of affordable accommodation meant many were forced to leave the city. In July 1961, H. Bond Jones, the director of welfare, estimated redevelopment was forcing two hundred families out of Halifax every month. "You drive along the road, you see a house is coming down, you say 'Isn't that nice the slum is being demolished,' and we know the buildings of low standards should be demolished; but how many times have you heard anyone say, 'What happened to the people?'" he asked the city's Housing Policy Review Committee.[42]

As the minutes of the Works Committee meetings reveal, there was little or no resistance to the implementation of the Stephenson plan: insofar as property owners took issue with redevelopment, it was with the compensation they received or the length of time they were given to vacate their buildings. Some, like lawyer Ralph Medjuck, who represented twelve property owners in the Jacob Street Redevelopment Area, including himself, wanted the city to negotiate with them on an individual basis – presumably rather than applying a formula for compensation. "We feel this Redevelopment program is a very good thing," he told city council in 1959. "But there first should be individual negotiations for these properties. There are other instances where properties are more valuable and should be discussed on an individual basis."[43]

Tenants who were threatened with displacement had no legal standing to contest expropriation and demolition. Insofar as they appeared before the Committee on Works, they did so to give testimony regarding the state of the buildings they occupied.[44] Indeed, it was not until the late 1960s that there was any organized resistance to redevelopment in downtown Halifax, and it came from heritage advocates who opposed the construction of Harbour Drive, fearing the loss of the city's historic waterfront.[45]

The situation in Africville was strikingly different. Not only was there opposition from residents, but they also managed to attract the attention and support of human rights activists. Furthermore, the process Halifax authorities put in place to deal with Africvillers was more liberal than the one it used with people in other redevelopment areas. They chose not to pass on the costs of redevelopment to residents by enforcing Ordinance No. 50 and the sections of the city charter in Africville.[46] Instead, the city negotiated with individual owners to expropriate their property, hiring a social worker to do so, and it also compensated the propertyless – those who were tenants, boarded, or lived with relatives. In addition, it created a special subcommittee of city council, which included the African–Nova Scotian members of the Halifax Human Rights Advisory Committee, to review compensation agreements. Finally, the city agreed to help the relocated residents find housing and jobs as well as get the education they needed to open up opportunities.

To begin to understand why the residents of Africville were treated differently from, and in some ways better than, those in other redevelopment areas, we need to understand the community's history and the politics of race and rights in the postwar years. Settled in the 1840s by descendants of African-American refugees from the War of 1812, Africville was located at the northern end of the city (Figure 4.1). From the second half of the nineteenth century, it was subjected to the encroachment of industry. Railway tracks were laid through the middle of the community in the 1850s and expanded twice before the First World War, and a number of factories opened. As well, Africville was the location of the city's sewage disposal pits (1858), the infectious diseases hospital (1870s), and a dump (1950) from which some residents were forced to scavenge because of their poverty. The community, which accounted for less than one-half of 1 percent of the population of Halifax, received 10 percent of its welfare payments. More than a third of residents earned less than $1,000 per year, compared to a fifth of the Halifax population generally. By the time Stephenson came to Halifax, eighty families comprising nearly four hundred people – more than half of them under the age of fifteen – existed on a thirteen-acre site that had no paved roads, lacked piped water, and was not connected to the municipal sewage system. It was an example of "slow violence," the "incremental and accretive" harms visited upon the poor and the environments in which they live (Figure 4.6).[47]

Figure 4.6 As the "boil water" warning sign in this photo conveys, even in the mid-1960s Africville was not connected to the city's water or sewer system, an example of environmental racism and "slow violence." | Bob Brooks, Nova Scotia Archives and Records Management, Accession no. 1989-468, vol. 16, Negative no.: sheet 6, image 3

Africvillers were not passive in the face of their circumstances. From the mid-nineteenth century, they had petitioned the city for services other Haligonians had.[48] In 1961, with the demolitions in the Jacob Street Redevelopment Area in full swing, a few residents approached Jewish Labour Committee lawyer Sid Blum for help, complaining about the difficulties they had getting building permits to improve their houses because Africville was slated for redevelopment.[49] In addition, they reiterated their long-standing concerns about the lack of sewers and safe water in the community and the discrimination residents faced in finding jobs. All this resonated with Blum. In the late 1950s, he had visited Atlantic Canada on behalf of the Jewish Labour Committee to investigate unfair hiring and accommodation practices.[50] His work was part of what historian James W. St. G. Walker identified as the "Jewish phase" of the fight for racial equality in Canada, a moment "when Canadian Jews and Jewish organizations were fundamental to the conceptualization and implementation of human rights policy," recognizing that racism hurt all workers.[51]

While Blum advised residents to organize themselves and to continue to press the city for what they wanted, he also dispatched a human rights lawyer to Halifax. Alan Borovoy saw his job as helping to put Africvillers "in a position where they had some strength and would not be screwed."[52] To that end, in August 1962 Borovoy brought residents together with representatives from the city's civil rights organizations hoping that some sort of coalition might emerge.[53] The result was the formation of the Halifax Human Rights Advisory Committee (HHRAC), whose core membership of ten consisted of a group of well-connected, middle-class white and black professionals and Africville residents.

The middle-class members of the HHRAC, both white and black, were liberals who shared a commitment to civil rights, something that led them to join the committee in the first place. Donald Maclean, the HHRAC's secretary, first came to see the impact of racial segregation when he worked for a summer in Washington, DC. The experience shaped his time working in adult education for the province, delivering programs to Nova Scotia's black community. He was also active in numerous rights organizations, including the Interracial Council, the Nova Scotia Human Rights Federation, and its successor, the Nova Scotia Civil Liberties and Human Rights Association. Fran Maclean, his wife, conducted surveys of black employment and employment placement in Halifax with the Voice of Women, something that heightened her awareness of racial discrimination and the need to address it. Fred Brodie, a trade unionist and active member of the provincial New Democratic Party (NDP), came to the HHRAC through his position as chair of the Human Rights Committee of the Halifax-Dartmouth Labour Council. Like Brodie, Lloyd Shaw was also a member of the Nova Scotia NDP, serving as its vice-president. Shaw was a prominent businessman and developer whose concern for Africville was, in part, an extension of his faith: his church worked with the Seaview Baptist Church in Africville.[54]

The three non-resident black members of the HHRAC, H.A.J. "Gus" Wedderburn, George Davis, and Charles Coleman, were equally committed to civil rights and came to their work in Africville for personal and professional reasons. A teacher by training and later a lawyer, Wedderburn held executive positions with a number of human rights organizations in Halifax and, at the time he joined the HHRAC, was president of the Nova Scotia Association for the Advancement of Coloured People. He came to the HHRAC because he was appalled that "members of my race were being treated unfairly." George Davis, a securities lawyer with the province, saw his work with the HHRAC as a way to eliminate segregation, to place residents "in a position where they would not be a separate community but a part of a larger community in which they would be competing as far as work, education, [and] housing were concerned." Charles Coleman was the pastor of Cornwallis Street Baptist Church. An American, he was influenced by the work of Martin Luther King, Jr., and understood Africville through that lens. The HHRAC also had three other active black members, residents of Africville who were not representative of the majority of residents. Drawn from among the community's older, respectable, church-going families, they were "conditioned to seek allies among White liberals."[55]

For the middle-class members of the Halifax Human Rights Advisory Committee particularly, Africville was primarily a civil rights issue, and an issue of spatial injustice rather than poverty. The committee was a way to combat racism and, specifically, the isolation of segregation. As Donald Maclean recalled, "At that time ... segregation was very much a completely unacceptable thing. In the United States, at least at that time, it was a flaming issue. There, there were segregated busses, schools, employment, and housing."[56] Fran Maclean challenged people to "imagine not having running water. Imagine being so much cut off, being part of the city, and yet, not really a part of it." Lloyd Shaw "didn't feel that any group of people should be living anywhere in that kind of condition," a sentiment Gus Wedderburn shared. Wedderburn's motives were also "personal." Although he had arrived in Halifax from Jamaica only in 1957, he saw Africville as a manifestation of the discrimination black people were subjected to around the world. According to George Davis, the goal of the Human Rights Advisory Committee was to address that discrimination through integration. For Fran Maclean, the opportunities that would come from integration constituted "having rights to be a full citizen," something necessary for "the development of the latent talents of all people."[57]

Over the next five years, the HHRAC acted as a liaison between Africville and municipal authorities, even though it had no formal mandate from the community to speak for it.[58] Like Borovoy, the committee viewed its task as ensuring that residents were treated fairly. It not only pushed for clarification about the reasons for relocation and the city's plans for the Africville lands, but it also argued the neighbourhood could be rehabilitated rather than razed. When the city refused, the HHRAC explored various possibilities for housing Africvillers in a way that would allow their community to continue to exist, whether it was through the provision of homes the city might build and sell to them at prices they could afford, through a cooperative housing arrangement, or by creating public housing that would be exclusively for them.[59]

The HHRAC might not have had a mandate to speak for Africville, but it did have influence: the city returned its calls, answered its letters, and solicited its advice. Perhaps the best example of the HHRAC's power came in September 1963, when the city agreed to consult with University of Toronto housing expert Albert Rose about Africville. Retaining Rose was Lloyd Shaw's idea: through his work with the Community Planning Association of Canada, he had become familiar with what Rose had done in Toronto's Regent Park, Canada's first public housing project. He had no hesitation recommending him and convincing a key alderman, Allan O'Brien, to support the HHRAC's proposal.[60] Having failed to get the city to take up its ideas for alternative housing, the HHRAC hoped an outside expert of Rose's stature would provide advice that the city would listen to and that would further the cause of Africville's residents.

Although he spent just two hours in Africville, Rose's time there left a deep and lasting impression and one that would shape the community's future. He was shocked. "Here was a group of Canadians that were entombed, entrapped, as ever I had even dreamed about ... Even in downtown Toronto, it seemed to me that what we called slums bore no resemblance to the impression that I got of Africville."[61] He could not imagine a way for residents to continue to live there. Indeed, to allow them to do so would be to perpetuate the appalling racial segregation that had produced Africville in the first place. He told them so at a meeting convened by the HHRAC at the Cornwallis Street Baptist Church in late November 1963. "Can a modern urban metropolis tolerate within its midst a community or grouping of dwellings which are physically and socially inadequate, not served with pure water and sewage disposal facilities?" he asked. "Can a minority group be permitted to reconstitute itself as a segregated community at a time in our history, at a time in the social history of western industrialized urban nations, when segregation either de jure (in law) or de facto (in fact) is almost everywhere condemned?"[62]

Based on what he saw and his interviews with city staff, university and community specialists, and the members of the HHRAC, Rose recommended that "the community of Africville ... be expropriated and cleared during the period commencing April 1, 1964 (or shortly thereafter) and that this process will be completed not later than December 31, 1966." More specifically, he called for the city to design a relocation program in consultation with the HHRAC and administered by the Development Department. Furthermore, he proposed that special funds be allocated for relocation, ones that would be used for three main purposes; first, to hire a social worker or social scientist to visit each family and document their situation and needs; second, to create a registry of available housing; and third, to create a fund to assist families who needed furniture or other equipment. In addition, he urged the city to recognize the complex pattern of land ownership and occupation in Africville that meant many residents did not have formal deeds. In his view, they nevertheless deserved some compensation.[63]

Rose's recommendations emerged from his recognition of Africville's "unique situation." Because razing the community and relocating its residents would take away from many "not merely their housing and their sense of community, but their employment and means of livelihood as well (in this case, scavenging on the adjacent city rubbish disposal area)," the city had to deal with Africville as a multidimensional welfare problem, not just one of compensation or housing.[64] Acknowledging Africville's "unique situation" also meant recognizing that strictly equal treatment was unfair. What Rose was asking for was equitable treatment for Africville's residents. "The coloured man is entitled to no less and no more consideration than the white resident of an urban redevelopment area," he concluded. But, "at the same time, because his needs are greater in nature and amount (education, employment, civil rights) he should and will receive greater consideration."[65]

The HHRAC and the majority of the forty-one Africvillers who met to consider the Rose report in January 1964 approved of it – albeit reluctantly. Confronted with resistance on the part of residents, Gus Wedderburn recalled that "we on the Committee tried at all times to explain that we had explored just about every alternative, every possibility, and ... to the best of our judgement at the time felt that the Rose Report ... was the best thing."[66] Shortly thereafter, the city also approved Rose's report, voting to relocate Africville's residents within the timeframe he suggested. It also created a committee to consider Rose's recommendations further and to suggest a phasing of the relocation program. In the view of the Director of Development, the housing expert had produced "a document that was clear, brief, well-written, and worth every cent of the five-hundred dollars that the City paid for it."[67]

The enthusiasm with which the city greeted Rose's report is not surprising: it wanted people out of Africville and, to its delight, it got an expert – one chosen by the community's advocates – who approved of that end and thus helpfully legitimated its plans. Indeed, city councillors believed clearing Africville could happen reasonably quickly and cheaply. Almost all the buildings in the area could be demolished at the owners' expense under various municipal ordinances. Because land title in Africville was "in a chaotic state," expropriation would not pose a large financial burden on the city: with just thirteen registered deeds on file and the cost of establishing ownership through the courts prohibitive, few residents would be able to claim more compensation.[68]

Remarkably, however, these fiscal arguments did not carry the day. In its own report on Africville, written six months *before* Rose submitted his to the mayor and city council, the Development Department argued that, because of the area's history, it could not treat Africville residents like it did those in the other redevelopment areas. It was referring to the history of neglect and discrimination that had created the conditions in Africville, and to a history of long-standing occupation.

Experts as well as municipal authorities claimed a kind of indigeneity for Africville residents that justified differential treatment. Gordon Stephenson called them "old Canadians" who could trace their roots in Africville back "well over a century."[69] In its study of the black population of Halifax, Dalhousie University's Institute of Public Affairs called attention to the "considerable stability in house tenure in Africville," despite the lack of clarity around land ownership. It estimated that over half of its eighty families had lived in their present houses for more than ten years; others had lived elsewhere in Africville for that long or even longer.[70] This "historicity" struck sociologists Donald H. Clairmont and Dennis Magill as unusual: in other North American cities, the length of residence in redevelopment areas usually averaged less than ten years.[71] Thus, relocation of Africville residents would be a great hardship, destroying the connections that sustained them.[72]

Africville's history was enough to convince the city's director of development to approach its expropriation differently. "While unfortunate precedents can be established by deviating from the strict letter of the Law, there seems to be some merit in some deviation in the case of Africville," Robert Grant argued. "Africville is unique ... Many of the families in Africville have occupied quarters in the area for generations." Rather than do only what it was legally required to, the city would come up with an expropriation process that was just: "Absolute implementation of strict legal responsibility and authority does not in itself appear to provide a suitable solution to the total problem." And, in a sentence that could have appeared in the Rose report, it continued, "Africville is a unique area and, in the interests of history and fair treatment to the residents, the approach should be tempered with natural justice."[73] Insofar as municipal authorities framed Africville as a rights issue, the rights in question were historical rather than universal, stemming from "historical relations rather than abstract definitions."[74]

Natural justice meant that the city would compensate residents with possessory title to the buildings and land they occupied and not just those with formal deeds. It also meant providing nominal compensation to those who owned no property but rented, boarded, or lived with relatives. Beyond this, natural justice required helping residents after they were relocated, assisting them with housing, jobs, education, and adjusting more generally.[75]

But natural justice did not mean replacing a home with a home or rehousing residents together as they wished. The idea was repugnant to the director of the Development Department. Interviewed in 1969, Robert Grant recalled taking "the view that I wasn't going to be party to rebuilding a coloured ghetto."[76] In short, doing the right thing for Africville meant integrating its residents into the city. Redevelopment was an act of spatial justice that would ensure they would no longer "live a life apart," enabling them to overcome the isolation that prevented them from fulfilling their potential.[77] But as to the quality of that life, Grant had little to say. He, along with his colleagues, believed that Africville residents' lives would automatically be improved through desegregation. Their belief was shared by Africville's advocates. As the HHRAC's Donald Maclean put it, "It would have been unthinkable, in those days, the days of the relocation, to have moved everybody to another location, to have relocated the entire community, so to speak," he recalled in 1995. "That would have been segregation, and that was what all of us were opposed to."[78]

The convergence of Rose's recommendations and those of Halifax's Development Department reflected a growing concern with discrimination in Canada in the 1950s and 1960s, one spurred in part by knowledge of what had happened during the war, namely, the genocide of Jews in Europe and the internment of Japanese Canadians. The civil rights movement in the United States also heightened awareness in Canada about the extent and pernicious effects of racism. Although overt discrimination was becoming less acceptable in the postwar years, something no modern society could countenance, historian Dominique Clément reminds us that Canada's "rights revolution" was a conservative one: it was led by middle-class white professionals and focused on addressing and preventing violations of individual civil and political rights by the state rather than addressing broader structural questions of social citizenship and inclusion.[79] Nevertheless, the period was marked by important legislative changes and, in some jurisdictions, comprehensive provincial human rights legislation. In 1960, the Conservative government of John Diefenbaker passed a federal Bill of Rights that, although flawed, contained many of the provisions that would appear later in the 1982 Charter of Rights and Freedoms.

Nova Scotia's history of human rights followed the same trajectory. It was shaped in part by Viola Desmond's refusal in 1946 to sit in the blacks-only section of a New Glasgow theatre, an act that led to a court case highlighting the existence of segregationist practices, and by the foundational work of Reverend W.P. Oliver and Conservative premier Robert Stanfield. Beginning in the 1940s, Oliver organized black communities and promoted self-help, bringing the situation of African Nova Scotians to the public's attention. Stanfield made human rights a priority when he was elected in 1956. In 1962, his government created an intergovernmental committee on human rights to explore ways of improving the situation of African Nova Scotians. The next year, it ushered in the province's first human rights act.[80]

As in the rest of Canada, Nova Scotia's human rights movement in the '50s and '60s was both progressive and conservative, with the emphasis being on legislative change and self-help. Notably, in Nova Scotia the movement's early leadership was partly drawn from the black community: in addition to Oliver, Carrie Best and Gus Wedderburn also played key roles in advancing a human rights agenda in the province, Best through her two newspapers, the *Clarion* and the *Negro Citizen,* and Wedderburn through his work as president of the Nova Scotia Association for the Advancement of Coloured People. Interestingly, however, while prominent individuals such as Oliver and Wedderburn involved themselves in the HHRAC, black organizations did not participate to any great extent in helping Africville residents or pressuring the city on the issue.[81] In part, this was due to class divisions among African Nova Scotians: many viewed Africville the same way white Haligonians did – as a slum, a place of illicit activity, an embarrassment. In these conservative, "pre-militant days," as Albert Rose characterized them, Africville had not yet become a rallying point for a black community because that community was not unified.[82]

The context of race and rights thus helps explain the convergence of views on Africville – that is, why advocates for the community could find their arguments for why residents deserved special consideration reflected in the city's recommendations for how to proceed with the acquisition of Africville lands. At a time when critics of urban renewal in the United States were casting it as "Negro removal," Halifax officials were particularly aware of the meaning and consequences of their actions, and they justified them in terms of desegregation.[83] Certainly they showed no such sensitivity when it came to dealing with the more numerous poor and working-class Haligonians who lived in its other redevelopment areas, including the racially mixed North End, site of the Uniacke Square project. Indeed, looking back on urban renewal, Robert Grant observed that, "in terms of compensation and in terms of personal attention, Africville received much more consideration than the others [other redevelopment areas], even though there were probably more blacks involved in the other programmes."[84] If the buildings in Africville had been anywhere else in the city, "they would have been ordered down at the expense of the owners. As a matter of fact, during those years, we did order down about seven hundred houses at the owners' expense, and that would have been the case [in Africville] except for colour."[85]

Had combatting poverty rather than racism been their primary concern, the HHRAC and the city would have been more attentive to the plight of the thousands of residents of other redevelopment areas who lost their homes to urban renewal with no compensation. But they lived in a class-based ghetto, not a racial one. However sympathetic the members of the HHRAC and city authorities may have been to them, their situation and treatment did not raise the same kind of concerns. For the liberal members of the HHRAC, poverty and class discrimination were not violations of individual rights; racial segregation was.

Setting out the approach the city would take in acquiring the land in Africville was one thing; implementing it was another, particularly when title was in a chaotic state and the city wished to compensate the owners of buildings as well as those without property. Rather than assign a real estate assessor to do the job, as it did in other redevelopment areas, the Development Department hired a social worker, recognizing that a different kind of expertise was required to remove Africville's residents. Seconded from his job working in child welfare and juvenile probation in Sydney,

Figure 4.7 Two Halifax city officials, one holding a rolled plan of Africville, outside an Africville house, prior to demolition of the community, ca. 1965. | Bob Brooks, Nova Scotia Archives and Records Management, Accession no. 1989-468, vol. 16, Negative no.: sheet 5, image 25

provincial social worker Peter MacDonald found himself at the sharp end of expropriation: he had the task of actually negotiating compensation with residents, of coming to agreements that were in keeping with the city's commitment to natural justice. Doing so depended on his personal and professional skills in building relationships.[86]

Authorities were explicit about why MacDonald had been chosen: in the absence of land and tax records, Africville was "illegible" to the state, to use James C. Scott's term.[87] The local knowledge that MacDonald would gather through his relationships with residents, and the quality of those relationships themselves, would be crucial to compensating them and clearing them out. As Nova Scotia's deputy minister of Public Welfare recalled, he had recommended MacDonald because he was someone "who can meet and talk to people, and that was what we needed. Someone who could go into Africville and talk to people on their own level. Peter was the person who had these skills"[88] (Figure 4.7).

For his own part, MacDonald saw the relocation and his role in it as a way to address racism. Ending segregation was a way to "break down prejudices," something that would allow residents, especially the children, to "reach [their] potential."[89] Like Gordon Stephenson, he believed that Africville was an "indictment of society and not its inhabitants."[90] In fact, MacDonald was more specific about who was to blame. "Probably the City of Halifax was ninety-five per cent at fault for even allowing such conditions to exist, and for even allowing such a condition to begin ... Why something was not done by the City Fathers, I don't know," he confessed. "If the City had the interests of the people actually at heart, they wouldn't have allowed it. If they were going to allow it [the city should have] put in some kind of sewer and water system, so that the people could live decently."[91]

Before being seconded to work for the city, MacDonald had little knowledge of Africville, and he took some time to get to know the community and its residents. Six months in, toward the end of 1964, he felt he could begin negotiations. His boss, Director of Development Robert Grant, estimated that it took three to four months on average for MacDonald to come to an agreement with each individual or family. Part of that time was spent simply trying to ascertain what was being negotiated – that is, exactly what land and buildings were being claimed by whom. As MacDonald explained, he first "tried to get the story from the owner" and then searched through city records for corroboration. Rather than deny claims when he could find no records, the social worker accepted what he was told. "When there were no actual deeds ... [we] pretty well went along with the story ... the people would give," he recalled. "[We] went along pretty well with the status quo as it was in the community."[92] Deviating from the usual process and dispensing natural justice to Africville's residents was thus possible only because of the local knowledge they provided (Figure 4.8).

As important as local knowledge about property holdings was to compensating and ultimately expropriating Africville residents, other factors played a role in shaping the financial settlements they received, including the age of the householders, the number of children in the family, and whether the adults were employed. According to the director of development, "there was no formula." The first settlements set a precedent for the ones that followed. In Grant's view, the amounts paid out were in excess of what residents would have received through the usual process the city used. "It was certainly an artificial calculation in legal terms, because there was no way in which we could possibly justify any of the amounts we paid, if it were on a strictly legal basis."[93]

Once MacDonald concluded each negotiation, he submitted his recommendation to the Africville subcommittee of city council for a specific

Figure 4.8 Africville resident orienting two city officials to their rolled plan of Africville, spread out on the hood of a City of Halifax car, ca. 1965. | Bob Brooks, Nova Scotia Archives and Records Management, Accession no. 1989-468, vol. 16, Negative no.: sheet 5, image 30

amount to be paid out. The formation of this body represented another way municipal authorities diverged from their usual practice and tried to do the right thing for residents. Its membership consisted of three aldermen and three black members of the HHRAC as well as Robert Grant and Peter MacDonald.[94] The presence of Gus Wedderburn, George Davis, and Charles Coleman was meant to safeguard residents' interests, but it also was meant to lend legitimacy to the city's process.[95] In explaining why the HHRAC had chosen these men to sit on the subcommittee, Donald Maclean revealed that "the first consideration was that these people were Negro; otherwise it would look again like White people were doing the whole thing." As well, they had "first-hand knowledge about the community, particularly about persons, and would be able to assess claims in terms of persons and their backgrounds." The Africville members of the HHRAC, who had real "first-hand knowledge," were deemed ineligible because they were negotiating their own settlements with MacDonald and thus would have been in a conflict of interest.[96]

The subcommittee's deliberations underscored the subjective nature of the compensation process and revealed its paternalism, something particularly evident in its discussions about "character" and "reputation." As one alderman recalled, "Sometimes a Committee member would indicate that a certain fellow had a reputation as being very irresponsible, even though he had a family. If he got a grant of so much money, it would end up back in the provincial coffers via the liquor store, or something like that." While he admitted that such a judgment was "playing God," he felt justified in doing so: "In those cases we felt that nothing would be served by giving that person a larger grant. Whereas you had a fellow who had ... a good steady job and was of fairly good character, you would stake him."[97]

Given Africville's illegibility, any compensation process the city put in place was bound to be discretionary. But the amount of discretion Peter MacDonald was able to exercise was increased by the lack of community cohesion in Africville. There was no collective bargaining; instead, residents dealt with MacDonald individually and on their own. Few availed themselves of the free legal advice the city provided, sought an independent real estate assessment, or even talked about compensation with their neighbours. According to one Africviller, the silence spoke to a lack of trust that ultimately undermined their position: "A lot of suspicion came along with this [relocation]. One [resident] was getting more than the other. I think it would have been a lot better if they had stuck together. My wife and I ..., we tried to stick together. We would have done a lot better if all had stuck together."[98]

In all, MacDonald concluded ninety-eight compensation agreements with Africville's residents and another thirty-eight with non-resident owners. The total cost of relocating Africville's residents was $613,425 (Tables 4.1 and 4.2).[99] As Rose had recommended, the city made payments to people with deeds as well as to those without, and to renters. As well as compensation for buildings and land, those payments included amounts for welfare, the waiving of tax and hospital bills, a furniture allowance, and sundry costs related to moving. Like their black counterparts in the rest of Halifax, the majority of Africville residents owned their homes. Not surprisingly, they received the largest settlements, averaging nearly $10,000 each. Those without property got the least, $1,600 on average: their settlements included a nominal payment of $500 each plus amounts for welfare, a furniture allowance, and moving costs.

Table 4.1 Settlements with Africville relocatees

Category	Propertyless $n = 28$	Renters with claims $n = 10$	Homeowners $n = 19$	Home and land owners $n = 32$	Homeowners with multiple claims $n = 9$	Total $n = 98$
Financial compensation	–	$20,825.55	$41,636.66	$269,896.80	$66,758.32	$399,117.33
Welfare payments	$21,271.04	$5,984.12	$20,337.33	$13,452.76	$6,171.14	$67,216.39
Furniture allowance	$18,360.35	$5,573.95	$10,658.54	$19,337.01	$5,471.96	$59,401.81
Sundry costs	$4,750.00	–	$175.00	$748.00	$239.50	$5,908.50
Hospital bills waived	–	$1,506.63	$2,543.83	$9,395.22	$313.95	$13,759.63
Tax bills waived	–	$311.11	$183.89	$4,263.78	$223.42	$4,982.20
Total	$44,381.39	$34,201.36	$75,535.25	$317,093.57	$79,178.29	$550,385.86

Reproduced from Clairmont and Magill, *Africville Relocation Report,* 279–80.

Table 4.2 Settlements with non-relocatees, $n = 38$

Category	Amount
Financial compensation	$57,471.35
Welfare payments	$1,255.19
Furniture allowance	$2,475.93
Hospital bills waived	$877.90
Tax bills waived	$986.71
Total	$63,067.08

Reproduced from Clairmont and Magill, *Africville Relocation Report,* 279–80.

When MacDonald left Halifax to go back to Cape Breton in October 1967, he had come to settlements with almost all of Africville's residents. Ironically, the last was paid from the city's sewer account and his property expropriated in November 1968.[100]

In the wake of the Stephenson report, municipal authorities in Halifax recognized that, because of Africville's history, urban renewal would affect its residents differently than it did those who lived in other redevelopment areas. The city would have to take a different approach to acquiring their land, one that was meant to be gentler and more generous than the usual legal process of expropriation and in keeping with an emerging consciousness among authorities as well as the community's advocates of the need to address racial discrimination and particularly segregation. Extending social citizenship to Africville's residents required physically integrating them into Halifax and providing them with better housing and increased opportunities.

Significant as the city's efforts were to understanding how this growing consciousness of racism manifested itself, they did not necessarily result in better outcomes. In May 1967, even before the relocation was completed, the provincial Department of Public Welfare initiated discussions with the Institute of Public Affairs (IPA) at Dalhousie University to do a study of the relocation. It was prompted in part by the questions that continued to be raised by the public about whether the city was justified in acting as it did. But, as was the case in Newfoundland with resettlement, it was also motivated by a kind of reflexiveness characteristic of modernity; in this case, an "administrative desire, in keeping with the best modern practice, to have a contemporary record and critical review of a major, planned, social change."[101]

Conducted by sociologists Donald Clairmont and Dennis Magill for the IPA, the study revealed a significant level of dissatisfaction among former residents. Although Peter MacDonald believed that residents largely accepted the settlements he reached, the interviews that Clairmont and Magill conducted told a different story: 80 percent of residents were unhappy with what they had received, and an even higher proportion of them felt that funds had not been fairly distributed.[102] But their main disappointment was that the promises MacDonald had made about the help they would receive after being relocated were not kept. While the city committed to helping residents find housing and jobs and improve their education, its efforts fell short of what was needed. A survey done at the end of 1968 revealed the struggles many former residents were experiencing: some who had managed to buy new homes had lost them or were in danger of losing them to foreclosure; tenants found themselves living in worse conditions and paying more in rent; the number of families headed by women had increased from one in six to one in three; and the number of Africville residents receiving welfare had increased by 40 percent from the time Albert Rose visited in 1963.[103] In the view of many former residents at the time, "The relocation of Africville has turned out to be simply a real estate operation instead of a project of social renewal."[104]

In part, the lack of support for former residents was the result of "bureaucratic buck-passing" and a shift in focus among their long-standing advocates.[105] MacDonald's secondment ended in the fall of 1967, and his departure meant a loss of continuity in the implementation of the post-relocation program. The city's new Social Planning Department eventually took over in 1968, assigning social worker Alexa Shaw to the task, but its efforts were also ineffective: few former residents enrolled in the education program it offered, so it was discontinued; and the credit union it helped establish to assist residents in securing loans floundered. With the terms of the Africville relocation set and the negotiation process underway, the non-resident members of the HHRAC moved on to other civil rights issues, focusing on minimum wage legislation and the creation of a provincial human rights commission.[106]

These shortcomings speak to the limited approach Nova Scotia's authorities took to addressing poverty compared to the efforts being made in rural Canada. Unlike what happened in the North, Newfoundland, and Quebec, there were no attempts at community development in Africville – that is, there were no initiatives aimed at cultivating leadership and collective decision making.[107] People such as Sid Blum and Alan Borovoy told residents they had to organize to protect their interests, but when it came time to deciding what to do and giving the city hell, it was the non-resident, middle-class professionals of the HHRAC who did so. As one Africville member of the committee put it in explaining the dominance of outsiders, "Talking is their business, and it's hard to beat them at it."[108]

But the shortcomings of planned social change in Africville also speak to the limits of the approach the state and the community's advocates took to making a good life. Both the city of Halifax and Albert Rose agreed that Africville was much more than a housing problem: it was an issue of rights and welfare. Africville garnered special attention because its existence was evidence of racial discrimination, of a violation of residents' civil rights. But the solution – integration – did little to address residents' poverty or the racism they confronted. While municipal authorities and the HHRAC did attend to the welfare of Africville residents, they conflated the provision of decent housing with the provision of social security. While many poor and working-class white Haligonians also lost their homes to redevelopment, racism meant that black Haligonians faced greater obstacles in being rehoused. Arguments like the one Leon Steed offered against being moved into public housing made no sense, particularly at a time when segregation was considered a social evil: "We all live in our own homes out there [in Africville], detached homes, where our children can run around," he told a reporter in 1963. "We couldn't go and live in no apartments today – segregated or not segregated – discriminated [against] that we are. First thing that happens, they're going to blame us: 'the Negroes is who done it!'"[109]

Rationalizing land use, compensating people more generously, integrating and rehousing them did nothing to redistribute power, nor did the solutions that both Rose and the city offered to former residents – help with jobs, education, and access to capital through a credit union. They put the onus on people to improve their own condition. The liberal welfare state would assist, but in the end it was up to individuals to make the most of these opportunities, to make a good life for themselves.

And they did – thanks to the politicization of the black community in the late 1960s. Influenced by the American Black Power movement, a new generation of activists in Halifax indigenized its critique, laying the foundation for the kind of cross-class solidarity among African Nova Scotians that had been lacking. They seized upon Africville as a symbol of black oppression. In moving away from the "integrationist philosophy" held by the members of the HHRAC and leaders such as W.P. Oliver to a "cultural nationalist philosophy," more radical activists such as Burnley "Rocky" Jones moved the discussion of poverty away from its focus on individual self-help and toward a recognition of the effects of systemic racism and the barriers it posed to extending social citizenship.[110]

Both the province and the federal government were unnerved by the growing politicization of the black community, fearing that racial violence might come to Nova Scotia as it had many American cities in the 1960s. In this context, the Trudeau cabinet agreed to a request for funding from the Black United Front (BUF), a moderate organization, hoping that such funding would undermine support for more radical groups like Jones's African-Canadian Liberation Movement.[111] In making the funding announcement, Minister of Health John Munro echoed what Donald Snowden said about Northern Affairs' support for Arctic cooperatives: "The Federal government is giving money to the Negro community (in Halifax) to structure themselves so they can protest, and to 'raise hell.'"[112]

Regardless of their differences, both BUF and Jones were in agreement about the importance of self-determination. As BUF noted, "One of the most basic needs of Black people is to have a vital role in the making of decisions which affect their daily lives and social status." To that end, the group aimed to "develop an organization controlled and operated by Black people" and to "assist Black people to identify their needs, plan for solutions and develop suitable plans of action based on the Black people's perception of their needs and on their relevance to their socio-economic status."[113] In short, and to return to T.H. Marshall, BUF sought to define social citizenship and particularly to set the "standards prevailing in society" that determined what "the life of a civilized being" was. Jones echoed these sentiments, noting that "what we learn from the States in particular, and from the African independence movements, is that Black people should be in control of their own affairs." In his view, black self-determination had lessons for the white population: "In rejecting white leadership, we were actually challenging the whites who were coming around, we were challenging their own racism, and we were taking the position that we don't want you to come and organize in the Black community and we don't want you to come and organize us. We want you to go back into the white community and organize whites in such a way that they would be more conducive to allowing more Black people to move in and move up."[114]

Community organizing of the kind Jones described came too late for the residents of Africville. In contrast, what happened in Vancouver's East Side exemplifies the potential power of citizen participation. With their neighbourhood slated for clearance, the residents of Strathcona mobilized to stop it. Their success was due to their own efforts, of course, but also to a shift in attitude, not just about the benefits of urban renewal, but also about how best to address urban poverty. Instead of top-down, expert-driven planning, governments embraced their grassroots – to different ends and with mixed results.

5

"A Fourth Level of Government"? Urban Renewal, State Power, and Democracy in Vancouver's East Side

"SHE IS A TINY GIRL, ink-black hair falling to her waist, covering more than half of her green micro-dress, which is matched by pale green hose. She is in second year at Simon Fraser," observed *Vancouver Sun* columnist Allan Fotheringham in November of 1968. "'The city has a responsibility to my parents,' she pleads. Suddenly, Shirley Chan converts the dry council chamber ... into a people chamber for a few short minutes. There's silence and attention."[1]

Concerned about the impact of urban renewal on her neighbourhood of Strathcona and perhaps heartened by the recent successful fight against a freeway that would have destroyed Vancouver's Chinatown, Shirley Chan had come to speak to the visiting Federal Task Force on Housing and Urban Development. She told Paul Hellyer, the minister responsible for housing, that, like many older residents, her parents wouldn't be able to get a mortgage to buy another home if they were forced to move. More fundamentally, they didn't understand why they had to leave – nor did she: "I didn't know this was a slum until the city told me it was."[2]

Like Africville and the Jacob Street Redevelopment Area of Halifax, Vancouver's East Side, of which Strathcona was a part, had long been iden fied as one of the city's "pariah spaces."[3] Settled in the late nineteenth cer it was a poor working-class neighbourhood and home to a culturally and racialized population that included Chinese. It was also ta clearance and redevelopment, thanks to another 1957 plan writte

British-trained planner and funded by the Central Mortgage and Housing Corporation (CMHC) through the National Housing Act.

But the parallels end there. The fact that Shirley Chan appeared before the task force and emerged as one of the chief advocates for her neighbourhood points to a key difference: as the literature makes clear, Vancouver's East Side residents played a central role in opposing urban renewal through their own grassroots organization, the Strathcona Property Owners and Tenants Association (SPOTA). By sticking together and forging alliances with key outsiders while maintaining control of its agenda, not only did SPOTA stop urban renewal and convince the federal government to fund the rehabilitation of Strathcona, but it also came to represent the neighbourhood's interests to the city and province and to run its own not-for-profit cooperative housing. More than a group dedicated to preserving a neighbourhood, SPOTA aimed to reform democracy: it considered itself "a fourth level of government."[4]

As important as grassroots organization and alliances were to saving Strathcona, the neighbourhood was able to avoid the "federal bulldozer" because by 1968 it was running out of gas.[5] Once considered the salvation of cities, by the mid-1960s urban renewal had attracted its share of critics, many of whom raised questions about its expense and some of its fundamental assumptions about the effectiveness of separating a city's functions (residential, commercial, industrial, transportation, and recreation), replacing single-family housing and small tenements with high-rise apartments, and ignoring the opinions of those who would be affected.[6]

Among the apostates were some of the very people who had implemented urban renewal, many of whom did not mince their words. In summarizing the main ideas to emerge at the Urban Renewal Research Seminar held by the Canadian Council on Urban and Regional Research in 1965, executive director Alan Armstrong observed that planners "suffered from a demolition syndrome." University of Toronto lecturer Hans Blumenfeld, who had worked in Europe and the United States before serving as a senior planner in Ottawa, Toronto, and Vancouver, was equally blunt: "Why care for people with ragged pants by tearing them off? Why not repair them?" Albert Rose, a proponent of Regent Park, Canada's first public housing project and consultant to the city of Halifax on Africville, made the case that urban renewal projects "cannot succeed if they are not couched in terms of the background of human respondents." Others, like Vancouver's director of planning W.E. Graham, demurred. The social problems associated with redevelopment were difficult, if not impossible, to deal with because "there is no adequate technique to predict *exactly* what human beings will do under changed circumstances."[7]

The idea that urban planners might improve their understanding of "what human beings will do under changed circumstances" by talking to them was not something to which Graham or his colleagues gave much thought. In contrast to rural redevelopment, particularly in Quebec, urban planning was a more explicitly top-down enterprise pursued by credentialed professionals. Indeed, since the early twentieth century, municipal authorities across North America considered things like transportation, zoning, and urban land use planning as technical matters best left in the hands of experts and bureaucrats who would administer them more effectively. Not only did city councillors often lack the expertise necessary to make good decisions, the fact they were accountable to an electorate rendered their judgment even more suspect, subject as it was to politics. Thus, while rural redevelopment projects aimed to involve and, in fact, create citizens by democratizing planning, urban redevelopment did not – until the late 1960s.

Fights against urban renewal, whether against destroying neighbourhoods or building freeways, were part of a transnational moment of protest and challenge to expert authority that characterized "the global sixties." As the editors of a collection of essays on the period argue, it was a time when "people worked to become the active creators or re-creators of their own lives and societies. They demanded a place as subjects rather than as objects of history."[8] Groups of people who historically had been disenfranchised claimed and, in many cases, took power, among them women, workers, Indigenous people, and members of ethno-cultural communities. They did so from a state that had, to that point, been able to argue it knew best. These protests democratized society by forcing the inclusion of new groups in the formal political process and more broadly by exposing the particular values that underlay assertions of the "public interest" and the expertise in whose name and on whose authority the state claimed to act.

Certainly, this is how the fight to save Strathcona has been framed.[9] As its scholars and those of Vancouver's Chinatown, which adjoined the neighbourhood, argue, the debate over urban renewal was not just about the physical form of the city. It was also about how the state intervened; ultimately, it was about the kind of democracy people wanted. But just which people is a point of contention. Some scholars point to the influence of those who lived outside the areas affected by renewal in saving Strathcona and stopping the construction of the Chinatown freeway, be they academics, architects, social workers, or a new generation of activists.[10] In contrast, historian Michael Bruce and sociologist Jo-Anne Lee emphasize the crucial role played by the poor and working-class residents of the neighbourhood itself. They show how SPOTA engaged in "hybrid forms of community-based activism" that played on male politicians' egos and built on its members' cultural capital.[11] For instance, Shirley Chan "dressed to deceive," engaging in strategic flirtation to get politicians to go on specially designed walking tours aimed at showing them that the neighbourhood was not a slum.[12] The group also built on the Chinese custom of gift exchange, or *guanxi,* and hosted banquets to build reciprocal relationships with politicians.[13] SPOTA, with its Chinese Canadian executive and culturally diverse membership, was a "new breed of group" that emerged in the late sixties and effected change through "people power."[14]

Powerful and convincing, the emphasis on activism and protest in the historical literature has tended to overshadow how the global sixties also shaped how the state exercised power. Many politicians and bureaucrats evinced the same desire to democratize Canadian society as those who demonstrated against them did. As much as the fight over urban renewal in Strathcona was evidence of people power, it was also about the kinds of democracy the state cultivated.

In what follows, I explore the changing manifestations and meanings of citizen participation and empowerment that emerged with the implementation of urban renewal in Vancouver. In many ways, for the state, "people power" was also disciplinary power, a form of government that enabled dissent and change even as it reinscribed existing political structures and hierarchies.

The chapter begins with a discussion of how Vancouver's East Side came to be seen as a problem whose solution lay in urban renewal. It then examines the opposition to the city's plans for the area, something that began in the late 1950s. Doing so helps contextualize SPOTA's emergence and achievements in the longer history of resistance to urban renewal on the East Side and in the efforts of the municipal state to engage citizens in redevelopment. The concluding section makes the case that SPOTA's success was not just due to its strong grounding in the community and the effectiveness of its activism but also to a newly articulated desire on the part of the federal government in the late 1960s to cultivate citizen participation as a way to govern more effectively and, in its view, more democratically.

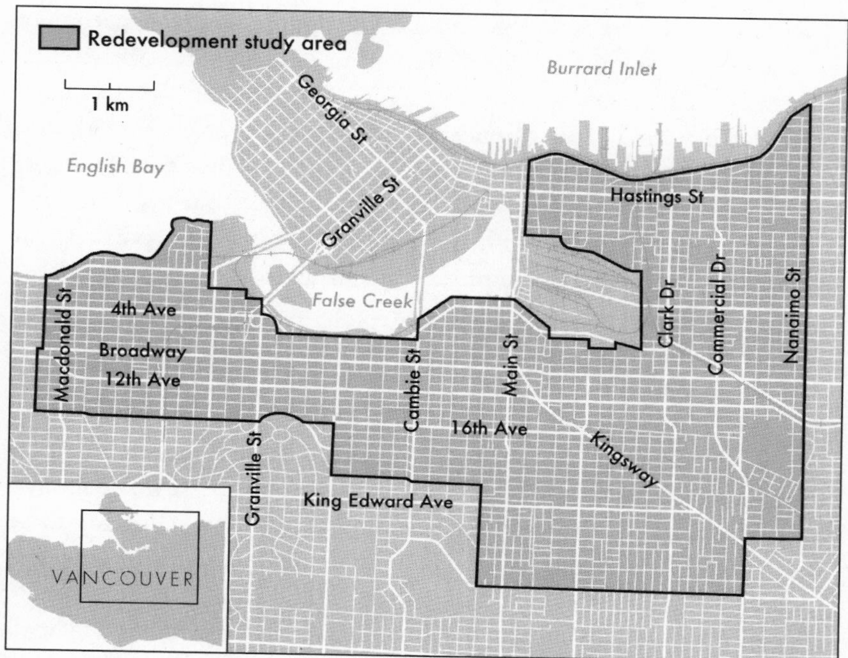

Figure 5.1 The 1957 *Vancouver Redevelopment Study* encompassed a large portion of the city, an area whose structures were vulnerable to blight if not already blighted.

Urban renewal in Vancouver followed the same general trajectory as that of Halifax, focusing on separating and rationalizing land use through zoning, eliminating blighted housing, and making better provisions for traffic. But rather than engage an outside consultant to guide it, the municipal government relied on its recently created Planning Department. Staffed by professionals and overseen by director Gerald Sutton Brown, it conducted a comprehensive redevelopment study in 1956 funded with federal monies.[15] Jamaican-born, British-educated Sutton Brown was a civil engineer by training and, like Gordon Stephenson, had worked on reconstructing war-damaged cities before taking the job in Vancouver in 1952. According to historian Will Langford, Sutton Brown was a classic high modernist, committed to "expert-managed technical solutions to perceived urban problems that involved the drastic alteration, regulation, standardization, and modernization of city space."[16]

The 1957 *Vancouver Redevelopment Study* encompassed a large portion of the city, an area bounded roughly by Burrard Inlet to the north, 33rd Avenue to the south, Bayswater Street to the west, and Semlin and McLean Drives to the east (Figure 5.1). City planners estimated that 44 percent of the buildings within those boundaries were vulnerable to blight, with 10 percent already showing signs of "incipient blight" and 7 percent "fully blighted." In a city as young as Vancouver (established in 1886), this was a worrisome state of affairs, and one that called for immediate action guided by a long-term plan.[17]

Like Stephenson's report on Halifax, Vancouver's was a twenty-year plan. It targeted four areas (A, B, C, and D) for "comprehensive redevelopment," by which it meant the total clearance of 718 acres and the displacement of nearly 24,000 people. Municipal authorities would also carry out "limited redevelopment" in a further 75 acres scattered through the city, displacing nearly 1,500 additional people. When comprehensive and limited redevelopment was completed, there would be fewer people living in these areas; approximately 12,000 instead of more than 25,000, making for a "net displacement" of 13,303.[18]

Despite its geographic scope, the *Vancouver Redevelopment Study* focused on the East Side, one of the areas targeted for comprehensive redevelopment. For the city's planners, the area bounded by Burrard Inlet, False Creek flats, Main Street, and Semlin and McLean Drives served as a laboratory to work out the techniques of urban renewal (Figure 5.2). Home to just over 15,000 people, or 60 percent of the population that would be affected by redevelopment, the "East End Survey Area" was the subject of a "detailed physical, economic and social investigation" to "illustrate the methods and procedures which might be applied generally throughout a twenty-year programme of redevelopment."[19]

Although 90 percent of the survey area was zoned for industrial or commercial use, it was predominately residential, home to an ethnically mixed, poor, and working-class population consisting mainly of North Americans, non-English-speaking Europeans (60 percent), and a sizable proportion of Chinese (30 percent), all of whom were attracted by low rents and social and cultural ties. Although families predominated, a significant number of the survey area's residents were single men, both pensioners and seasonal resource workers. Whether families or single persons, many were new to the East Side: a third had lived in the survey area for less than a year, and would likely move on again. That said, there was also a core of long-term residents, some 16.7 percent, who had lived there for more than ten years.[20]

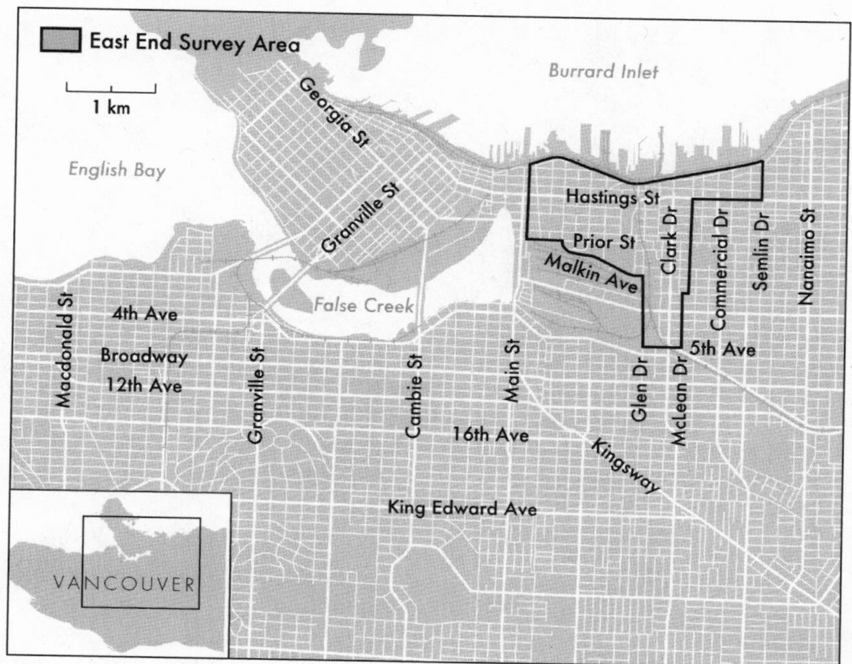

Figure 5.2 The East End Survey Area

The same technocratic social science approach that contributed to localizing and materializing poverty in Halifax was even more in evidence in Vancouver's redevelopment report, perhaps because the humanitarianism Stephenson expressed in his report was largely absent. Although Sutton Brown believed planning was a powerful tool for social improvement, he tended to ignore "social concerns and [the] qualitative features of urban life ... because they resisted rational, engineering-style interpretation."[21] Indeed, the *Vancouver Redevelopment Study* insisted that redevelopment was not about rehabilitating people.[22] Insofar as urban renewal addressed social problems it did so indirectly, by "enabl[ing] the constructive efforts of official and voluntary social agencies to be conducted in an hopeful environment."[23] Instead, its main purpose was to maximize the economic value of city lands. Planners estimated that the comprehensive renewal of the East End Survey Area would increase the tax revenue accruing from that part of the city by two or three times.[24]

Through tables, maps, statistics, and photographs, the *Vancouver Redevelopment Study* pinpointed the areas of the city that were most in need

Figure 5.3 Housing like this convinced planners that Strathcona was in need of urban renewal, ca. 1960–80. | City of Vancouver Archives, CVA 780-309

of renewal. The East End Survey Area represented just 5 percent of the city's population but was home to 20 percent of those on social assistance.[25] Moreover, it contained nearly three times the number of active tuberculosis cases compared to the city as a whole, perhaps because of the level of overcrowding, estimated to be 15 percent.[26] Not surprisingly, the survey also revealed that 85 percent of the dwellings were among the oldest in the city, built between 1900 and 1915, and some 60 percent of the "dwelling units" (rooms) were "sub-standard" in terms of both their physical condition and their sanitary facilities (Figure 5.3). While this assessment came from a "windshield check" – a once-over by an assessor working from a car and using a standardized set of criteria – rather than a more thorough examination of each property, it not only went unchallenged but also came to have significant rhetorical power and material effect.[27]

While blight affected all of the East Side, it wasn't homogeneous; the report identified three districts within the survey area, two of which would become industrial lands, and one of which – Strathcona – would be rebuilt as a residential area.[28] In presenting a "sketch scheme" for Strathcona,

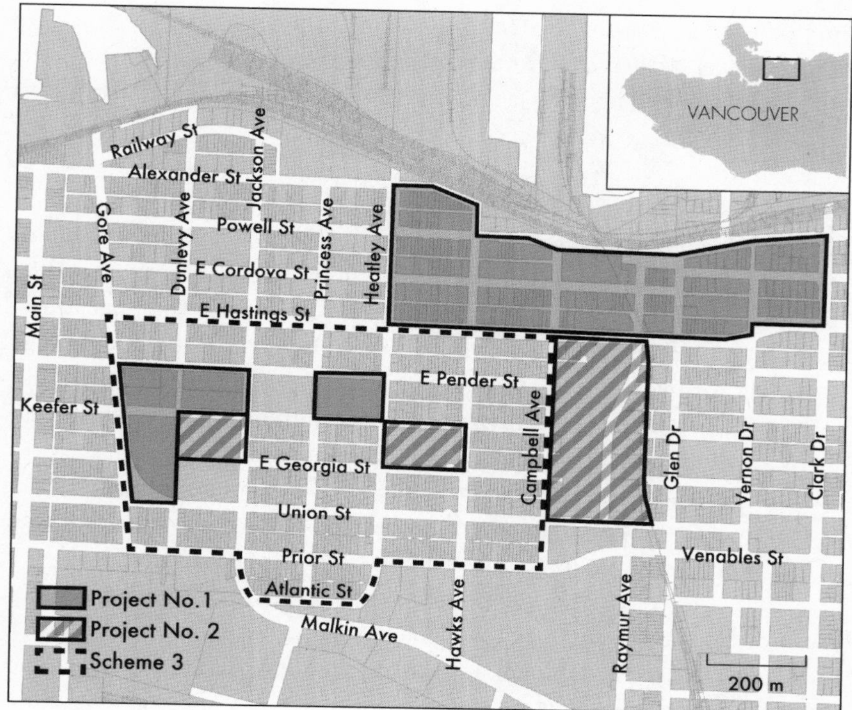

Figure 5.4 The three phases of redevelopment in the Strathcona area (Project No. 1, Project No. 2, and Scheme 3, as they were officially known) were projected to displace more than six thousand people.

Vancouver's planners drew on a report the city had commissioned from Leonard Marsh in 1950, which identified the same area for slum clearance and rebuilding because of its strategic importance to the city, located as it was near the waterfront and central business district. Like Marsh's report, the city's "sketch scheme" was meant to "show what a desirable type of development would look like." Built by government and private developers, two-storey row houses, three-storey walk-up apartments, and high-rise apartments, as well as hostels for single men, replaced the single-family detached homes and rooming houses that had once characterized the area. A shopping centre, park, school, and community centre provided the focal points of the new planned, modern neighbourhood.[29]

In all, clearing the East Side's blighted districts would necessitate relocating more than 6,000 people in three phases. Project 1 (approved in 1960) would disrupt approximately 1,380 people, Project 2 (approved in 1963) approximately 1,700, and Scheme 3 (approved in 1967), 3,000 (Figure 5.4). Some of those who lost their homes to renewal would be rehoused in one of three new public housing facilities that were also part of the redevelopment plans: McLean Park, Skeena Terrace, and Raymur Place.[30]

While historians have focused on SPOTA's opposition to the third phase of urban renewal, its efforts were preceded by a decade of dissent over the first two. Perhaps because the Chinese community was unsuccessful in stopping the initial phases of redevelopment, this opposition is not much explored.[31] Yet doing so helps contextualize SPOTA's achievements. More important for my purposes, this early resistance forced the state to grapple with how it would engage citizens on the question of urban renewal; thus analyzing this resistance also helps historicize and differentiate the structure, function, and meanings of citizen participation over the 1960s and early 1970s.

From its adoption, the *Vancouver Redevelopment Study* provoked concern, largely from the immigrant Chinese, who used an existing infrastructure of resistance, a legacy of their experience over the twentieth century fighting the racist laws and policies of the Canadian state.[32] In addition to making their views on redevelopment known through the Chinese Benevolent Association and various family organizations, they also established new groups in response to the threat of urban renewal. As well, individuals and organizations that provided social services to those who lived in the East End Survey Area also lent their support to the Chinese.

Formed in 1958, ten years before SPOTA, the Area "A" Property Owners Association raised concerns that were taken up by other organizations over the 1960s.[33] It argued that the city's plans would impose particular hardships on the Chinese. Urban renewal would erode their security by destroying "a social pattern based on the desire to associate and live in a community manner with other persons of common cultural background." Forcing the Chinese to move from Strathcona would also deprive them of easy access to the services available in Vancouver's Chinatown, which adjoined it. Such access was "particularly important in the case of older, low-income Chinese who are unable to use public transportation facilities because of their inability to speak and read English." While displaced residents would be accommodated in public housing, the Area "A" Property Owners Association worried about racism or, as it put it, "the possibility of social friction arising in part from living in apartment-type dwellings with other people." Thus, while it insisted it supported "a programme of civic improvement," it urged the city to realize it through "a less radical process," one that allowed residents to rehabilitate their homes and continue to live in the area.[34]

Other organizations and individuals also pursued these social security and cultural arguments through the 1960s. Retained by a number of Chinese organizations that opposed the city's redevelopment plans, lawyer Charles Locke told the mayor and council in 1960 that expropriation and clearing would seriously disrupt and impoverish the community, limiting its ability to take care of its own and to integrate newcomers. In the view of his clients, that ability stemmed as much from the extent of property ownership among Strathcona's residents as from the area's proximity to Chinatown: "To the Chinese has at last come ownership of a piece of land and the stability that goes with it. This is not provided by rented accommodation, no matter how good."[35] Home ownership was the basis of social security for the entire community and not just individuals. It allowed the Chinese to engage in self-help and not become dependent on welfare, something that Charles F. Barton believed made them model Canadians. Indeed, the principal of Strathcona School argued that redevelopment threatened to destroy what the Chinese had achieved – and what many people wanted, namely, "a consolidated happy family, independent of subsidy, industrious, studious, and law-abiding." In his view and that of his teachers, Strathcona was not a slum, and its residents were "not a typical unsettled slum people. These are respected citizens, over 7000 of them, and they are our people."[36]

The importance of property ownership also lay at the root of critiques of public housing. Writing on behalf of the Chinese Canadian Citizens Association in 1961, W.P. Wong expressed his organization's belief that despite its assurances, the government would eventually get out of the public housing business, leaving tenants at the mercy of landlords who would charge more than they could afford.[37]

The Chinese Benevolent Association's Dean Leung also insisted public housing was not an appropriate solution for those displaced by redevelopment, albeit for cultural, rather than economic, reasons. "The Vancouver citizens of Chinese origin are essentially believers in the system of private enterprise," he told the city in 1963. They wished to own, not rent, and for that reason he urged the mayor and council to make provision for the private development of residential units on the lands it cleared in Area "A." These could be purchased by those who were displaced by urban renewal but wished to remain in the neighbourhood.[38] Indeed, the Strathcona Area Council, a group supported by the Community Chest and Councils of the Greater

Vancouver Area and which consisted of representatives of various non-governmental social services organizations in the neighbourhood, echoed Leung and suggested that condominiums might be a solution. "Many of the Chinese population are familiar with the condominium concept because of its use in China," it noted. Moreover, in contrast to cooperative housing – which had also been discussed for the neighbourhood – condominiums offered individual buyers more control over their investment: "The purchaser of a unit can decide what size of mortgage loan he wishes to borrow and he is not responsible if other owners default on their mortgages."[39]

Of course, the ability to purchase another home of any kind depended on the compensation property owners received from the city, something that was also a point of contention. While many argued that it was impossible to compensate people for their sense of loss, the Chinatown Property Owners' Association did manage to come up with a figure, suggesting the city add 10 percent for "sentimental value" to its offers.[40] More fundamentally, however, some contended that the existing practice of basing compensation on market value was problematic because it did not capture the particular economies at work in Strathcona. Chinese often paid more than what properties in the neighbourhood were worth on the market because they wanted to live near Chinatown.[41] In any case, compensation at market value in an area slated for redevelopment was not sufficient to allow owners to purchase another house elsewhere in Vancouver. Instead of market value, what Fred Soon and other property owners affected by the second phase of renewal wanted was replacement value, a "home for a home," preferably in the same area.[42]

For many older residents, houses did not just provide shelter: they were also a significant source of income. As Ng Jung Yen and his wife Siu Gum Hin could attest, losing a house meant losing a livelihood. The sixty-three-year-old invalid and his wife had managed to buy a house on East Pender Street in 1957, the year the city's redevelopment study was done. By renting rooms to five families, they managed to make the mortgage payments and have a little money left over each month – until it became apparent their house was in an area targeted for eventual clearance. All but one of their tenants moved out, and no one wanted to buy the property. When his wife could no longer find work picking potatoes and berries, Yen became desperate. He feared he would lose his house before the city began the process of negotiating with owners in his neighbourhood. It was, as he put it, "a most serious predicament."[43]

As in Halifax, tenants in Vancouver were the group with the fewest rights when it came to urban renewal – and the fewest advocates. That said, the Strathcona Area Council did call attention to the needs of the neighbourhood's many single elderly tenants. The East End Survey revealed that 40 percent of the population of Area "A," some six thousand people, were single, and half of them were over the age of sixty-five. As A.D. Geach, the city's assistant director of urban renewal observed, this posed a potential problem as the National Housing Act only made reference to the city's obligation to rehouse *families* displaced by urban renewal.[44] Given this, the Strathcona Area Council urged the city to encourage Chinese organizations to meet the needs of this population by building hostel accommodation, particularly for those who "prefer[red] to remain in an ethnic environment."[45]

The impacts of redevelopment on the Chinese in Strathcona led some to argue that it was a form of discrimination, amounting to ethnic clearance. The Chinese Canadian Citizens Association noted that its constituents "thought that they were happy that they can got out [sic] from their homeland to live in this free country 'Canada' comfortably for the rest of their time but unfortunately this [urban renewal] happens to them." It warned that, "if the government use[s] force to buy them out, they will complain that the government is a dogmatic government, the government oppresses the people, especially the Chinese people ... and the poor in the Area 'A.'"[46] Rather than see Strathcona as a racial ghetto whose residents needed to be integrated, Dean Leung urged the city to capitalize on its tourist potential by investing in a rebuilding program (his own) that "introduced some typical Chinese architecture" to the neighbourhood, something that would turn it into a "'show place' and added attraction for all people."[47] His plan for an "Oriental City" consisting of seventy-two units for families would feature "moongate windows, pagoda roofs, and landscapes of bamboo, Chinese maples, cherries, and tea gardens."[48]

Presented with the concerns raised by the Chinese community, Gerald Sutton Brown responded with paternalistic sympathy and an assertion of his authority both as a planner and, by that point, one of the city's two commissioners, and the one in charge of Vancouver's budget. "I know that if I heard a big, impersonal City was going to pull my house down I'd be very upset," he told the *Chinatown News* in 1961. "But we're sure the Chinese will be very surprised when they find they can have modern Western accommodation at prices they can afford ... It is true that their mode of life will change, but it can't be helped. We're not spending public money where it isn't necessary."[49]

Sutton Brown's attitude reflected his personality: meeting him, "the most powerful person in city hall," was said to be like "being granted an audience with the Queen."[50] But more than simply an inherent characteristic, his imperiousness was rooted in the high regard the public had for planning expertise, something that historian Christopher Klemek argues was both crucial to and characteristic of a transnational "urban renewal order." Spurred by the emergence of modernism as the dominant architectural style and the increased scope and intensity of state power at the municipal level, professional planners fundamentally transformed North American and European cities from the 1920s to the 1960s. Gerald Sutton Brown was Vancouver's version of what Klemek calls a "local public entrepreneur," a bureaucrat who, in the tradition of New York's infamous planner, Robert Moses, turned his municipal planning department into a machine for creating a modern city.[51]

From 1951, when Vancouver created a Department of Planning and subsequently appointed Sutton Brown its first director, until the late 1960s, planners occupied a central role in shaping the city.[52] To a significant extent, their power in Vancouver also rested on the structure of government, something that was itself the product of a broader North American urban-reform movement that had its origins in the late nineteenth and early twentieth centuries. Led by business interests, that movement sought in part to take politics out of municipal affairs, seeing it as a corrupting influence and hence a threat to continued economic growth. Instead, proponents of civic reform believed experts and expertise should inform policy and decision making. The job of elected officials was simply to see that public money was spent responsibly and to do so by exercising their own judgment and conscience rather than being influenced by any party line.[53]

As historian Paul Rutherford argues, these beliefs led urban reformers to pin their hopes on the "bureaucratic method" to achieve their ends. Founded on the science of statistics, it "seemed able to rationalize the complex and mysterious world created by the new urban-industrial order." Businessman Herbert Ames's study of living conditions in Montreal's working-class neighbourhoods exemplified the bureaucratic method and the progressive impulse in Canada more generally. His *The City Below the Hill* (1897) revealed residents' needs in statistical form, a representation that both captured their problems as a whole and broke them down into constituent parts that could be managed. Doing so required an independent and specialized civil service.

As Rutherford observed, "To reformers, expert knowledge was a near panacea. This was the beginning of the age of the specialist and the professional."[54]

According to political scientist Paul Tennant, Vancouver was "an extreme example" of the non-partisanship – and, I would argue, of the reliance on expertise – that characterized the Progressive reform movement. The city abolished wards in 1935 and instituted an at-large system of representation to limit the power of neighbourhoods. Soon after, in 1937, some of the city's real estate and businesspeople came together to form the Non-Partisan Association (NPA), a loosely formed political party that would dominate city council and the mayor's office for more than thirty years.[55]

While, historically, the majority of municipalities in Canada discharged their administrative responsibilities through standing committees consisting of city councillors that made policy recommendations to the mayor and council as a whole, under the NPA the power of the civic bureaucracy grew while that of elected officials declined.[56] Staffed increasingly by professionals, the municipal civil service was, council believed, better placed to make the kinds of complex policy decisions about transportation and land use, particularly in a growing city. From 1941 to 1971, Vancouver's population increased by 55 percent, from 275,353 to 426,256, compounding its housing shortage.[57] Meeting the challenge of urbanization and suburbanization required specialized, technical knowledge as well as time, which most elected officials did not have – but planners on the municipal payroll did.

In Vancouver, establishing a Department of Planning in 1951 to replace the citizen-staffed Town Planning Commission that had existed since 1926 was only the first step in building an administrative structure that placed decision making in the hands of unelected and politically unaccountable experts. At the same time that council voted to establish this department and hire Sutton Brown as its first director, it also created a Technical Planning Board consisting of the heads of the city's other departments and chaired by the director of planning. Designed to increase coordination among the different arms of government and thus achieve better recommendations, the Technical Planning Board's detailed reports to council only increased the administrative load the city's elected officials were expected to carry.

To alleviate this burden, in 1956 council voted to create what was essentially a council-manager form of government.[58] A Board of Administration consisting of two appointed city commissioners, the mayor, and one alderman, who acted in an ex-officio capacity, managed all of the city's administrative and service functions. The board was allowed to define its own duties and, after 1959, to hold its meetings in secret. As Langford points out, the immense power of the Board of Administration lay in its ability to decide what matters it would send to council and when, and which it would dispense with on its own. When it did send issues to council, councillors would usually refer them to the board for further investigation, asking it to report back. "In sum," Langford notes, "council generally dealt with problems twice, yet rarely generated the policies it endorsed."[59]

In 1961, council voted to eliminate elected officials from the board altogether to reduce their own workload further. This left the administration of the city's affairs in the hands of two appointed commissioners, who split the responsibilities. One of them was Gerald Sutton Brown. Promoted from his job as director of planning, he had responsibility for the city's budget, social services, health, building, and planning. His counterpart, John Oliver, had oversight of electrical, engineering, civil defence, fire, and court duties. The two commissioners shared control over the city clerk's office, finance, and legal matters.[60]

By 1961, then, civic government in Vancouver, with its at-large system of representation and powerful unelected Board of Administration, looked like what, in a very different context, political scientist Timothy Mitchell calls "the rule of experts."[61] Given that, it might seem surprising that, over the decade, the city also sought advice from citizens on urban renewal. The ways it did so reveal how the municipal state understood the meaning and purpose of citizen participation. In 1961, the Board of Administration recommended the city establish the mayor's Redevelopment Consultative Committee, a body whose job was to advise the director of planning on redevelopment in Area "A."[62] Together, twelve members representing "interested groups" of citizens acted as a liaison between residents and the city, passing on "objections or problems" and making recommendations to council and the director of planning.[63] In addition, in 1964 the Department of Planning sought guidance on how it might improve the role and mandate of the Redevelopment Consultative Committee prior to embarking on the second phase of renewal. It sent out a questionnaire to municipal governments across North America describing the committee and asking how these other jurisdictions involved their citizens in redevelopment.[64] It learned that, while American cities had formed similar committees, largely because active citizen participation in urban renewal programs was a prerequisite for federal funding, Canadian cities had not. Of those that responded, none had done what Vancouver had – or anything else – to engage citizens.[65]

Despite appearances, however, the creation of the Redevelopment Consultative Committee and the city's desire to clarify and improve its workings were not motivated by a democratic impulse to share power or counterbalance the influence of planners and the Board of Administration in decision making. Instead, it was entirely consistent with the "rule of experts." The committee's membership, purpose, and actions reveal how, in this period, the city deployed citizen participation as a technique of government, using it to reinforce the relations of ruling, not to alter them.

The groups the city identified as having an interest in urban renewal largely reflected the East Side's demography and the social services it drew on. There were four representatives from the Chinese community (a banker, a realtor, and two journalists, all with connections to different Chinese organizations) and two from the Italian community (an accountant who wrote for the Italian-language newspaper and an architect). They were joined by the principal of Strathcona School, the Anglican pastor of the Good Shepherd Mission in Chinatown, an African-Canadian social worker, and the Ukrainian-Canadian executive director of the Civic Unity Association, a group dedicated to fighting discrimination.[66] These choices spoke to the kinds of citizens the city thought it important to consult with and how it conceived of citizen participation in planning. Rather than choose residents of Area "A" who presumably had an interest in redevelopment, the city appointed people whom, by virtue of their standing and networks, it considered were in a position to ascertain and influence the views of those who lived in the areas designated for renewal.

Indeed, such individuals were crucial to the kind of consultation in which the city wished to engage. The purpose of citizen participation was not to alter the shape or course of its plans in any meaningful way or to build consensus. Instead, citizen participation was a communications strategy. Insofar as the city tried to elicit support for redevelopment, it was by disseminating its message more effectively. Confident in the merit of his plans and that his rationality would prevail, Sutton Brown believed that opposition to urban renewal was due to a lack of information and ultimately to poor communication. Referring to the reaction of the Chinese, he told the CMHC's Urban Renewal seminar in 1959 that "to a large measure this opposition is due to misunderstanding of the processes and safeguards and is also due in part to some prejudice. Had we been able to proceed more quickly with our project and had we been able to establish an information centre in the redevelopment area, I feel sure that this problem would not have arisen to the same degree." While he did not think the community's resistance would derail renewal, it would cause "unnecessary difficulties" and require the assistant director of redevelopment to combine the administrative and technical skills he possessed as a planner with those of "an accomplished speaker and soother of ruffled feelings."[67]

Appointing well-connected individuals to the Redevelopment Consultative Committee would help get the city's message out and let planners know what residents thought of it. To that end, the committee advertised its role and prepared publicity releases on the first phase of renewal. Its members also appeared on television to talk about renewal and attended meetings of various citizens' groups to hear their concerns. In addition, it advised the city on which organizations should be sent detailed information about the second phase of renewal and then reported on their reactions to council in 1963.[68]

More than a reporting body, however, the Redevelopment Consultative Committee also did its own investigative work. Concerned about the apparent exodus of Chinese from Strathcona, especially the better-off working- and middle-class families, it conducted a survey in 1964 to ascertain why this was the case, with an eye to advising the city how it might proceed in the second phase of renewal. If Chinese were leaving because they saw Strathcona as a "stepping stone" in a move to a better neighbourhood, that was one thing. If, however, people were moving because they could not find accommodation in the redeveloped neighbourhood, that was another – and something that necessitated that the city do more than just provide public housing if it were to avoid creating a class ghetto.[69]

Short of such policy advice, the committee also provided what might be considered political guidance to the city aimed at preventing it from unnecessarily provoking residents already anxious and angry about renewal. For instance, when the city proposed holding a sod-turning ceremony at the site of the future McLean Park public housing project, the members of the Redevelopment Consultative Committee advised against it: the area had just been cleared, and at least some residents were in a less-than-celebratory mood. Instead, it suggested the city mark the completion of redevelopment projects – which it did, holding an opening ceremony at Skeena Terrace, where some of those dislocated from Strathcona would be housed in 1963.[70]

In addition to helping the city communicate with the residents of Area "A" more effectively, the Redevelopment Consultative Committee also heard complaints. The solutions it facilitated, while meaningful to the individuals involved, did not require, much less lead to, changes in the city's approach to urban renewal. For instance, it helped the elderly owners of a small grocery store on the fringes of the area targeted for renewal with the compensation process and made a case for assisting the Yens with their predicament described above. As well, when it learned that tenants were being told, wrongly, by their landlords to vacate immediately because their building was slated for demolition, the committee asked to be informed of when expropriation negotiations on individual properties were completed so it could advise and assist those who were facing eviction. The city's supervisor of property and insurance agreed.[71]

Rather than reconfiguring political power, then, citizen participation was a way the city enhanced and reinforced its control: the Redevelopment Consultative Committee delivered the city's message and helped solve problems in a way that highlighted the discretionary power of its members and that of municipal authorities. Equally importantly, by keeping planners informed of residents' concerns, the committee helped the experts anticipate reactions and avoid confrontations. In that sense, citizen participation was a kind of risk management, a way for the city to evaluate the social and political terrain on which it operated so it could navigate it more effectively.

Beyond acknowledging the need to consult on urban renewal, the city also recognized it would have to engage the residents of Area "A" to deal with its social problems, ones that were exacerbated by redevelopment even if their causes lay elsewhere. Although conventional city planning was conceived of as a humanitarian enterprise aimed at improving the lives of citizens, in the mid-twentieth century it did not deal particularly well with humans. Sutton Brown realized doing so required a different set of skills and a new administrative structure; specifically, it called for the expertise of a *social* planner working in a municipal department dedicated to that purpose. As he told council in 1965, Vancouver spent approximately $400,000 yearly on physical planning but nothing on social planning.[72] In response to the Board of Administration's arguments, council established a Department of Social Planning and Development in November 1966. Its first director was appointed effective January 1968.[73]

Conceived as a complement to physical planning, social planning focused on people, attending to their needs and well-being. The new department worked at a local scale to deal with social change by coordinating services and engaging in community development. Specifically, municipal social planners were "to strengthen individual and family life and to enrich neighbourhood and city living by helping to plan, develop, coordinate and integrate health, education, welfare, recreational, and community renewal programs; and ... to foster citizen self-help and community-betterment programs." It did so, in part, by building capacity, "encourag[ing] residents to assume personal responsibilities for improving the social and economic conditions of their community."[74]

While city councillor Walter Hardwick believed the new department was a sort of "Distant Early Warning system" designed to alert government to potential problems, it was meant to be far more than that.[75] Ultimately, the aim of social planning was not simply to react to existing problems but to help create communities that never acquired them. In that sense, it was a technology of government aimed at producing particular subjects. As the Board of Administration described it, the city's social planners assisted in "the development of the social fabric of the community" by organizing programs "to facilitate the development of individuals through group activities, etc."[76] Sociologist Karen Bridget Murray argues that community centres in particular were key institutions and sites for producing citizens on Vancouver's East Side, reinforcing the norm of the "two-parent, heterosexual, breadwinner family." It was an idea that had its origins in the argument Leonard Marsh made in his 1950 report on Strathcona, in which he insisted that "rebuilding a neighbourhood" required more than constructing housing: it required initiatives that developed different kinds of affect and affiliation to overcome the "apathetic dreary living" that defined slums and threatened "every aspect of healthy citizenship."[77] The city's efforts captured the attention of outsiders, who lauded them as innovative. Searching for a "social planning prototype" that could guide its members, in 1974 the American Society of Planning Officials chose Vancouver's department, a measure of the regard that professionals had for what the city had achieved.[78]

Nevertheless, by the late 1960s, it was clear to the members of council that opposition to urban renewal was only growing, despite the efforts of the Redevelopment Consultative Committee and the establishment of the Department of Social Planning. Indeed, the ongoing opposition of the Chinese community to slum clearance and that of a broad-based coalition of citizens, including the Chinese, to the city's plans to build a freeway through Vancouver's East Side in 1967 forced municipal authorities to rethink how they engaged citizens.[79]

As a result, in 1969 the city disbanded the Redevelopment Consultative Committee and the other citizens' advisory committees it had created and consolidated citizen participation in a reconfigured Town Planning Commission (TPC). The newly restructured TPC was meant to act "as a public sounding board to advise Council as spokesmen of the citizens." Urban renewal and redevelopment would be dealt with by one of the TPC's three subcommittees, whose members were drawn from its own ranks and supplemented by invited outsiders "with special skills and knowledge related to renewal and redevelopment."[80]

Despite these changes, city bureaucrats continued to understand opposition to its redevelopment plans as a communications problem and to conceive of citizen participation primarily as a means of managing risk. In supporting calls for the role of the TPC to be reviewed in light of "new attitudes to planning," both its chairman and the director of planning noted that "it is obvious that there is still a gap in communication between Council, its advisers and officials at City Hall, outside organizations and the general public, despite serious attempts by City Council, the Town Planning Commission, and the Director of Planning to improve the situation." Although they saw the restructured TPC as providing better "two-way" exchanges, they did not discuss how the city's plans might be changed or improved by such input. Instead, they reiterated the idea that the commission's role was to help the city anticipate the public's response and, in so doing, implement its plans more effectively. "If the broader planning policies can be resolved in this way, then specific projects will become easier to assess and citizen reactions become more predictable."

By the time the third, and potentially most disruptive, phase of urban renewal was scheduled to start in Vancouver, there had been a shift in opinion in Ottawa about the wisdom of centralized policymaking. Concerned about this and about the rising costs and questionable efficacy of urban renewal, in 1968 the federal minister responsible for housing established the Task Force on Housing and Urban Development. Paul Hellyer and his executive assistant, Lloyd Axworthy, travelled across Canada in the fall, hearing from city representatives, people who lived in public housing, and those who had been affected by urban renewal. As Hellyer explained, "We are finding out from people themselves what they think, talking to them in their neighbourhoods. This is not a Task Force that will make up its mind only through written evidence or expert testimony. We are trying to absorb the character of Canadians as they seek to find a decent life in a very complicated world."[81]

When it reported in early 1969, the task force made forty-seven recommendations, most of which dealt with housing. Of particular relevance to the fate of Strathcona was its recommendation that research on the economic, social, and psychological effects of public housing was necessary – so much so that, "until such study is completed and assessed, no new large projects should be undertaken."[82] Because the provision of public housing was a requirement for federally funded redevelopment projects, this essentially signalled the end of urban renewal. In August 1969, Hellyer's successor, Robert Andras, made it official.[83]

In the course of its travels across Canada, the task force received submissions from many people, including Shirley Chan. It wouldn't be the last time its members heard from her. Following its visit, Chan and the residents of Strathcona met privately and publicly to discuss what they could do about the last phase of urban renewal, scheduled to begin in 1969. In mid-December 1968, the Strathcona Property Owners and Tenants Association was formed at a community meeting of some five hundred people. In May 1969, it presented a brief to the mayor and city council, rejecting renewal and making the case for rehabilitating their neighbourhood: "As residents of an area which has been marked for 'a clearance and rebuilding program' we are tired of waiting for the bulldozer. Instead, we are prepared to begin a program for rehabilitation of existing structures providing the Federal Government is willing to utilize the money available for mass demolition and convert this money to ready grants and loans for our homeowners."[84]

A multigenerational, multicultural, and multilingual organization, SPOTA had both the local knowledge and relationships that came from its familiarity with the neighbourhood and the neighbours, and the linguistic and political skills to deal with outsiders, thanks largely to the involvement of a university-educated younger generation and its well-connected presidents.[85] Walter Chan, the first president of SPOTA, wrote articles for the *Chinese Times* encouraging its readers to come to public meetings and to join the organization. His wife, Mary, who spoke little English, and her friend Bessie Lee organized a "block captain" system, assigning individuals to knock on doors and leaflet each house in every block in the neighbourhood. Both set an example for others by taking their turn pounding the pavement. Their daughters, university students Shirley Chan and Jo-Anne Lee, were also active SPOTA members. As a member of its executive and public relations secretary, Shirley Chan played an important role in lobbying key politicians and bureaucrats at all levels of government. SPOTA was also helped by the political connections its second president, Chinatown businessman Harry Con, brought to the job. He was a member of the Non-Partisan Association and of the federal Liberal Party.[86]

Cultivating relationships with officials and bureaucrats at all levels of government proved to be one of the keys to SPOTA's success. Vancouver's first director of social planning, Maurice Egan, and particularly one of his new employees, local area coordinator Darlene Marzari, proved to be especially important allies. Sutton Brown may have conceived of the new Social Planning Department as an instrument to fashion governable subjects, but, in its first years of operation, it played an important role in helping SPOTA make its case against urban renewal and top-down planning. City engineer Bill Curtis called the department a "commando group" that worked to ensure social concerns were taken into account in developing and implementing municipal policy. Peter Leckie, the director of finance, considered that the job of the social planner was to "act almost as a goad or needle to keep the rest of us honest on the social aspects, because social aspects can so easily be dropped from consideration."[87]

Hired to assist Strathcona residents to find new homes, one of the "commandos," Darlene Marzari, encouraged SPOTA's formation and became directly involved in the group's lobbying efforts, helping Shirley Chan show Paul Hellyer and his entourage around Strathcona in November 1968. When Marzari emerged from the two-car motorcade returning the group to their hotel after the tour, Maurice Egan recalled there was a "collective murmur" of surprise from the crowd of fifty city employees who had gathered to meet their Ottawa guests. Egan soon found himself in front of Sutton Brown. He survived.[88]

So did Marzari, who continued to work on behalf of the residents of Strathcona, extending their network of allies: she found them a lawyer – future BC premier Mike Harcourt – and connected SPOTA with some of the area's charitable organizations that were doing community development work.[89] Future city councillor and member of Parliament Margaret Mitchell, then at Alexandra Neighbourhood House, agreed to help engage Strathcona's residents on the issue of urban renewal, provided they find her a Cantonese-speaking community development worker to partner with.[90] They did. Paid by Mitchell's Neighbourhood Services Association funds, Jonathan Lau proved invaluable: not only did he have the necessary language skills, but

Figure 5.5 Shirley Chan (centre), at a SPOTA dinner in the summer of 1969, with Robert Andras (to her right), the federal minister in charge of housing, with the executive of the Chinese Benevolent Association. | Hayne Wai, private collection

he also lived in McLean Park public housing. A trusted figure, he played a crucial role in building support for SPOTA among residents.[91]

The walking tours SPOTA designed and the banquets it hosted were opportunities for residents to appeal directly to politicians. City councillors and planners were regular guests, as were provincial and federal politicians and CMHC bureaucrats (Figure 5.5).[92] While Michael Bruce highlights the effectiveness of these non-confrontational forms of protest and how they set SPOTA apart from other groups critical of urban renewal, Jo-Anne Lee goes further and argues that SPOTA's tactics were part of "a unique campaign that successfully overturned the grand designs of planners, engineers, politicians and developers."[93]

As important as the efforts of SPOTA and its allies were in convincing the federal government to stop urban renewal and instead fund the rehabilitation of housing in Strathcona, we need to ask why politicians like Hellyer gave grassroots organizations the time and attention they did. Why were task force members willing to go on a neighbourhood tour – especially one that started "at 6 o'clock in the freaking morning"?[94] Why did Hellyer's successor, Robert Andras, and other politicians regularly accept invitations to SPOTA's banquets and tea parties? These are not questions the organization's scholarly chroniclers ask, focused as they are on analyzing SPOTA's strategies.

Posing them not only helps contextualize SPOTA's achievements, but it also reveals other understandings of citizen participation in the late 1960s. In contrast to Vancouver's civic bureaucrats, federal politicians in particular had a different view of how ordinary people might be involved in policymaking, one that was rooted in a greater commitment to participatory democracy. However, empowering the grassroots was not an end itself but a means to another one. Federal politicians saw citizen participation as a way to leverage their own power against the Sutton Browns of Ottawa; in other words, engaging ordinary people would democratize decision making by empowering elected politicians against an entrenched and politically unaccountable bureaucracy. Groups like SPOTA nevertheless benefited from the federal government's embrace of citizen participation and did so in ways that expose the meanings, possibilities, and limits of such participation.

According to Lloyd Axworthy, pressure to democratize policymaking came from within the ranks of the federal government as well as from outside them. Recalling the 1960s, he noted that the instrument Hellyer chose to study Canada's housing problem, the task force, was a new vehicle of policymaking, one whose use increased under the Trudeau regime. Like the Kennedy administration in the United States a few years earlier, the Liberal government had become concerned about the slowness of policymaking and the difficulty of bringing new kinds of knowledge and expertise that were not available within the ranks of the civil service to bear on problems. Indeed, Axworthy argues that ministers in the Trudeau government considered the civil service a brake on the kind of policymaking required for a rapidly changing Canada. It was too conservative, committed to particular ways of doing things and particular positions, and it was unaccountable.[95] For Axworthy, the task force was "a different device for policymaking ... It was not an instrument controlled by the civil service or greatly informed by the Ottawa policymaking establishment. Instead, it was an instrument based on the concept of political populism. It sought answers from the kinds of people that rarely are consulted in policymaking. It was in fact a means of giving some life to the philosophy of participatory democracy."[96]

Using a task force to bring ordinary people into the policymaking process and thus "reassert power … over the civil servant" was part of a broader moment of democratization in North America.[97] Spurred by an increasing dissatisfaction with the leadership class and with the forms and practices of representative democracy, both of which were deemed to be unresponsive, elitist, and self-serving, in the early to mid-1960s activists representing a diversity of concerns called for "power to the people" to counter and defeat that of "the Establishment." The success of the civil rights, women's, and students' movements spoke to the capacity of "participatory democracy" to reform public and private institutions and make the kinds of changes and worlds that were once unimaginable. As political philosopher Frank Cunningham notes, the phrase was coined as the student movement was gaining momentum and figured in the 1962 Port Huron Statement by Students for a Democratic Society, which served as that group's manifesto. Students fought for, and in many cases won, roles for themselves in governing the university, whether it was serving on hiring committees or shaping curriculum and grading policy. Their successes led other proponents of people power to argue for similarly democratizing decision making in the family, workplace, and neighbourhood. As commentators at the time noted, participatory democracy had become "a kind of panacea for contemporary political discontent."[98]

As Axworthy's comments about the purpose of the task force suggest, those who worked within the formal institutions of the state also embraced citizen participation as a way to make better decisions and better policy. About the same time Hellyer began his task force, two of his ministerial colleagues undertook consultations with First Nation organizations across Canada as part of the process of revising the Indian Act. As historian Sally M. Weaver observes, Indigenous peoples had long complained about being left out of the process of defining the policies that governed their lives. In the climate of the 1960s, it would have been hard not to include them.[99]

This obligation to consult with ordinary Canadians was particularly pressing as the Trudeau government had been elected in 1968 promising a "just society," in which participatory democracy occupied a central place. As historian Paul Litt argues, Trudeau capitalized on the belief that "no society that restricted its citizens' access to the political process could be truly just." He urged "people to engage in politics, to make democracy work by taking responsibility for their futures themselves." As he told his fellow Liberals, "Basically, what we try to do in government is to sit down with the people and discuss the facts of the situation." For Trudeau, participatory democracy was "a way of working together; it's a way of looking for solutions together. And, if you're a free man, if you're a free people, you don't want to be governed without knowing the reasons why and you don't want solutions fed to you. You want to participate in the solution-making process."[100]

Paradoxically, Trudeau's commitment to participatory democracy led him to consolidate power. One of his first actions as prime minister was to reorganize the Prime Minister's Office and the Privy Council Office in a way that centralized power by, among other things, creating a policy and planning division. It funded social science research that provided the cabinet with advice independent of government departments, including information about Canadians' views on a variety of issues that would inform government policy. While this was hardly the kind of citizen participation in policymaking that participatory democrats called for, the Liberal government constructed it as such. As the press release announcing the change explained, "The Prime Minister recalled that during the recent election campaign he had repeatedly stressed the importance of increased participation by the public in the actual processes of government ... The changes being instituted are intended to provide a greater sensitivity by government to the will of the people and to facilitate speedier decision-making and more efficient service." To that end, the reorganized PMO had "units responsible for policy advice, for maintaining close contacts with individuals and groups in all regions of the country, for initiation of policy proposals and for information."[101] The irony of governments consolidating power in the name of participatory democracy wasn't limited to Ottawa but was something that was apparent in how citizen participation was structured in Strathcona, as we will see.

Even before Trudeau's election, the federal government facilitated and funded citizen participation through community development initiatives aimed at giving ordinary people more control over the decisions that affected their collective lives. The best-known of these was the Company of Young Canadians (1966), an organization modelled on the US Peace Corps.[102] Its volunteers did a range of grassroots social service work in urban and rural Canada, from developing food co-ops and drop-in centres to engaging in civil rights and anti-poverty activism, much of which was aimed at helping people take charge of and govern their own lives.

The National Film Board of Canada also made community development a priority with its Challenge for Change program (1967–80), a participatory video project.[103] As discussed in Chapter 2, participatory filmmaking was a way to forge the kind of awareness and consensus that could lead to collective action and citizen-initiated social change. As one filmmaker put it, "It was beautiful democracy at work."[104]

The principles of citizen participation and community development also informed two community-based job-creation programs established in 1971, Opportunities for Youth and the Local Initiatives Program. Consistent with the idea of citizen control, federal government funds for these programs, from the Secretary of State and the Department of Manpower and Immigration, respectively, went directly to local organizations, enabling them to "manage their own solutions" to the problems confronting them.[105]

Community development and citizen participation also left their imprint on one of the federal government's largest bureaucracies. In 1964, it became a priority in the Department of Indian Affairs. According to Hugh Shewell, Walter Rudnicki pitched such policies in a way that would resonate with the politics of the time, emphasizing how they would end welfare dependency among Indigenous peoples and make them equal citizens. In practice, however, community development on reserves was carried out in ways similar to that in the North, where Rudnicki had worked previously – ways that were soon considered subversive by some of his colleagues. He intended community development workers hired by Indian Affairs "to be the spearhead of giving Indian people back their 'heads' ... so that they could start challenging what ... we were doing." Although the program foundered, George Manuel, who worked as a community development assistant and later became chief of the Assembly of First Nations, insisted it had a lasting legacy: "On every reserve where the Community Development program had a measure of success, people had a new measure of their own individual and collective capacities, and a new yardstick by which to measure would-be friends."[106]

Given these initiatives, it was completely in keeping with the federal government's commitment to citizen participation in community development that Lloyd Axworthy urged Chinese Canadians to organize. Speaking for Hellyer in April 1969, he told the national conference on urban renewal as it affected Chinatowns that change "will not happen just by having a conference and talking about it." The critics of urban renewal were right to point out that it served the interests of business. But there was a lesson in that for the Chinese: "Businessmen in the community are well-organized. They know how to play local politics. They know how to gain their interests."[107]

According to Axworthy, what the federal government wanted was "some better competition and that the poor, and the different racial and ethnic communities, the downtown people, make their point heard, and do it in a way that is going to count." The usual process was for governments to present their initiatives to the public and ask for its acquiescence. That was "backwards." Instead, citizens needed to be engaged from the start in setting the direction for policy as well as contributing to its substance.[108] But citizen participation also required building capacity. As Axworthy told the conference delegates, "There should be the kind of self-development within the community, the kind of participation which says 'this is the kind of community we want, these are the kinds of things we want to take place, and this is what we are prepared to do.' We have not done very much of that in this country."[109]

That was about to change. Well-represented at the conference, SPOTA led Strathcona's residents through the kinds of discussions Axworthy said were necessary for effective citizen participation. Not only did the members of its executive act as facilitators, engaging the neighbourhood in discussions of what it wanted and needed, but it also built capacity among residents, using seating plans at its banquets to encourage the more reticent and deferential to engage with authorities and, in so doing, develop "a sense of ownership" of the issues among them. It also surveyed neighbourhood opinion to back up the association's demands and push them forward.[110] As a result, the executive secured a role for SPOTA in developing a rehabilitation program for Strathcona and in implementing it.

SPOTA was able to make a place for itself by dint of its own hard work, but also because of the influence and interventions of the federal government. Through its control of a significant portion of the funding for urban renewal, Ottawa created the space for ordinary people to participate in the planning and implementation of policies that affected them. SPOTA itself recognized this, noting the power of the federal purse. As Shirley Chan recalled, while urban renewal was "proposed, planned, studied, and administered at the local level," Ottawa could effect change through its financial contribution: "Even this limited control is useful as it gives protesting citizens like the ones in Strathcona someone outside of the local government to appeal to."[111]

Significantly, despite the freeze on urban renewal that had been put in place following the completion of the Hellyer task force's hearings, the minister responsible for housing and urban development made it known to municipal authorities that he was willing to consider a revised urban renewal plan for Strathcona, provided it emphasized rehabilitation rather than the acquisition and clearance of land, and that it was agreeable to residents as well as the city, province, and CMHC. Committed to completing the redevelopment of Area "A," the city indicated its willingness to take the minister up on his offer in April 1969. Thus, when SPOTA submitted its brief to council a month later asking that funds for urban renewal be used for rehabilitating the neighbourhood and detailing a plan for doing so, municipal authorities responded differently than they had earlier in the decade, when other organizations had asked for the same thing. Rather than dismiss the request, in July 1969 the director of planning asked for and received "authority to negotiate" with SPOTA to explore the feasibility of neighbourhood rehabilitation through a pilot project.[112]

While the city retained the services of a professional who would carry out the building inspections for the "crash survey," it turned to SPOTA to inform residents, choose the blocks that would be surveyed in the pilot program, and provide individuals who would accompany the inspector and translate between English and Chinese or English and Italian as necessary. Since the feasibility of a rehabilitation program depended in part on the ability of residents to contribute their own resources to it, the city also asked SPOTA to provide it with information on people's incomes. As Max Cross, the deputy director of planning, put it to Bessie Lee, SPOTA's secretary, "We are relying on your Association to investigate the financial resources of the residents in order, in the case of tenants, to assess their ability to pay increased rents should such result from rehabilitation costs; also in the case of property owners, to assess their ability to bear increased costs that would be involved in private rehabilitation."[113]

Although the survey left the city doubtful about its feasibility, rehabilitation nevertheless went ahead, in large part because of the intervention of the federal minister, Robert Andras, and the provincial minister of municipal affairs, Dan Campbell.[114] SPOTA found itself on the Strathcona Working Committee, chaired by Vancouver's director of social planning, Maurice Egan, an appointment that Shirley Chan felt signalled a change in direction for the city.[115] Along with high-ranking representatives from the city, province, and CMHC, it was tasked with designing and administering a rehabilitation program for the entire neighbourhood. It was jubilant. "Urban renewal is out the window," SPOTA's executive announced at a public meeting in September 1969. "Everything is up to us. The three levels of government have to deal with us."[116]

Not only did SPOTA get a place at the table, it was also given a booster seat in the form of funding from the three levels of government to attend meetings and to hire its own expert consultants so it could meet the city's planners on even ground. Birmingham and Wood, a Vancouver architectural firm, acted as what SPOTA called its "civil service." With its advice and guidance, SPOTA initiated a number of projects aimed at generating ideas with residents about what a rehabilitation program might look like.[117] Reporting at the end of 1970, Birmingham and Wood concluded that rehabilitation was feasible and that it would cost a minimum of $4,000 to bring each house up to standard, given the long history of government neglect in the area. After several rounds of hard negotiation, all parties agreed to "rehabilitation through cooperation," the plan the architects laid out at the end of July 1971.[118]

The Birmingham and Wood report was the basis for a legal agreement between the three levels of government in January 1972 that established a $5 million rehabilitation program for Strathcona and an administrative structure that would implement it over a three-year period.[119] The Strathcona Rehabilitation Committee (SRC) replaced the Strathcona Working Committee but retained its membership structure: it consisted of one representative each from SPOTA, the city, the province, and the CMHC, and advised the three levels of government, coordinated the rehabilitation program, and made recommendations on applications for rehabilitation assistance from residents. Its decisions were reached by consensus, a practice that allowed differences among the parties to be aired and discussed. A project coordinator oversaw the day-to-day operations and reported to the city's Planning Department.[120]

Having created the space for SPOTA to participate in planning a neighbourhood rehabilitation program, the federal government then financed its further involvement. Recognizing that SPOTA's executive were volunteers, the CMHC agreed to pay its representatives and the association's professional advisers for the time they spent attending Rehabilitation Committee meetings, to a maximum of $6,000 per year. Equally importantly, it provided SPOTA with a grant of $50,000 to "cover paying salaries and setting up a community office" to facilitate its work.[121]

Over its life, the Strathcona Rehabilitation Committee disbursed nearly $1 million to renovate 382 dwellings and 212 homes, representing some

Figure 5.6 House under renovations in Strathcona, August 1973. | City of Vancouver Archives, COV S511-CVA 780-345

30 percent of all dwellings and 62 percent of all single-family homes in the neighbourhood (Figure 5.6).[122] The program was voluntary, and the overwhelming majority of recipients of the grants and loans (84 percent) were Chinese, most of them older: while their average age was sixty, 11 percent were over seventy-five. Most of the repairs they undertook were cosmetic, improvements to the exterior or interior of the houses done at the request of homeowners rather than ones mandated by the city to correct health and

safety concerns. In addition, the committee also approved expenditures for recreational facilities, mainly parks, and above- and below-ground services for the neighbourhood, including street lighting, sidewalks, and sewer and water mains.[123]

SPOTA's involvement with neighbourhood rehabilitation captures the possibilities and limits of citizen participation as a vehicle for social change. Unlike the members of the Redevelopment Consultative Committee, SPOTA's representatives were active participants in shaping urban renewal: rather than simply being consulted by municipal authorities, they, along with senior representatives from the three levels of government, set the terms of the rehabilitation program for the neighbourhood in which they lived and then implemented them. Indeed, through its work, the committee broadened the meaning of "rehabilitation" beyond housing. Over the course of the program's life, the SRC received all kinds of concerns, complaints, and suggestions about what the neighbourhood needed, so much so that, in the judgment of the consultants hired to assess the project, it "assume[d] a role as unofficial planning board for Strathcona," acting as a conduit for residents to make their concerns known to the city bureaucracy.[124]

In addition, the Strathcona project shaped housing policy at a national level. In a 1972 brief for Councillor Marianne Linnell, the city's Planning Department noted that it was "a model for new federal legislation in community upgrading and residential rehabilitation."[125] Shortly after the CMHC sent its policy planning head, Walter Rudnicki, to Vancouver to see the Rehabilitation Committee in action, it introduced the Neighbourhood Improvement Program and the Residential Rehabilitation Assistance Program, programs that historian Pierre Filion argues "differed from prior forms of renewal by emphasizing the preservation of the built environment and citizen participation in neighbourhood planning."[126] In fact, for the government officials involved, the importance of the Strathcona rehabilitation program lay in changing attitudes toward citizen involvement; specifically, it convinced them "that decisions for neighbourhoods could no longer be made in 'ivory towers,' that is, by people outside the community with little understanding of its dynamics."[127]

Comments like these support the arguments made by SPOTA's scholars that what set the group apart from others that opposed urban renewal was its commitment to fighting "for the right to participate equally in civic democracy" and its desire to effect "systemic change in politics and government." Rather than simply preserving their neighbourhood, SPOTA's members brought about "genuine democratic reform."[128] As I have suggested, however, SPOTA succeeded where others failed in large part because it was able to capitalize on the growing disillusionment with urban renewal and the federal government's embrace of citizen participation in the late 1960s.

But assessing whether SPOTA's achievements amounted to systemic change and genuine reform requires more than contextualizing them in the political and ideological landscape of the global sixties. As scholars of citizen participation argue, it is also important to think critically about "empowerment"; specifically, to ask who was empowered to do what and the extent to which power relations were reconfigured as a result of citizen participation.[129] The members of SPOTA's executive were the people who were literally empowered as a result of the group's opposition to urban renewal. They spoke for the community; negotiated with officials from the city, province, and CMHC; helped design the rehabilitation program, monitored its progress, and disbursed its funds; and were paid for their efforts.

Although the three levels of government recognized SPOTA as "the accredited representative of the property owners and tenants in the urban renewal area," it was never clear who had provided that accreditation.[130] Not surprisingly, city officials raised questions about its representativeness – no doubt in an attempt to undermine SPOTA's claims, but also out of some genuine concern.[131] As geographers David Ley, Kay Anderson, and Doug Konrad point out, after the threat of demolition disappeared, so too did much of SPOTA's membership: it was seldom more than two hundred.[132] While Vancouver authorities raised questions about how the state could be sure that a community group like SPOTA was representative, Homer Borland expressed "some doubts as to the claimed cohesiveness of neighbourhoods." The former director of the CMHC's Urban Renewal and Public Housing Division insisted he supported citizen participation but worried about whether the voices that his planners were "constantly charged with violating" were those of the neighbourhood or a "vocal minority." More fundamentally, he asked, "Can a community speak with one voice or do various elements present their views?"[133]

The city also worried about the impact of empowering some citizens over others. In its view, the rehabilitation program had the potential to violate the rights of individual residents by "surrender[ing] many of the city's legal powers and the council's policy-making powers with respect to the Strathcona area" to a non-elected and potentially non-representative group.[134] This concern about contravening the rights of residents by empowering

SPOTA only grew as the association made the transition from opposing government policies to proposing them. As the city's Planning Department observed, when initiating new ideas there was a tendency for decision making to become concentrated among a small group whose knowledge of and familiarity with the issues rapidly outdistanced that of the people they represented. Impatient with the relatively slow response from their constituents, there was a temptation among the executive to avoid taking issues back to the larger group or even to ignore or manipulate it. As the Planning Department noted, "Both attitudes are a denial of the basic premise of citizen participation."[135]

While its lack of enthusiasm for citizen participation means we should take the Planning Department's assessment of SPOTA with a grain of salt, the concerns it raised about elitism were shared by the group's executive itself, some of the association's supporters, and some outsiders, particularly as SPOTA revealed plans to move into the housing business. Even as the rehabilitation program was underway, its executive started to plan its next initiative, heartened perhaps by the defeat of the NPA in 1972 and the election of a new civic government committed to citizen participation, the Electors Action Movement (TEAM).

In its successful application to the CMHC for funding "Operation Total Involvement of the Neighbourhood," SPOTA observed that "power means being a part of the decision-making set up ... Power and democracy mean not just being near the action, but being right in the action." The action SPOTA wanted to be in was planning, and particularly housing. While it argued for "total involvement of the neighbourhood," what it actually asked for was more power for itself to engage in community development (Figure 5.7). Specifically, it wanted to provide more affordable housing in the neighbourhood in order to serve residents' needs and to attract former residents back to Strathcona, and it wanted to do so in a way that would build their capacity. To that end, SPOTA proposed instituting a training program to upgrade the skills of residents for employment purposes, for continuing the maintenance of rehabilitated houses, and for developing new houses in the rehabilitation area.[136] Doing all of this would necessitate acquiring cleared land from the province, deciding what form of housing should be built, negotiating with the CMHC for financing, and setting up the legal arrangements so it could act as a housing authority – not to mention hiring the full-time staff to do it. In other words, "being right in the action" required SPOTA to

Figure 5.7 Shirley Chan addresses one of SPOTA's community meetings in the spring of 1973. Note the bilingual agenda on the blackboard. | Hayne Wai, private collection

become a developer, landlord, and neighbourhood government, something that gave some of its own members and outside observers pause.[137]

SPOTA's self-consciousness about exercising power was evident at a meeting of its Housing Committee in July 1973. Reflecting on previous discussions, social worker Jonathan Lau noted that SPOTA had always imagined its role as helping to organize housing initially and then letting go of the project, allowing residents to set up their own organizations. Others wondered if SPOTA should retain and even exercise more control, whether it "should pick the people, set the rules, [and] manage" and ultimately "grow and control the whole community" – in other words, whether it should become the fourth level of government it claimed it was. While Lau noted there was "still the power trip fear" among some in the group, architect Joe Wai, who would design SPOTA's infill and cooperative housing, told the meeting that exercising such power was "what a neighbourhood government is supposed to come to." In "shying away from community control," he asked, were they "all [being] good liberals?"[138]

The way citizen participation was structured in Vancouver empowered SPOTA's executive over other residents and, at the same time, limited the influence it wielded over the three levels of government. Indeed, as SPOTA itself noted in making its case for the "total involvement of the neighbourhood" in planning, despite its participation in the Rehabilitation Project, it was "still not an official decision-making group in the eyes of the governments of Canada, the Province, or City Hall." It noted that the rehabilitation grant "did not go to SPOTA but to the City of Vancouver. It is not administered by us residents but by city hall. Its staff are not our people, meeting our requirements, but City Hall, CMHC requirements. Although we are on the Strathcona Rehabilitation Committee among representatives of three governments, we are often 'put in our place' by the fact that our representatives are paid $25 per meeting so 'what are they kicking about?'"[139]

Indeed, one could argue that, as it was manifested in Vancouver's East Side, citizen participation reinscribed existing hierarchies and structures of power. SPOTA engaged in the hybrid forms of community activism Lee and Bruce analyze, but it also reinforced conventional understandings of authority when it hired its own experts – lawyers and architects – to fight the city's. As well, although SPOTA liked to think of itself as a fourth level of government, it came close to achieving that status only in a specific and time-limited, albeit important, context – namely, in the design and implementation of the rehabilitation program.

Given the reluctance of the city's bureaucrats to consult meaningfully with residents, SPOTA's securing seats on the Strathcona Working Committee and then the Strathcona Rehabilitation Committee was a significant achievement, yet the focus on equal representation masked a fundamental inequity. As one CMHC official observed, of the four groups on the SRC, "SPOTA was the only group without money, although they had a lot of sweat equity and enthusiasm."[140] The injection of government funds to pay SPOTA's representatives and consultants and to provide the group with an office and staffing went some distance to addressing this imbalance, as did the consensus form of decision making the committees adopted. Nevertheless, it did not render the four partners equal.

Moreover, an analysis of the decisions taken by the SRC reveals other limitations on SPOTA's power. While it had a say in the allocation of funds in the areas of housing rehabilitation and improvements to recreation, these represented less than 20 percent of the total funds disbursed, some $760,000. SPOTA had little to no influence in making decisions about above- and below-ground services – things like street lighting and sewer and water mains – that constituted 62.5 percent of total project expenditures, or $2.5 million. Instead, government representatives, relying on technical help from their own bureaucracies, controlled both the implementation of policy and the disbursement of funds in these two costly areas.[141]

Citizen participation thus seemed to be greatest where expenditures were the least, and particularly where they "affected a relatively individualistic aspect of the total project," like renovations to specific houses. As David Ley points out, governments often responded to demands for participation by addressing and fulfilling the particular interests of citizen groups rather than their communal goals, and in so doing they lessened their power. SPOTA members wanted housing rehabilitation, and they got it. Indeed, they even secured a role in shaping the program and allocating its funds. As a result, the three levels of government could, and did, point to this as a successful instance of citizen participation, despite the fact that the larger goal of citizen control and neighbourhood government remained elusive.[142]

As well, the way decision making was structured on the Rehabilitation Committee actually allowed the city to achieve some of what it had wanted when it first proposed urban renewal for Strathcona. Although it was prevented from acquiring properties and clearing the land, it did manage to get the street improvements and the below-ground services that would support a higher population density, something envisioned in the Marsh "sketch scheme" of 1950 and incorporated into the city's plans for redevelopment.[143] While increased density was not something residents wanted, it was consistent with the city's long-standing vision for the area and "the unquestioned assumption [on the part of all three levels of government] that servicing should be done not for the existing level of population density but for much higher densities in the future." Moreover, the potential for increased density increased the value of the land and its potential for real estate development, both of which had been goals of urban renewal. In the view of the consultants who assessed the rehabilitation program, Strathcona represented "a market oriented notion of neighbourhood rehabilitation which ... differed little (if at all) from that of urban renewal."[144]

Interviewed by SPOTA as part of a CMHC-mandated self-evaluation exercise, Steven Rosell, former special assistant to Minister Robert Andras, was invited to assess the association's accomplishments. He hedged a bit and then was blunt, pointing out the limits to the kinds of social change that were possible, given how citizen participation was structured. "I wouldn't say you did as well as you could have done, but you did well," he began. "I'm not saying that you can't accomplish things. What I'm saying is that the model we're using is just worse than useless. It doesn't work." He continued, "I guess that's really my overall impression of this whole Strathcona exercise when you get down to it. It's a really good representation of how that model works: it doesn't work! ... I honestly don't think that you can say that realistically you can expect to get much more than you have got out of it, out of this way of doing things."[145] What the "model" or the "game," as he also called it, of citizen participation did do was allow the state to decentralize certain kinds of decision making. It was a kind of democratic reform that enabled dissenting voices to be heard and even to make a material difference, while at the same time limiting the difference they could make.

More than that, citizen participation, as it was manifested in the Strathcona Rehabilitation Program, also had some of the same kinds of disciplinary effects as were imagined for the rural redevelopment projects discussed in some of the previous chapters. Participation led residents to form connections beyond family and to forge the kinds of affiliations that would lead to political engagement.[146] Social service workers in the area commented on the heightened community awareness and the emergence of an Indigenous leadership group that came in its wake.[147] Those who worked at the Rehabilitation Project's site office argued that participation in the project helped integrate residents, particularly the Chinese, into the broader community: "Nothing in the Chinese people's history in Canada had done as much as the SRP [Strathcona Rehabilitation Project] to expose the Chinese to 'mainstream' Canadian society and bring them in closer contact with it."[148] Historian Wing Chung Ng also notes the "upsurge in local consciousness among Vancouver Chinese" in the wake of SPOTA's formation and success in stopping urban renewal. Three Chinese candidates ran for civic office in the elections of 1968 and 1970, and, although they were unsuccessful, their participation pointed to a significant shift in identity as Canadians, and, I would argue, the disciplinary effects of citizen participation. As a result of the fight over urban renewal, "ethnic Chinese were all now Vancouver residents with civic responsibility to vote their representatives into government."[149]

SPOTA's members echoed this sentiment, observing that the Rehabilitation Project had "brought them a new level of awareness about the government people involved and about the ways in which governments operate. They now saw the people involved as individual persons."[150] Indeed, both the politicians interviewed about the project and the consultants who evaluated it noted how the capacity of SPOTA members, and particularly its executive, grew in ways that speak to how rehabilitation created political subjects. Using language not dissimilar from that of the government agents describing effects of cooperatives on the Inuit, they noted that "previously, most people were unused to and frightened of politics and had roles mainly focused on their responsibilities as housewives, workers, etc. Now, most of the executive are confident in dealing with government."[151]

Thus, while it would be an exaggeration to call citizen participation "the new tyranny," as some scholars have done, its transformative potential in Strathcona spoke to how the liberal state could share power and at the same time reinforce its own.[152]

Conclusion

TOGETHER, THE CASE STUDIES IN THIS BOOK encompass a range of different people who aren't usually brought within the same analytical framework: Inuit in the central Arctic, Newfoundland fishers, Gaspé loggers and farmers, black Haligonians, and the Chinese Canadian residents of Vancouver's East Side. But if historians haven't focused their gaze upon them collectively, Canada certainly did. For all their differences, they were poor people who lived in poor places. As such, they found themselves moved by the state.

During Canada's *trente glorieuses,* authorities used forced relocation to combat rural and urban poverty and to make good on the welfare state's promise of universality. If it couldn't deliver services to the poor, it would deliver the poor to services. While attending to the social security of all citizens benefited many, it was also one of the ways the welfare state exercised power. Uprooting people against their wills so they could realize their potential as individuals captures the violence and contradiction inherent in extending the "liberal order" that Ian McKay argues characterizes Canada.[1] In extending social citizenship in the name of spatial justice, the state ran roughshod over other notions of freedom that were embedded in places like Ennadai Lake, Francois, and Saint-Paulin-Dalibaire. They were invisible to well-meaning outsiders such as Gus Wedderburn, who later admitted he supported the relocation of Africville's residents because he "did not see the flowers," the good that was rooted in that community.[2]

The pursuit of social security through spatial justice didn't end with relocation. Nor did the exercise of state power. People were rarely left alone after being displaced. The communities that received them didn't escape attention, nor did those that rejected relocation when given the choice, like the outports on Fogo Island. In the postwar period, the state's "will to improve" manifested itself in attempts to empower the residents of impoverished regions to determine their own futures, to make good lives for themselves.[3]

"Development" often began with the state deploying expertise to understand the nature and scope of the problem: it marshalled different kinds of specialists to make the poor and the places they lived in legible and thus targets for particular kinds of intervention. In the North, Newfoundland, eastern Quebec, Halifax, and Vancouver, social scientists and planners "rendered society technical" through resource surveys, isolation indices, ethnographies, and estimates of overcrowding, for instance.[4] Where such surveys fell short, the state also relied on expert knowledge of a different kind – that possessed by local people. Africville residents provided Peter MacDonald with information about who owned what in the neighbourhood, thus making it possible for the city to deviate from its standard expropriation process. Similarly, the Strathcona Property Owners and Tenants Association (SPOTA) provided authorities in Vancouver with information on residents' incomes, something crucial to the feasibility of the rehabilitation program.

Whatever the specific problems identified by these technical studies were – an apparent mismatch of resources and population, an obsolete settlement pattern, or blight – the solution seemed to lie in transforming the beliefs and behaviour of the poor. Government bureaucrats and university social scientists believed a "culture of poverty" prevented Inuit, Newfoundlanders, Gaspesians, Africvillers, and Vancouver's East Siders from prospering. While they concerned themselves with providing the poor with the means of empowerment – things like education and access to credit – those involved in development were also fundamentally concerned with instilling confidence and building solidarities that extended beyond family, place, faith, and race. Creating different scales of affect and affiliation would allow people who were strangers to each other to come together and imagine a different future for themselves, to be able to say collectively, as Lloyd Axworthy told an audience of Chinese Canadians, "'This is the kind of community we want, these are the things we want to take place, and this is what we are prepared to do.'"[5]

For those engaged in development in the 1960s and 1970s, participation was the way to cultivate this "capacity to aspire" among the poor and, through it, the kind of modern community government wanted.[6] Rather than having to have the ability to participate in decision making before doing so, they believed the poor would learn by doing. Like their counterparts in international development, the Department of Northern Affairs and National Resources, the Extension Department at Memorial University, the Bureau d'aménagement de l'Est du Québec, the Secretary of State, and the Central Mortgage and Housing Corporation (CMHC) all embraced participation and deliberative democracy as engines of progress.[7] Along with the growth pole theory, these elements were the "travelling rationalities" of development. Regional and community development work focused on "helping people to help themselves," whether by establishing cooperatives, local development committees, or télé-clubs; deploying film and *animation sociale;* or funding cultural and neighbourhood organizations like the Black United Front and SPOTA. Specifically, such work focused on teaching targeted populations to articulate their views, share them, deal with differences, and make choices about how to shape the future they wanted. By making the poor active participants in their own development rather than passive recipients of it, participation democratized decision making.

But according to philosopher Jay Drydyk, participation, empowerment, and democracy could be "fickle friends": one didn't necessarily lead to the others.[8] As we've seen, poverty and social security were entry points for the postwar welfare state to extend its control. Development disciplined as it enabled; it was a technique of governmentality that aimed to inculcate a set of values associated with modernity. Once internalized, these values made people self-regulating and thus facilitated the ongoing imposition of a liberal order.

Being modern meant embracing the market and industrialization by mechanizing, specializing, and working for wages. It also meant actively seeking opportunities, taking risks, and being mobile – like capital – but not rootless. For regional and community development workers, modernization was about instilling a different sense of belonging in the poor, a sense of community that included and transcended place. To be modern was to have a more expansive horizon of aspiration that included region, province, and country; it was to see diversity as a safeguard of rather than a threat to social security.

Paradoxically, however, the kind of development that the liberal welfare state engaged in also involved encouraging the poor to challenge the very authorities that empowered and disciplined them. As Donald Snowden insisted, development projects like the Arctic cooperatives were meant to "make it possible for the Eskimos to give us Hell!"[9] Federal funding for the Black United Front in Nova Scotia was meant to have the same purpose.[10] Such challenges were directed toward and contained within the existing practices and institutions of deliberative democracy and, as the example of citizen participation in rehabilitating Strathcona suggested, accommodating them could even reinforce state power.

Nevertheless, disciplinary power didn't determine outcomes. Inuit saw their experience with cooperatives as a springboard for their politicization, preparation for self-government. Encouraging eastern Quebecers to become "artisans of their destiny" through participatory planning led to the largest mass demonstrations in the history of rural Quebec when the people's plan wasn't implemented. In response to les Opérations Dignité, the provincial government instituted a regime of integrated resource management that included *fermes forestières,* local resource-development corporations, and cooperatives that the people of the region felt served their interests better than did the government's intial proposals.

All this would have pleased Walter Rudnicki, Robert Williamson, Donald Snowden, Roger Guy, Peter MacDonald, and Lloyd Axworthy – people who were agents of the state's project of rule but also progressives, and who saw no contradiction in that. But we know far less about them than we do the other activists of the global sixties, the ones who assailed the institutions of power from the outside rather than walking in their corridors. And finding out about them isn't easy: few of the people involved in carrying out forced relocations and development have spoken or written about their experiences, and fewer still have left behind an archival record – with one notable exception: Walter Rudnicki (1925–2010).[11] We first encountered him when he was dispatched to Eskimo Point (Arviat) in 1958 to assess the starving inland Inuit who had been relocated there. For all its exceptionality, his career encapsulates something of the nature of state power and the character and political culture of postwar Canada.

Rudnicki was a federal civil servant who worked for the Department of Northern Affairs and National Resources, the Department of Indian Affairs, the CMHC, and the Privy Council Office – all institutions implicated in the forced relocations and development projects I've discussed. From the time he entered the public service in 1955, he distinguished himself. Northern Affairs had been created just two years earlier, and when it hired the thirty-year-old it gave him what he described as a "broad and unfocussed mandate."[12] He used it to design a social welfare system for northern Canada, one that many historians argue was a central part of the machinery of postwar colonization, severing the connection Indigenous peoples had with the land and assimilating them. For instance, while Rudnicki recognized the role colonialism had played in creating the situation that led to starvation in the central Arctic, he also insisted that, if Inuit were to have a good life in the modern North, they would have to be "rehabilitated." He meant that in a medical sense; Inuit suffering from the effects of starvation or diseases like tuberculosis would have to be brought back to health. But he also meant it in a broader sense: at rehabilitation centres across the Arctic, which he helped establish, Inuit would be restored for "normal" life, as defined by the values of the time – namely, "punctuality and regular attendance [at work], saving of money, and how to get along with employers."[13]

Rudnicki was proud of what he accomplished in the North, something he considered qualified him for other positions that required policy analysis and planning expertise. After his stint at Northern Affairs, he went to work with Citizenship and Immigration (a larger bureaucracy) as its first director of planning for Indian affairs. At the time, welfare policies for Indigenous peoples were shifting toward defining social welfare entitlements in terms of citizenship. Soon afterwards, he was seconded to the Privy Council Office, where he was made deputy director of the Special Planning Secretariat in charge of waging Canada's "War against Poverty." One of the things he did in that capacity was to help the government of Newfoundland establish a new department to oversee its massive resettlement program, the Department of Community and Social Development. When that project was completed, he became the chief adviser on housing and urban issues to Robert Andras, the minister in charge of housing, and at the same time served as executive director of policy planning at the CMHC in the aftermath of Hellyer's Task Force on Housing and Urban Development, a key juncture in the evolution of Canadian housing policy and urban affairs.[14]

As this brief sketch suggests, by all appearances Walter Rudnicki was the very model of the modern organization man: he was a career bureaucrat, "the man in the grey flannel suit" – or just "the Man," to use the label that became popular in the 1960s to describe authority. But appearances can be deceiving. Rudnicki was a more complex and contradictory figure than his résumé suggests, as was the power he wielded. He believed in using the resources of the state to empower people so they could play a role in making the decisions that shaped their own lives and collective futures. He did this by championing community development. For Rudnicki, the self-determination it fostered was the key to "a good life," and he dedicated himself to helping others achieve it.

While at Citizenship and Immigration, Rudnicki introduced and developed "the concept of consultation with Indians" in relation to the provision of welfare services. This was one of the influences that led to the creation of provincial and national Indigenous organizations that were instrumental in fighting for Aboriginal rights, including the National Indian Brotherhood, a precursor to the Assembly of First Nations.[15] At the CMHC, Rudnicki helped move the agency away from its emphasis on urban renewal and toward investing resources to help poor people rehabilitate the places in which they lived, through two initiatives – the Neighbourhood Improvement Program and the Residential Rehabilitation Assistance Program.[16]

But making a good life for everyone required more than the efforts of the disadvantaged to pull themselves up by their own bootstraps. Rudnicki also believed that Canadians, including his colleagues in government and the civil service, needed to change their attitudes about poverty – starting with becoming aware of its existence and their own negative stereotypes about it. While he was head of the Welfare Division of Northern Affairs, he chastised his colleagues in the Industrial Division for their paternalism, an orientation "based essentially on the well known, well worn and outdated thesis that 'them folks ain't ready yet for responsibility.'"[17] He also leaked information to Farley Mowat about the circumstances that led to the starvation and relocation of Inuit in the central Arctic, information that Mowat used to write *The Desperate People* (1959), a criticism of government neglect of the North and its peoples.[18] In waging war against poverty, under Rudnicki's watch the Special Planning Secretariat at the Privy Council Office funded the National Film Board to make films about poverty that were meant to humanize the poor. These included the ones made by Colin Low and Donald Snowden on Fogo Island that were discussed in Chapter 2. The Newfoundland project became the basis for the NFB's Challenge for Change program, which aimed not only to alter public opinion about poverty but also to transform and mobilize the poor.[19]

As director of planning for Indian Affairs, Rudnicki pushed back against assimilationist arguments about the need for "integration," making the case that what Indigenous peoples, and, more generally, those on the social and economic margins of society, needed first was control over their own affairs and security.[20] By that he meant a secure place from which to engage with the mainstream, where people could be who they were. Security was rooted in making the places people lived socially and economically viable through regional and community development. These places included Indian reserves, but, as we've seen, they also included outports, rural villages, and inner-city neighbourhoods. It was security of the kind that was later represented in the images of houses being towed across Newfoundland's bays or trucked to larger villages in the Gaspé, or captured in the phrase "safe as houses"; it was security of the kind Leon Steed gestured to in making an argument against public housing; it was security of the kind that underlay Shirley Chan's apparent desire for more Chinese to move to Strathcona.[21]

But, as much as people needed to come together to develop their own communities, create their own security, and make their own case for the futures they wanted, Rudnicki also believed government needed to do more to invite participation and, more importantly, to act on what it heard. Neo-liberalism would come later; in the 1960s and 1970s, Rudnicki and his colleagues believed in a big state and an activist one – and was grateful that many Canadians did as well.

Reflecting on his career in the civil service with *New Yorker* writer Edith Iglauer in 1963, one of those colleagues, Donald Snowden, marvelled at the capaciousness of Canadians' sense of community, something signalled by their willingness to pay people like him to design and implement projects aimed at helping individuals who lived almost beyond the pale of most people's imaginations. "What you saw with us was a very insignificant part of what this nation is trying to do in its northern parts," he told her. "You did not hear about the type of person who plays a *really* important part in the north . . . and certainly that most significant of all persons, the man who foots the bill." He continued:

> Whenever I get angry with this country, disturbed by its hibernation, worried by its gentle ways, angry at its vacillations, frustrated by its indecision, and ALL READY TO LEAVE one thing always brings me back to my senses: that in this nation, at this time, there is a genuine interest in our north, and most of all in its people. And I say thanks to those I will never know who foot the bills, not so much because they keep me alive, but because they are willing to spend their money to make it possible for others of this country to learn to come through a time of confusion and change.[22]

As he told his boss, Arthur Laing, the minister of Northern Affairs and National Resources, "A nation which puts such a heavy investment in the productive well-being of a small group of people seems to me to be a decent place to live."[23] The encompassing community of concern that Snowden was so appreciative of was exactly what development was supposed to create among the poor.

If the Canadian public was supportive of the development efforts of Snowden, Rudnicki, and their colleagues, their superiors weren't always equally so. Snowden left the public service in 1965 for what he believed to be the less constraining confines of the university, where he could do the kind of work he wanted to. Rudnicki carried on, but his commitment to citizen participation eventually cost him his job. On learning that Rudnicki had shown an allegedly confidential cabinet document to the leadership of the Native Council of Canada, the president of the CMHC promptly fired him in 1973. He was unconvinced by Rudnicki's argument that, in order to have meaningful input and participation from Indigenous people on housing, they had to know what the government had planned for them.[24] While Rudnicki's firing made national news, his blacklisting didn't, at least not initially. In a confidential memo written two years before the episode that led to his dismissal, the solicitor general named Rudnicki and twenty other bureaucrats as members of an "Extra-Parliamentary Opposition" group "who appear to have as their aim the destruction of the existing political and social structure of Canada."[25]

For many historians, career bureaucrats such as Walter Rudnicki are representative of "the Man," but, for many of his colleagues in the federal government and the public service, Rudnicki wasn't that at all. Instead, he was a disrupter – and probably a royal pain. The Indigenous peoples for whom he worked agreed, and loved him for it. They considered Rudnicki an important ally in their fight for Aboriginal rights, and in many ways to be one of them. In 1983 the Stoney Nation in Alberta honoured him in a ceremony in which he was given a chief's headdress and the name Wanbli-Waha Cunka, or Eagle Shield.[26]

Rudnicki won a wrongful dismissal case, was awarded damages by the court, and eventually returned to the federal civil service in 1983, ten years after he was fired. He considered his re-hiring a further exoneration of his position, and until he retired, and well afterwards, he continued to see his work as "helping people to help themselves." In many ways, he remained the man described in one of his first job evaluations. According to his supervisor at the Crease Clinic, a mental health facility at which he worked before joining the civil service, Rudnicki was someone "sincerely interested" in "the provision of all social services for those in need and in the necessary social action to implement this." However, he was "somewhat intolerant of obstacles and inclined at times to think in terms of using pressure methods to overcome barriers if he considers that the goal warrants it."[27]

Walter Rudnicki was a man who coloured inside the lines while moving them. For those interested in how "state power" was exercised, understanding how he and people like him navigated a world of imperfect choices is crucial. Many forces shaped the path they took, perhaps the most obvious being the racist and classist assumptions about what constituted a good life. As influential as those assumptions were, that path was also lit by hope. Rudnicki's actions over the course of his career and those of people like Snowden, Williamson, Guy, MacDonald, and Axworthy speak to the power of hope, one of the key, yet largely unacknowledged, influences shaping postwar Canada.

As much as this is an era we associate with affluence and anxiety, growth and containment, it was also a time when people believed governments could and, more importantly, should change the lives of their citizens for the better, when politicians could talk about "eliminating poverty" and "the right to a good life" and be believed. It was a time when those who wanted to change the world could imagine doing so from within a government bureaucracy or a university. Rudnicki was one such person, as was his colleague and friend Robert Williamson. Then an amateur anthropologist, he leapt at the chance to leave his comfortable post at the National Museum in Ottawa for a position as a welfare office in Rankin Inlet in the late 1950s because "there was so much to be done" and "one had to respond to one's responsibility to make use of one's knowledge."[28]

This was also a time when governments invested in expertise, most notably from the social sciences, and in citizen participation as vehicles for policy-making. Indeed, in the postwar period, one of the ways the state became more present in the lives of the poor was through interventions aimed at, among other things, encouraging them to put limits on its power.

The hope evinced by the people I've introduced you to wasn't just a feeling, a desire, or an aspiration. Instead, it was a place from which to assess the world critically, one whose power was rooted in three historically specific things: a conviction that the key to eliminating poverty was to unlock the potential in people; a belief in the effectiveness of state intervention, that "government could succeed," as the environmental advocate Gus Speth said of the '60s; and faith in the transformative power of knowledge.[29] Indeed, hope generated knowledge – about, for instance, the Inuit and their capacity for change, social relations in outport Newfoundland, the mentality of rural Quebecers, and the experience of inner-city residents relocated by urban renewal. Because this knowledge was the basis for action, hope didn't just inspire a critique of poverty and government policy, it was also a creative force for change. Hope was power.

Thinking about hope historically, as a perspective from which people saw, evaluated, and took action in the world in which they lived, helps to characterize the postwar state and the postwar years. But equally importantly, it helps historicize ourselves. State-sponsored relocation isn't a dead letter. Economic exigency has led the government of Newfoundland to reactivate a version of its resettlement program as a cost-saving measure. The multiple challenges confronting Indigenous peoples on northern reserves has led some commentators to argue that their future lies in abandoning their communities. The ensuing debates are as furious as the ones from fifty years ago, and in many ways echo them. Some of the most resonant voices remind us that, for many people, a good life is a place. When places disappear, so too does that life. Having voted to shut down their community, the people of Williams Harbour in Labrador nevertheless insisted on re-shingling their church before leaving in November 2017. As one commentator noted, "The ties to this community run deep. Everyone has family buried on the island and they themselves want to be buried next to them." Until that time, Cliff Russell will be fishing its waters every summer, "making a living, keeping the name on the map."[30]

For Veronica Broomfield of St. Brendan's, an outport of just over one hundred that's serviced by a ferry at a yearly cost of $6 million, the provincial government's arguments for resettlement ignore what for her is Newfoundland's identity and reality: it's an island. In her view, she and her neighbours have the same right to a good life as other islanders. "If you cut out rural Newfoundland, there will be no Newfoundland," she insists. "We live in Newfoundland, and Newfoundland is an island ... I'm not worried about what it costs people to live in Burnside [on the Eastport peninsula in Bonavista Bay]. Or what it costs people to live in St. John's. So why are they worried about us?"[31]

When *Maclean's* columnist Scott Gilmore suggested in 2016 that the solution to the poverty and misery of some northern reserves was for

Indigenous people to be assisted to move to cities in southern Canada, the critical response was immediate and echoed arguments made most explicitly during the Africville relocation, namely, that the very conditions that justified removal had been created by the state, and more fundamentally by systemic racism and colonialism. Moreover, arguments like these ignored the fact that urbanization is no cure-all. Indigenous peoples who live in Canada's cities experience the worst levels of poverty in the country.[32] The statistics that the government of Canada found brutal fifty years ago have not improved appreciably.

When he became the first minister of Regional Economic Expansion in the 1970s, Jean Marchand argued that his department's job, and that of the federal government, was to reduce regional inequality so everyone didn't have to live in Toronto.[33] But, beyond that, he and his colleagues struggled to determine how far the government should go in upholding the right to a good life. Then, as now, these are political questions that reflect the extent to which we think the state should intervene and the extent to which we believe human potential is realized in place and are willing to pay for its realization through our taxes.

But, more than that, our answers to these questions reflect our expectations for the state, the commitments we make to each other through the state, and ultimately the boundaries of our community of concern – who "we" consider ourselves to be. They reflect our hope, the standpoint from which we see the world. As Kevin O'Reilly's comments make clear, those expectations, commitments, and boundaries have changed, and so too has the hope that sustains them. Reflecting on the pressure being brought to bear on the people of St. Brendan's to move, he observed, "There's no way to defend your home, you know, if they look at you as an expense."[34]

We've travelled a long way from thinking about the state and its agents as forces for positive change, not just managing expenses. The distance only makes the differences – the hope and the bureaucratic activism – stand out all the more clearly as markers of a distinct period in the political culture and history of Canada.

Notes

Introduction

1 Farley Mowat and John de Visser, *This Rock within the Sea: A Heritage Lost* (Boston: Little, Brown, 1968). The ellipses are in the original. The book is unpaginated. The quote is from the chapter entitled "The Heritage."
2 Farley Mowat, "People of the Coasts," *Atlantic Advocate* 57, 11 (1967): 49–50.
3 Mowat and de Visser, *This Rock within the Sea,* [2].
4 Key academic works include Frank J. Tester and Peter Kulchyski, *Tammarniit (Mistakes): Inuit Relocation in the Eastern Arctic, 1939–1963* (Vancouver: UBC Press, 1994); Raymond B. Blake, *Lions or Jellyfish: Newfoundland-Ottawa Relations since 1957* (Toronto: University of Toronto Press, 2015), chaps. 3 and 4; Bruno Jean, ed., *Le BAEQ revisité: un nouveau regard sur la première expérience de développement régional au Québec* (Laval, QC: Presses de l'Université Laval, 2016); Jennifer J. Nelson, *Razing Africville: A Geography of Racism* (Toronto: University of Toronto Press, 2008); and Jo-Anne Lee, "Gender, Ethnicity, and Hybrid Forms of Community-Based Urban Activism in Vancouver, 1957–1978: The Strathcona Story Revisited," *Gender, Place and Culture* 14, 4 (2007): 381–407.
5 Frédéric Laugrand, Jarich Oosten, and David Serkoak, "'The Saddest Time of My Life': Relocating the Ahiarmiut from Ennadai Lake (1950–1958)," *Polar Record* 46, 2 (2010): 117–18.
6 All quotations are from *Chez nous, c'est chez nous,* directed by Marcel Carrière (Ottawa: National Film Board of Canada, 1972) and translated by the author.
7 *Remember Africville,* directed by Shelagh Mackenzie (Ottawa: National Film Board of Canada, 1991).
8 "Hellyer Disgusted by Poverty Tales," *Vancouver Sun,* 8 November 1968, and *Vancouver Province,* 8 November 1968, 6, cited in Michael Bruce, "'A New Breed of Group': Community Activism in Vancouver's Strathcona Neighbourhood, 1968–1972" (master's thesis, University of British Columbia, 2005), 24.
9 E.P. Thompson, *The Making of the English Working Class* (New York: Pantheon Books, 1964), 12.
10 T.H. Marshall, "Citizenship and Social Class," in *Citizenship and Social Class,* ed. T.H. Marshall and Tom Bottomore (London: Pluto Press, 1992), 8.

11 Quoted in R.A.J. Phillips, *Canada's North* (Toronto: Macmillan, 1967), 169.

12 See Smallwood's 1946 speech at http://www.revparl.ca/english/issue.asp?param=141&art=928.

13 See Blake, *Lions or Jellyfish,* chaps. 3 and 4.

14 Gordon Stephenson, *A Redevelopment Study of Halifax, 1957* (Halifax: Corporation of the City of Halifax, 1957), 27–28.

15 Pierre Elliott Trudeau, *Federalism and the French Canadians* (New York: St. Martin's Press, 1968), 147.

16 Ralph R. Krueger, "Regional Disparities and Regional Development in Canada," in *Regional Patterns: Disparities and Development,* ed. Ralph R. Krueger, Robert M. Irving, and Colin Vincent (Toronto: Canadian Studies Foundation and Canadian Association of Geographers, 1975), 18.

17 The literature on the attempts to deal with regional inequality in Canada is large. Some places to begin are Anthony G.S. Careless, *Initiative and Response: The Adaptation of Canadian Federalism to Regional Economic Development* (Montreal and Kingston: McGill-Queen's University Press and the Institute of Public Administration of Canada, 1977), chaps. 2 and 3; Benjamin Higgins and Donald J. Savoie, "Canada," chap. 16 in *Regional Development Theories and Their Application* (New Brunswick, NJ: Transaction Publishers, 1995), especially 276–80; and P.E. Bryden, "'Pooling Our Resources': Equalization and the Origins of Regional Universality, 1937–1957," *Canadian Public Administration* 57, 3 (2014): 401–18.

18 Bryden, "'Pooling Our Resources,'" 402–3, 416. Section 36 of the Constitution Act, 1982 reads in part: "Parliament and the [provincial] legislatures, together with the government of Canada and the provincial governments, are committed to (a) promoting equal opportunities for the well-being of Canadians; (b) furthering economic development to reduce disparity in opportunities; and (c) providing essential public services of reasonable quality to all Canadians." See Constitution Act, 1982 at http://laws-lois.justice.gc.ca/eng/Const/page-16.html.

19 Economic Council of Canada, *Second Annual Review: Towards Sustained and Balanced Economic Growth* (Ottawa: Queen's Printer, December 1965), 100–9, and Krueger, "Regional Disparities," 5–10.

20 Economic Council of Canada, *Second Annual Review,* 105.

21 See Higgins and Savoie, "Canada." Despite the fact that relocation was part of many regional development projects, there has been little historical work exploring this aspect of such projects. An exception is Ronald Rudin's work on the establishment of Kouchibouguac National Park. Established in 1969 as part of a regional development program for New Brunswick, it entailed the forced relocation of some 1,200 residents. See his *Kouchibouguac: Removal, Resistance, and Remembrance at a Canadian National Park* (Toronto: University of Toronto Press, 2016).

22 James N. McCrorie, *ARDA: An Experiment in Development Planning* (Ottawa: Canadian Council on Rural Development, 1969), 15.

23 James C. Scott, *Seeing like a State: How Certain Schemes to Improve the Human Condition Have Failed* (New Haven, CT: Yale University Press, 1998).

24 R.A.J. Phillips, *The Elimination of Poverty* (Ottawa: Special Planning Secretariat, Privy Council Office, 1967), 3. He estimates that poverty afflicted one in four Canadians. The Economic Council of Canada put the figure at one in five. See Economic Council of Canada, *Fifth Annual Review: The Challenge of Growth and Change* (Ottawa: Queen's Printer, September 1968), 110.

25 Economic Council of Canada, *Fifth Annual Review,* 112.

26 Ibid., 121n2.

27 Michael Harrington, *The Other America: Poverty in the United States* (1962; New York: Penguin Books, 1981), 3–5.

28 Ken Lefolii, "Why Canada Too Should Declare War on Chronic Poverty," *Maclean's*, 22 February 1964, 4; David Suderman, "Poverty: A National Challenge," *Canadian Business*, May 1966, 67.

29 John Porter, *The Vertical Mosaic: An Analysis of Social Class and Power in Canada* (Toronto: University of Toronto Press, 1965), and Rick Helmes-Hayes, *Measuring the Mosaic: An Intellectual Biography of John Porter* (Toronto: University of Toronto Press, 2010), chap. 7.

30 A. Alan Borovoy, "Human Rights in Canada," *Canadian Labour*, December 1967, 5; Phillips, *The Elimination of Poverty*, 5; Economic Council of Canada, *Fifth Annual Review*, 103; and "What the Ministers Are Saying about Poverty," *Canadian Welfare*, March–April 1970, 18.

31 Canada, Speech from the Throne, 5 April 1965, 4, at https://www.poltext.org/sites/poltext.org/files/discours/tcan1965.pdf.

32 Canada, Privy Council Office, Special Planning Secretariat, *Fighting Poverty in 1966* (Ottawa: Queen's Printer, August 1967), 4.

33 For more on the SPS, see David Tough, "'At Last! The Government's War on Poverty Explained': The Special Planning Secretariat, the Welfare State, and the Rhetoric of Poverty in the 1960s," *Journal of the Canadian Historical Association* 25, 1 (2014): 177–200.

34 As the Special Senate Committee on Poverty noted, "The poor have a right to participate, to be heard, and, indeed, to share in the organization and administration of programs created for them ...; for too long the poor have been people to whom and for whom things were done by others." Canada, Senate, *Highlights from the Report of the Special Senate Committee on Poverty* (Ottawa: Information Canada, 1971), 14. On the need for more research, see Senate of Canada, *Poverty in Canada: Report of the Special Senate Committee on Poverty* (Ottawa: Information Canada, 1971), pt. 2, chap. 3. Also see Economic Council of Canada, *Fifth Annual Review*, 132.

35 Tania Murray Li, *The Will to Improve: Governmentality, Development, and the Practice of Politics* (Durham, NC: Duke University Press, 2007).

36 Emma Crewe and Richard Axelby, *Anthropology and Development: Culture, Morality and Politics in a Globalised World* (Cambridge: Cambridge University Press, 2013), 4.

37 Ibid., 6.

38 Michael E. Latham, "Introduction: Modernization, International History, and the Cold War World," in *Staging Growth: Modernization, Development, and the Global Cold War*, ed. David Engerman, Nils Gilman, Mark H. Haefle, and Michael E. Latham (Amherst: University of Massachusetts Press, 2003), 2.

39 Nils Gilman, "Modernization Theory: The Highest Stage of American Intellectual History," in Engerman et al., *Staging Growth*, 62–70.

40 Daniel Immerwahr, *Thinking Small: The United States and the Lure of Community Development* (Cambridge, MA: Harvard University Press, 2015), 4.

41 Mark H. Haefle, "Walt Rostow's Stages of Economic Growth: Ideas and Action," in Engerman et al., *Staging Growth*, 81–83.

42 Crewe and Axelby, *Anthropology and Development*, 31–38; and James Ferguson, "Anthropology and Its Evil Twin: 'Development' in the Constitution of a Discipline," chap. 7 in *The Anthropology of Development and Globalization: From Classical Political Economy to Contemporary Neoliberalism*, ed. Marc Edelman and Angelique Haugerud (Malden, MA: Blackwell, 2005).

43 Cited in Latham, "Introduction," 1.

44 Ibid., 7.

45 Paul C. Rosier, "Crossing New Boundaries: American Indians and Twentieth Century US Foreign Policy," *Diplomatic History* 39, 5 (2015): 955–66.

46 David Meren, "'Commend Me the Yak': The Colombo Plan, the Inuit of Ungava, and 'Developing' Canada's North," *Histoire sociale / Social History* 50, 102 (2017): 368–69.

47 Oscar Lewis, "The Culture of Poverty," in *On Understanding Poverty: Perspectives from the Social Sciences,* ed. Daniel P. Moynihan (New York: Basic Books, 1969), 189–92.

48 Economic Council of Canada, *Fifth Annual Review,* 104.

49 "Challenge and Response, Part II," *Labour Gazette* 65, 12 (1965): 1171–72.

50 See R.A.J. Phillips, *Community Development: The Principles* (Ottawa: Special Planning Secretariat, Privy Council Office, 1966).

51 The Sauvé quote on community development is from United Nations, *Community Development and National Development: Report by an Ad Hoc Group of Experts Appointed by the Secretary-General of the United Nations* (New York: United Nations Department of Economic and Social Affairs, 1963), 4.

52 Timothy Mitchell, *Rule of Experts: Egypt, Techno-Politics, Modernity* (Berkeley: University of California Press, 2002); and Li, *The Will to Improve.*

53 Hugh L. Keenleyside, *Memoirs of Hugh L. Keenleyside,* vol. 2, *On the Bridge of Time* (Toronto: McClelland and Stewart, 1982), 309.

54 See Sarah Bonesteel, *Canada's Relationship with Inuit: A History of Policy and Program Development* (Ottawa: Prepared by Public History, Inc. for the Department of Indian and Northern Affairs Canada, 2006); Tester and Kulchyski, *Tammarniit;* David Damas, *Arctic Migrants / Arctic Villagers: The Transformation of Inuit Settlement in the Central Arctic* (Montreal and Kingston: McGill-Queen's University Press, 2004); and Alan Marcus, *Relocating Eden: The Image and Politics of Inuit Exile in the Canadian Arctic* (Hanover, NH: University Press of New England, 1995).

55 Frances Abele, "Canadian Contradictions: Forty Years of Northern Political Development," *Arctic* 40, 4 (1987): 312.

56 Damas, *Arctic Migrants;* and Tester and Kulchyski, *Tammarniit.*

57 John David Hamilton, *Arctic Revolution: Social Change in the Northwest Territories, 1935–1994* (Toronto: Dundurn Press, 1994).

58 Abele, "Canadian Contradictions," 312.

59 Hamilton, *Arctic Revolution,* 93.

60 Ibid., 65.

61 David Craig and Doug Porter, *Development beyond Neoliberalism: Governance, Poverty Reduction and Political Economy* (Abingdon, UK: Routledge, 2006), 120.

62 Alfonso Gumucio Dagron and Thomas Tufte, eds., *Communication for Social Change Anthology: Historical and Contemporary Readings* (South Orange, NJ: Communication for Social Change Consortium, 2006), 488–94.

63 Metra Consultants Ltée, *Relocalisation de population dans l'Est du Québec: étude critique d'une expérience pilote, proposition d'une equisse de programme général* (Montreal: Metra Consultants, November 1970), 18.

64 Bureau d'aménagement de l'Est du Québec, *Development Plan for the Pilot Region: Lower St. Lawrence, Gaspé, and Îles-de-la-Madeleine – A Summary* (Ottawa: Rural Development Branch, Department of Forestry and Rural Development, June 1967), 1.

65 Pierre Filion, "The Neighbourhood Improvement Program in Montréal and Toronto: Two Approaches to Publicly Sponsored Upgrading," in *The Changing Canadian Inner City: Essays on Canadian Urban Process and Form,* vol. 4, ed. Trudi E. Bunting and Pierre Filion (Waterloo, ON: Department of Geography, University of Waterloo, 1988), 88.

66 Leonard Marsh, *Report on a Demonstration Slum-clearance and Urban Rehabilitation Project in a Key Central Area in Vancouver* (Vancouver: University of British Columbia, 1950), 23.

67 Rhodri Windsor-Liscombe, "Leonard Marsh and the Vancouver Modern," *Architecture and Ideas* 1, 1 (1996): 40–51.

68 Zachary Spicer, "The Rise and Fall of the Ministry of State for Urban Affairs: A Re-Evaluation," *Canadian Political Science Review* 5, 2 (2011): 121.
69 Ian McKay, "The Liberal Order Framework: A Prospectus for a Reconnaissance of Canadian History," *Canadian Historical Review* 81, 4 (2000): 624 (emphasis in original).

Chapter 1: "No More Canadians Will Starve!"

1 The key academic works dealing with the forced relocation of Inuit in Canada are Sarah Bonesteel, *Canada's Relationship with Inuit: A History of Policy and Program Development* (Ottawa: Public History, Inc., for Indian and Northern Affairs Canada, June 2006); David Damas, *Arctic Migrants, Arctic Villagers: The Transformation of Inuit Settlement in the Central Arctic* (Montreal and Kingston: McGill-Queen's University Press, 2002); Frédéric Laugrand, Jarich Oosten, and David Serkoak, "'The Saddest Time of My Life': Relocating the Ahiarmiut from Ennadai Lake (1950–1958)," *Polar Record* 46, 2 (2010): 113–35; Alan Marcus, *Relocating Eden: The Image and Politics of Inuit Exile in the Canadian Arctic* (Hanover, NH: University Press of New England, 1995); and Frank James Tester and Peter Kulchyski, *Tammarniit (Mistakes): Inuit Relocation in the Eastern Arctic, 1939–63* (Vancouver: UBC Press, 1994).
2 Sandra Martin, "Richard Harrington, Photographer, 1911–2005," *Globe and Mail,* 13 October 2005, S7.
3 Richard Harrington, *Padlei Diary, 1950: An Account of the Padleimiut Eskimo in the Keewatin District West of Hudson Bay during the Early Months of 1950,* ed. Edmund Carpenter (New York: Rock Foundation, 2000), 28, 66.
4 Richard Harrington, *The Face of the Arctic: A Cameraman's Story in Words and Pictures of Five Journeys into the Far North* (New York: Abelard Schuman, 1952), 261, 237.
5 James C. Scott, *Seeing like a State: How Certain Schemes to Improve the Human Condition Have Failed* (New Haven, CT: Yale University Press, 1998), 2.
6 Bonesteel, *Canada's Relationship with Inuit,* 38–39.
7 Farley Mowat, *People of the Deer* (Boston: Little Brown, 1952).
8 Canada, House of Commons, *Debates, First Session: Twenty-Second Parliament, 2–3 Elizabeth II,* vol. 1, *1953–54* (Ottawa: Queen's Printer, 1954), 773.
9 R. Quinn Duffy, *The Road to Nunavut: The Progress of the Eastern Arctic Inuit since the Second World War* (Montreal and Kingston: McGill-Queen's University Press, 1988), 16.
10 Alvin Finkel, *Social Policy and Practice in Canada: A History* (Waterloo, ON: Wilfrid Laurier University Press, 2006), chaps. 7–11. Also see Liza Piper, "From Subsistence to Nutrition: The Canadian State's Involvement in Food and Diet in the North, 1900–1970," in *Ice Blink: Navigating Northern Environmental History,* ed. Stephen Bocking and Brad Martin (Calgary: University of Calgary Press, 2017), 181–222.
11 For an overview of the welfare measures that were undertaken for the Inuit, see Damas, *Arctic Migrants,* chap. 5.
12 Press release, "Eskimos Fly to New Hunting Grounds," 24 May 1957, cited in Tester and Kulchyski, *Tammarniit,* 220.
13 Laugrand, Oosten, and Serkoak, "'The Saddest Time of My Life.'"
14 For a discussion of the starvations, see Tester and Kulchyski, *Tammarniit,* chaps. 5–7. They are also covered more briefly and in a different interpretive frame in Damas, *Arctic Migrants,* 87, 91–92. "State of nature" is from Frances Abele, "Canadian Contradictions: Forty Years of Northern Political Development," *Arctic* 40, 4 (1987): 312.
15 Quoted in R.A.J. Phillips, *Canada's North* (Toronto: Macmillan, 1967), 169.
16 Cited in C.S. Mackinnon, "The 1958 Government Policy Reversal in Keewatin," in *For Purposes of Dominion: Essays in Honour of Morris Zaslow,* ed. Kenneth S. Coates and William R. Morrison (North York, ON: Captus University Publications, 1989), 166.

17 Damas, *Arctic Migrants.*

18 In February 1958, Northern Affairs flew thirty-three starvation survivors from the Henik Lake relocation to Eskimo Point. Later that year, in June, it relocated the survivors of the Garry Lake famine to Baker Lake. Later in the year, a total of seventy Inuit were moved again, to Rankin Inlet. This latter group consisted of the famine survivors as well as other Garry Lake families who were resident in Baker Lake. See Laugrand, Oosten, and Serkoak, "'The Saddest Time of My Life,'" 126; Tester and Kulchyski, *Tammarniit,* 290; and F.G. Vallee, *Kabloona and Eskimo in the Central Keewatin* (Ottawa: Northern Coordination and Research Centre, Department of Northern Affairs and National Resources, 1962), 8.

19 Gordon Robertson, "The Future of the North," *North* 8, 2 (1961): 13.

20 Gordon Robertson, "Administration for Development in Northern Canada: The Growth and Evolution of Government," *Canadian Public Administration* 3, 4 (1960): 355 and 362.

21 P. Whitney Lackenbauer and Daniel Heidt, introduction to *The Advisory Committee on Northern Development: Context and Meeting Minutes, 1948–66* (Calgary and Waterloo, ON: Centre for Military and Strategic Studies, University of Calgary, and Centre on Foreign Policy and Federalism, St. Jerome's University, 2015).

22 In 1954, the in-house publication for the Department of Northern Affairs and National Resources noted that thirteen Inuit from Chesterfield Inlet were employed in surface work at the North Rankin Nickel Mine. See *Northern Affairs Bulletin* 1, 5 (1954): 6. On the North Rankin mine, see Arn Keeling and Patricia Boulter, "From Igloo to Mine Shaft: Inuit Labour and Memory at the Rankin Inlet Nickel Mine," in *Mining and Communities in Northern Canada: History, Politics, and Memory,* ed. Arn Keeling and John Sandlos (Calgary: University of Calgary Press, 2015), 35–58.

23 "Report: Field Trip to Eskimo Point, 1958," Appendix C, "Thematic Apperception Test," 2, University of Manitoba Archives and Special Collections (UMASC), Walter Rudnicki fonds, MSS 331, box 81, folder 1.

24 "Eskimo Rehabilitation Centre: Justification for Welfare Officer II Position," n.d. [1959], attached to Memorandum from R.J. Green, Superintendent, Eskimo Rehabilitation Centre, for Mr. Delaute, re: staff estimates 1960–61, Frobisher Bay, NWT, 26 May 1959, UMASC, Walter Rudnicki fonds, MSS 331, box 98, folder 2.

25 "Rehabilitation Case Example," n.d., UMASC, Walter Rudnicki fonds, MSS 331, box 98, folder 2. For an overview of Frobisher Bay and the rehabilitation work done there, see *An Introduction to Frobisher Bay, Baffin Island* (Ottawa: Department of Northern Affairs and National Resources, Editorial and Information Division, 1962). In addition to Frobisher Bay and Itivia, Keewatin, there was a third rehabilitation centre at Inuvik. The Frobisher one appears to have been the largest and the one in operation for the longest. It's hard to find out much about the Inuvik rehabilitation centre beyond the fact that it existed. The Department of Northern Affairs and National Resources established the Frobisher rehabilitation in 1956 as "a 'half-way house' for Eskimos returning north after prolonged medical care in southern Canada." It was closed in 1964. See Sheila Keith MacBain, "The Evolution of Frobisher Bay as a Major Settlement in the Eastern Arctic" (master's thesis, McGill University, 1970), 57 and 59. The Inuvik rehabilitation centre is mentioned in Indian and Northern Affairs Canada, *The Changing Eskimo* (Ottawa: Department of Northern Affairs and National Resources, 1964), 15.

26 Walter Rudnicki, "Report: Field Trip to Eskimo Point, March 1958, Findings," 1, UMASC, Walter Rudnicki fonds, MSS 331, box 81, folder 1.

27 Ibid., 2.

28 Robertson to E.L. Harvie, 17 June 1957, cited in Richard J. Diubaldo, "You Can't Keep the Native Native," in Coates and Morrison, *For Purposes of Dominion,* 180.

29 For an overview, see Katy Gardner and David Lewis, *Anthropology, Development and the Post-Modern Challenge* (London: Pluto Press, 1996).

30 V.F. Valentine and J.R. Lotz, "Northern Co-ordination and Research Centre of the Canadian Department of Northern Affairs and National Resources," *Polar Record* 11 (1963): 419–22.

31 Memorandum for Mr. A.C. Wimberley from F.A.G. Carter, for the Director, Re: Transfer of R.G.H. Williamson to Rankin Inlet, n.d. [March 1958], University of Saskatchewan Archives (USA), Robert G. Williamson fonds, MG 216, box 3, file Transfer of Williamson to Rankin Inlet.

32 The information in this paragraph is from R.G. Williamson, "A Personal Retrospective on Anthropology Applied in the Arctic," 1988, and the biography that is part of the finding aid for the Robert G. Williamson fonds at the University of Saskatchewan Archives. See USA, Robert G. Williamson fonds, MG 216, box 4, and http://scaa.usask.ca/gallery/northern/en_finding_aid_display.php?filename=williamson&title=Robert%20Williamson%20fonds. Also see "Robert Williamson (1931–2012)," *Etudes Inuits / Inuit Studies* 36, 1 (2012): 231–33.

33 See James Ferguson, "Anthropology and Its Evil Twin: 'Development' in the Constitution of the Discipline," in *International Development and the Social Sciences: Essays on the History and Politics of Knowledge*, ed. Frederick Cooper and Randall M. Packard (Berkeley: University of California Press, 1997), 150–75. For a Canadian example, see Peter Kulchyski, "Anthropology in the Service of the State: Diamond Jenness and Canadian Indian Policy," *Journal of Canadian Studies* 28, 2 (1993): 21–50.

34 Robert G. Williamson, *Eskimo Underground: Socio-Cultural Change in the Canadian Central Arctic* (Uppsala: Institutionen för allmän och jämförande etnografi vid Uppsala Universitet, 1974).

35 David D. Gow, "Anthropology and Development: Evil Twin or Moral Narrative?" *Human Organization* 61, 4 (2002): 299.

36 Williamson, "A Personal Retrospective," 46.

37 Keeling and Boulter, "From Igloo to Mine Shaft," 39–42.

38 "Northwest Territories Newest Mine," *Northern Affairs Bulletin* 1, 2 (1954): 51; "Vocational Vignettes," *Northern Affairs Bulletin* 2, 9 (1955): 3–4 and *Northern Affairs Bulletin* 3, 2 (1956): 3–4; and "Vocational Training for Eskimos," *Northern Affairs Bulletin* 4, 3 (1957): 5. For Inuit involvement in industrial employment, see Edward R. Weick, "The Eskimos of Canada's Northwest Territories: A Problem of Development" (master's thesis, University of Ottawa, 1971), chap. 5.

39 R.G. Williamson, "Eskimos in the Modern World," 1970, 9, USA, Robert G. Williamson fonds, MG 216, box 24, file I7-1, International Nickel Co.

40 Mines Staff, "North Rankin Nickel Mines," *Canadian Mining Journal* 70, 8 (1957): 97.

41 Williamson, "A Personal Retrospective," 46–47. Williamson went on to make the Rankin miners the subject of his doctoral research. For his comments on the work rotation system at the mine, see Williamson, *Eskimo Underground*, 116–19.

42 Robert G. Williamson, "The Notion of Cultural Commuting: Evaluation of Short-Term Feasibility," n.d., USA, Robert G. Williamson fonds, MG 216, box 12.

43 "Shooting Script for a Canada Carries On Film on the Rankin Inlet Community," National Film Board of Canada Archives, AI 2015-2016-1, 51.

44 Weick, "The Eskimos of Canada's Northwest Territories," 142.

45 Northern Service Officer D.W. Grant had reported that the mine could close by the end of the 1959 shipping season. Memorandum for Mr. C.M. Bolger, Administrator of the Arctic, from D.W. Grant, Re: North Rankin Nickel Mines, Ltd., 16 March 1959, 1, Library and Archives Canada (LAC), RG 85, vol. 1962, file A-1009-10/184.

46 D.M. Brack and D. McIntosh, *Keewatin Mainland Economic Survey and Regional Appraisal* (Ottawa: Projects Section, Industrial Division, Department of Northern Affairs and National

Resources, March 1963), 135; and Confidential [no title; recommendations of the Keewatin Conference, 1962], vol. 6, 1, LAC, RG 85, vol. 1148, file 1000/184. R.G. Robertson, the deputy minister of Northern Affairs and National Resources, said 560, not 520, Inuit were affected by the mine shutdown. R.G. Robertson, Deputy Minister, Memorandum for the Minister re: Keewatin Region Crisis, 19 April 1962, LAC, Donald Snowden fonds, MG 31 D163, vol. 1.

47 "Rankin Inlet Questionnaires: Post Close-Down Interviews, Genealogies," USA, Robert G. Williamson fonds, MG 216, box 32.

48 A numerical breakdown of the survey results is given in Williamson, *Eskimo Underground*, 131.

49 "Rankin Inlet Questionnaires: Post Close-Down Interviews, Genealogies."

50 For overviews of these relocations, see D.S. Stevenson, *Problems of Eskimo Relocation for Industrial Employment: A Preliminary Study* (Ottawa: Northern Science Research Group, Department of Indian Affairs and Northern Development, 1968); R.G. Williamson, *Eskimo Relocation in Canada* (Saskatoon: University of Saskatchewan, Institute of Northern Studies, 1974).

51 Speech by the Honorable Jean Chrétien, PC, MP, Minister of Indian Affairs and Northern Development, to the Yellowknife Board of Trade, Monday, 10 November 1969, 3, Prince of Wales Northern Heritage Centre (PWNHC), Alexander Stevenson fonds, N-1992-023, box 25, file 9; A. Stevenson, "Sociological Aspects: Northern Development," presented at the Arctic Petroleum Operators Association Arctic Environmental Workshop, Gulf Theatre, Gulf Oil Building, Calgary, 27–28 October 1971, ibid., box 23, file 7.

52 Robert C. Dailey and Lois A. Dailey, *The Eskimo of Rankin Inlet: A Preliminary Report* (Ottawa: Northern Coordination and Research Centre, Department of Northern Affairs and National Resources, 1961), 94–95.

53 Jean Malaurie, *Hummocks: Journeys and Inquiries among the Canadian Inuit,* trans. Peter Feldstein (Montreal: McGill-Queen's University Press, 2007), 321, 325. The Inuit interviewed in 2011 by Arn Keeling and Patricia Boulter gave a more complex portrait of their experience working in the North Rankin mine. Rather than being the story of "deculturation," their experience was in many ways one of enculturation: mining and the mine were incorporated into their identity as Inuit. See Keeling and Boulter, "From Igloo to Mine Shaft."

54 Williamson, *Eskimo Relocation,* 54.

55 Stevenson, *Problems of Eskimo Relocation,* 8.

56 Restricted – Keewatin Conference, 22–28 February 1962, NCRC Community Planning Group, LAC, R216-128-4-E, vol. 1660, file part 1, NR4/2-9, 13.

57 Nelson H.H. Graburn, "The Discovery of Inuit Art: James Houston – Animateur," *Inuit Art Quarterly* 2, 2 (1987): 3–5.

58 Restricted – Keewatin Conference, 22–28 February, 13.

59 My summary of Northern Affairs' arts and crafts initiative for the Keewatin is drawn from the following: Stacey Neale, "Rankin Inlet Ceramics, Part 1: A Study in Development and Influence," *Inuit Art Quarterly* 14, 1 (1999): 4–17; "The Rankin Inlet Ceramics Project, Part Two: The Quest for Authenticity and Market Share," *Inuit Art Quarterly* 14, 2 (1999): 6–16; Stacey Neale, "The Rankin Inlet Ceramics Project: A Study in Development and Influence" (master's thesis, Concordia University, 1997); Claude Grenier, "Some Wonderful, Creative Years in Rankin Inlet," *About Arts and Crafts* 5, 1 (1982): 28–34; and W.T. Larmour and the Junior League of Toronto, *Keewatin Eskimo Ceramics '67* (Toronto: Bryant Press, 1967).

60 Claude Grenier to the Industrial Division [Department of Northern Affairs and National Resources], re: Report 1964–65, LAC, RG85, vol. 1058, file 255-5/164, part 3, Arts and Crafts – Rankin Inlet.

61 Quote from Neale, "Rankin Inlet Ceramics, Part 1," 10.

62 Ibid., 10, 8, 12.

63 Neale, "The Rankin Inlet Ceramics Project, Part Two."

64 Edith Iglauer, "Donald Snowden, 1928–1984" [obituary], *Arctic* 37, 3 (1984): 317.

65 See John Sandlos, *Hunters at the Margin: Native Peoples and Wildlife Conservation in the Northwest Territories* (Vancouver: UBC Press, 2014), chap. 7; Peter Kulchyski and Frank Tester, *Kiumajut (Talking Back): Game Management and Inuit Rights, 1900–1970* (Vancouver: UBC Press, 2014), chaps. 2, 3, and 4; and Tina Loo, "Political Animals: Barren Ground Caribou and the Managers in a 'Post-Normal' Age," *Environmental History* 22, 3 (2017): 433–59.

66 Brack and McIntosh, *Keewatin Mainland Economic Survey,* 116 and, more generally, 113–19.

67 Ibid., 116.

68 R.G. Williamson to Walter Rudnicki, 21 November 1960, 12, USA, Robert G. Williamson fonds, MG 216, box 34, file Walter Rudnicki.

69 Memo from R. Mulligan re: Move to Daly Bay, January 1964, LAC, RG85, 1997-98/076 20, file 251-9/1059, Specialty Foods, Daly Bay Cannery (project file).

70 Brack and McIntosh, *Keewatin Mainland Economic Survey,* 137.

71 R.G. Robertson, Deputy Minister, Memorandum for the Minister re: Keewatin Region Crisis, 19 April 1962.

72 Northern Affairs had experience with implementing the "organized resource harvesting of arctic char" in the eastern Arctic. See Donald Snowden, "Eskimo Commercial Fisheries," *Polar Record* 10, 67 (1961): 382–84.

73 Quoted in Edith Iglauer, "A Change of Taste: A Reporter at Large," *New Yorker*, 24 April 1965, 122.

74 Edith Iglauer, "Donald Snowden" [obituary], *Inuktitut Magazine,* Summer 1984, 56–57.

75 "Arctic Circle Specialty Foods," n.d. [1969], PWNHC, Alexander Stevenson fonds, N-1992-023, box 30, file 6. Also see A.W. Lantz, "Fish Cannery in Northwest Territories," Trade News [Department of Fisheries of Canada], October 1965, 12–13, ibid., file 5. For details on the char fishery operating from Rankin Inlet, see H.M. Budgell, Report on the Keewatin Project, Ottawa, 4 June 1962, LAC, RG 85, vol. 1448, file 1000/184, vol. 7.

76 Community Development Committee, Second Meeting, 7 June 1966, 3, LAC, RG 85, vol. 1948, file A-560-1-5, pt. 4.

77 Northern Administration Branch, Branch Policy Directive No. 32, Subject: Community Development in the North, n.d. [1964], 3, ibid.

78 Bibliography of Community Development, Area and Community Planning Section, Industrial Division, 23 May 1961, LAC, RG 85, vol. 1946, file A-501-1, pt. 1. For a brief overview of the history of community development, see Alice K. Johnson Butterfield and Benson Chisanga, "Community Development," in *Encyclopedia of Social Work,* ed. Terry Mizrahi and Larry Davis, vol. 1 (New York: Oxford University Press, 2008), 376–77.

79 Northern Administration Branch, Branch Policy Directive No. 32, 1.

80 R.D. Currie, *Western Ungava: An Area Economic Survey* (Ottawa: Industrial Division, Department of Indian Affairs and Northern Development, 1968), 75.

81 D.M. Brack, "The Keewatin Region: Preliminary Report," 3 October 1962, 14, LAC, RG 85, vol. 1448, file 1000/184, vol. 8.

82 Andrew Moemeka, "Radio Strategies for Community Development: A Critical Analysis," in *Communication for Social Change Anthology: Historical and Contemporary Readings,* ed. Alfonso Gumucio-Dagron and Thomas Tufte (South Orange, NJ: Communication for Social Change Consortium, 2006), 432–41.

83 See, for instance, "CBC: Rankin Inlet News and Commentary," USA, Robert G. Williamson fonds, MG 216, box 8, file 1, and Williamson, "A Personal Retrospective," 48–49.

84 Gordon R. Wensley, *Comminterphone – Rankin Inlet: A Report of Research for the Department of Communications, Government of Canada, Ottawa* (Saskatoon: University of Saskatchewan Institute for Northern Studies, June 1973), 1, 4.

85 Wensley, *Comminterphone*, 2, 82.

86 Ian MacPherson, introduction to *Each for All: A History of the Co-operative Movement in English Canada, 1900–1945* (Toronto: Macmillan, 1979). The companion book is Ronald Rudin, *In Whose Interest? Quebec's Caisses Populaires, 1900–1945* (Montreal: McGill-Queen's University Press, 1990).

87 Paul Godt, "The Role of Co-operatives," 25 August 1960, 5, PWNHC, Alexander Stevenson fonds, N-1993-023, box 30, file 10.

88 MacPherson, *Each for All*, 130–32.

89 Address to the Yellowknife Education Conference, 3 February 1966, cited in Glenn Fields and Glenn Sigurdson, *Northern Co-operatives as a Strategy for Community Change: The Case of Fort Resolution* (Winnipeg: Centre for Settlement Studies, University of Manitoba, May 1972), 5.

90 *The Annanacks*, directed by René Bonnière (Ottawa: National Film Board of Canada, 1964).

91 Godt, "The Role of Co-operatives," 5.

92 R. Gordon Robertson, *Memoirs of a Very Civil Servant: Mackenzie King to Pierre Trudeau* (Toronto: University of Toronto Press, 2000), 179, 190.

93 This is one of the many provocative arguments of her book *From Talking Chiefs to a Native Corporate Elite: The Birth of Class and Nationalism among Canadian Inuit* (Montreal and Kingston: McGill-Queen's University Press, 1996).

94 Director, Northern Administration Branch, Branch Policy Directive No. 13, Community Development and Local Organization, 25 October 1961, 3, LAC, RG 85, vol. 1962, file A-1012-9, vol. 2.

95 Bonnière, *The Annanacks*.

96 Northern Administration Branch, Branch Policy Directive No. 32, 3.

97 "Northern Cooperatives," Department of Northern Affairs and National Resources Information Services Division, December 1964, 1, PWNHC, Alexander Stevenson fonds, N-1992-023, box 30, file 10.

98 R.J. Wickware, "Northern Co-operative Development," paper presented to the NAACL Annual Meeting, 5–8 July 1971, St. John's, NL, 1–2, PWNHC, Alexander Stevenson fonds, N-1992-023, box 30, file 10.

99 M. Stopp, *The Northern Co-operative Movement in Canada*, submission reports, vol. 2, report no. 2009-22 (Ottawa: Historic Sites and Monuments Board of Canada, Spring 2009), 670.

100 Economist E.F. Schumacher came up with the idea of "intermediate technology" in his critique of development aid. Such aid often failed to achieve the desired results because it funded projects – technologies – inappropriate to the needs and skills of people in the societies in which they were located. He called instead for "intermediate technologies." See "How to Help Them Help Themselves," *Observer* (UK), 29 August 1965, at http://www.centerforneweconomics.org/content/how-help-them-help-themselves.

101 Alexander F. Laidlaw, "Cooperatives in the Canadian Northland," *North/Nord*, November–December 1963, 12. Mitchell analyzes the effects of cooperatives on Inuit and argues that these organizations were crucial to creating class divisions and facilitated the emergence of a "corporate elite." See her *From Talking Chiefs*.

102 Laugrand, Oosten, and Serkoak, "'The Saddest Time of My Life,'" 121–22; the quote is from R.A.J. Phillips, Memorandum for the Director Re: Movement of Henik Lake Eskimos, 15 January 1958, cited on 125.

103 Edith Iglauer, "Conclave at Frobisher: A Reporter at Large," *New Yorker*, 23 November 1963, 192.

104 Snowden to Edith Hamburger, n.d. [appears to be in response to a letter from her dated 1 November 1963], LAC, Donald Snowden fonds, MG 31 D 163, vol. 14, file 34, Northern Affairs, Miscellaneous, 1961–64 (emphasis in original).

105 Stopp, *The Northern Co-operative Movement,* 671, 684.

Chapter 2: "The Governmentality Game"

1 The key academic works on resettlement in Newfoundland and Labrador are Raymond Blake, *Lions or Jellyfish: Newfoundland-Ottawa Relations since 1957* (Toronto: University of Toronto Press, 2015), chaps. 3 and 4; Noel Iverson and D. Ralph Matthews, *Communities in Decline: A Study of Household Resettlement in Newfoundland* (St. John's: Memorial University of Newfoundland Institute of Social and Economic Research, 1968); George Withers, "Reconstituting Rural Communities and Economies: The Newfoundland Fisheries Household Resettlement Program, 1965–1970" (PhD diss., Memorial University of Newfoundland, 2016); and Miriam Wright, *A Fishery for Modern Times: The State and the Industrialization of the Newfoundland Fishery, 1934–1968* (Toronto: Oxford University Press, 2000), chap. 7. The Newfoundland and Labrador Heritage website also features a number of useful articles on resettlement. These include "Centralization," "Outports," "The Resettlement Program," "Resettlement," "The Second Resettlement Program," "Was Resettlement Justified," and "Rural Depopulation." See https://www.heritage.nf.ca.

2 Report Diary, Week Beginning 17 November 1969, Memorial University of Newfoundland Archives and Special Collections (MUNASC), Fred W. Earle Collection, Coll-399, file 5.01.

3 Report Diary, Week Beginning 15 September 1968, ibid.

4 Robert Johnson, "Outporters Go 'Inport,'" *Atlantic Advocate* 61 (September 1970): 29.

5 Sandra Gwyn, "The Newfcult Phenomenon," *Saturday Night,* April 1976, 38–45.

6 The latest work on resettlement, by George Withers, labels resettlement as "high modern." See Withers, "Resettlement of Newfoundland Inshore Fishing Communities, 1954–72: A High-Modernist Project" (master's thesis, Memorial University, 2009) and his "Reconstituting Rural Communities," 17.

7 Testimony of H. Carl Goldenberg, counsel for the province of Newfoundland, in Canada, *Royal Commission on Canada's Economic Prospects: Hearings Held at St. John's, Newfoundland, October 18, 1955* (Ottawa: Queen's Printer, 1955), 34.

8 Robert Wells, *Report on Resettlement in Newfoundland* (St. John's, 1960), 5, Provincial Archives of Newfoundland and Labrador (PANL), GN 34/2, box 29, file 12/62/1E.

9 William N. Rowe, "The Newfoundland Resettlement Program: A Case Study of Regional Development and Social Adjustment," Harrison Liberal Conference, Harrison Hot Springs, BC, 21–23 November 1969, 6.

10 Iverson and Matthews, *Communities in Decline,* 1–2.

11 Parzival Copes, *The Resettlement of Fishing Communities in Newfoundland* (Ottawa: Canadian Council on Rural Development, 1972), 7.

12 Ibid.

13 Department of Fisheries, Ottawa, Fisheries Development Programme, Newfoundland, Discussion on Centralization of Industry and Population, 19 January 1965, 2, Library and Archives Canada (LAC), RG 124, vol. 27, file 168-N5, part 1.

14 Parzival Copes, "Community Resettlement and Rationalization of the Fishing Industry in Newfoundland," paper presented at Annual Meeting of the Canadian Economics Association, St. John's, 4 June 1971, 3.

15 The figure was calculated on the basis of data from Copes, *The Resettlement of Fishing Communities,* 189.

16 M.W. Graesser, "Review Essay: *The Political Economy of Newfoundland, 1929–1972,* by Peter Neary, *The Resettlement of Fishing Communities in Newfoundland,* by Parzival Copes, and *Regional Policy and Settlement Strategy in Newfoundland's Experience,* by Parzival Copes and Guy Steed," *Canadian Journal of Political Science* 8, 1 (1975): 150.

17 Ralph Matthews, "The Smallwood Legacy: The Development of Underdevelopment in Newfoundland, 1949–1972," *Journal of Canadian Studies* 13, 4 (1978–79): 90.

18 United Nations, Department of Economic and Social Affairs, Population Division, *World Population Prospects: The 2017 Revision,* http://esa.un.org/unpd/wpp/Excel-Data/fertility.htm, and Copes, *The Resettlement of Fishing Communities,* 12.

19 Matthews, "The Smallwood Legacy," 96.

20 Copes, "Community Resettlement," 2.

21 Copes, *The Resettlement of Fishing Communities,* 12.

22 Transfers "subsidized improvement in Newfoundland's living standards" and, in so doing, worked "to make life in the province more attractive and to lessen the pressure for out-migration." See ibid., 17. For those influenced by dependency theory, this was an example of the "modernization of under-development." See Graesser, "Review Essay," 149.

23 Rowe, "The Newfoundland Resettlement Program," 5.

24 Copes, *The Resettlement of Fishing Communities,* 174, Table 1: Population, Natural Increase and Net Migration for Newfoundland, for Inter-Censal Periods, 1921–1966.

25 Briefing Notes, Newfoundland Fisheries Resettlement Programme, for Minister's Speech, 28 November 1969, 3, LAC, RG 124, vol. 27, file 168-N5, part 5.

26 Iverson and Matthews, *Communities in Decline,* 136.

27 Rosemary E. Ommer and Nancy J. Turner, "Informal Rural Economies in History," *Labour/Le travail* 53 (2004): 152.

28 Rosemary Ommer, "One Hundred Years of Fisheries Crises in Newfoundland," *Acadiensis* 23, 2 (1994): 11.

29 Ottar Brox, *Maintenance of Economic Dualism in Newfoundland* (St. John's: Memorial University of Newfoundland, Institute of Social and Economic Research, 1969), 62–63.

30 Timothy Mitchell, *Rule of Experts: Egypt, Techno-Politics, Modernity* (Berkeley: University of California Press, 2002), 210.

31 See, for instance, Frederick W. Rowe, *A History of Newfoundland and Labrador* (Toronto: McGraw-Hill Ryerson, 1980), 131; Kevin Major, *As Near to Heaven by Sea: A History of Newfoundland and Labrador* (Toronto: Penguin Books, 2001), 419; and John C. Kennedy, "At the Crossroads: Newfoundland and Labrador Communities in a Changing International Context," *Canadian Review of Sociology and Anthropology* 34, 3 (1997): 309.

32 James McLeod, "James McLeod Lauds NL's Nationalist Identity, Outlines Impending Poverty Struggles," *St. John's Telegram,* 17 November 2017, http://www.thetelegram.com/news/james-mcleod-lauds-nls-nationalist-identity-outlines-impending-poverty-struggles-162850/.

33 David Alexander, "Newfoundland's Traditional Economy and Development," *Acadiensis* 5, 2 (1976): 56.

34 Gordon Handcock, "The Commission of Government's Land Settlement Scheme in Newfoundland," in *Twentieth Century Newfoundland: Explorations,* ed. James Hiller and Peter Neary (St. John's: Breakwater, 1994), 123–52.

35 Memorial University of Newfoundland, Newfoundland and Labrador Heritage, "Argentia," at http://www.heritage.nf.ca/law/argentia_base.html.

36 Robert Wells, *What You Need to Know about the Government's Policy on Centralizing the Population* (St. John's: Office of the Premier, Province of Newfoundland, 1959). Although this document suggests the province wanted to know where potential resettlers were going, there was no list of designated communities to which they were encouraged to resettle, as there would be later, when the federal government became involved.

37 Newfoundland Resettlement Program, "Report to the Joint Planning Committee from the Newfoundland Resettlement Committee," n.d. [1973], 2, PANL, GN 59/7/A box 2, file 2.
38 See, for instance, Memorandum to Cabinet, Newfoundland – Centralization of Fishermen, 19 February 1965, 1, LAC, RG 124, vol. 27, file 168-N5, part 1; Lemieux to Davidson, 28 July 1966, 1, ibid., part 1.; and Smallwood to Pearson, 12 January 1967, 1, ibid., part 2. Also see Blake, *Lions or Jellyfish,* chaps. 4 and 5.
39 The name of the program changed over the decade it was in operation. Initially called the Fisheries Household Resettlement Program, toward the end of the first resettlement agreement it was called the Newfoundland Resettlement Program. That name remained until 1972, when it became known as the Community Consolidation Program. For details on the payments made to people who resettled, see Blake, *Lions or Jellyfish,* 133 and 144–45.
40 Bernard Higgins and Donald Savoie, *Regional Development Theories and Their Application* (New Brunswick, NJ: Transaction Publishers, 1995), 89.
41 "Travelling rationality" is from David Craig and Doug Porter, *Development Beyond Neoliberalism: Governance, Poverty Reduction, and Political Economy* (London: Routledge, 2006). Michael Staveley, "Resettlement and Centralisation in Newfoundland," in *Policies of Population Distribution,* ed. John W. Webb, Arvo Naukkarinen, and Leszek A. Kosinski (Oulu, FI: Geographical Society of Northern Finland for the International Geographical Union on Population Geography, 1981), 160.
42 Higgins and Savoie, *Regional Economic Development Theories,* 89–90.
43 Cited in ibid., 103.
44 Ibid., 91–97; also François Perroux, "Economic Space: Theory and Applications," *Quarterly Journal of Economics* 64, 1 (1950): 89–104.
45 Perroux, "Economic Space," 89.
46 Maloney to Robichaud, 22 January 1968, 2, LAC, RG 124, vol. 133, file 168-N5, part 6, and Minutes of Meeting of the Fisheries Household Resettlement Subcommittee, 17 July 1967, 2–4, PANL, GN 34/2, file 12/62/1A, vol. 1.
47 Blake, *Lions or Jellyfish,* 145.
48 Ian Whitaker, "A Projected Institute for Social and Economic Research in Newfoundland: Needs and Aims," 12 November 1960, 2, MUNASC, Institute of Social and Economic Research (ISER), Coll-454, file 1.01.012, Institute, 1962–1969.
49 Royal Commission on the Economic Prospects of Newfoundland and Labrador, *Report of the Royal Commission on the Economic Prospects of Newfoundland and Labrador* (St. John's: Queen's Printer, 1967), 34.
50 Minutes of Meeting of Fisheries Household Resettlement Subcommittee, 3 October 1967, 1, LAC, RG 124, vol. 27, file 168-N5, part 2.
51 The numbers are from Canada, Department of Regional Economic Expansion, *Statistics: Federal-Provincial Resettlement Program, Community Consolidation Program – First Resettlement Agreement (1965–1970) and Second Resettlement Agreement (1970–1975), Completed to April 30, 1975* (Ottawa: Department of Regional Economic Expansion, 1975).
52 See, for instance, PANL, GN 39/1, Department of Rural Development – Resettlement, files H737, H6369, and H7533.
53 Francis to Kent, 30 September 1970, 1, LAC, RG 124, vol. 133, file 168-N5-2; Selection Criteria for Receiving Communities outside Special (Designated) Areas, as modified by the JPC 10 September 1970, included in the Minutes of the Resettlement Committee for Newfoundland, 5 October 1970, PANL, GN 59/7/A, box 4, file 2.
54 Notes of a meeting held 23 November 1966, 10:30AM in the ADB Board Room, of a Subcommittee of the Interdepartmental Committee on Centralization of Newfoundland Fishing Communities, 25 November 1966, LAC, RG 124, vol. 27, file 168-N5, part 1.
55 Meeting on the Development of the Newfoundland Fisheries, 21–22 August 1968, Outline

and Progress Report: Topographical and Statistical EDP Inventory System on Nfld Outports, V.P. Rossiter, Consultant, 1, ibid., vol. 28, file 168-N5-1, part 1.

56 Department of Regional Economic Expansion, *Summary Description: Isolation Criteria Program, Newfoundland and Labrador Unincorporated Communities* (Ottawa: Department of Regional Economic Expansion, November 1970), 1.

57 See, for instance, PANL, GN 39/1, Department of Rural Development – Resettlement, file H3777. On where Smallwood's electoral support lay, see Parzival Copes, "The Fishermen's Vote in Newfoundland," *Canadian Journal of Political Science* 3, 4 (1970): 579–604.

58 See, for instance, Jamieson to Marchand, 30 June 1971, LAC, RG 124, vol. 133, file 168-N5, part 4.

59 Memorandum from G. Adams to A.D. Crerar, 1 June 1970, Re: Comments by Doug Day and Ian McAllister on the Newfoundland Resettlement Agreement, 3, ibid., vol. 27, file 168-N5, part 6.

60 Minutes of the Resettlement Committee for Newfoundland, 6 October 1970, 3 and 5, PANL, GN 59/7/A, box 4, file 2.

61 Minutes of the Resettlement Meeting, 7 December 1972, 1, 2, ibid., box 4, file 4.

62 DREE Development Plan for Newfoundland, Seminar, Ottawa, 1 November 1969. Draft – Confidential, 4, LAC, RG 124, vol. 27, file 168-N5, part 5.

63 Ninth meeting of the Federal-Provincial Interdepartmental Committee on Centralization of Newfoundland Communities, 26 November 1968, Appendix 4, Newfoundland Community Evacuation Progress, 1945–1968, 25, PANL, GN 34/2, box 80.

64 Newfoundland Resettlement Program, Report to the Joint Planning Committee from the Newfoundland Resettlement Committee, n.d. [1973], 7, ibid., GN59/7/A, box 2, file 2.

65 The number of receiving communities was calculated from Canada, Department of Regional Economic Expansion, *Statistics: Federal-Provincial Resettlement Program.* The quotation is from "Newfoundland Resettlement Program: A Critique of the Existing Program and Some Guidelines for a New Program," n.d. [1969], 9, LAC, RG 124, vol. 27, file 168-N4, part 4, and Copes, *The Resettlement of Fishing Communities,* 110.

66 For the procedures under the first resettlement agreement, see Newfoundland, Department of Fisheries, Fisheries Household Resettlement Division, "Outline of a Policy Regarding Resettlement of Isolated Communities," ca. 1965, at http://www.mun.ca/mha/resettlement/documents_full_view.php?img=068_outline_of_policy&galleryID=Doc1; for the second agreement, see Canada, Department of Regional Economic Expansion, *Canada-Newfoundland Second Resettlement Agreement, 1970,* PANL, GN 59/7/A, box 2, file 4; for the 1966 amendment, see Record of Cabinet Decision, Meeting of 10 August 1966, Newfoundland Fisheries Resettlement Program, Appendix A, Minutes of the Meeting of the Interdepartmental Committee on Centralization of Newfoundland Communities, 16 November, 1966, LAC, RG 124, vol. 27, file 168-N5, part 1.

67 Record of Cabinet Decision, Meeting of August 10, 1966, Newfoundland Fisheries Resettlement Program, Appendix A, Minutes of the Meeting of the Interdepartmental Committee on Centralization of Newfoundland Communities, 16 November 1966, LAC, RG 124, vol. 27, file 168-N5, part 1.

68 Crerar to Francis, 21 January 1973, 1, LAC, RG 124, vol. 28, file 168-N5, part 8; Robichaud to Maloney, 31 October 1967, 1, ibid., vol. 133, file 168-N5, part 6; Maloney to Robichaud, 22 January 1968, 2, ibid., vol. 133, file 168-N5, part 6; Adams to Crerar, 1 June, 1970, 3, ibid., vol. 27, file 168-N5, part 6; and McIntyre to Bryden, 14 September 1973, 1, ibid., vol. 28, file 168-N5, part 9.

69 Crerar to Jamieson, 13 February 1973, 1, ibid., part 8. The number of individual households applying for resettlement came as a surprise to the program's administrators, who, at one point, contemplated capping them, worried that thousands of people would be moved

without any communities actually being abandoned. See Newfoundland Fisheries Household Resettlement Committee, Meeting with Dr. Weeks, Mr. McClure, Mr. August, Mr. Rossiter, Mr. Hart, 22 July 1969, 2–3, ibid., vol. 168-N5-1, part 2.

70 Kent to Jamieson, 18 June 1970, cited in Blake, *Lions or Jellyfish,* 137.

71 The number of sending communities was calculated from Canada, Department of Regional Economic Expansion, *Statistics: Federal-Provincial Resettlement Program.* The number of totally evacuated or abandoned communities is taken directly from that report. Of the 148 that were totally evacuated, 119 were abandoned in the first five years of the resettlement program.

72 Tenth Meeting of the Federal Interdepartmental Committee on Centralization of Newfoundland Communities, 13 May 1969, 4, LAC, RG 124, vol. 28, file 168-N5-1, part 2.

73 Withers, "Resettlement of Newfoundland Inshore Fishing Communities"; Withers, "Reconstituting Rural Communities and Economies," Introduction and chap. 1; and Blake, *Lions or Jellyfish,* 102.

74 Ommer, "One Hundred Years of Fisheries Crises," 17 and 15.

75 Withers, "Reconstituting Rural Communities and Economies," chap. 8. Sally Hermansen and I also discuss this case in "Belonging to Place," in *The Otter / La loutre,* the NiCHE (Network in Canadian History and Environment / Nouvelle initiative Canadienne en histoire de l'environnement) blog: http://niche-canada.org/2018/03/07/belonging-to-place/.

76 Ross to Crerar, 13 April 1973, 1, LAC, RG 124, vol. 28, file 168-N5, part 8, notes the shift in provincial policy away from centralization and towards "making the rural environment more attractive and economical." The resettlement program officially expired on 31 March 1977. See Harnum to G--, 17 October 1977, PANL, GN 59/7/A, box 3A, file 2.

77 Minutes of Resettlement Committee Meeting, 1 November 1971, 2, PANL, GN 59/7/A, box 4, file 2.

78 Newfoundland, Department of Fisheries, "What You Need to Know about the Fisheries Household Resettlement Program," n.d., reproduced in Iverson and Matthews, *Communities in Decline,* Appendix A.

79 Jeff A. Webb, *Observing the Outports: Describing Newfoundland Culture, 1950–1980* (Toronto: University of Toronto Press, 2015), 199–200, 203–4, and 228.

80 Ralph Matthews, "Ethical Issues in Policy Research: The Investigation of Community Resettlement in Newfoundland," *Canadian Public Policy* 1, 2 (1975): 207.

81 Iverson and Matthews, *Communities in Decline,* 138.

82 Matthews, "Ethical Issues in Policy Research," 207.

83 Davis to Marchand, 12 March 1969, 1, LAC, RG 124, vol. 27, file 168-N5, part 4.

84 A. Leslie Robb and Roberta Edgecombe Robb, *A Cost-Benefit Analysis of the Newfoundland Resettlement Program* (St. John's: Memorial University of Newfoundland Institute of Social and Economic Research, 1969), 24 and 138.

85 W. Irwin Gillespie, *The Redistribution of Income in Canada* (Agincourt, ON: Gage Publishing in association with the Institute of Canadian Studies, Carleton University, 1980), 98.

86 Copes, *The Resettlement of Fishing Communities,* 170.

87 Iverson and Matthews, *Communities in Decline,* 136 and 139.

88 Webb, *Observing the Outports,* chap. 4, discusses ISER's community ethnographies in depth.

89 Cato Wadel, *Communities and Committees: Community Development and the Enlargement of the Sense of Community on Fogo Island, Newfoundland* (St. John's: Extension Service, Memorial University of Newfoundland, 1969), 56.

90 See, for instance, James C. Faris, *Cat Harbour: A Newfoundland Fishing Settlement* (St. John's: Memorial University of Newfoundland/Institute of Social and Economic Research, 1966), part 3 and especially chap. 11; and Melvin M. Firestone, *Brothers and Rivals: Patrilocality in Savage Cove* (St. John's: Memorial University of Newfoundland/Institute of Social and

Economic Research, 1967), chap. 5. For an explicit and detailed discussion of how alien the resettlement process would have been to outport residents, see Ralph Matthews, "The Sociological Implications of Resettlement: Some Thoughts on the Power and Responsibility of Planners," paper presented to the Annual Meeting of the Canadian Institute of Planners, Halifax, 6 August 1979, 8–11.

91 Cited in David Curran, "Citizen Participation and Public Policy in Rural Development: The Rural Development Association Movement in Newfoundland and Labrador" (master's thesis, Saint Mary's University, 1992), 76–77.

92 Memorial University of Newfoundland, Extension Service Media Unit, "The Fogo Process," 1984, 1, MUNASC, H.A. Williamson Collection, Coll-347, file 3.02.012.

93 Donald Snowden, "CONFIDENTIAL: A Proposed Involvement between Memorial University of Newfoundland and the National Film Board of Canada," 1967, 2, ibid., file 3.02.006; Don Snowden, "A Report on the Extension Service of Memorial University of Newfoundland," April 1975, LAC, Donald Snowden fonds, MG 31 D 163, vol. 17, file 14: Extension Services: A Report on the Film Unit and VTA, 1975; United Nations Economic and Social Council, Document E/2931, 18 October 1956, cited in Donald Snowden and Miss Edna Baird, "Summary of Community Development Training and Activities Undertaken by Extension Services of Some Canadian Universities," compiled for the Annual Meeting of CADESS, Montreal, 8–11 May 1967 (St. John's: Memorial University, Extension Service, 1967), 1.

94 Tony Williamson, "Don Snowden, Participatory Communications and People-Centred Development," 26 October 1998, MUNASC, H.A. Williamson Collection, Coll-347, file 3.07.054; *What Now: The 1975 Dag Hammarskjöld Report on Development and International Cooperation* (Uppsala, FI: Dag Hammarskjöld Foundation), 27.

95 Tony Williamson, Transcript of his remarks to the Extension Staff Conference, n.d. [ca. 1967], 2, MUNASC, H.A. Williamson Collection, Coll-347, 3.01.002.

96 Minutes, Meeting of Federal-Provincial Fisheries Household Resettlement Committee, 4–5 April 1968, 3, LAC, RG 124, vol. 28, file 168-N5-1, part 1.

97 Federal-Provincial Meeting on Centralization of Industry and Population in Newfoundland, 10–11 March 1966, 24, ibid., vol. 27, file 168-N5, part 1.

98 Newfoundland, The Department of Community and Social Development Act, 1966, ibid., part 2.

99 Directors Meeting No. 130, Department of Community and Social Development, 14 September 1970, 4, PANL, GN 59/7/A, box 4, file 1.

100 Included in Hart to Francis, 16 December 1970, 3, LAC, RG 124, vol. 28, file 168-N5, part 7.

101 Lemieux to Davidson, 28 July 1966, 1, ibid., vol. 27, file 168-N5, part 1. Also see Memorandum from the Rural Development Branch (ARDA), Department of Forestry and Rural Development, to Interdepartmental Committee on Centralization of Newfoundland Communities, n.d., Appendix F, 4–5, Minutes of the Meeting of the Interdepartmental Committee on Centralization of Newfoundland Communities, 16 November, 1966, ibid.

102 On Extension, see Jeff Webb, "The Rise and Fall of Memorial University's Extension Service, 1959–91," *Newfoundland and Labrador Studies* 29, 1 (2015): 84–116; and Gwyn, "The Newfcult Phenomenon."

103 Susan Newhook, "The Godfathers of Fogo: Donald Snowden, Fred Earle, and the Roots of the Fogo Island Films, 1964–1967," *Newfoundland and Labrador Studies* 24, 2 (2009): 177.

104 Memorandum from Greg L. Donovan to W. Jobbins, J.W. Fisher, J. Kemeny, B. Nemetin, re: Community Change for Fogo Island through a NFB Production-Distribution team, 4 August 1967, 1, NFB Archives, Fogo Films, AI 2015-14-4.

105 Peter Wiesner, "Media for the People: The Canadian Experiments with Film and Video in Community Development," typescript, 1989, 48, enclosed in Wiesner to Colin Low, 21 February 1989, LAC, Colin Low fonds, R5667, box 173, files 25 and 26.
106 Donald Snowden, "The Co-operative Movement in Newfoundland: An ARDA Study of Co-operative Organization from the Viewpoint of Industrial and Social Development," prepared for the Government of Newfoundland by the Co-operative Union of Canada under the direction of Donald Snowden (1965), 37.
107 Robert L. DeWitt, *Public Policy and Community Protest: The Fogo Case* (St. John's: ISER Books, 1969), 13.
108 Colin Low, "A Report on Information, Government, and Three-Dimensional Communication (an Adaptation of Fogo)," for the Office of Economic Opportunity, n.d., 19, LAC, Colin Low fonds, box 253, file 34.
109 *Fogo Island Improvement Committee,* directed by Colin Low (Montreal: National Film Board of Canada in Collaboration with Memorial University of Newfoundland, 1967); Wadel, *Communities and Committees,* 61, 23–27.
110 Wadel, *Communities and Committees,* 24.
111 Fred Earle Collection Finding Aid, Coll-399, Centre for Newfoundland Studies, Queen Elizabeth II Library, Memorial University of Newfoundland.
112 Bill Nemtin and Colin Low, "Fogo Island Film and Community Development Project," n.d. [1968], 4, NFB Archives, Fogo Films, AI 2015-16-4.
113 *The Mercer Family,* directed by Colin Low (Montreal: National Film Board of Canada in collaboration with Memorial University of Newfoundland, 1967).
114 *Some Problems of Fogo,* directed by Colin Low (Montreal: National Film Board of Canada in collaboration with Memorial University of Newfoundland, 1967).
115 *Andrew Britt [Brett] at Shoal Bay,* directed by Colin Low (Montreal: National Film Board of Canada in collaboration with Memorial University of Newfoundland, 1967).
116 *The Merchant and the Teacher,* directed by Colin Low (Montreal: National Film Board of Canada in collaboration with Memorial University of Newfoundland, 1967).
117 *A Woman's Place,* directed by Colin Low (Montreal: National Film Board of Canada in collaboration with Memorial University of Newfoundland, 1967).
118 Wadel, *Committees and Community,* 62.
119 *Dan Roberts on Fishing,* directed by Colin Low (Montreal: National Film Board of Canada in collaboration with Memorial University of Newfoundland, 1967).
120 *Jim Decker Builds a Longliner,* directed by Colin Low (Montreal: National Film Board of Canada in collaboration with Memorial University of Newfoundland, 1967).
121 *The Story of the Up Top,* directed by Colin Low (Montreal: National Film Board of Canada in collaboration with Memorial University of Newfoundland, 1967).
122 *Brian Earle on Merchants and Welfare,* directed by Colin Low (Montreal: National Film Board of Canada in collaboration with Memorial University of Newfoundland, 1967).
123 *The Mercer Family,* directed by Colin Low (Montreal: National Film Board of Canada in collaboration with Memorial University of Newfoundland, 1967).
124 *Billy Crane Moves Away,* directed by Colin Low (Montreal: National Film Board of Canada in collaboration with Memorial University of Newfoundland, 1967).
125 *Some Problems of Fogo,* directed by Colin Low (Montreal: National Film Board of Canada in collaboration with Memorial University of Newfoundland, 1967).
126 Wendy Quarry, "The Fogo Process: An Interview with Donald Snowden," *Interaction* 2, 3 (1984): 61.
127 Nemtin and Low, "Fogo Island Film and Community Development Project," 1.
128 Mammoth Notebook – Fogo Island, 3, LAC, Colin Low fonds, R5667-0-E, box 253, file Fogo Island Project, 1967–72, file 8 of 13.

129 Ibid.

130 Bill Nemtin, "Fogo Island Film and Community Development Project," National Film Board of Canada, May 1968, 9, NFB Archives, Fogo Films, 2015-16-4; Nemtin and Low, "Fogo Island Film and Community Development Project," 22 and 24.

131 Nemtin and Low, "Fogo Island Film and Community Development Project," 24.

132 Wadel, *Communities and Committees,* 49 (emphasis in original).

133 H. Anthony Williamson, "The Fogo Process: User-Oriented Communications Systems and Social Development – The Canadian Experience. Summary of Presentation at the UNESCO Meeting on the Planning and Management of New Communications Systems, Paris, October 8–12, 1973," 2, MUNASC, Fred Earle Collection, Coll-399, file 2.01.159.

134 Donald Snowden, "A Proposed Involvement between Memorial University of Newfoundland and the National Film Board of Canada for Follow-Up Filming on Fogo Island, February 1971," 14, MUNASC, H.A. Williamson Collection, Coll-347.

135 Ibid., 15–16.

136 Tony Williamson, "Screening Report on Initial Showing of Labrador films," 31 January 1970, 6, MUNASC, Fred Earle Collection, Coll-399, file 2.01.159.

137 Snowden, "A Proposed Involvement between Memorial University of Newfoundland and the National Film Board of Canada," 9.

138 Memorial University of Newfoundland, Extension Service Media Unit, "The Fogo Process," 1984, 4, MUNASC, H.A. Williamson Collection, Coll-347, file 3.02.12.

139 Ibid., 8.

140 "An Interview with the Honorable Eric Kierans, Minister of Communications and Memorial University of Newfoundland Extension Service on Communications on the Coast of Labrador," Ottawa, 4 December 1970, 1, MUNASC, Fred Earle Collection, Coll-399, file 2.01.159.

141 [H.A. Williamson,] "Presentation to Fieldworkers by Anthony H. Williamson," n.d., 3, ibid. In general, see J.C. Crosbie, "Local Government in Newfoundland," *Canadian Journal of Economics and Political Science* 22, 3 (1956): 332–46.

142 R.D. Currie, *Western Ungava: An Area Economic Survey* (Ottawa: Industrial Division, Department of Indian Affairs and Northern Development, 1968), 75; and [Williamson,] "Presentation to Fieldworkers," 8.

143 J.D. House, "Does Community Really Matter in Newfoundland and Labrador? The Need for Supportive Capacity in the New Regional Development," in *Retrenchment and Regeneration in Rural Newfoundland,* ed. Reginald Byron (Toronto: University of Toronto Press, 2003), 230.

144 H.A. Williamson and D. Snowden, "Aspects of Community Development in Newfoundland: The Views of the Extension Service of the Memorial University of Newfoundland, 22 December 1967," 5, MUNASC, H.A. Williamson Collection, Coll-347, file 3.01.002.

145 Snowden, "A Report on the Extension Service of Memorial University of Newfoundland," 2.

146 Michel Foucault, "Governmentality," in *The Foucault Effect: Studies in Governmentality,* ed. Graham Burchell, Colin Gordon, and Peter Miller (Chicago: University of Chicago Press, 1991), 87–104.

Chapter 3: "Artisans of Their Destiny"

1 *Les smattes,* directed by Jean-Claude Labrecque (Montreal: Les Films Mutuels, 1972). All translations from French films and literature in this chapter are the author's.

2 The key works on the BAEQ and its development planning in eastern Quebec as well as the protest it inspired are Charles Banville, *Les Opérations Dignité* (Quebec: Université Laval, 1977); Clermont Dugas, "Le développement regional de l'Est du Québec de

1963 à 1972," *Cahier de géographie de Québec* 17, 41 (1973): 283–316; Alain-G. Gagnon, *Développement régional, état et groupes populaires: le cas de l'Est du Québec* (Hull, QC: Éditions Asticou, 1985); Alain-G. Gagnon, ed. *Les Opérations Dignité: naissance d'un mouvement social dans l'Est du Québec* (Montreal: Les Éditions Leméac, 1981); Bruno Jean, ed., *Le BAEQ revisité: un nouveau regard sur la première experience de développement regional au Québec* (Laval, QC: Presses de l'Université Laval, 2016); and Dominique Morin, "Le BAEQ, la légende et l'esprit du développement régionale," in *Pouvoir et territoire au Québec depuis 1850,* ed. Harold Berubé and Stéphane Savard (Quebec: Les Éditions du Septentrion, 2017), 265–309.

3 *Populorum Progressio: Encyclical of Pope John VI on the Development of Peoples,* 26 March 1967, ss. 25–29, and 76, http://www.vatican.va/holy_father/paul_vi/encyclicals/documents/hf_p-vi_enc_26031967_populorum_en.html.

4 See particularly Dugas, "Le développement regional de l'Est du Québec de 1963"; Gagnon, *Développement régional;* Jacques Godbout, *La participation contre la démocratie* (Montreal: Éditions coopératives Albert Saint-Martin, 1983); and Jean-Jacques Simard, *La longue marche des technocrates* (Montreal: Éditions coopératives Albert Saint-Martin, 1979).

5 Jean-François Simard, "Le BAEQ: réhabiliter un moment phare de la révolution tranquille," in Jean, *Le BAEQ revisité,* 157. Dominique Morin also discusses the negative interpretations of BAEQ in "Le BAEQ, la légende et l'esprit du développement régionale," 269. Perhaps the most important of these is Simard, *La longue marche des technocrates.*

6 Simard, "Le BAEQ," 155–95, and Lawrence Desrosiers, "La contribution du BAEQ au développement regional et au développement de la société Québécoise," in Jean, *Le BAEQ revisité,* 107–30, quote from 107.

7 Hugues Dionne, "Le Bureau d'aménagement de l'Est du Québec (BAEQ) revisité: Acte fondateur québécois de planification régionale et démocratique," in *Choix publics et prospective territorial: Horizon 2025, La Gaspésie – futurs anticipés,* ed. Danielle Lafontaine (Rimouski: Groupe de recherche interdisciplinaire sur le développement regional de l'Est du Québec (GRIDEQ), Université du Québec à Rimouski, 2001), 123.

8 Serge Courville, *Quebec: A Historical Geography,* trans. Richard Howard (Vancouver: UBC Press, 2008), 51, 179–82.

9 Georges-Henri Dubé, "Le BAEQ et les paroisses marginales," in Jean, *Le BAEQ revisité,* 51.

10 Jean-Claude Lebel, "Le plan du BAEQ est un plan de rattrapage," 75 and 77, Bibliothèque et Archives nationales du Québec (BAnQ), Jean-Claude Lebel fonds, P730. Another source puts the percentage of personal income provided by government transfers at 31 percent and notes the provincial average was 12 percent. See "Le Bureau d'aménagement de l'Est du Québec," *Le BAEQ vous informe . . . 1 Information générale* (Mont-Joli, QC: BAEQ, September 1965), 16.

11 Michel Doray, "Méthodes et techniques d'animation," *Les cahiers de l'ICEA,* nos. 4–5 (September 1967): 26.

12 "Aménagement," Document I, *Dimensions de l'aménagement,* Bureau d'aménagement de l'Est du Québec, June 1964, cited in Martin Poulin, "Planification et animation sociale," *Les cahiers de l'ICEA,* nos. 4–5 (September 1967): 34. The second quote is from Rural Development Branch, Department of Forestry and Rural Development, *Development Plan for the Pilot Region: Lower St Lawrence, Gaspé, and the Iles-de-la-Madeleine, Bureau d'aménagement de l'Est du Québec. A Summary* (Ottawa: Rural Development Branch, Department of Forestry and Rural Development, June 1967), 2.

13 "Le Bureau d'aménagement de l'Est du Québec," 7. Also see Georges-Henri Dubé, "Le BAEQ revisité par un acteur de premier plan: le témoignage du président du BAEQ," in Jean, *Le BAEQ revisité,* 39.

14 Rural Development Branch, Department of Forestry and Rural Development, *Development Plan for the Pilot Region,* ii.

15 The first agreement provided $258 million for development. See *Entente générale de coopération sur la réalisation du plan de développement de la région du Bas Saint-Laurent, de la Gaspésie et des Îles de la Madeleine* (Ottawa: Ministère des forêts et du développement rural, 1968). It was renegotiated in 1971 and the amount increased to $411 million. The agreement remained in place until 1976.

16 "The overall growth objective for the pilot region is to catch up with the province of Quebec, and thus virtually to eliminate disparities in employment, productivity, and income." See Rural Development Branch, Department of Forestry and Rural Development, *Development Plan for the Pilot Region,* 1.

17 Lebel, "Le plan du BAEQ est un plan de rattrapage."

18 Rural Development Branch, Department of Forestry and Rural Development, *Development Plan for the Pilot Region,* 8–9.

19 Bureau d'aménagement de l'Est du Québec, *Plan de développement. Région-pilote: Bas St-Laurent, Gaspésie et Îles-de-la-Madeleine,* cahier 9, chap. 6, *L'espace regional et les objectifs du plan* (Mont Joli: Bureau d'aménagement de l'Est du Québec, 1966), 123–25.

20 Dubé, "Le BAEQ et les paroisses marginales," 60.

21 Metra Consultants Ltée., *Relocalisation de population dans l'Est du Québec: étude critique d'une expérience pilote, proposition d'une esquisse de programme général* (Montreal: Metra Consultants Ltée., November 1970), 10–16.

22 Gouvernement du Québec, Arrêté en Conseil 2525, Concernant une expérience-pilote de fermeture de territoires marginaux et de relocalisation de population dans la région de l'Est du Québec, 27 August 1969. The marginal communities "eligible" for relocation were:

Saint-Thomas-de-Cherbourg in Matane County
Saint-Paulin-Dalibaire in Matane County
Rang IV – les Méchins in Matane County
Saint-Octave-de-l'Avenir in Gaspé-Nord
Sacré-Coeur-Deslandes in Gaspé-Nord
Sainte-Bernadette-de-Pellegrin in Gaspé-Sud
Saint-Charles-Garnier-de-Pabos-Nord in Gaspé-Sud
Saint-Edmond-de-Pabos in Gaspé-Sud
Saint-Gabriel-de-Rameau in Gaspé-Sud
Saint-Jean-de-Brébeuf in Bonaventure County.

23 Metra Consultants, *Relocalisation de population dans l'Est du Québec,* 16.

24 Ibid., 18.

25 Ibid., 37.

26 Ibid., 46–47.

27 In eight of the ten communities identified by the province in 1969 as marginal, the vote to leave passed by a margin of at least 90 percent. In a ninth, the vote was more than 85 percent in favour of relocation. Sacré-Coeur-Deslandes was the single outlier, and, even there, relocation still received the support of 65 percent of residents. Ibid., 29.

28 Ibid., 47 and 18.

29 Pierre De Bané, "Le BAEQ et ses suites: le regard d'un député engagé," in Jean, *Le BAEQ revisté,* 94.

30 Robin d'Anjou, "Le BAEQ et ses retombées: le regard d'un agent de relocalisation devenu un administrateur public des ententes de développement regional," in Jean, *Le BAEQ revisité,* 67–68.

31 I have already mentioned Lebrecque's film *Les smattes.* In addition, the closure of marginal parishes was the subject of *Chez nous, c'est chez nous,* directed by Marcel Carrière (Montreal:

National Film Board of Canada, 1972). Musician Jocelyn Berubé also made those closures the subject of his album *Nil en ville* (1976).

32 *La participation,* directed by Raymond Garceau (Ottawa: ARDA and the National Film Board of Canada, 1965).

33 BAEQ received visitors from twenty different countries in June 1965. They came as part of the Economic Development Institute, which organized annual courses in several languages for senior officials from developing countries. "Le Bureau d'aménagement de l'Est du Québec vous informe," television broadcast, 6 June 1965, BAnQ, FN01618.

34 Garceau, *La Participation.*

35 Doray, "Méthodes et techniques d'animation," 27.

36 Cited in Simard, "Le BAEQ," 174.

37 Cited in ibid.

38 Benoit Lévesque, ed. *Animation sociale, entreprises communautaires et coopératives* (Laval, QC: Les Éditions coopératives Albert Saint-Martin, 1979), 8.

39 André Tétrault, "Quelques clarifications sur la notion d'animation," *Les cahiers de l'ICEA,* nos. 4–5 (September 1967): 13–17.

40 Ibid., 15.

41 Bureau d'aménagement de l'Est du Québec, *Plan de développement. Région-pilote: Bas St-Laurent, Gaspésie et Îles-de-la-Madeleine,* cahier 1, chap 1, *Les grands objectifs du plan* (Mont Joli: Bureau d'aménagement de l'Est du Québec, 1966), xv.

42 On "agents of change," see *Le BAEQ vous informe,* 24–26; on "harnessing," see Doray, "Méthodes et techniques d'animation," 27.

43 Simard, *La longue marche des technocrates,* xx.

44 Desrosiers, "La contribution du BAEQ," 117.

45 Godbout, *La participation contre la démocratie,* 56.

46 For background on Roger Guy, see "Discours de la rectrice de l'UQAT et du directeur de la Chaire Desjardins à la Cérémonie de la Médaille d'Honneur," *Info Chaire Desjardins: bulletin d'information* 4, special issue, June 2014, http://uqat.ca/chairedesjardins/medias/uploads/misc/ChDjsBulletinspecial2014.pdf.

47 Roger Guy, "Mon expérience d'animateur au BAEQ," in Lévesque, *Animation sociale,* 59–60.

48 Ibid., 61. Morin discusses these tensions in BAEQ. See "Le BAEQ, la légende et l'esprit du développement régionale," 278–85.

49 Rural Development Branch, Department of Forestry and Rural Development, *Development Plan for the Pilot Region,* ii.

50 *Le BAEQ vous informe,* 24–26 and 32.

51 "Toujours les mêmes," *L'aménagement,* 15 January 1965, 4.

52 Rural Development Branch, Department of Forestry and Rural Development, *Development Plan for the Pilot Region,* 192.

53 Gilles Picard and Albert Juneau, *Étude sociologique des changements agricoles dans le Bas-St-Laurent et la Gaspésie* (Mont-Joli, QC: Bureau d'aménagement de l'Est du Québec, 1966), 1–10 and 89.

54 Rural Development Branch, Department of Forestry and Rural Development, *Development Plan for the Pilot Region,* 186 and 194. Also see Alain-G. Gagnon, *Développement régional,* 99.

55 *Le BAEQ vous informe,* 37.

56 Ibid., 37–38. Frère Untel, or Brother Anonymous, was Jean-Paul Desbiens, a Marist brother, who was critical of the church-controlled public education system in Quebec. He published his views as *Les insolences du Frère Untel* in 1960. The book was important in shaping educational reform in the ensuing Quiet Revolution.

57 Télé-Club broadcast, 24 February 1965, BAnQ DVD, FN08521.
58 Ibid.
59 Télé-Club broadcast, 10 March 1965, BAnQ DVD, FN08523.
60 Office national du film du Canada, *Soirée Raymond Garceau* (Montreal: Office national du film du Canada, 27 January 1966).
61 Ibid.
62 Léo Bonneville, "Entretien avec Raymond Garceau," in *Séquences: la revue de cinéma* 57 (1969): 47.
63 Office national du film du Canada, *Soirée Raymond Garceau.*
64 *Le Milieu,* directed by Pierre Lemelin, 16 mm (Ottawa: ARDA and the National Film Board of Canada, 1965).
65 Ibid.
66 *Les coopératives,* directed by Pierre Lemelin (Ottawa: ARDA and the National Film Board of Canada, 1965).
67 Ibid.
68 Lemelin, *Le milieu.*
69 Garceau, *La participation.*
70 Ibid.
71 Paul-André Linteau, René Durocher, Jean-Claude Robert, and François Ricard, *Quebec since 1930* (Toronto: James Lorimer, 1991), 388.
72 Cited in Gagnon, *Développement régional,* 55.
73 Godbout, *La participation contre la démocratie,* 51–52.
74 *Le BAEQ vous informe,* 24 and 45.
75 Banville, *Les Opérations Dignité,* 23.
76 Ibid., 25–28.
77 Ibid., 17–18, 26–27. Also see Annexe II: Projet de mémoire sur la mise en valeur des ressources forestières du Bas-Saint-Laurent et de la Gaspésie, Louis-Jean Lussier, ing. for. (Quebec, September 1970), 111–17.
78 Pierre Vallée, "Hommage à Léonard Otis : l'homme de la forêt," *Le Devoir,* 8 March 2008.
79 Banville, *Les Opérations Dignité,* 17.
80 Ibid., 18–21.
81 Cited in ibid.
82 Comité d'aménagement de Sainte-Paule, "La vérité sur le projet des fermes forestières à Sainte-Paule," 9 March 1970, in Léonard Otis in collaboration with Paul Larocque, Jean Larrivée, and Augustine Lavoie, *Une forêt pour vivre: témoignage d'un sylviculteur* (Rimouski: Groupe de recherche interdisciplinaire en développement de l'Est-du-Québec de l'Université du Québec à Rimouski, 1989), 26.
83 Ibid., v.
84 Banville, *Les Opérations Dignité,* 33.
85 Ibid., 40–42.
86 See "Irving Explains Cabano Action," *Montreal Gazette,* 20 August 1970, and "Town Discounts Any Link with Liberation Movement," *Bangor Daily News,* 23 October 1970.
87 Richard Cleroux, "A Dream Came True This Week for a Small Gaspe Town That Fought for Its Life," *Globe and Mail,* 23 September 1972, 8; and Jean-François Lépine, "Les promoteurs du projet de cartonnerie populaire de Cabano" (master's thesis, Université de Québec à Montréal, 1979).
88 Banville, *Les Opérations Dignité,* 61.
89 Ibid., 63.
90 Ibid., 65.

91 "Prise de position du clergé devant la situation économique de la région de l'action entreprise par la population, 27 septembre 1970, Archives du diocèse de Rimouski," Annexe 1 in Banville, *Les Opérations Dignité,* 107 (emphasis in original).
92 *Populorum Progressio,* ss. 25–29, and 76.
93 Vincent Cosmao, O.P., "Louis Joseph Lebret, O.P., 1897–1966: From Social Action to the Struggle for Development," *New Blackfriars* 51, 597 (1970): 62–68.
94 *Populorum Progressio,* ss. 50 and 65.
95 Ibid., s. 50.
96 Ibid., ss. 64 and 65.
97 Convention de travail entre l'OPDQ et le FRUL, 20 August 1971, cited in Banville, *Les Opérations Dignité,* 79.
98 Gouvernement du Québec, Arrêté en conseil 2874-72, Concernant un programme d'aide aux migrants applicable à l'arrière-pays de la région de l'Est du Québec, 27 September 1972.
99 Jacques Lemay, "La question des paroisses marginales: une analyse de contenu de la presse régionale," in Jean, *Le BAEQ revisité,* 153, gives the number of people relocated as 2,178.
100 Gagnon, ed. *Les Opérations Dignité,* 149–51.
101 Gouvernement du Québec, Arrêté en conseil 1452-74, Concernant la suspension du programme d'aide aux migrants prévue par l'Arrêté en conseil 2874-72 du 27 septembre 1972.
102 Ibid., s. 6.
103 This is one of Gagnon's points in *Développement régional.*
104 Morin, "Le BAEQ, la légende et l'esprit du développement régionale."
105 "Le ministre Kevin Drummond dit non aux fermes forestières," *Rimouski Progrès-Echo,* 14 October 1970, cited in Otis et al., *Une forêt pour vivre,* 28.
106 Cited in Gagnon, *Développement régional,* 79.
107 Banville, *Les Opérations Dignité,* 17.
108 Gilles Roy, "L'animation sociale et la mise en place d'entreprises autogestionnaires: le point de vue d'un animateur," in Lévesque, *Animation sociale,* 36.
109 Jay Drydyk, "Participation, Empowerment, and Democracy: Three Fickle Friends," in *New Directions in Development Ethics: Essays in Honor of Denis Goulet,* ed. Charles K. Wilber, Amitava Krishna Dutt, and Theodore M. Hesburgh (Notre Dame, IN: University of Notre Dame, 2010), 333–56.
110 Carrière, *Chez nous, c'est chez nous.*

Chapter 4: "Deviating from the Strict Letter of the Law"

1 The key work on Africville is Donald H. Clairmont and Dennis W. Magill, *Africville Relocation Report* (Halifax: Dalhousie University, Institute of Public Affairs, 1971), http://dalspace.library.dal.ca/handle/10222/55960?show=full, a large portion of which was reprinted as *Africville: The Life and Death of a Canadian Black Community* (Toronto: Canadian Scholars' Press, 1999). As will become apparent, I have relied heavily on it because it contains many of the key primary sources for the study of Africville that are not easily accessed. Other key works include Tina Loo, "Africville and the Dynamics of State Power in Postwar Canada," *Acadiensis* 39, 2 (2010): 23–47; Howard McCurdy, "Africville: Environmental Racism," in *Faces of Environmental Racism: Confronting Issues of Global Justice,* 2nd ed., ed. Laura Westra and Bill E. Lawson (London: Rowman and Littlefield Publishers, Inc., 2005), 95–112; Jennifer J. Nelson, *Razing Africville: A Geography of Racism* (Toronto: University of Toronto Press, 2008); and Ted Rutland, *Displacing Blackness: Planning, Power, and Race in Twentieth-Century Halifax* (Toronto: University of Toronto Press, 2018).
2 Jennifer J. Nelson, "'Panthers or Thieves': Racialized Knowledge and the Regulation of Africville," *Journal of Canadian Studies* 45, 1 (2011): 121–42.

3 Rutland, *Displacing Blackness*, 14.
4 T.H. Marshall, *Citizenship and Social Class* (London: Pluto Press, 1992), 8.
5 Pierre Elliott Trudeau, *Federalism and the French Canadians* (New York: St. Martin's Press, 1968), 147.
6 "Africville," City of Halifax Development Department Report, 23 July 1962, in Clairmont and Magill, *Africville Relocation Report*, Appendix A, A7.
7 Rutland, *Displacing Blackness*, 23.
8 Michel F. Girard, *L'écologisme retrouvé: essor et déclin de la Commission de la conservation du Canada* (Ottawa: Presses de l'Université d'Ottawa, 1994), 188–89.
9 Michael Simpson, "Thomas Adams in Canada, 1914–1930," *Urban History Review* 11, 2 (1982): 4, 6–11.
10 Research Committee of the League for Social Reconstruction, *Social Planning for Canada* (Toronto: Thomas Nelson, 1935), 218.
11 Ibid., 452.
12 Ibid., 453 and 460.
13 Urban growth during the war was three times what it had been before the war. Advisory Committee on Reconstruction, Report IV, Housing and Community Planning, *Final Report of the Subcommittee, March 24, 1944* (Ottawa: Edmond Cloutier, Printer to the King's Most Excellent Majesty, 1944), 133.
14 Ibid., 132. Also see John Bacher, "From Study to Reality: The Establishment of Public Housing in Halifax, 1930–1953," *Acadiensis* 18, 1 (1988): 128–35.
15 Advisory Committee on Reconstruction, *Final Report*, 135.
16 Ibid., 160.
17 H. Peter Oberlander and Arthur L. Fallick, *Housing a Nation: The Evolution of Canadian Housing Policy* (Vancouver: Centre for Human Settlements, University of British Columbia for Canada Mortgage and Housing Corporation, June 1992), 35–37.
18 The term "urban renewal" dates from the 1950s. See Kevin J. Cross and Robert W. Collier, *The Urban Renewal Process in Canada: An Analysis of Current Practice* (Vancouver: School of Regional Planning Studies, University of British Columbia, 1967), 1; and Colin Gordon, "Blighting the Way: Urban Renewal, Economic Development, and the Elusive Definition of Blight," *Fordham Urban Law Journal* 31, 2 (2003): 314.
19 Helen Meller, *Towns, Plans, and Society in Modern Britain* (Cambridge: Cambridge University Press, 1997), 67. Stephen Bocking argues that, from 1940 to 1970, urban expertise "was perhaps most unchallenged." See his "Constructing Urban Expertise: Professional and Political Authority in Toronto, 1940–1970," *Journal of Urban History* 33, 1 (2006): 52.
20 Gordon Stephenson, *A Redevelopment Study of Halifax, Nova Scotia, 1957* (Halifax: Corporation of the City of Halifax, 1957), vii–viii. The statistic on the number of urban renewal projects is from Pierre Filion, "The Neighbourhood Improvement Program in Montreal and Toronto: Two Approaches to Publicly Sponsored Upgrading," in *The Changing Canadian Inner City*, ed. Trudi E. Bunting and Pierre Filion (Waterloo: University of Waterloo Department of Geography, 1988), 88. There is a large literature on urban renewal, much of it case studies of particular cities. A few places to start for overviews are Christopher Klemek, *The Transatlantic Collapse of Urban Renewal: Postwar Urbanism from New York to Berlin* (Chicago: University of Chicago Press, 2011); Jon C. Teaford, *The Rough Road to Renaissance: Urban Revitalization in America, 1940–1985* (Baltimore, MD: Johns Hopkins University Press, 1990); Samuel Zipp and Michael Carriere, "Introduction: Thinking through Urban Renewal," *Journal of Urban History* 39, 3 (2013): 359–65, and that issue in general; and Samuel Zipp, *Manhattan Projects: The Rise and Fall of Urban Renewal in Cold War New York* (New York: Oxford University Press, 2010).

21 John C. Bacher, *Keeping to the Marketplace: The Evolution of Canadian Housing Policy* (Montreal and Kingston: McGill-Queen's University Press, 1993), 214.

22 Ibid., vii.

23 Marcus Paterson, "Slum Clearance in Halifax: The Role of Gordon Stephenson" (master's research project, School of Planning, Dalhousie University, 2009), 34 and part 2 generally.

24 Jenny Gregory and David L.A. Gordon, "Introduction: Gordon Stephenson, Planner and Civic Designer," *Town Planning Review* 83, 3 (2012): 269–78.

25 Quoted in Paterson, "Slum Clearance in Halifax," 10.

26 Quoted in Jill L. Grant and Marcus Paterson, "Scientific Cloak / Romantic Heart: Gordon Stephenson and the Redevelopment Study of Halifax, 1957," *Town Planning Review* 83, 3 (2012): 322.

27 Gordon Stephenson, *Compassionate Town Planning*, ed. Hugh Stretton (Liverpool: Liverpool University Press, 1996) and Gordon Stephenson, *On a Human Scale: A Life in City Design*, ed. Christina DeMarco (South Fremantle, Western AU: Fremantle Arts Centre Press, 1992). The quote from Le Corbusier is cited in Jenny Gregory and David L.A. Gordon, "Conclusion: Reflecting on the Career of a 'Technical Man,'" *Town Planning Review* 83, 3 (2012): 398.

28 Mayor Leonard Kitz, foreword in Stephenson, *A Redevelopment Study of Halifax*, v.

29 Stephenson, *A Redevelopment Study of Halifax*, 21.

30 Grant and Paterson, "Scientific Cloak." Average incomes were $1,800 per year: nowhere else in the city were incomes below $2,200. See Stephenson, *A Redevelopment Study of Halifax*, 32.

31 Stephenson, *A Redevelopment Study of Halifax*, 32, 46, and 69. The number of people who would be displaced by the twelve redevelopment schemes Stephenson set out was 6,480 and was calculated from the table on 56. On 58, he gives a different figure, noting 7,000 would have to be rehoused.

32 Ibid., 56, 25–26. In 1998, the city, province, and Downtown Halifax Business Commission commissioned a report that recommended the demolition of the interchange. It is currently underway, https://www.halifax.ca/about-halifax/regionalcommunityplanning/construction projects/cogswelldistrict

33 Alderman Abbie Lane in city council minutes, City of Halifax, 3 December 1958, 666. See http://legacycontent.halifax.ca/archives/HalifaxCityMinutes/index.php.

34 City council approved the Jacob Street demolitions on 20 February 1958. Bacher, *Keeping to the Marketplace*, 216.

35 The acreage is from Joan Parsons Doehler, "Scotia Square: Its Impact on the Downtown Core" (master's thesis, Dalhousie University, 2001, 17). The number of dwelling units demolished is from City of Halifax, Works Department, Ordinance No. 50 and Building Demolition Statistics, 31 March 1965, Halifax Regional Municipality Archives (hereafter HRMA), Committee on Works Records, Building Inspectors correspondence and subject files, Ordinance 50 Implementation [Dilapidated Buildings], File 102-3-L-1. The population figure was calculated by multiplying the number of dwelling units demolished by an average household size of 3.5. That figure was itself an average of household size in Halifax generally (2–3 persons) and the household size of black families living in the downtown area (5–6).

36 Christopher Parsons, "'The Civic Bible for Future Development': Power, Planning, and Expertise in Halifax, 1956–1962" (honours thesis, University of King's College, 2009), 42.

37 In addition to Jacob Street, the other redevelopment projects initiated by the city before it began acquiring and clearing properties in Africville were Maitland Street (1958, involving 139 people), Spring Garden South (1958, involving 384 people), the Downtown Waterfront (1960, involving 44 people), and Uniacke Square (1962, involving 4,090 people). On Maitland Street, see Resolution, 18 March, HRMA, 102-42B, file B10 (which gives different figures: 115 people and 25 families) and Memorandum from G.F. West, Commissioner of Works and

Buildings to His Worship Mayor Vaughan, Chairman, and Members of the Housing Committee, 5 September 1958, re: Gottingen Street Shopping Centre and Parking – Block 17 Submission, 2, HRMA, 102-42A. I have taken the figures from the latter document. On Spring Garden South, see Minutes of a meeting of the Redevelopment Committee, 11 March 1960, 11ff., HRMA, 102-42A; on the Downtown Waterfront, see Minutes of a meeting of the Redevelopment Committee, 31 March 1960, 6ff., HRMA, 102-42A; and on Uniacke Square, see City of Halifax, "Uniacke Square Redevelopment Project Report," 19 April 1961, 7 and 13, HRMA, 102-42D, File D1.

38 Ordinance No. 50 Respecting Minimum Standards for Housing Accommodation, 1956, HRMA, 102-1D. It was revised in 1962 and made applicable to all buildings, not just those built before 1945. See HRMA, 102-1D, Ordinance No. 50-1962. The sections of the city charter relating to dangerous and dilapidated buildings were ss. 754 to 757. See *Halifax City Charter, 1931* (Halifax: Commissioner of Public Works, 1931), 338–40.

39 See, for instance, Minutes of the Committee on Works, 1 April 1958, 43-52, HRMA, 102-39A.

40 Bacher, *Keeping to the Marketplace,* 216.

41 "Rentals in Slums Show Sharp Rise in the Last 12 Months," *Halifax Mail-Star,* 25 January 1961, cited in Parsons, "The Civic Bible for Future Development," 39.

42 Minutes of a meeting of the Housing Policy Review Committee, 11 July 1961, 1, HRMA, 102-68, file 2.

43 City Council Minutes, City of Halifax, 25 June 1959, 457.

44 See, for instance, Committee on Works Minutes, 26 May 1958, 116, HRMA, 102-39A.

45 Doehler, "Scotia Square," 95. Also see Rutland, *Displacing Blackness,* 157–62, and Danielle Robinson, "'The Streets Belong to the People': Expressway Disputes in Canada, ca. 1960–75" (PhD diss., McMaster University, 2012), chap. 6.

46 I have been able to find only one occasion in which Ordinance No. 50 was applied in Africville and that was in June 1960, when "dwellings" were ordered demolished by the Committee on Works. See "Ordered Demolished, 1960," 1, in HRMA, 102-39L, file 1.

47 For a description of Africville, see Loo, "Africville." The statistics on welfare are from Memorandum re: Africville from Dr. A.R. Morton, Commissioner of Health and Welfare, to Mr. P.F.C. Byars, City Manager, 28 August 1962, 1, HRMA, City Manager's Correspondence, Africville, 1954–65, file 102-4A.5.1. Figures on income and population are from Institute of Public Affairs, Dalhousie University, *The Condition of the Negroes of Halifax City, Nova Scotia* (Halifax: Institute of Public Affairs, Dalhousie University, 1962), 11, 7. On "slow violence," see Rob Nixon, *Slow Violence and the Environmentalism of the Poor* (Cambridge, MA: Harvard University Press, 2013).

48 Clairmont and Magill, *Africville Relocation Report,* 74.

49 In 1961, the Committee on Works recommended withholding a building permit for a dwelling in Africville pending the outcome of discussions on redeveloping the area. Memorandum from G.F. West, Commissioner of Works and Buildings, to the Mayor and Members of the Redevelopment Committee, 23 August 1961, re: Application for a Building Permit – 1803 Barrington Street, HRMA 104-42B, file B49.

50 Loo, "Africville," 28–29.

51 James W. St. G. Walker, "The 'Jewish Phase' in the Movement for Racial Equality in Canada," *Canadian Ethnic Studies* 34, 1 (2002): 1–2.

52 Cited in Loo, "Africville," 29.

53 Alan Borovoy, *At the Barricades: A Memoir* (Toronto: Irwin Law, 2013), 76.

54 Clairmont and Magill, *Africville Relocation Report,* 179–85.

55 Ibid., 185–97 generally, and 359.

56 Verbatim transcript of a tape-recorded interview conducted by Scott Roxborough with Donald F. Maclean, 5 June 1995, 1, Halifax Human Rights Advisory Committee, HRMA, CR 5.2.
57 Clairmont and Magill, *Africville Relocation Report,* 182, 184, 186, 188.
58 It met forty times and held an additional seven meetings with Africville residents at the Seaview Baptist Church. See ibid., 177.
59 Ibid., 209–10.
60 Ibid., 211.
61 Cited in ibid., 214.
62 "Report of a Visit to Halifax with Particular Respect to Africville, November 24–26, 1963," in ibid., Appendix F, A62.
63 Ibid., A66–A67.
64 Ibid., A63.
65 Ibid., A67.
66 Cited in ibid., 230.
67 Ibid., 232 and 226.
68 "Africville," City of Halifax Development Department Report, A7, A3, and A4.
69 Stephenson, *A Redevelopment Study of Halifax,* 27–28.
70 Institute of Public Affairs, *The Condition of Negroes of Halifax City,* 16.
71 Clairmont and Magill, *Africville Relocation Study,* 63.
72 Institute of Public Affairs, *The Condition of the Negroes of Halifax City,* 16.
73 "Africville," City of Halifax Development Department Report, A7 and A5.
74 E.A. Heamon, "Rights Talk and the Liberal Order Framework," in *Liberalism and Hegemony: Debating the Canadian Liberal Revolution,* ed. Jean-François Constant and Michel Ducharme (Toronto: University of Toronto Press, 2009), 155.
75 As the city manager reminded members of council, "In essence, the City of Halifax committed itself to compensate the residents of the area for all legal and moral claims to ownership to property, to provide alternate housing at reasonable rentals and to provide guidance and casework service with regard to employment, education, and personal problems." Memorandum re: Africville from P.F.C. Byars to Members of the Sub-Committee on Africville – Confidential, 12 November 1964, 1, HRMA, City Manager's Correspondence, Africville, 1954–1965, file 104-4A.5.1.
76 Cited in Clairmont and Magill, *Africville Relocation Report,* 163.
77 Stephenson, *A Redevelopment Study of Halifax,* 27.
78 Interview conducted by Scott Roxborough with Donald F. Maclean, 4.
79 Dominique Clément, *Canada's Rights Revolution: Social Movements and Social Change, 1937–82* (Vancouver: UBC Press, 2009).
80 Wanda Thomas Bernard and Judith Fingard, "Black Women at Work: Race, Family, and Community in Greater Halifax," in *Mothers of the Municipality: Women, Work, and Social Policy in Post–1945 Halifax,* ed. Judith Fingard and Janet Guildford (Toronto: University of Toronto Press, 2005), 205; and Bridglal Pachai, ed., *Nova Scotia Human Rights Commission – 25th Anniversary, 1967–1992: A History* (Halifax: The Commission, 1992).
81 Clairmont and Magill, *Africville Relocation Report,* 357.
82 Cited in ibid., 216. On Africville's reputation among Black Haligonians, see 356.
83 Ibid. In a 1963 interview, American social critic James Baldwin argued that urban renewal was "Negro removal." See Kenneth B. Clark, "A Conversation with James Baldwin," in *Conversations with James Baldwin,* ed. Fred L. Standley and Louis H. Pratt (Jackson: University Press of Mississippi, 1989), 42.
84 In 1959, the black population in Halifax outside of Africville was 1,227. It was concentrated in the "mid-city" area, just north and east of the Citadel. This was not a segregated area;

most had white neighbours. See Institute of Public Affairs, *The Condition of the Negroes of Halifax City*, 5, 15; R.B. Grant, Director of Development, to Kell Antoft, Assistant Director, Administration, Institute of Public Affairs, Dalhousie University, re: Africville Relocation Report, 26 November 1971, 2, HRMA, City Manager's Correspondence, file 102-4A.129.

85 Cited in Clairmont and Magill, *Africville Relocation Report*, 238.

86 Ibid., 245.

87 Scott argues that "an illegible society ... is a hindrance to any effective intervention by the state." James C. Scott, *Seeing like a State: How Certain Schemes to Improve the Human Condition Have Failed* (New Haven, CT: Yale University Press, 1998), 78 and Part 1 generally.

88 Clairmont and Magill, *Africville Relocation Report*, 245.

89 Cited in ibid., 256 and 309.

90 Stephenson, *A Redevelopment Study of Halifax*, 28.

91 Cited in Clairmont and Magill, *Africville Relocation Report*, 256.

92 Ibid., 274–75.

93 Ibid., 274.

94 Ibid., 270.

95 In setting out the function of the subcommittee, City Manager P.F.C. Byars noted it would "insure that the City's commitments to the community are carried out and, at the same time, [communicate] the implications of and the actions which will be carried out by the City [with respect to residents]." Memorandum re: Africville from P.F.C. Byars, City Manager, to Members of the Sub-Committee on Africville, 19 June 1964, 2, HRMA, City Manager's Correspondence, Africville 1954–1965, file 102-4A.5.1.

96 Clairmont and Magill, *Africville Relocation Report*, 267–68, 272.

97 Cited in ibid., 274.

98 Ibid., 265–66.

99 Memorandum re: Africville Relocation Scheme from C. McC. Henderson, City Manager, to His Worship the Mayor and Members of City Council, 8 February 1971, HRMA, City Manager's Correspondence, file 102-4A.129.

100 Memorandum re: Transfer of Overfunding to Africville Account, from S.A. Ward, City Manager, to His Worship the Mayor and Members of the Finance and Executive Committee, 17 October 1969, City Manager's Correspondence, file 102-4A.129, Halifax and Halifax Regional Municipality; Memorandum re: Africville Relocation – Mr. [redacted], from S.A. Ward, City Manager, to A.W. Churchill, Administrative Assistant, 7 January 1970, HRMA, City Manager's Correspondence, file 102-4A.129. The former site of Africville currently has one resident. Eddie Carvery was born in Africville and returned there after it was bulldozed. See Jon Tattrie, *The Hermit of Africville: The Life of Eddie Carvery* (Halifax: Pottersfield Press, 2010).

101 Clairmont and Magill, *Africville Relocation Report*, viii.

102 Ibid., 283.

103 Africville Follow-Up Proposal submitted by Social Planning Staff, City of Halifax, 4 February 1969, 4, HRMA, City Manager's Correspondence, file 102-4A.129.

104 Africville Action Committee, 29 October 1970, 2, HRMA, City Manager's Correspondence, file 102-4A.129.

105 Clairmont and Magill, *Africville Relocation Report*, 311.

106 Ibid., 307–12. Alexa Shaw (McDonough) was the daughter of Lloyd Shaw and a future leader of the federal New Democratic Party.

107 There were, however, community development efforts being carried out in black communities outside Halifax. See Bernard and Fingard, "Black Women at Work," 206–7.

108 Cited in Clairmont and Magill, *Africville Relocation Report*, 196.

109 Featured in *Remember Africville,* directed by Shelagh Mackenzie (Montreal: National Film Board of Canada, 1991).

110 Burnley "Rocky" Jones and James W. St. G. Walker, *Burnley "Rocky" Jones, Revolutionary: An Autobiography* (Halifax: Roseway Publishing, 2016), 103.

111 Confidential Memorandum to the Cabinet from John Munro, Minister of National Health and Welfare, and Gérard Pelletier, Secretary of State, 16 June 1969, Library and Archives Canada (LAC), RG 2, vol. 6349, file 636/69, and Memorandum to Cabinet, 30 July 1969, re: Black United Front, ibid., vol. 6352, file 839/69.

112 James W. St. G. Walker, "Black Confrontation in 1960s Halifax," in *Debating Dissent: Canada and the Sixties,* ed. Lara Campbell, Dominique Clément, and Gregory S. Kealey (Toronto: University of Toronto Press, 2012), 186.

113 "Submission for Developmental Phase Demonstration Project," n.d., 1, LAC, Jewish Labour Committee of Canada fonds, MG 28 V 75, vol. 41, file 1.

114 Jones and Walker, *Burnley "Rocky" Jones,* 102 and 104.

Chapter 5: "A Fourth Level of Government"?

1 Cited in SPOTA Early History, Chislett-Robinson Report (draft with comments), n.d., City of Vancouver Archives (CVA), Strathcona Property Owners and Tenants Association (SPOTA) fonds, AM-734-S1, box 583-B-5, file 5, 14.

2 "Hellyer Disgusted by Poverty Tales," *Vancouver Sun,* 8 November 1968 and *Vancouver Province,* 8 November 1968, 6, cited in Michael Bruce, "'A New Breed of Group': Community Activism in Vancouver's Strathcona Neighbourhood, 1968–1972" (master's thesis, University of British Columbia, 2005), 24.

3 Sean Purdy, "Constructing Pariah Spaces in the Americas North and South: Newspaper Representations of Slums, Ghettos and Favelas in the 1960s," in *New World Coming: The Sixties and the Shaping of Global Consciousness,* ed. Karen Dubinsky, Catherine Krull, Susan Lord, Sean Mills, and Scott Rutherford (Toronto: Between the Lines, 2009), 220.

4 Bessie Lee, "Strathcona Property Owners and Tenants Association," in *Opening Doors: Vancouver's East End,* ed. Carole Itter and Daphne Marlatt (Victoria, BC: Aural History Program, 1979), 184.

5 The phrase is Martin Anderson's. See his *The Federal Bulldozer: A Critical Analysis of Urban Renewal, 1949–1962* (Cambridge, MA: MIT Press, 1965).

6 There is a very large literature on urban renewal. For an overview of its rise and fall, see Christopher Klemek, *The Transatlantic Collapse of Urban Renewal: Postwar Urbanism from New York to Berlin* (Chicago: University of Chicago Press, 2011).

7 Canadian Council on Urban and Regional Research, Urban Renewal Research Seminar, Montreal, 13–15 May 1965, 18, 4, 5, 9, and 3, CVA, City of Vancouver fonds, S648, Director of Planning, General Files, box 926-E-3, file 5 (emphasis in the original).

8 Dubinsky et al., *New World Coming,* 4.

9 The key works on urban renewal on the East Side and in Strathcona, particularly, are Kay J. Anderson, *Vancouver's Chinatown: Racial Discourse in Canada, 1875–1980* (Montreal and Kingston: McGill-Queen's University Press, 1991), 188–210; Bruce, "'A New Breed of Group"; Jo-Anne Lee, "Gender, Ethnicity, and Hybrid Forms of Community-Based Urban Activism in Vancouver, 1957–1978: The Strathcona Story Revisited," *Gender, Place and Culture* 14, 4 (2007): 381–407; David Ley, Kay Anderson, and Doug Konrad, "Chinatown-Strathcona: Gaining an Entitlement," in *Neighbourhood Organizations and the Welfare State,* ed. Shlomo Hasson and David Ley (Toronto: University of Toronto Press, 1994), 112–36; and Wing Chung Ng, *The Chinese in Vancouver: The Pursuit of Identity and Power* (Vancouver: UBC Press, 1999), 97–102.

10 Ley, Anderson, and Konrad, "Chinatown-Strathcona."
11 Bruce, "'A New Breed of Group,'" and Lee, "Gender, Ethnicity, and Hybrid Forms of Community-Based Urban Activism."
12 Darlene Marzari interview, cited by Bruce, "'A New Breed of Group,'" 25.
13 Lee, "Gender, Ethnicity, and Hybrid Forms of Community-Based Urban Activism," and Bruce, "'A New Breed of Group,'" chaps. 7, 8, and 9.
14 Kay Alsop, "She Thrives on Involvement," *Vancouver Province,* 7 January 1972, 20.
15 William Langford, "'Is Sutton Brown God?' Planning Expertise and the Local State in Vancouver, 1952–1973" (master's thesis, University of British Columbia, 2011), 10–11.
16 Ibid., 11–12 and 20.
17 City of Vancouver Planning Department for the Housing Research Committee, *Vancouver Redevelopment Study* (Vancouver: City of Vancouver Planning Department, December 1957), 1.
18 Ibid., 4, 55, 56, 59.
19 Ibid., 6.
20 Ibid., 48.
21 Langford, "'Is Sutton Brown God?'" (thesis), 17.
22 *Vancouver Redevelopment Study,* 52.
23 Ibid., 8.
24 Ibid., 13.
25 Ibid., 91 and 7.
26 The incidence of active TB cases was 642 per 100,000 on the East Side and 231 per 100,000 in Vancouver as a whole. Ibid., 7 and 39.
27 Ibid., 28, 41, and 22–25.
28 Strathcona was a thirty-five-block area bounded by Raymur Avenue to the east, Gore Avenue to the west, Hastings Street to the north, and Union Street to the south.
29 Ibid., 84ff. Also see Rhodri Windsor-Liscombe, "Leonard Marsh and the Vancouver Modern," *Architecture and Ideas* 1, 1 (1996): 40–51.
30 The three phases were officially known as Project 1, Project 2, and Scheme 3. The dates noted are when the three levels of government approved the redevelopment plan. See Memorandum, Project 1 Clearance Areas (as revised 12 July 1960), CVA, City of Vancouver fonds, S648, box 925-E-2, file 10, Redevelopment – general – public relations and liaison with Chinese community, 1956–63; Draft Memorandum re: Redevelopment Project No. 2 and Subsequent Projects Relocation and Associated Activity, 18 February 1965, ibid., box 924-D-6, folder 1, Urban renewal – social planning, 1962–1965; "She's Got a Thing about Bulldozers … and Their Levelling Approach," *Vancouver Province,* 21 May 1969; and City of Vancouver, *City of Vancouver Urban Renewal Program Under the National Housing Act: Estimated Principal Activities to 1970* (Vancouver: City of Vancouver Planning Department, September 1965), CVA, PD-2085.
31 Two exceptions are Anderson, *Vancouver's Chinatown,* 188–210, and Ng, *The Chinese in Vancouver,* 97–102.
32 Interestingly, Vancouver's local-born Chinese, or *tusheng,* supported redevelopment, arguing it would help "deghettoize" the area. In their view, the ethnic enclave had served its purpose, helping newcomers adjust. Ng, *The Chinese in Vancouver,* 50 and 99.
33 Area "A" was the part of the East Side targeted for comprehensive redevelopment.
34 Area "A" Property Owners' Association to Mayor and Council, 14 July 1959, 1–2, CVA, City of Vancouver fonds, S648, box 925-E-2, file 10.
35 Submission of the Chinese Community to the Mayor and Council of the City of Vancouver Regarding the Vancouver Re-Development Scheme, Charles C. Locke, Counsel, 30 September 1960, 4, ibid.

36 Carl F. Barton, Principal, Strathcona School, to R. Thompson, City Clerk, n.d. [stamped received 12 October 1960], 2, ibid.

37 W.P. Wong, President, Chinese Canadian Citizens Association, 108 E. Pender Street, to the Mayor and Council, 26 April 1961, 1, ibid.

38 Leung to the Mayor and Council, 30 January 1963, 1, CVA, City of Vancouver fonds, S648, box 926-E-3, file 3.

39 Brief to City Council, City of Vancouver, re: Urban Renewal Plans for the Strathcona Area (Comments on the Summary Report, Urban Renewal Scheme No. 3), from Strathcona Area Council, Committee on Redevelopment and Relocation, n.d. [but the Strathcona Area Council was not established until 1965], 7–8, ibid., box 926-F-3, file 2.

40 Brief of the Chinatown Property Owners Association, 17 July 1961, Royal Commission on Expropriation Laws and Procedures, 3, ibid., box 925-E-2, file 10.

41 Lawyer Charles Locke told the regional supervisor for the CMHC, the provincial housing commissioner, and the city's planner that "some Chinese had paid comparatively high prices for property which had a special locational advantage for their race." Confidential, Memorandum of Meeting held in the offices of Messrs. Ladner, Downs, Ladner, Locke, Clark, and Lenox, Barristers and Solicitors, 17 May 1960, re: Housing, Redevelopment, Section 23, National Housing Act, 3, ibid.

42 A Brief on Housing, sent to Mr. W.E. Graham, 8 November 1965, W.E. Graham, Director of Planning, to Mr. Dai Foon Soon, 626 E. Pender Street, re: Redevelopment Project No. 2: Alternative Housing; and "Redevelopment Upsets Owner," *Vancouver Sun,* 28 October 1965, CVA, City of Vancouver fonds, S648, CVA, box 925-E-7, file 3.

43 Ng Jung Yen and Siu Gum Hin, 653 E. Pender Street, to George D. Wong, Chairman, Mayor's Consultative Committee, 22 November 1961, ibid, box 926-E-3, folder 2.

44 A.D. Geach, Notes for the Guidance of Attendants at the City of Vancouver's Exhibit on Redevelopment at the PNE, August to September 1960, 17 August 1960, 3, ibid., box 926-F-3, file 5.

45 Brief to City Council, City of Vancouver, re: Urban Renewal Plans for the Strathcona Area (Comments on the Summary Report, Urban Renewal Scheme No. 3), from Strathcona Area Council, Committee on Redevelopment and Relocation, n.d., ibid., box 926-F-3, file 2.

46 W.P. Wong, President, Chinese Canadian Citizens Association, 108 E. Pender Street, to the Mayor and Council, 26 April 1961, 1, ibid., box 925-E-2, file 10.

47 Leung to the Mayor W.G. Rathie Re: Redevelopment in Area "A," 8 February 1963, 1, ibid., box 926-E-3, file 3.

48 Cited in Anderson, *Vancouver's Chinatown,* 196–97.

49 *Chinatown News,* 18 February 1961, cited by Anderson, *Vancouver's Chinatown,* 195.

50 Cited in Will Langford, "'Is Sutton Brown God?' Planning Expertise and the Local State in Vancouver, 1952–73," *BC Studies* 173 (Spring 2012): 14.

51 Klemek, *The Transnational Collapse of Urban Renewal,* part 1 and 19.

52 Langford, 'Is Sutton Brown God?' (article), 15–26.

53 For an overview on urban reform, see Robert Wiebe, *The Search for Order* (New York: Hill and Wang, 1967); Samuel Hays, "The Politics of Reform in Municipal Government in the Progressive Era," *Pacific Northwest Quarterly* 55, 4 (1964): 3–26; and Sam Bass Warner, Jr., "If All the World Were Philadelphia: A Scaffold for Urban History, 1774–1930," *American Historical Review* 74, 1 (1968): 26–43.

54 Paul Rutherford, "Tomorrow's Metropolis: The Urban Reform Movement in Canada, 1880–1920," Canadian Historical Association *Historical Papers* 61 (1971): 213–14.

55 Paul Tennant, "Vancouver Civic Politics, 1929–1980," *BC Studies* 46 (1980): 6–11.

56 On forms of municipal government in Canada, see Thomas J. Plunkett, *Urban Canada and Its Government: A Study of Municipal Organization* (Toronto: Macmillan, 1968). See his comments on the council-committee system, 16.

57 Patricia Roy, "Table II: Vancouver City as a Proportion of Greater Vancouver, 1901–1971," in *Vancouver: An Illustrated History* (Toronto: Lorimer, 1980), 168.

58 Plunkett calls it a "Council–City Commissioner System" largely because administrative duties were split between two commissioners rather than vested in a single city manager. Given the power of the commissioners, and particularly one of them – Gerald Sutton Brown – it is more accurate to call Vancouver's form of government a council-manager system, rather like those in the United States, which are characterized by a powerful city manager. Plunkett, *Urban Canada and Its Government,* 143ff.

59 Langford, "'Is Sutton Brown God?'" (article), 29.

60 Ibid., 28.

61 Timothy Mitchell, *Rule of Experts: Egypt, Techno-Politics, Modernity* (Berkeley: University of California Press, 2002).

62 Confidential Memorandum, from Mr. A.D. Geach, Assistant Director of Redevelopment, to Mr. W.E. Graham, Director of Planning, cc: Mr. H.W. Pickstone, Deputy Director of Planning, re: Redevelopment Consultative Committee, 3 December 1963, 1, CVA, City of Vancouver fonds, S648, box 926-E-3, file 8.

63 The goals of the Redevelopment Consultative Committee were listed in an article in *L'Eco D'Italia,* 2 August 1961, ibid., file 2.

64 Draft of Inquiry to be circulated to various cities for reply, re: Citizen Participation in the City of Vancouver Urban Renewal Program Under Section 23 of the National Housing Act of the Federal Government of Canada, 9 July 1964, 2, ibid., file 4.

65 Summary of Replies to the Questionnaire on Citizen Participation in Urban Renewal, n.d. [1964], and Canadian Experience with Citizens Committees, n.d. [1964], ibid., file 8.

66 In addition, there was a member and former chair of the Greater Vancouver Tourism Association and a downtown lawyer. Specifically, the committee members were George D. Wong (chair), Faye Leung, William Kan, Wong Foon Sien, Marino Culos, John D'Appolonia, Charles F. Barton, Rev. Thomas Speed, Rosemary Brown (Gus Wedderburn's sister), Mrs. E. Ostapchuk, Harry Duker (secretary), and R.P. Anderson. Mayor's Re-Development Consultative Committee, Official Publicity Release of Mayor's Consultative Committee, n.d. [but cover letter with the release is dated 21 June 1961], ibid., file 2.

67 Cited by Will Langford, "Gerald Sutton Brown and the Discourse of City Planning Expertise in Vancouver, 1953–1959," *Urban History Review* 41, 2 (2013): 37.

68 W.E. Graham, Director of Planning to Board of Administration, 2 November 1964, re: Redevelopment Consultative Committee Revised Terms of Reference (interim report), Appendix: Summary of Principal Actions, Redevelopment Consultative Committee, CVA, City of Vancouver fonds, S648, box 926-E-3, file 8.

69 Report of the Sub-Committee Investigating Reports on Exodus of Chinese from the Strathcona Area, Excerpted from the Meeting of the Re-development Co-ordinating Committee, 26 August 1964, ibid., file 4.

70 W.E. Graham, Director of Planning to Board of Administration, 2 November 1964.

71 Ibid.

72 "City Considers New 'Social' Department," *Vancouver Province,* 6 August 1965.

73 For its administrative history, see the City of Vancouver Archives webpage on the Department of Social Planning, at http://searcharchives.vancouver.ca/vancouver-b-c-social-planning-department.

74 Joint Technical Committee, Department of Social Planning and Development to His Worship the Mayor and Members of Council, 7 May 1968, re: Terms of Reference, and 1968 Program and Budget of Social Planning and Development, Attachment A, 1, CVA, City of Vancouver fonds, S571, Social Planning Department Administrative and Subject Files, box 101-A-4, file 10. Also see City of Vancouver, Community Services, *Social Planning: Celebrating Thirty Years, 1968–1998* (Vancouver: Community Services, City of Vancouver, 1998), 5, and Maurice Egan, "Social Planning in Vancouver," *Plan Canada* 17, 2 (1977): 118–26.

75 Walter G. Hardwick and David F. Hardwick, "Civic Government: Corporate, Consultative or Participatory?" in *Community Participation and the Spatial Order of the City*, ed. D. Ley (Vancouver: Tantalus Research Ltd., 1974), 91.

76 Memorandum by the Board of Administration in Support of the Concept of a Social Development Board and a Department of Social Planning and Development, 28 June 1965, 1–2, CVA, City of Vancouver fonds, S648, box 924-D-6, file 1.

77 Karen Bridget Murray, "Making Space in Vancouver's East End: From Leonard Marsh to the Vancouver Agreement," *BC Studies* 169 (Spring 2011): 13.

78 Egan, "Social Planning in Vancouver," 126.

79 On the freeway fights in Vancouver, see Ken MacKenzie, "Freeway Protests in Vancouver, 1954–1972" (master's thesis, Simon Fraser University, 1985); and Danielle Robinson, "'The Streets Belong to the People': Expressway Disputes in Canada, ca. 1960–75" (PhD diss., McMaster University, 2012), chap. 2.

80 Memo from the Planning Department to the Board of Administration, re: Town Planning Commission – organization, 4 February 1969, 3 and 5, CVA, City of Vancouver fonds, S648, box 926-E-3, file 6. The TPC members assigned to the Urban Renewal Subcommittee were Roy Lisogar, a hotelier and philanthropist; Peter S. Bullen, a UBC academic; and Helen Boyce, a Parks Board commissioner. See Memorandum from Miss F.M. Ross, Secretary, to All Members Town Planning Commission, 22 July 1969, ibid., S623, box 162-B-7, file 1. I have not been able to identify the other members of the subcommittee who were not members of the TPC but drawn from the citizenry at large. However, one can get a sense of who they might be from the director of planning's "suggested list of organizations with city-wide interests from whom representatives on the Town Planning Commission could be selected." They included the Amalgamated Construction Association of British Columbia, the BC Society of Landscape Architects, the Community Planning Association of Canada, the Downtown Business Association, United Community Services, and the Vancouver and District Labour Council, among others. There were no representatives of neighbourhood citizens' associations. Instead there were organizations that may have represented their interests and concerns, whether they be work, housing, or social services. See W.E. Graham, Director of Planning, to Chairman and Members, Special Committee, re: Town Planning Commission – Organization, 12 March 1968, ibid., Series S623, box 162-B-6, file 4.

81 Paul Hellyer, speech to the Canadian Real Estate Board, 1968, cited by N. Lloyd Axworthy, "The Task Force on Housing and Urban Development: A Study of Democratic Decision-Making in Canada" (Ph.D diss., Princeton University, 1972), 112.

82 Canada, *Report of the Federal Task Force on Housing and Urban Development* (Ottawa: Queen's Printer, 1969), 55.

83 James David Lowden, "Urban Renewal in Canada: A Post-Mortem" (master's thesis, University of British Columbia, 1970), 16–17.

84 Brief to Vancouver City Council from Strathcona Property Owners and Residents Association, 16 May 1969, 1, CVA, City of Vancouver fonds, series 648, box 924-E-4, file 5.

85 Shirley Chan, quoted in *Vancouver Province*, 7 January 1972, cited by Bruce, "'A New Breed of Group,'" 119–21.

86 SPOTA Early History – Chislett-Robinson Report (draft with comments), 33–34.
87 Daniel Lauber, "Social Planning, Vancouver," *Planning* 41 (March–April 1975): 19.
88 Ken Cameron and Mike Harcourt, *City Making in Paradise: Nine Decisions That Saved Vancouver* (Vancouver: Douglas and McIntyre, 2007), 48.
89 Ibid., 36. On the involvement of the charitable organizations and specifically the Neighbourhood Services Association in community development in Vancouver and Strathcona specifically, see Margaret A. Mitchell, *Don't Rest in Peace, Organize! A Community Development Scrapbook Reviewing Five Years' Experience with Vancouver Citizens* (Vancouver: Neighbourhood Services Association of Greater Vancouver, 1975), 47–66. Alexandra Neighbourhood House (later Alexandra Neighbourhood Services) was established by the Woman's Christian Temperance Union in 1892 as a home for motherless children. Over the course of the twentieth century, it transformed itself into a "neighbourhood house" that offered social and recreational services for the Kitsilano area and was part of the Community Chest and Councils of the Greater Vancouver Area.
90 Darlene Marzari, "Presentation at Women Warriors Workshop," *West Coast Line* 42, 2 (2008): 50–52.
91 "Bessie Lee's Story: An Interview with Bessie Lee Transcribed by Jo-Anne Lee," *West Coast Line* 42, 2 (2008): 47.
92 A list of some of SPOTA's meetings, banquets, and tea parties and their invited guests is given in "Questions and Answers or an Analysis of the Strathcona Rehabilitation Project's Planning Process," Submitted to CMHC from SPOTA, September 1973, 13–14, CVA, SPOTA fonds, AM-734-S4, box 538-E-7, file 4.
93 Bruce, "'A New Breed of Group,'" chap. 9; and Lee, "Gender, Ethnicity, and Hybrid Forms of Community-Based Urban Activism," 381.
94 Darlene Marzari quoted in Bruce, "'A New Breed of Group,'" 25.
95 Axworthy, "The Task Force on Housing and Urban Development," chap. 1.
96 Ibid., 3.
97 Ibid., 18.
98 Frank Cunningham, *Theories of Democracy: A Critical Introduction* (London: Routledge, 2002), 141 and chap. 7 generally; Richard Flacks and Nelson Lichtenstein, Introduction in *The Port Huron Statement: Sources and Legacies of the New Left's Founding Manifesto* (Philadelphia: University of Pennsylvania Press, 2015); Paul Litt, *Trudeaumania* (Vancouver: UBC Press, 2016), 249.
99 Sally M. Weaver, *Making Canadian Indian Policy: The Hidden Agenda, 1968–70* (Toronto: University of Toronto Press, 1981), introduction and chap. 2 particularly.
100 Litt, *Trudeaumania*, 249–50.
101 Fred Schindeler and C. Michael Lanphier, "Social Science Research and Participatory Democracy in Canada," *Canadian Public Administration* 12, 4 (1969): 481–98, the quote is from 491.
102 Carrie A. Dickenson and William J. Campbell, "Strange Bedfellows: Youth Activists, Government Sponsorship, and the Company of Young Canadians (CYC), 1965–1970," *European Journal of American Studies* 3, 2 (2008): 1–22; and Kevin Brushett, "Making Shit Disturbers: The Selection and Training of Company of Young Canadian Volunteers 1965–1970," in *The Sixties in Canada: A Turbulent and Creative Decade*, ed. M. Athena Palaeologu (Montreal: Black Rose Books, 2009), 246–69.
103 Thomas Waugh, Michael Brendan Baker, and Ezra Winton, eds., *Challenge for Change: Activist Documentary at the National Film Board of Canada* (Montreal and Kingston: McGill-Queen's University Press, 2010).
104 Dorothy Todd Hénault, "Interview with Léonard Forest," in ibid., 43.

105 Jennifer Keck and Wayne Fulks, "Meaningful Work and Community Betterment: The Case of Opportunities for Youth and Local Initiatives Program, 1971–1973," in *Community Organizing: Canadian Experiences,* ed. Brian Wharf and Michael Clague (Toronto: Oxford University Press, 1997), 112.

106 Hugh Shewell, "Bitterness behind Every Smiling Face: Community Development and Canada's First Nations, 1954–1968," *Canadian Historical Review* 83, 1 (2002): 6, 9, and 14.

107 "Luncheon Address by Lloyd Axworthy, representing the Honourable Mr. Paul Hellyer," in *National Conference on Urban Renewal as It Affects Chinatown, Sponsored by the Sien Lok Society of Calgary, 6–9 April 1969,* 78, CVA, SPOTA fonds, AM734-S4, box 583-E-8, file 10.

108 Ibid.

109 Ibid., 77.

110 Bruce, "'A New Breed of Group,'" 34; Leslie Bella and Penelope Stewart, A Systems Analysis of Community Action (December 1968), 54, CVA, SPOTA fonds, AM734-S4, box 583-E-08, file 1; and Brief, from SPOTA to Vancouver City Council, 16 May 1969, CVA, City of Vancouver fonds, S648, box 924-E-4, file 5.

111 Shirley Y. Chan, for Action Research, Secretary of State Department, Vancouver, BC, "An Overview of the Strathcona Experience with Urban Renewal by a Participant," 31 March 1971, 22, CVA, SPOTA fonds, AM734-S5, box 583-C-3, file 2.

112 Memorandum from the Director of Planning to the Board of Administration, 31 July 1969 re: Communication dated 16 May 1969 from Strathcona Property Owners and Tenants Association and Extract from Council Minutes, 22 July 1969, 1, CVA, City of Vancouver fonds, S648, box 924-E-4, file 5.

113 M.M. Cross, Deputy Director of Planning to Mrs. B. Lee, SPOTA, 24 July 1969, Re: Urban Renewal Scheme 3: Strathcona Rehabilitation Survey, 1, CVA, City of Vancouver fonds, box 924-E-4, file 5.

114 Chan, "An Overview of the Strathcona Experience," 15; and Strathcona Rehabilitation Project Evaluation, Stage II, Preliminary Draft (Ptarmigan Planning Associates, Vancouver, [ca. 1976]), 10, CVA, SPOTA fonds, AM734-S4, box 583-E-8, file 4.

115 Chan, "An Overview of the Strathcona Experience," 15.

116 SPOTA Minutes, 11 September 1969, cited in SPOTA Early History – Chislett-Robinson Report [draft with comments], CVA, SPOTA fonds, AM734-S1, box 583-B-5, file 5, 57.

117 Birmingham and Wood, "Supporting Document – Rehabilitation through Cooperation in Strathcona," draft, December 1970, for submission to Vancouver City Council for information, CVA, City of Vancouver fonds, S40, City Clerk's Office, box 120-E-4, file 308, 30.

118 The $4,000 per house figure is from Strathcona Rehabilitation Project Evaluation, Stage II, preliminary draft, 15, CVA, SPOTA fonds, AM734-S4, box 583-E-8, file 4. Also see Birmingham and Wood, *Report: "Rehabilitation through Cooperation" in Strathcona, Draft, December 1970,* vols. 1 and 2 (December 1970), CVA, City of Vancouver fonds, S40, box 120-E-4, file 308.

119 The $5 million budget represented the unexpended remainder of the renewal funds. Strathcona Rehabilitation Project Evaluation, Stage II, preliminary draft, 20. Its last regular meeting was in June 1976. See ibid., 60.

120 Ibid., 25; and Agreement between Central Mortgage and Housing Corporation and the City of Vancouver and the Province of British Columbia, 6 January 1972, CVA, City of Vancouver fonds, S648, box 854-A-4, file 2.

121 The Strathcona Rehabilitation Project, Year One Perspective, prepared for Ald. Linnell for visit to Ottawa, 28 July 1972, 7, ibid., box 854-A-4, file 2. Also see Strathcona Rehabilitation Project Evaluation, Stage II, preliminary draft, 25.

122 Larry I. Bell and Richard Moore, *The Strathcona Rehabilitation Project: Documentation and Analysis* (Vancouver: United Way of Greater Vancouver, Social Policy and Research, December 1975), 1.

123 Strathcona Rehabilitation Project Evaluation, Stage II, preliminary draft, ii–iii and 101–2.

124 Ibid., 28.

125 The Strathcona Rehabilitation Project, Year One Perspective, 1.

126 Newsletter IV, May 1973, Newsletter of the Strathcona Property Owners and Tenants Association, 6, CVA, City of Vancouver fonds, S648, box 854-A-4, file 6; and Pierre Filion, "The Neighbourhood Improvement Plan: Montreal and Toronto – Contrasts between a Participatory and a Centralized Approach to Urban Policy Making," *Urban History Review* 17, 1 (1988): 16.

127 Strathcona Rehabilitation Project Evaluation, Stage II, preliminary draft, 98.

128 Lee, "Gender, Ethnicity, and Hybrid Forms of Community-Based Urban Activism," 394; and Bruce, "'A New Breed of Group,'" 38.

129 Sherry R. Arnstein, "A Ladder of Citizen Participation," *Journal of the American Planning Association* 34, 5 (1969): 216–24. There is a very large literature on citizen participation that addresses these issues of power. Some starting points are Bill Cooke and Uma Kothari, eds., *Participation: The New Tyranny?* (New York: Zed Books, 2001); Samuel Hickey and Giles Mohan, eds., *Participation: From Tyranny to Transformation?* (New York: Zed Books, 2004); and Brian Christens and Paul Speer, "Review Essay. Tyranny/Transformation: Power and Paradox in Participatory Development," *Forum Qualitative Sozialforschung/Forum: Qualitative Social Research* [online] 7, 2 (31 March 2006), available at http://www.qualitative-research.net/index.php/fqs/article/view/91/189.

130 Agreement between Central Mortgage and Housing Corporation and the City of Vancouver and the Province of British Columbia, 6 January 1972, 12.

131 Bell and Moore, *The Strathcona Rehabilitation Project,* 18.

132 Ley, Anderson, and Konrad, "Chinatown-Strathcona," 126.

133 Address by Mr. Homer Borland (former director Urban Renewal and Public Housing Division Central Mortgage and Housing Corporation) to Canadian Association of Renewal Officials, 3 March 1970, 19, CVA City of Vancouver fonds, S648, box 926-E-1, file 6.

134 "Questions and Answers or Analysis of the Strathcona Rehabilitation Project's Planning Process," submitted to CMHC from SPOTA, September 1973, 55, CVA, SPOTA fonds, AM734-S4, box 583-E-7, file 4.

135 The Strathcona Rehabilitation Project, Year One Perspective, 6.

136 Total Neighbourhood Involvement II, Application to CMHC, Part V for Second Year, 7 August 1973, 5, CVA, City of Vancouver fonds, S648, box 583-B-6, file 11.

137 SPOTA: Operation Total Involvement of the Neighbourhood, draft proposal, n.d., 1-2, CVA, SPOTA fonds, AM734-S1, box 583-B-6, file 11.

138 Partial Transcript of Meeting, Wednesday, 18 July [1973?], 1, ibid., file 10.

139 SPOTA: Operation Total Involvement of the Neighbourhood, draft proposal, n.d., 2.

140 Strathcona Rehabilitation Project Evaluation, Stage II, preliminary draft, 124.

141 Ibid., 117–19.

142 David Ley, "Problems of Co-optation and Idolatry in the Community Group," in Ley, *Community Participation and the Spatial Order of the City,* 75–88.

143 Strathcona Rehabilitation Project Evaluation, Stage II, preliminary draft, 121.

144 Ibid., 118.

145 Interview with Steve Rosell, special assistant to Robert Andras, 1970–72, CVA, SPOTA fonds, AM 734-S4, 1980-250.03.1.

146 Strathcona Rehabilitation Project Evaluation, Stage II, preliminary draft, 101.
147 Ibid., 105.
148 Ibid., 99.
149 Ng, *The Chinese in Vancouver,* 102.
150 Strathcona Rehabilitation Project Evaluation, Stage II, preliminary draft, 100.
151 Ibid., 101.
152 Bill Cooke and Uma Kothari, eds., *Participation: The New Tyranny?* (London: Zed Books, 2001).

Conclusion

1 Ian McKay, "The Liberal Order Framework: A Prospectus for a Reconnaissance of Canadian History," *Canadian Historical Review* 81, 4 (2000): 616–45.
2 *Remember Africville,* directed by Shelagh Mackenzie, DVD (Montreal: National Film Board of Canada, 1991).
3 Tania Murray Li, *The Will to Improve: Governmentality, Development, and the Practice of Politics* (Durham, NC: Duke University Press, 2007).
4 Tania Murray Li, "Rendering Society Technical: Government through Community and the Ethnographic Turn at the World Bank in Indonesia," in *Adventures in Aidland: The Anthropology of Professionals in International Development,* ed. David Mosse (Oxford: Berghahn Books, 2011), 57–80.
5 "Luncheon Address by Lloyd Axworthy, Representing the Honourable Mr. Paul Hellyer," in *National Conference on Urban Renewal as It Affects Chinatown, Sponsored by the Sien Lok Society of Calgary, 6–9 April 1969,* 77, City of Vancouver Archives (CVA), Strathcona Property Owners and Tenants Association (SPOTA) fonds, AM734-S4, box 583-E-8, file 10.
6 Arjun Appadurai, "The Capacity to Aspire: Culture and the Terms of Recognition," in *Culture and Public Action,* ed. Vijayendra Rao and Michael Walton (Stanford, CA: Stanford University Press, 2004), 59–84.
7 Michael E. Latham, "Introduction: Modernization, International History, and the Cold War World," in *Staging Growth: Modernization, Development, and the Global Cold War,* ed. David C. Engerman, Nils Gilman, Mark H. Haefle, and Michael E. Latham (Amherst: University of Massachusetts Press, 2003), 4.
8 Jay Drydyk, "Participation, Empowerment, and Democracy: Three Fickle Friends," in *New Directions in Development Ethics: Essays in Honor of Denis Goulet,* ed. Charles K. Wilber, Amitava Krishna Dutt, and Theodore M. Hesburgh (Notre Dame, IN: University of Notre Dame, 2010), 333–56.
9 Edith Iglauer, "Conclave at Frobisher: A Reporter at Large," *New Yorker,* 23 November 1963, 192.
10 James W. St. G. Walker, "Black Confrontation in 1960s Halifax," in *Debating Dissent: Canada and the Sixties,* ed. Lara Campbell, Dominique Clément, and Gregory S. Kealey (Toronto: University of Toronto Press, 2012), 186.
11 University of Manitoba Archives and Special Collections (UMASC) holds the Walter Rudnicki fonds, over ninety metres of textual and other material. See https://main.lib.umanitoba.ca/walter-rudnicki-fonds.
12 "History Outline," 7, UMASC, Walter Rudnicki fonds, MSS 331, box 1, folder 1.
13 Cited in Frank James Tester, "Integrating the Inuit: Social Work Practice in the Eastern Arctic, 1955–63," in *Social Fabric or Patchwork Quilt: The Development of Social Policy in Canada,* ed. Raymond B. Blake and Jeffrey Keshen (Toronto: Broadview Press, 2006), 243.

14 "History Outline," 1, 4, 6–7. On Rudnicki's involvement in helping establish Newfoundland's Department of Community and Social Development, see Rudnicki to F.W. Rowe, Minister of Community and Social Development, Re: Proposals re: the Department of Community and Social Development, 30 March 1967, UMASC, Walter Rudnicki fonds, box 112, folder 2.

15 "History Outline," 7.

16 Ibid., 4.

17 Walter Rudnicki, Chief, Welfare Division, Memorandum for the Director, re: Rankin Inlet et al., 11 October 1961, 2, Library and Archives Canada (LAC), RG 85 vol. 1447, file 1000/184, pt 5.

18 "Walter Rudnicki," *Late Show*, episode 1, CBC Radio One, 14 June 2010, http://www.cbc.ca/thelateshow/2010/06/episode-1---walter-rudnicki---july-1-and-july-4.html.

19 Susan Newhook, "The Godfathers of Fogo: Donald Snowden, Fred Earle and the Roots of the Fogo Island Films, 1964–1967," *Newfoundland and Labrador Studies* 24, 2 (2009): 174–75.

20 Hugh Shewell, "'Bitterness behind Every Smiling Face': Community Development and Canada's First Nations, 1954–1968," *Canadian Historical Review* 83, 1 (2002): 1–15.

21 Ev Brown Interview, n.d. [16 March 1973?], CVA, SPOTA fonds, AM734-S4, 1980-250.02.

22 Snowden to Edith Hamburger [Iglauer], n.d. [but it appears to be in response to a letter from her dated 1 November 1963], Donald Snowden fonds, LAC, MG 31 D 163, vol. 14, file 34 (emphasis in original).

23 Snowden to Arthur Laing, Ottawa, 25 June 1964, ibid.

24 For an overview, see "William Teron vs Walter Rudnicki: How Ottawa Does Its Business," *City Magazine,* November 1976, 14–25, UMASC, Walter Rudnicki fonds, MSS 331, box 6, folder 1.

25 W5, transcript [of a program dealing with the dismissal of Walter Rudnicki], 23 January 1983 (includes newspaper clippings), n.p., ibid., box 21, folder 2.

26 Rudnicki Biography by Millie Poplar (draft), 1998, 2, ibid., box 1, folder 5; Amanda Brooke Sinclair Linden, "The Advocate's Archive: Walter Rudnicki and the Fight for Indigenous Rights in Canada, 1955–2010" (master's thesis, University of Manitoba, 2016), 81n61.

27 Miss Alice K. Carroll, Provincial Supervisor, Psychiatric Social Work, Crease Clinic of Psychological Medicine, to Walter Rudnicki, 18 June 1953, UMASC, Walter Rudnicki fonds, MSS 331, box 1, folder 1.

28 R.G. Williamson, "A Personal Retrospective on Anthropology Applied in the Arctic" (1988), University of Saskatchewan Archives, Robert G. Williamson fonds, MG 216, box 4.

29 "Five Questions for Gus Speth on His Environmental Evolution," *Yale Environment 360,* 2 December 2014, http://environment.yale.edu/news/article/five-questions-for-gus-speth/.

30 "'I'm Going to Miss It': William's Harbour Residents Bid Farewell and Begin Relocation," *The Current,* CBC Radio, 9 November 2017, http://www.cbc.ca/radio/thecurrent/the-current-for-november-9-2017-1.4393302.

31 Ibid.

32 Scott Gilmore, "La Loche Shows Us It's Time to Help People Escape the North," *Maclean's,* 27 January 2016, http://www.macleans.ca/news/canada/la-loche-shows-us-its-time-to-help-people-escape/ and Chelsea Vowell, "Scott Gilmore and the Imaginary Indian," *Canadaland,* 29 January 2016, http://www.canadalandshow.com/scott-gilmore-and-imaginary-indian/.

33 Analysis and Liaison Branch, Department of Regional Economic Expansion, "Economic Opportunity and Regional Development: Recognizing Regional Economic Trends in Formulating Canadian Objectives for Development," 3 October 1977, 8, LAC, RG 124-B-1, Acc. BAN 1987-88/178, box 26, file 1200-1 NFLD, vol. 1, pt 1/2.
34 "'I'm Going to Miss It.'"

Bibliography

Archival Sources

Bibliothèque et Archives nationales du Québec
Jean-Claude Lebel fonds
Télé-Club broadcast, 24 February 1965, BAnQ DVD, FN08521
Télé-Club broadcast, 10 March 1965, BAnQ DVD, FN08523

City of Vancouver Archives
City of Vancouver fonds, S40, City Clerk's Office
City of Vancouver fonds, S571, Social Planning Department, Administrative and Operational Subject files
City of Vancouver fonds, S623, City Planning Commission Minutes and Other Records
City of Vancouver fonds, S648, Planning, Operational Records
Strathcona Property Owners and Tenants Association (SPOTA) fonds, AM-734

Halifax Regional Municipal Archives
Africville Subcommittee Minutes, 102-42C
Building Inspectors' Correspondence, 102-39L
City Manager's Correspondence, 102-4A
Committee on Works Records, 102-39A
Halifax Human Rights Advisory Committee, CR 5.2
Housing Policy Review Committee, 102-68
Redevelopment Committee Minutes, 102-42A
Redevelopment Committee, Reports, etc., 102-42D
Redevelopment Committee, Submissions and Staff Reports, 102-42B

Library and Archives Canada
Cabinet documents, RG 2
Colin Low fonds, LAC, R5667-0-E
Department of Fisheries, RG124
Department of Indian Affairs and Northern Development fonds, R216-128-4-E and RG 85
Donald Snowden fonds, LAC, MG 31 D163
Jewish Labour Committee fonds, LAC, MG 28 V 75

Memorial University of Newfoundland, Archives and Special Collections
Fred W. Earle Collection, Coll-399
H.A. Williamson Collection, Coll-347

Prince of Wales Northern Heritage Centre, Yellowknife
Alexander Stevenson fonds, N-1992-023

Provincial Archives of Newfoundland and Labrador
Department of Rural, Agricultural and Northern Development, GN 59/7/A
Department of Rural Development – Resettlement, GN 39/1
Fisheries Household Resettlement Committee, GN 34/2

University of Manitoba Archives and Special Collections
Walter Rudnicki fonds, MSS 331

University of Saskatchewan Archives
Robert G. Williamson fonds, MG 216

Published Primary Sources

Alsop, Kay. "She Thrives on Involvement." *Vancouver Province,* 7 January 1972, 20.

d'Anjou, Robin. "Le BAEQ et ses retombées: le regard d'un agent de relocalisation devenu un administrateur public des ententes de développement regional." In *Le BAEQ revisité: un nouveau regard sur la première experience de développement régional au Québec,* edited by Bruno Jean, 65–90. Laval: les Presses de l'Université Laval, 2016.

Arnstein, Sherry R. "A Ladder of Citizen Participation." *Journal of the American Planning Association* 34, 5 (1969): 216–24.

Banville, Charles. *Les Opérations Dignité.* Quebec: Université Laval, 1977.

Bell, Larry I., and Richard Moore. *The Strathcona Rehabilitation Project: Documentation and Analysis.* Vancouver: United Way of Greater Vancouver, Social Policy and Research, December 1975.

"Bessie Lee's Story: An Interview with Bessie Lee transcribed by Jo-Anne Lee." *West Coast Line* 42, 2 (2008): 44–49.

Bonneville, Léo. "Entretien avec Raymond Garceau." *Séquences: la revue de cinéma* 57 (1969): 44–54.

Borovoy, Alan. *At the Barricades: A Memoir.* Toronto: Irwin Law, 2013.

–. "Human Rights in Canada." *Canadian Labour,* December 1967, 5, 29–30.

Brack, D.M., and D. McIntosh. *Keewatin Mainland Economic Survey and Regional Appraisal.* Ottawa: Projects Section, Industrial Division, Department of Northern Affairs and National Resources, March 1963.

Bureau d'aménagement de l'Est du Québec. *Development Plan for the Pilot Region: Lower St. Lawrence, Gaspé, and Îles-de-la-Madeleine: A Summary.* Ottawa: Rural Development Branch, Department of Forestry and Rural Development, June 1967.
–. "Le Bureau d'aménagement de l'Est du Québec." In *Le BAEQ vous informe … 1 Information générale.* Mont-Joli, QC: Bureau d'aménagement de l'Est du Québec, September 1965.
Canada. Advisory Committee on Reconstruction, Report IV, Housing and Community Planning. *Final Report of the Subcommittee, March 24, 1944.* Ottawa: Edmond Cloutier, Printer to the King's Most Excellent Majesty, 1944.
–. Department of Northern Affairs and National Resources. *An Introduction to Frobisher Bay, Baffin Island.* Ottawa: Department of Northern Affairs and National Resources, Editorial and Information Division, 1962.
–. Department of Regional Economic Expansion. *Summary Description: Isolation Criteria Program, Newfoundland and Labrador Unincorporated Communities.* Ottawa: Department of Regional Economic Expansion, November 1970.
–. *House of Commons Debates, First Session, Twenty-Second Parliament, 2–3 Elizabeth II.* Volume 1. *1953–54*. Ottawa, Queen's Printer, 1954.
–. Ministère des forêts et du développement rural. *Entente générale de coopération sur la réalisation du plan de développement de la région du Bas Saint-Laurent, de la Gaspésie et des Îles de la Madeleine.* Ottawa: Ministère des forêts et du développement rural, 1968.
–. Privy Council Office, Special Planning Secretariat. *Fighting Poverty in 1966.* Ottawa: Queen's Printer, August 1967.
–. *Report of the Federal Task Force on Housing and Urban Development.* Ottawa: Queen's Printer, 1969.
–. *Royal Commission on Canada's Economic Prospects: Hearings Held at St. John's, Newfoundland, October 18, 1955.* Ottawa: Queen's Printer, 1955.
–. Rural Development Branch, Department of Forestry and Rural Development. *Development Plan for the Pilot Region: Lower St Lawrence, Gaspé, and the Îles-de-la-Madeleine, Bureau d'aménagement de l'Est du Québec: A Summary.* Ottawa: Rural Development Branch, Department of Forestry and Rural Development, June 1967.
–. Senate. *Highlights from the Report of the Special Senate Committee on Poverty.* Ottawa: Information Canada, 1971.
–. Senate. *Poverty in Canada: Report of the Special Senate Committee on Poverty.* Ottawa: Information Canada, 1971.
"Challenge and Response, Part II." *Labour Gazette* 65, 12 (1965): 1165–75.
"City Considers New 'Social' Department." *Vancouver Province,* 6 August 1965.
City of Vancouver. Community Services. *Social Planning: Celebrating Thirty Years, 1968–1998.* Vancouver: Community Services, City of Vancouver, 1998.
City of Vancouver Planning Department for the Housing Research Committee. *Vancouver Redevelopment Study.* Vancouver: City of Vancouver Planning Department, December 1957.
Clairmont, Donald H., and Dennis W. Magill. *Africville: The Life and Death of a Canadian Black Community.* Toronto: Canadian Scholars' Press, 1999.
Clark, Kenneth B. "A Conversation with James Baldwin." In *Conversations with James Baldwin,* edited by Fred L. Standley and Louis H. Pratt, 38–58. Jackson: University Press of Mississippi, 1989.
Copes, Parzival, "Community Resettlement and Rationalization of the Fishing Industry in Newfoundland." Paper presented at Annual Meeting of the Canadian Economics Association in St. John's, 4 June 1971. Simon Fraser University Department of Economics and Commerce, 1971.

–. "The Fishermen's Vote in Newfoundland." *Canadian Journal of Political Science* 3, 4 (1970): 579–604.
–. *The Resettlement of Fishing Communities in Newfoundland.* Ottawa: Canadian Council on Rural Development, 1972.
Cross, Kevin J., and Robert W. Collier. *The Urban Renewal Process in Canada: An Analysis of Current Practice.* Vancouver: School of Regional Planning Studies, University of British Columbia, 1967.
Currie, R.D. *Western Ungava: An Area Economic Survey.* Ottawa: Industrial Division, Department of Indian Affairs and Northern Development, 1968.
Dailey, Robert C., and Lois A. Dailey. *The Eskimo of Rankin Inlet: A Preliminary Report.* Ottawa: Northern Coordination and Research Centre, Department of Northern Affairs and National Resources, 1961.
Dalhousie University. Institute of Public Affairs. *The Condition of the Negroes of Halifax City, Nova Scotia.* Halifax: Institute of Public Affairs, Dalhousie University, 1962.
De Bané, Pierre. "Le BAEQ et ses suites: le regard d'un député engage." In *Le BAEQ revisité: un nouveau regard sur la première experience de développement régional au Québec,* edited by Bruno Jean, 91–104. Laval, QC: Presses de l'Université Laval, 2016.
DeWitt, Robert L. *Public Policy and Community Protest: The Fogo Case.* St. John's: ISER Books, 1969.
Doray, Michel. "Méthodes et techniques d'animation." *Les cahiers de l'ICEA,* no. 4–5 (September 1967): 25–37.
Dubé, Georges-Henri. "Le BAEQ et les paroisses marginales." In *Le BAEQ revisité: un nouveau regard sur la première experience de développement régional au Québec,* edited by Bruno Jean, 51–63. Laval: Presses de l'Université Laval, 2016.
–. "Le BAEQ revisité par un acteur de premier plan: le témoignage du président du BAEQ." In *Le BAEQ revisité: un nouveau regard sur la première experience de développement régional au Québec,* edited by Bruno Jean, 25–50. Laval: Presses de l'Université Laval, 2016.
Egan, Maurice. "Social Planning in Vancouver." *Plan Canada* 17, 2 (1977): 118–26.
Economic Council of Canada. *Fifth Annual Review: The Challenge of Growth and Change.* Ottawa: Queen's Printer, September 1968.
–. *Second Annual Review: Towards Sustained and Balanced Economic Growth.* Ottawa: Queen's Printer, December 1965.
Faris, James C. *Cat Harbour: A Newfoundland Fishing Settlement.* St. John's: Memorial University of Newfoundland, Institute of Social and Economic Research, 1966.
Fields, Glenn, and Glenn Sigurdson. *Northern Co-operatives as a Strategy for Community Change: The Case of Fort Resolution.* Winnipeg: Centre for Settlement Studies, University of Manitoba, May 1972.
Firestone, Melvin M. *Brothers and Rivals: Patrilocality in Savage Cove.* St. John's: Memorial University of Newfoundland, Institute of Social and Economic Research, 1967.
Godbout, Jacques. *La participation contre la démocratie.* Montreal: Les Éditions coopératives Albert Saint-Martin de Montréal, 1983.
Graburn, Nelson H.H. "The Discovery of Inuit Art: James Houston – Animateur." *Inuit Art Quarterly* 2, 2 (1987): 3–5.
Grenier, Claude. "Some Wonderful, Creative Years in Rankin Inlet." *About Arts and Crafts* 5, 1 (1982): 28–34.
Guy, Roger. "Mon expérience d'animateur au BAEQ." In *Animation sociale, entreprises communautaires et coopératives,* edited by Benoit Lévesque, 59–62. Laval: Éditions coopératives Albert Saint-Martin, 1979.

Harrington, Michael. *The Other America: Poverty in the United States.* 1962; New York: Penguin Books, 1981.

Harrington, Richard. *The Face of the Arctic: A Cameraman's Story in Words and Pictures of Five Journeys into the Far North.* New York: Abelard Schuman, 1952.

–. *Padlei Diary, 1950: An Account of the Padleimiut Eskimo in the Keewatin District West of Hudson Bay during the Early Months of 1950,* edited by Edmund Carpenter. New York: Rock Foundation, 2000.

Hénault, Dorothy Todd. "Interview with Léonard Forest." In *Challenge for Change: Activist Documentary at the National Film Board of Canada,* edited by Thomas Waugh, Michael Brendan Baker, and Ezra Winton, 41–51. Montreal and Kingston: McGill-Queen's University Press, 2010.

Iglauer, Edith. "A Change of Taste: A Reporter at Large." *New Yorker,* 24 April 1965, 121–62.

–. "Conclave at Frobisher: A Reporter at Large." *New Yorker,* 23 November 1963, 188–232.

–. "Donald Snowden" [obituary]. *Inuktitut Magazine* (Summer 1984), 55–62.

–. "Donald Snowden, 1928–1984" [obituary]. *Arctic* 37, 3 (1984): 316–17.

"Irving Explains Cabano Action." *Montreal Gazette,* 20 August 1970.

Iverson, Noel, and D. Ralph Matthews. *Communities in Decline: A Study of Household Resettlement in Newfoundland.* St. John's: Memorial University of Newfoundland Institute of Social and Economic Research, 1968.

Johnson, Robert. "Outporters Go 'Inport.'" *Atlantic Advocate* 61 (September 1970): 25–31.

Jones, Burnley "Rocky," and James W. St. G. Walker. *Burnley "Rocky" Jones, Revolutionary: An Autobiography.* Halifax: Roseway Publishing, 2016.

Keenleyside, Hugh L. *Memoirs of Hugh L. Keenleyside.* Volume 2. *On the Bridge of Time.* Toronto: McClelland and Stewart, 1982.

Laidlaw, Alexander F. "Cooperatives in the Canadian Northland." *North/Nord,* November–December 1963, 11–14.

Larmour, W.T., and the Junior League of Toronto. *Keewatin Eskimo Ceramics '67.* Toronto: Bryant Press, 1967.

Lauber, Daniel. "Social Planning, Vancouver." *Planning* 41 (March–April 1975): 19–21.

Lee, Bessie, and Tom Mesic. "Strathcona Property Owners and Tenants Association." In *Opening Doors: Vancouver's East End,* edited by Carole Itter and Daphne Marlatt, 180–84. Victoria: Aural History Program, 1979.

Lefolii, Ken. "Why Canada Too Should Declare War on Chronic Poverty." [editorial]. *Maclean's,* 22 February 1964, 4.

Lévesque, Benoit, ed. *Animation sociale: entreprises communautaires et coopératives.* Laval, QC: Les Éditions coopératives Albert Saint-Martin, 1979.

Lewis, David Stein. "The Counter-Attack on Diehard Racism." *Maclean's,* 20 October 1962, 26–27, 91–93.

Lewis, Oscar. "The Culture of Poverty." In *On Understanding Poverty: Perspectives from the Social Sciences,* edited by Daniel P. Moynihan, 187–200. New York: Basic Books, 1969.

Malaurie, Jean. *Hummocks: Journeys and Inquiries among the Canadian Inuit,* translated by Peter Feldstein. Montreal and Kingston: McGill-Queen's University Press, 2007.

Marcus, Alan. *Relocating Eden: The Image and Politics of Inuit Exile in the Canadian Arctic.* Hanover, NH: University Press of New England, 1995.

Marsh, Leonard. *Report on a Demonstration Slum-clearance and Urban Rehabilitation Project in a Key Central Area in Vancouver.* Vancouver: University of British Columbia, 1950.

Marzari, Darlene. "Presentation at Women Warriors Workshop." *West Coast Line* 42, 2 (2008): 50–52.

McCrorie, James N. *ARDA: An Experiment in Development Planning.* Ottawa: Canadian Council on Rural Development, 1969.

Metra Consultants Ltée. *Relocalisation de Population dans l'Est du Québec: étude critique d'une expérience pilote, proposition d'une equisse de programme général.* Montreal: Metra Consultants, November 1970.

Mines Staff. "North Rankin Nickel Mines." *Canadian Mining Journal* 70, 8 (1957): 97.

Mitchell, Margaret A. *Don't Rest in Peace, Organize! A Community Development Scrapbook Reviewing Five Years' Experience with Vancouver Citizens.* Vancouver: Neighbourhood Services Association of Greater Vancouver, 1975.

Mowat, Farley. "People of the Coasts." *Atlantic Advocate* 57, 11 (1967): 49–56.

–. *People of the Deer.* Boston: Little Brown, 1952.

Mowat, Farley, and John de Visser. *This Rock within the Sea: A Heritage Lost.* Boston: Little, Brown, 1968.

"Northwest Territories Newest Mine." *Northern Affairs Bulletin* 1, 2 (1954): 51.

Office national du film du Canada. *Soirée Raymond Garceau.* Montreal: Office national du film du Canada, 27 January 1966.

Otis, Léonard, in collaboration with Paul Larocque, Jean Larrivée, and Augustine Lavoie. *Une forêt pour vivre: témoignage d'un sylviculteur.* Rimouski: Groupe de recherche interdisciplinaire en développement de l'Est-du-Québec de l'Université du Québec à Rimouski, 1989.

Perroux, François. "Economic Space: Theory and Applications." *Quarterly Journal of Economics* 64, 1 (1950): 89–104.

Picard, Gilles, and Albert Juneau. *Étude sociologique des changements agricoles dans le Bas-St-Laurent et la Gaspésie.* Mont-Joli: Bureau d'aménagement de l'Est du Québec, 1966.

Phillips, R.A.J. *Canada's North.* Toronto: Macmillan, 1967.

–. *Community Development: The Principles.* Ottawa: Special Planning Secretariat, Privy Council Office, 1966.

–. *The Elimination of Poverty.* Ottawa: Special Planning Secretariat, Privy Council Office, 1967.

Porter, John. *The Vertical Mosaic : An Analysis of Social Class and Power in Canada.* Toronto: University of Toronto Press, 1965.

Poulin, Martin. "Planification et animation sociale." *Les Cahiers de l'ICEA,* nos. 4–5 (September 1967): 41–50.

Québec. Arrêté en conseil 1452-74. Concernant la suspension du programme d'aide aux migrants prévue par l'Arrêté en conseil 2874-72 du 27 septembre 1972.

–. Arrêté en conseil 2525. Concernant une expérience-pilote de fermeture de territoires marginaux et de relocalisation de population dans la région de l'Est du Québec, 27 August 1969.

–. Arrêté en conseil 2874-72. Concernant un programme d'aide aux migrants applicable à l'arrière-pays de la région de l'Est du Québec, 27 September 1972.

Research Committee of the League for Social Reconstruction. *Social Planning for Canada.* Toronto: Thomas Nelson, 1935.

Robb, A. Leslie, and Roberta Edgecombe Robb. *A Cost-Benefit Analysis of the Newfoundland Resettlement Program.* St. John's: Memorial University of Newfoundland Institute of Social and Economic Research, 1969.

Robertson, Gordon. "Administration for Development in Northern Canada: The Growth and Evolution of Government." *Canadian Public Administration* 3, 4 (1960): 354–62.

–. "The Future of the North." *North* 8, 2 (1961): 1–13.

–. *Memoirs of a Very Civil Servant: Mackenzie King to Pierre Trudeau.* Toronto: University of Toronto Press, 2000.

Rowe, William N. "The Newfoundland Resettlement Program: A Case Study of Regional Development and Social Adjustment." Harrison Liberal Conference, Harrison Hot Springs, BC, 21–23 November 1969.

Roy, Gilles. "L'animation sociale et la mise en place d'entreprises autogestionnaires: le point de vue d'un animateur." In *Animation sociale, entreprises communautaires et coopératives*, edited by Benoît Lévesque, 21–36. Montreal: Éditions coopératives Albert Saint-Martin, 1979.

Schindeler, Fred, and C. Michael Lanphier. "Social Science Research and Participatory Democracy in Canada." *Canadian Public Administration* 12, 4 (1969): 481–98.

Schumacher, E.F. "How to Help Them Help Themselves," *Observer*, 29 August 1965, at http://www.centerforneweconomics.org/content/how-help-them-help-themselves.

"She's Got a Thing about Bulldozers ... and Their Levelling Approach." *Vancouver Province*, 21 May 1969.

Snowden, Donald. "Eskimo Commercial Fisheries." *Polar Record* 10, 67 (1961): 382–84.

Stephenson, Gordon. *Compassionate Town Planning*, edited by Hugh Stretton. Liverpool: Liverpool University Press, 1996.

–. *On a Human Scale: A Life in City Design*, edited by Christina DeMarco. South Fremantle, Western AU: Fremantle Arts Centre Press, 1992.

–. *A Redevelopment Study of Halifax, 1957*. Halifax: Corporation of the City of Halifax, 1957.

Stevenson, D.S. *Problems of Eskimo Relocation for Industrial Employment: A Preliminary Study.* Ottawa: Northern Science Research Group, Department of Indian Affairs and Northern Development, 1968.

Suderman, David. "Poverty: A National Challenge." *Canadian Business*, May 1966, 66–73.

Tétrault, André. "Quelques clarifications sur la notion d'animation." *Les cahiers de l'ICEA*, nos. 4–5 (September 1967): 11–21.

"Toujours les mêmes." *L'aménagement*, 15 January 1965.

"Town Discounts Any Link with Liberation Movement." *Bangor Daily News*, 23 October 1970.

Trudeau, Pierre Elliott. *Federalism and the French Canadians*. New York: St. Martin's Press, 1968.

United Nations. *Community Development and National Development: Report by an Ad Hoc Group of Experts Appointed by the Secretary-General of the United Nations*. New York: United Nations Department of Economic and Social Affairs, 1963.

Valentine, V.F., and J.R. Lotz. "Northern Co-ordination and Research Centre of the Canadian Department of Northern Affairs and National Resources." *Polar Record* 11 (1963): 419–22.

Vallee, F.G. *Kabloona and Eskimo in the Central Keewatin*. Ottawa: Northern Coordination and Research Centre, Department of Northern Affairs and National Resources, 1962.

Vallée, Pierre. "Hommage à Léonard Otis: L'homme de la forêt." *Le Devoir*, 8 March 2008.

"Vocational Training for Eskimos." *Northern Affairs Bulletin* 4, 3 (1957): 5.

"Vocational Vignettes." *Northern Affairs Bulletin* 2, 9 (1955): 3–4.

"Vocational Vignettes." *Northern Affairs Bulletin* 3, 2 (1956): 3–4.

Wadel, Cato. *Communities and Committees: Community Development and the Enlargement of the Sense of Community on Fogo Island, Newfoundland*. St. John's: Extension Service, Memorial University of Newfoundland, 1969.

Wells, Robert. *What You Need to Know about the Government's Policy on Centralizing the Population*. St. John's: Office of the Premier, Province of Newfoundland, 1959.

Wensley, Gordon R. *Comminterphone – Rankin Inlet: A Report of Research for the Department of Communications, Government of Canada, Ottawa*. Saskatoon: University of Saskatchewan Institute for Northern Studies, June 1973.

"What the Ministers Are Saying about Poverty." *Canadian Welfare,* March–April 1970, 18.

Williamson, R.G. *Eskimo Relocation in Canada.* Saskatoon: University of Saskatchewan, Institute of Northern Studies, 1974.

Williamson, Robert G. *Eskimo Underground: Socio-Cultural Change in the Canadian Central Arctic.* Uppsala, FI: Institutionen för allmän och jämförande etnografi vid Uppsala Universitet, 1974.

Secondary Sources

Abele, Frances. "Canadian Contradictions: Forty Years of Northern Political Development." *Arctic* 40, 4 (1987): 310–20.

Alexander, David. "Newfoundland's Traditional Economy and Development." *Acadiensis* 5, 2 (1976): 56–78.

Anderson, Kay J. *Vancouver's Chinatown: Racial Discourse in Canada, 1875–1980.* Montreal and Kingston: McGill-Queen's University Press, 1991.

Anderson, Martin. *The Federal Bulldozer: A Critical Analysis of Urban Renewal, 1949–1962.* Cambridge, MA: MIT Press, 1965.

Appadurai, Arjun. "The Capacity to Aspire: Culture and the Terms of Recognition." In *Culture and Public Action,* edited by Vijayendra Rao and Michael Walton, 59–84. Stanford, CA: Stanford University Press, 2004.

Axworthy, N. Lloyd. "The Task Force on Housing and Urban Development: A Study of Democratic Decision-Making in Canada." Ph.D diss., Princeton University, 1972.

Bacher, John. "From Study to Reality: The Establishment of Public Housing in Halifax, 1930–1953." *Acadiensis* 18, 1 (1988): 120–35.

–. *Keeping to the Marketplace: The Evolution of Canadian Housing Policy.* Montreal and Kingston: McGill-Queen's University Press, 1993.

Bernard, Wanda Thomas, and Judith Fingard. "Black Women at Work: Race, Family, and Community in Greater Halifax." In *Mothers of the Municipality: Women, Work, and Social Policy in Post-1945 Halifax,* edited by Judith Fingard and Janet Guildford, 189–225. Toronto: University of Toronto Press, 2005.

Blake, Raymond B. *Lions or Jellyfish: Newfoundland-Ottawa Relations since 1957.* Toronto: University of Toronto Press, 2015.

Bocking, Stephen. "Constructing Urban Expertise: Professional and Political Authority in Toronto, 1940–1970." *Journal of Urban History* 33, 1 (2006): 51–76.

Bonesteel, Sarah. *Canada's Relationship with Inuit: A History of Policy and Program Development.* Ottawa: Prepared by Public History, Inc. for the Department of Indian and Northern Affairs Canada, 2006.

Brox, Ottar. *Maintenance of Economic Dualism in Newfoundland.* St. John's: Memorial University of Newfoundland, Institute of Social and Economic Research, 1969.

Bruce, Michael. "'A New Breed of Group': Community Activism in Vancouver's Strathcona Neighbourhood, 1968–1972." Master's thesis, University of British Columbia, 2005.

Brushett, Kevin. "Making Shit Disturbers: the Selection and Training of Company of Young Canadian Volunteers 1965–1970." In *The Sixties in Canada: A Turbulent and Creative Decade,* edited by M. Athena Palaeologu, 246–69. Montreal: Black Rose Books, 2009.

Bryden, P.E. "'Pooling Our Resources': Equalization and the Origins of Regional Universality, 1937–1957." *Canadian Public Administration* 57, 3 (2014): 401–18.

Cameron, Ken, and Mike Harcourt. *City Making in Paradise: Nine Decisions That Saved Vancouver.* Vancouver: Douglas and McIntyre, 2007.

Careless, Anthony G.S. *Initiative and Response: The Adaptation of Canadian Federalism to Regional Economic Development.* Montreal and London: McGill-Queen's University Press and Institute of Public Administration of Canada, 1977.

Christens, Brian, and Paul Speer. "Review Essay. Tyranny/Transformation: Power and Paradox in Participatory Development." *Forum Qualitative Sozialforschung / Forum: Qualitative Social Research* [online] 7, no. 2 (31 March 2006). http://www.qualitative-research.net/index.php/fqs/article/view/91/189.

Clément, Dominique. *Canada's Rights Revolution: Social Movements and Social Change, 1937–82.* Vancouver: UBC Press, 2009.

Cooke, Bill, and Uma Kothari, eds. *Participation: The New Tyranny?* London: Zed Books, 2001.

Cosmao, Vincent, O.P. "Louis Joseph Lebret, O.P., 1897–1966: From Social Action to the Struggle for Development." *New Blackfriars* 51, 597 (1970): 62–68.

Courville, Serge. *Quebec: A Historical Geography,* translated by Richard Howard. Vancouver: UBC Press, 2008.

Craig, David, and Doug Porter. *Development beyond Neoliberalism: Governance, Poverty Reduction and Political Economy.* Abingdon, UK: Routledge, 2006.

Crewe, Emma, and Richard Axelby. *Anthropology and Development: Culture, Morality and Politics in a Globalised World.* Cambridge: Cambridge University Press, 2013.

Crosbie, J.C. "Local Government in Newfoundland." *Canadian Journal of Economics and Political Science* 22, 3 (1956): 332–46.

Cunningham, Frank. *Theories of Democracy: A Critical Introduction.* London: Routledge, 2002.

Curran, David. "Citizen Participation and Public Policy in Rural Development: The Rural Development Association Movement in Newfoundland and Labrador." Master's thesis, Saint Mary's University, 1992.

Dagron, Alfonso Gumucio, and Thomas Tufte, eds. *Communication for Social Change Anthology: Historical and Contemporary Readings.* South Orange, NJ: Communication for Social Change Consortium, 2006.

Damas, David. *Arctic Migrants / Arctic Villagers: The Transformation of Inuit Settlement in the Central Arctic.* Montreal and Kingston: McGill-Queen's University Press, 2004.

Desrosiers, Lawrence. "La contribution du BAEQ au développement régional et au développement de la société Québecoise." In *Le BAEQ revisité: un nouveau regard sur la première experience de développement régional au Québec,* edited by Bruno Jean, 107–30. Laval, QC: Presses de l'Université Laval, 2016.

Dickenson Carrie A., and William J. Campbell. "Strange Bedfellows: Youth Activists, Government Sponsorship, and the Company of Young Canadians (CYC), 1965–1970." *European Journal of American Studies* 3, 2 (2008): 1–22.

Dionne, Hugues. "Le Bureau d'aménagement de l'Est du Québec (BAEQ) revisité: acte fondateur québécois de planification régionale et démocratique." In *Choix publics et prospective territorial: Horizon 2025, La Gaspésie – futurs anticipés,* edited by Danielle Lafontaine, 123–34. Rimouski: Groupe de recherche interdisciplinaire sur le développement régional de l'Est du Québec (GRIDEQ), Université du Québec à Rimouski, 2001.

Diubaldo, Richard J. "You Can't Keep the Native Native." In *For Purposes of Dominion: Essays in Honour of Morris Zaslow,* edited by Kenneth S. Coates and William R. Morrison, 171–85. Toronto: Captus Press, 1989.

Doehler, Joan Parsons. "Scotia Square: Its Impact on the Downtown Core." Master's thesis, Dalhousie University, 2001.

Drydyk, Jay. "Participation, Empowerment, and Democracy: Three Fickle Friends." In *New Directions in Development Ethics: Essays in Honor of Denis Goulet,* edited by Charles K. Wilber, Amitava Krishna Dutt, and Theodore M. Hesburgh, 333–56. Notre Dame, IN: University of Notre Dame, 2010.

Duffy, R. Quinn. *The Road to Nunavut: The Progress of the Eastern Arctic Inuit since the Second World War.* Montreal and Kingston: McGill-Queen's University Press, 1988.

Dugas, Clermont. "Le développement régional de l'Est du Québec de 1963 à 1972." *Cahier de géographie de Québec* 17, 41 (1973): 283–316.

Ferguson, James. "Anthropology and Its Evil Twin: 'Development' in the Constitution of a Discipline." In *The Anthropology of Development and Globalization: From Classical Political Economy to Contemporary Neoliberalism,* edited by Marc Edelman and Angelique Haugerud, 140–54. Malden, MA: Blackwell, 2005.

Filion, Pierre. "The Neighbourhood Improvement Program in Montréal and Toronto: Two Approaches to Publicly Sponsored Upgrading." In *The Changing Canadian Inner City: Essays on Canadian Urban Process and Form.* Volume 4, edited by Trudi E. Bunting and Pierre Filion, 87–106. Waterloo, ON: Department of Geography, University of Waterloo, 1988.

Finkel, Alvin. *Social Policy and Practice in Canada: A History*. Waterloo, ON: Wilfrid Laurier University Press, 2006.

Flacks, Richard, and Nelson Lichtenstein, eds. *The Port Huron Statement: Sources and Legacies of the New Left's Founding Manifesto.* Philadelphia: University of Pennsylvania Press, 2015.

Foucault, Michel. "Governmentality." In *The Foucault Effect: Studies in Governmentality,* edited by Graham Burchell, Colin Gordon, and Peter Miller, 87–104. Chicago: University of Chicago Press, 1991.

Gagnon, Alain-G. *Développement régional, État et groupes populaires: le cas de l'Est du Québec.* Hull, QC: Éditions Asticou, 1985.

–, ed. *Les Opérations Dignité: naissance d'un mouvement social dans l'Est du Québec.* Montreal: Les Éditions Leméac, 1981.

Gardner, Katy, and David Lewis. *Anthropology, Development and the Post-Modern Challenge.* London: Pluto Press, 1996.

Gillespie, W. Irwin. *The Redistribution of Income in Canada.* Agincourt, ON: Gage Publishing in association with the Institute of Canadian Studies, Carleton University, 1980.

Gilman, Nils. "Modernization Theory, the Highest Stage of American Intellectual History." In *Staging Growth: Modernization, Development, and the Global Cold War,* edited by David C. Engerman, Nils Gilman, Mark H. Haefle, and Michael E. Latham, 47–80. Amherst: University of Massachusetts Press, 2003.

Girard, Michel F. *L'écologisme retrouvé: essor et déclin de la Commission de la conservation du Canada.* Ottawa: Presses de l'Université d'Ottawa, 1994.

Godbout, Jacques. *La participation contre la démocratie.* Montreal: Éditions coopératives Albert Saint-Martin, 1983.

Gordon, Colin, "Blighting the Way: Urban Renewal, Economic Development, and the Elusive Definition of Blight." *Fordham Urban Law Journal* 31, 2 (2003): 305–38.

Gow, David D. "Anthropology and Development: Evil Twin or Moral Narrative?" *Human Organization* 61, 4 (2002): 299–313.

Graesser, M.W. "Review Essay: *The Political Economy of Newfoundland, 1929–1972,* by Peter Neary, *The Resettlement of Fishing Communities in Newfoundland,* by Parzival Copes, and *Regional Policy and Settlement Strategy in Newfoundland's Experience,* by Parzival Copes and Guy Steed." *Canadian Journal of Political Science* 8, 1 (1975): 149–50.

Grant, Jill L., and Marcus Paterson. "Scientific Cloak / Romantic Heart: Gordon Stephenson and the Redevelopment Study of Halifax, 1957." *Town Planning Review* 83, 3 (2012): 319–36.

Gregory, Jenny, and David L.A. Gordon. "Conclusion: Reflecting on the Career of a 'Technical Man.'" *Town Planning Review* 83, 3 (2012): 397–406.

–. "Introduction: Gordon Stephenson, Planner and Civic Designer." *Town Planning Review* 83, 3 (2012): 269–78.

Gwyn, Sandra. "The Newfcult Phenomenon." *Saturday Night*, April 1976, 38–45.

Haefle, Mark H. "Walt Rostow's Stages of Economic Growth: Ideas and Action." In *Staging Growth: Modernization, Development, and the Global Cold War*, edited by David C. Engerman, Nils Gilman, Mark H. Haefle, and Michael E. Latham, 81–103. Amherst: University of Massachusetts Press, 2003.

Hamilton, John David. *Arctic Revolution: Social Change in the Northwest Territories, 1935–1994*. Toronto: Dundurn Press, 1994.

Handcock, Gordon. "The Commission of Government's Land Settlement Scheme in Newfoundland." In *Twentieth Century Newfoundland: Explorations*, edited by James Hiller and Peter Neary, 123–52. St. John's: Breakwater, 1994.

Hardwick, Walter G., and David F. Hardwick. "Civic Government: Corporate, Consultative or Participatory?" In *Community Participation and the Spatial Order of the City*, edited by David Ley, 89–95. Vancouver: Tantalus Research, 1974.

Hays, Samuel. "The Politics of Reform in Municipal Government in the Progressive Era." *Pacific Northwest Quarterly* 55, 4 (1964): 3–26.

Heamon, E.A. "Rights Talk and the Liberal Order Framework." In *Liberalism and Hegemony: Debating the Canadian Liberal Revolution*, edited by Jean-François Constant and Michel Ducharme, 147–75. Toronto: University of Toronto Press, 2009.

Helmes-Hayes, Rick. *Measuring the Mosaic: An Intellectual Biography of John Porter*. Toronto: University of Toronto Press, 2010.

Hickey, Samuel, and Giles Mohan, eds. *Participation: From Tyranny to Transformation?* New York: Zed Books, 2004.

Higgins, Benjamin, and Donald J. Savoie. *Regional Development Theories and Their Application*. New Brunswick, NJ: Transaction Publishers, 1995.

House, J.D. "Does Community Really Matter in Newfoundland and Labrador? The Need for Supportive Capacity in the New Regional Development." In *Retrenchment and Regeneration in Rural Newfoundland*, edited by Reginald Byron, 226–76. Toronto: University of Toronto Press, 2003.

Immerwahr, Daniel. *Thinking Small: The United States and the Lure of Community Development*. Cambridge, MA: Harvard University Press, 2015.

Jean, Bruno, ed. *Le BAEQ revisité: un nouveau regard sur la première expérience de développement régional au Québec*. Laval, QC: Presses de l'Université Laval, 2016.

Johnson Butterfield, Alice K., and Benson Chisanga. "Community Development." In *Encyclopedia of Social Work*. Volume 1, edited by Terry Mizrahi and Larry E. Davis, 376–77. New York: Oxford University Press, 2008.

Keck, Jennifer, and Wayne Fulks. "Meaningful Work and Community Betterment: The Case of Opportunities for Youth and Local Initiatives Program, 1971–1973." In *Community Organizing: Canadian Experiences*, edited by Brian Wharf and Michael Clague, 113–36. Toronto: Oxford University Press, 1997.

Keeling, Arn, and Patricia Boulter. "From Igloo to Mine Shaft: Inuit Labour and Memory at the Rankin Inlet Nickel Mine." In *Mining and Communities in Northern Canada: History, Politics, and Memory*, edited by Arn Keeling and John Sandlos, 35–58. Calgary: University of Calgary Press, 2015.

Kennedy, John C. "At the Crossroad: Newfoundland and Labrador Communities in a Changing International Context." *Canadian Review of Sociology and Anthropology* 34, 3 (1997): 297–317.

Klemek, Christopher. *The Transatlantic Collapse of Urban Renewal: Postwar Urbanism from New York to Berlin*. Chicago: University of Chicago Press, 2011.

Krueger, Ralph R. "Regional Disparities and Regional Development in Canada." In *Regional Patterns: Disparities and Development,* edited by Ralph R. Krueger, Robert M. Irving, and Colin Vincent, 1–36. Toronto: Canadian Studies Foundation and Canadian Association of Geographers, 1975.

Kulchyski, Peter. "Anthropology in the Service of the State: Diamond Jenness and Canadian Indian Policy." *Journal of Canadian Studies* 28, 2 (1993): 21–50.

Kulchyski, Peter, and Frank Tester. *Kiumajut (Talking Back): Game Management and Inuit Rights, 1900–1970*. Vancouver: UBC Press, 2014.

Lackenbauer, P. Whitney, and Daniel Heidt. *The Advisory Committee on Northern Development: Context and Meeting Minutes, 1948–66.* Calgary and Waterloo: Centre for Military and Strategic Studies, University of Calgary, and Centre on Foreign Policy and Federalism, St. Jerome's University, 2015.

Langford, Will. "Gerald Sutton Brown and the Discourse of City Planning Expertise in Vancouver, 1953–1959." *Urban History Review* 41, 2 (2013): 30–41.

–. "'Is Sutton Brown God?' Planning Expertise and the Local State in Vancouver, 1952–73." *BC Studies*, 173 (Spring 2012): 11–39.

–. "'Is Sutton Brown God?' Planning Expertise and the Local State in Vancouver, 1952–1973." Master's thesis, University of British Columbia, 2011.

Latham, Michael E. "Introduction: Modernization, International History, and the Cold War World." In *Staging Growth: Modernization, Development, and the Global Cold War,* edited by David C. Engerman, Nils Gilman, Mark H. Haefle, and Michael E. Latham, 1–22. Amherst: University of Massachusetts Press, 2003.

Laugrand, Frédéric, Jarich Oosten, and David Serkoak. "'The Saddest Time of My Life': Relocating the Ahiarmiut from Ennadai Lake (1950–1958)." *Polar Record* 46, 2 (2010): 113–35.

Lee, Jo-Anne. "Gender, Ethnicity, and Hybrid Forms of Community-Based Urban Activism in Vancouver, 1957–1978: The Strathcona Story Revisited." *Gender, Place and Culture* 14, 4 (2007): 381–407.

Lemay, Jacques. "La question des paroisses marginales: une analyse de contenu de la presse régionale." In *Le BAEQ revisité: un nouveau regard sur la première experience de développement régional au Québec,* edited by Bruno Jean, 131–53. Laval, QC: Presses de l'Université Laval, 2016.

Lépine, Jean-François. "Les promoteurs du projet de cartonnerie populaire de Cabano." Master's thesis, Université de Québec à Montréal, 1979.

Ley, David. "Problems of Co-optation and Idolatry in the Community Group." In *Community Participation and the Spatial Order of the City,* edited by David Ley, 75–88. Vancouver: Tantalus Research, 1974.

Ley, David, Kay Anderson, and Doug Konrad. "Chinatown-Strathcona: Gaining an Entitlement." In *Neighbourhood Organizations and the Welfare State,* edited by Shlomo Hasson and David Ley. Toronto: University of Toronto Press, 1994, 112–36.

Li, Tania Murray. "Rendering Society Technical: Government through Community and the Ethnographic Turn at the World Bank in Indonesia." In *Adventures in Aidland: The Anthropology of Professionals in International Development,* edited by David Mosse, 57–80. Oxford: Berghahn Books, 2011.

–. *The Will to Improve: Governmentality, Development, and the Practice of Politics.* Durham, NC: Duke University Press, 2007.

Linteau, Paul-André, René Durocher, Jean-Claude Robert, and François Ricard. *Quebec since 1930*. Toronto: Lorimer, 1991.

Litt, Paul, *Trudeaumania.* Vancouver: UBC Press, 2016.
Loo, Tina. "Africville: The Dynamics of State Power in Postwar Canada." *Acadiensis* 39, 2 (2010): 23–47.
–. "Political Animals: Barren Ground Caribou and the Managers in a 'Post-Normal' Age." *Environmental History* 22, 3 (2017): 433–59.
MacKenzie, Ken. "Freeway Protests in Vancouver, 1954–1972." Master's thesis, Simon Fraser University, 1985.
Mackinnon, C.S. "The 1958 Government Policy Reversal in Keewatin." In *For Purposes of Dominion: Essays in Honour of Morris Zaslow,* edited by Kenneth S. Coates and William R. Morrison, 159–70. North York, ON: Captus University Publications, 1989.
MacPherson, Ian. *Each for All: A History of the Co-operative Movement in English Canada, 1900–1945.* Toronto: Macmillan, 1979.
Major, Kevin. *As Near to Heaven by Sea: A History of Newfoundland and Labrador.* Toronto: Penguin Books, 2001.
Marcus, Alan. *Relocating Eden: The Image and Politics of Inuit Exile in the Canadian Arctic.* Hanover, NH: University Press of New England, 1995.
Marshall, T.H. "Citizenship and Social Class." In T.H. Marshall and Tom Bottomore, *Citizenship and Social Class.* London: Pluto Press, 1992.
Matthews, Ralph, "Ethical Issues in Policy Research: The Investigation of Community Resettlement in Newfoundland." *Canadian Public Policy* 1, 2 (1975): 204–16.
–. "The Smallwood Legacy: The Development of Underdevelopment in Newfoundland 1949–1972." *Journal of Canadian Studies* 13, 4 (1978–79): 89–108.
–. "The Sociological Implications of Resettlement: Some Thoughts on the Power and Responsibility of Planners." Paper presented to the Annual Meeting of the Canadian Institute of Planners, Halifax, 6 August 1979.
McCurdy, Howard. "Africville: Environmental Racism." In *Faces of Environmental Racism: Confronting Issues of Global Justice.* 2nd ed., edited by Laura Westra and Bill E. Lawson, 95–112. London: Rowman and Littlefield, 2005.
McKay, Ian. "The Liberal Order Framework: A Prospectus for a Reconnaissance of Canadian History." *Canadian Historical Review* 81, 4 (2000): 616–45.
Meller, Helen. *Towns, Plans, and Society in Modern Britain.* Cambridge: Cambridge University Press, 1997.
Meren, David. "'Commend Me the Yak': The Colombo Plan, the Inuit of Ungava, and 'Developing' Canada's North." *Histoire sociale / Social History* 50, 102 (2017): 343–70.
Mitchell, Marybelle. *From Talking Chiefs to a Native Corporate Elite: The Birth of Class and Nationalism among Canadian Inuit.* Montreal and Kingston: McGill-Queen's University Press, 1996.
Mitchell, Timothy. *Rule of Experts: Egypt, Techno-Politics, Modernity.* Berkeley: University of California Press, 2002.
Moemeka, Andrew. "Radio Strategies for Community Development: A Critical Analysis." In *Communication for Social Change Anthology: Historical and Contemporary Readings,* edited by Alfonso Gumucio Dagron and Thomas Tufte, 432–41. South Orange, NJ: Communication for Social Change Consortium, 2006.
Morin, Dominique. "Le BAEQ, la légende et l'esprit du développement régionale." In *Pouvoir et territoire au Québec depuis 1850,* edited by Harold Berubé and Stéphane Savard, 265–309. Quebec: Les Éditions du Septentrion, 2017.
Murray, Karen Bridget. "Making Space in Vancouver's East End: From Leonard Marsh to the Vancouver Agreement." *BC Studies* 169 (Spring 2011): 7–49.
Neale, Stacey. "The Rankin Inlet Ceramics Project: A Study in Development and Influence." Master's thesis, Concordia University, 1997.

–. "Rankin Inlet Ceramics Project, Part One: A Study in Development and Influence." *Inuit Art Quarterly* 14, 1 (1999): 4–17.

–. "The Rankin Inlet Ceramics Project, Part Two: The Quest for Authenticity and Market Share." *Inuit Art Quarterly* 14, 2 (1999): 6–16.

Nelson, Jennifer J. "'Panthers or Thieves': Racialized Knowledge and the Regulation of Africville." *Journal of Canadian Studies* 45, 1 (2011): 121–42.

–. *Razing Africville: A Geography of Racism.* Toronto: University of Toronto Press, 2008.

Newhook, Susan. "The Godfathers of Fogo: Donald Snowden, Fred Earle, and the Roots of the Fogo Island Films, 1964–1967." *Newfoundland and Labrador Studies* 24, 2 (2009): 171–97.

Nixon, Rob. *Slow Violence and the Environmentalism of the Poor.* Cambridge, MA: Harvard University Press, 2013.

Oberlander, H. Peter, and Arthur L. Fallick. *Housing a Nation: The Evolution of Canadian Housing Policy.* Vancouver: Centre for Human Settlements, University of British Columbia for Canada Mortgage and Housing Corporation, June 1992.

Ommer, Rosemary. "One Hundred Years of Fisheries Crises in Newfoundland." *Acadiensis* 23, 2 (1994): 5–20.

Ommer, Rosemary E., and Nancy J. Turner. "Informal Rural Economies in History." *Labour/Le travail* 53 (2004): 127–57.

Pachai, Bridglal, ed. *Nova Scotia Human Rights Commission, 25th Anniversary, 1967–1992: A History*. Halifax: The Commission, 1992.

Parsons, Christopher. "'The Civic Bible for Future Development': Power, Planning, and Expertise in Halifax, 1956–1962." Honours thesis, University of King's College, 2009.

Paterson, Marcus. "Slum Clearance in Halifax: The Role of Gordon Stephenson." Master's research project, Dalhousie University, 2009.

Piper, Liza. "From Subsistence to Nutrition: The Canadian State's Involvement in Food and Diet in the North, 1900–1970." In *Ice Blink: Navigating Northern Environmental History,* edited by Stephen Bocking and Brad Martin, 181–222. Calgary: University of Calgary Press, 2017.

Plunkett, Thomas J. *Urban Canada and Its Government: A Study of Municipal Organization.* Toronto: Macmillan, 1968.

Purdy, Sean. "Constructing Pariah Spaces in the Americas North and South: Newspaper Representations of Slums, Ghettos and Favelas in the 1960s." In *New World Coming: The Sixties and the Shaping of Global Consciousness,* edited by Karen Dubinsky, Catherine Krull, Susan Lord, Sean Mills, and Scott Rutherford, 219–28. Toronto: Between the Lines, 2009.

Quarry, Wendy. "The Fogo Process: An Interview with Donald Snowden." *Interaction* 2, 3 (1984): 28–63.

"Robert Williamson (1931–2012)." *Etudes Inuits/Inuit Studies* 36, 1 (2012): 231–33.

Robinson, Danielle. "'The Streets Belong to the People': Expressway Disputes in Canada, ca. 1960–75." PhD diss., McMaster University, 2012.

Rosier, Paul C. "Crossing New Boundaries: American Indians and Twentieth Century US Foreign Policy." *Diplomatic History* 39, 5 (2015): 955–66.

Rowe, Frederick W. *A History of Newfoundland and Labrador.* Toronto: McGraw-Hill Ryerson, 1980.

Roy, Patricia. *Vancouver: An Illustrated History.* Toronto: Lorimer, 1980.

Rudin, Ronald. *In Whose Interest? Quebec's Caisses Populaires, 1900–1945.* Montreal and Kingston: McGill-Queen's University Press, 1990.

–. *Kouchibouguac: Removal, Resistance, and Remembrance at a Canadian National Park.* Toronto: University of Toronto Press, 2016.

Rutherford, Paul. "Tomorrow's Metropolis: The Urban Reform Movement in Canada, 1880–1920." Canadian Historical Association *Historical Papers* 6, 1 (1971): 203–24.

Rutland, Ted. *Displacing Blackness: Planning, Power, and Race in Twentieth-Century Halifax.* Toronto: University of Toronto Press, 2018.

Sandlos, John. *Hunters at the Margin: Native Peoples and Wildlife Conservation in the Northwest Territories.* Vancouver: UBC Press, 2014.

Scott, James C. *Seeing like a State: How Certain Schemes to Improve the Human Condition Have Failed.* New Haven, CT: Yale University Press, 1998.

Shewell, Hugh. "Bitterness behind Every Smiling Face: Community Development and Canada's First Nations, 1954–1968." *Canadian Historical Review* 83, 1 (2002): 1–15.

Simard, Jean-François. "Le BAEQ: réhabiliter un moment phare de la revolution tranquille." In *Le BAEQ revisité: un nouveau regard sur la première experience de développement régional au Québec,* edited by Bruno Jean, 155–95. Laval, QC: Presses de l'Université Laval, 2016.

Simard, Jean-Jacques. *La longue marche des technocrates.* Montreal: Éditions coopératives Albert Saint-Martin, 1979.

Simpson, Michael. "Thomas Adams in Canada, 1914–1930." *Urban History Review* 11, 2 (1982): 1–16.

Spicer, Zachary. "The Rise and Fall of the Ministry of State for Urban Affairs: a Re-evaluation." *Canadian Political Science Review* 5, 2 (2011): 117–26.

Staveley, Michael. "Resettlement and Centralisation in Newfoundland." In *Policies of Population Distribution,* edited by John W. Webb, Arvo Naukkarinen, and Leszek A. Kosinski, 159–68. Oulu, FI: Geographical Society of Northern Finland for the International Geographical Union on Population Geography, 1981.

Stopp, M. *The Northern Co-operative Movement in Canada.* Submission reports vol. 2, Report no. 2009-22. Ottawa: Historic Sites and Monuments Board of Canada, Spring 2009.

Tattrie, Jon. *The Hermit of Africville: The Life of Eddie Carvery.* Halifax: Pottersfield Press, 2010.

Teaford, Jon C. *The Rough Road to Renaissance: Urban Revitalization in America, 1940–1985.* Baltimore, MD: Johns Hopkins University Press, 1990.

Tennant, Paul. "Vancouver Civic Politics, 1929–1980." *BC Studies* 46 (1980): 3–27.

Tester, Frank James. "Integrating the Inuit: Social Work Practice in the Eastern Arctic, 1955–63." In *Social Fabric or Patchwork Quilt: The Development of Social Policy in Canada,* edited by Raymond B. Blake and Jeffrey Keshen, 237–50. Toronto: Broadview Press, 2006.

Tester, Frank J., and Peter Kulchyski. *Tammarniit (Mistakes): Inuit Relocation in the Eastern Arctic, 1939–63.* Vancouver: UBC Press, 1994.

Thompson, E.P. *The Making of the English Working Class.* New York: Pantheon Books, 1964.

Tough, David. "'At Last! The Government's War on Poverty Explained': The Special Planning Secretariat, the Welfare State, and the Rhetoric of Poverty in the 1960s." *Journal of the Canadian Historical Association* 25, 1 (2014): 177–200.

Walker, James W. St. G. "Black Confrontation in 1960s Halifax." In *Debating Dissent: Canada and the Sixties,* edited by Lara Campbell, Dominique Clément, and Gregory S. Kealey, 173–91. Toronto: University of Toronto Press, 2012.

–. "The 'Jewish Phase' in the Movement for Racial Equality in Canada." *Canadian Ethnic Studies* 34, 1 (2002): 1–29.

Warner, Jr., Sam Bass. "If All the World Were Philadelphia: A Scaffold for Urban History, 1774–1930." *American Historical Review* 74, 1 (1968): 26–43.

Waugh, Thomas, Michael Brendan Baker, and Ezra Winton, eds. *Challenge for Change: Activist Documentary at the National Film Board of Canada.* Montreal and Kingston: McGill-Queen's University Press, 2010.

Weaver, Sally M. *Making Canadian Indian Policy: The Hidden Agenda, 1968–70.* Toronto: University of Toronto Press, 1981.

Webb, Jeff A. *Observing the Outports: Describing Newfoundland Culture, 1950–1980.* Toronto: University of Toronto Press, 2015.

–. "The Rise and Fall of Memorial University's Extension Service, 1959–91." *Newfoundland and Labrador Studies* 29, 1 (2015): 84–116.

Weick, Edward R. "The Eskimos of Canada's Northwest Territories: A Problem of Development." Master's thesis, University of Ottawa, 1971.

Wiebe, Robert. *The Search for Order.* New York: Hill and Wang, 1967.

Windsor-Liscombe, Rhodri. "Leonard Marsh and the Vancouver Modern." *Architecture and Ideas* 1, 1 (1996): 40–51.

Withers, George. "Reconstituting Rural Communities and Economies: The Newfoundland Fisheries Household Resettlement Program, 1965–1970." PhD diss., Memorial University of Newfoundland, 2015.

–. "Resettlement of Newfoundland Inshore Fishing Communities, 1954–1972: A High Modernist Project." Master's thesis, Memorial University of Newfoundland, 2009.

Wright, Miriam. *A Fishery for Modern Times: The State and the Industrialization of the Newfoundland Fishery, 1934–1968.* Toronto: Oxford University Press, 2000.

Zipp, Samuel. *Manhattan Projects: The Rise and Fall of Urban Renewal in Cold War New York.* New York: Oxford University Press, 2010.

Zipp, Samuel, and Michael Carriere. "Introduction: Thinking through Urban Renewal." *Journal of Urban History* 39, 3 (2013): 359–65.

Films

Andrew Britt [Brett] at Shoal Bay. Directed by Colin Low. Montreal: National Film Board of Canada in collaboration with Memorial University of Newfoundland, 1967.

The Annanacks. Directed by René Bonnière. Ottawa: National Film Board of Canada, 1964.

Billy Crane Moves Away. Directed by Colin Low. Montreal: National Film Board of Canada in collaboration with Memorial University of Newfoundland, 1967.

Brian Earle on Merchants and Welfare. Directed by Colin Low. Montreal: National Film Board of Canada in collaboration with Memorial University of Newfoundland, 1967.

Chez nous, c'est chez nous. Directed by Marcel Carrière. Ottawa: National Film Board of Canada, 1972.

Les coopératives. Directed by Pierre Lemelin. 16mm. Ottawa: ARDA and the National Film Board of Canada, 1965.

Dan Roberts on Fishing. Directed by Colin Low. Montreal: National Film Board of Canada in collaboration with Memorial University of Newfoundland, 1967.

Fogo Island Improvement Committee. Directed by Colin Low. Montreal: National Film Board of Canada in collaboration with Memorial University of Newfoundland, 1967.

Jim Decker Builds a Longliner. Directed by Colin Low. Montreal: National Film Board of Canada in collaboration with Memorial University of Newfoundland, 1967.

The Mercer Family. Directed by Colin Low. Montreal: National Film Board of Canada in collaboration with Memorial University of Newfoundland, 1967.

The Merchant and the Teacher. Directed by Colin Low. Montreal: National Film Board of Canada in collaboration with Memorial University of Newfoundland, 1967.

Le milieu. Directed by Pierre Lemelin. 16 mm. Ottawa: ARDA and the National Film Board of Canada, 1965.

La participation. Directed by Raymond Garceau. 16mm. Ottawa: ARDA and the National Film Board of Canada, 1965.

Remember Africville. Directed by Shelagh Mackenzie. Ottawa: National Film Board of Canada, 1991.

Les smattes. Directed by Jean-Claude Labrecque. Montreal: Films Mutuels, 1972.

Some Problems of Fogo. Directed by Colin Low. Montreal: National Film Board of Canada in collaboration with Memorial University of Newfoundland, 1967.

The Story of the Up Top. Directed by Colin Low. Montreal: National Film Board of Canada in collaboration with Memorial University of Newfoundland, 1967.

A Woman's Place. Directed by Colin Low. Montreal: National Film Board of Canada in collaboration with Memorial University of Newfoundland, 1967.

Websites

Clairmont, Donald, and Dennis W. Magill. *Africville Relocation Report*. Halifax: Dalhousie University, Institute of Public Affairs, 1971, Appendix F, A62. http://dalspace.library.dal.ca/handle/10222/55960?show=full.

"Discours de la Rectrice de l'UQAT et du Directeur de la Chaire Desjardins à la Cérémonie de la Médaille d'Honneur." *Info Chaire Desjardins: Bulletin d'Information* 4, special issue, June 2014. http://uqat.ca/chairedesjardins/medias/uploads/misc/ChDjsBulletinspecial2014.pdf.

"Five Questions for Gus Speth on His Environmental Evolution." *Yale Environment 360*, 2 December 2014. http://environment.yale.edu/news/article/five-questions-for-gus-speth/.

Gilmore, Scott, "La Loche Shows Us It's Time to Help People Escape the North." *Maclean's*, 27 January 2016. http://www.macleans.ca/news/canada/la-loche-shows-us-its-time-to-help-people-escape/.

"'I'm Going to Miss It': William's Harbour Residents Bid Farewell and Begin Relocation." *The Current*. CBC Radio, 9 November 2017. http://www.cbc.ca/radio/thecurrent/the-current-for-november-9-2017-1.4393302.

McLeod, James, "James McLeod Lauds NL's Nationalist Identity, Outlines Impending Poverty Struggles." *St. John's Telegram*, 17 November 2017. http://www.thetelegram.com/news/james-mcleod-lauds-nls-nationalist-identity-outlines-impending-poverty-struggles-162850/.

Memorial University of Newfoundland, Newfoundland and Labrador Heritage, "Argentia." http://www.heritage.nf.ca/law/argentia_base.html.

Newfoundland. Department of Fisheries, Fisheries Household Resettlement Division. "Outline of a Policy Regarding Resettlement of Isolated Communities," ca. 1965. http://www.mun.ca/mha/resettlement/documents_full_view.php?img=068_outline_of_policy&galleryID=Doc1.

Populorum Progressio: Encyclical of Pope John VI on the Development of Peoples. 26 March 1967. http://www.vatican.va/holy_father/paul_vi/encyclicals/documents/hf_p-vi_enc_26031967_populorum_en.html.

United Nations. Department of Economic and Social Affairs, Population Division. *World Population Prospects: The 2017 Revision.* http://esa.un.org/unpd/wpp/Excel-Data/fertility.htm.

Vowell, Chelsea. "Scott Gilmore and the Imaginary Indian." *Canadaland,* 29 January 2016. http://www.canadalandshow.com/scott-gilmore-and-imaginary-indian/.

"Walter Rudnicki." *The Late Show*. Episode 1. CBC Radio, 14 June 2010. http://www.cbc.ca/thelateshow/2010/06/episode-1---walter-rudnicki---july-1-and-july-4.html.

Index

Note: In subheadings, BAEQ refers to the Bureau d'aménagement de l'Est du Québec, CMHC to the Central Mortgage and Housing Corporation, HHRAC to the Halifax Human Rights Advisory Committee, and SPOTA to the Strathcona Property Owners and Tenants Association. "(f)" after a page number indicates a figure and "(t)" a table.

abandoned communities. *See* marginal and sending communities
Abele, Frances, 19
acculturation, 41
activism, 24, 108, 138, 154–55, 182. *See also* Halifax Human Rights Advisory Committee (HHRAC); Strathcona Property Owners and Tenants Association (SPOTA)
Adams, Thomas, 126, 127, 130
Adams, Willie, 52(f)
adaptation, 41, 42, 44, 47
Advisory Committee on Northern Development (Canada), 33–34
Advisory Committee on Reconstruction (Canada), 128
African Canadians, 173
African Nova Scotians: Halifax population outside Africville, 234*n*84; as HHRAC members, 137, 139–40, 145, 149; home ownership of, 132; politicization of, 154–55; in province's history of human rights, 145
African-Canadian Liberation Movement, 155
Africville: African Nova Scotians' view of, 145–46, 154; approach to, 25–26; building permits denied in, 233*n*49; cost of settlements in, 150, 151(t)–152(t); current resident on former site of, 235*n*100; definition of social security in, 6; history of, 137, 143–44; lack of community development and citizen engagement in, 124, 150, 153–54, 156; legibility of, 147, 150, 198; literature on, 122, 124; map of, 123(f); motivations for razing of, 8, 122; Ordinance No. 50 applied to, 233*n*46; photos of, 138(f), 147(f), 149(f); post-relocation study, 152–53; Rose's work in, 122, 141–43, 150; similarities with Strathcona, 157–58; social citizenship in, 124, 125, 126, 135, 152; social security in, 203; social workers in, 122, 125, 137, 146–49, 150, 152, 153, 198, 235*n*106; spatial justice and, 140; Stephenson's study and, 130, 132, 133. *See also* Halifax;

Halifax Human Rights Advisory Committee (HHRAC)
Africvillers: approach to, 197; compensation for, 125, 137, 142, 143, 144, 146–47, 148–50, 151(t)–152(t), 153; culture of poverty among, 198; as experts, 198; HHRAC and, 139, 140, 149, 154, 234*n*58; hope and, 206; indigeneity of, 143; interviews with, 6, 121, 150, 153, 154; motivations for relocation of, 8; photos of, 149(f); response to Rose report, 142; work with lawyers, 138–39. *See also* Halifax government: special treatment of Africville
Agricultural Rehabilitation and Development Administration. *See* ARDA (Agricultural Rehabilitation and Development Administration)
agriculture, 100, 104, 107–8, 110
Ahiarmiut peoples, 32, 54
Alaq (Inuit woman), 30, 31(f)
Alexander, David, 64
Alexandra Neighbourhood House, 241*n*89
amalgamation, 111
American Society of Planning Officials, 176
Ames, Herbert, 170
Anderson, Kay, 190
Andras, Robert, 178, 180(f), 181, 186, 194, 201
animation sociale, 22–23, 99, 100–2, 108, 116, 119. *See also* eastern Quebec residents: citizen engagement of
anthropologists: work in development generally, 15; work in Newfoundland, 68, 78, 86; work in the North, 37–42, 44, 51–52, 76, 205
Antigonish Movement, 53
applied anthropology, 37–38
Arctic. *See* North, the
Arctic Division, Department of Northern Affairs and National Resources, 19
ARDA (Agricultural Rehabilitation and Development Administration), 10–11, 22, 65, 95, 106
Area "A": defined, 237*n*33; demographics of, 169; Redevelopment Consultative Committee and, 172, 173, 174; resistance to redevelopment plans for, 167; social planning and, 175; Vancouver's commitment to completing redevelopment of, 186
Area "A" Property Owners Association, 166–67
Argentia, 65
Armstrong, Alan, 158
Arnalukjuak (Inuit woman), 30
Arnold's Cove, 57–58
artists: handicrafts program in the North, 44–45, 46(f), 47; works on eastern Quebec, 91–92, 98, 227*n*31; works on Newfoundland, 4, 5, 56, 58. *See also* films; North, the: artists' works on; television
Arts Centre (Rankin Inlet), 45, 46(f)
Asbestos Hill, 41
Assembly of First Nations, 184, 202
Atlantic Charter, 32
Atlantic Queen II, 85
Axworthy, Lloyd, 177, 181–82, 184–85, 198, 200, 205

BAEQ. *See* Bureau d'aménagement de l'Est du Québec (BAEQ)
Baker Lake, 213*n*18
Baldwin, James, 234*n*83
Bané, Pierre De, 98
Banville, Charles, 111, 114, 116
Barrenlands. *See* North, the
Barton, Charles F., 167
Batteau, 56
Bedford Bay, 122
Bell Canada, 88
Bell Northern Research Laboratories, 51
Berubé, Jocelyn, 227*n*31
Best, Carrie, 145
Betty (Newfoundlander), 84, 85
Bill of Rights (Canada), 145
Birmingham and Wood (company), 187
black people. *See* African Nova Scotians; Africvillers
Black Power, 154
Black United Front (BUF), 155, 199, 200
Blackwood, David, 58
Blake, Raymond, 58, 65
blight, 24, 127, 130, 161–62, 164
Blum, Sid, 138–39, 154
Blumenfeld, Hans, 158
Board of Administration (Vancouver), 171–72, 173, 175, 176
Bonaventure, 96
Borland, Homer, 190

Borovoy, Alan, 13, 139, 140, 154
Boucher, Randy, 58
Boulter, Patricia, 215*n*53
Bourassa, Robert, 109
Brack, D.M., 51, 52
Brett, Andrew, 84, 87
Brian Earle on Merchants and Welfare (film), 86
British Colonial Office, 88
British Columbia government, 27, 186–87, 189, 190, 193–94
Broadcasting Corporation of Newfoundland, 81
Brodie, Fred, 139
Broomfield, Veronica, 206
Brox, Ottar, 63
Bruce, Michael, 160, 180, 193
Bryden, Penny, 9
Budgell, Max, 49
building inspections, 135(f)
Bureau d'aménagement de l'Est du Québec (BAEQ): bureaucratic democracy of, 119; creation of, 95; failure of plan by, 118; *fermes forestières* and, 110; funding for, 22, 95; international visitors to, 99, 228*n*33; model of citizen participation practised by, 22–23, 98–99, 100–9, 111, 119–20, 199; positive legacy of, 92–93; relocation and development plan of, 91, 95–96, 109, 115, 227*n*16
bureaucratic method, 170
Burin, 73
Burnt Island, 57
Byars, P.F.C., 235*n*95
Byrne, Pat, 56

Cabano, 113–14
Campbell, Dan, 186
Canadian Arctic Producers, 50
Canadian Business, 12–13
Canadian Council on Urban and Regional Research, 158
Canadian government. *See* federal government
Canadian Wildlife Service, 48
Cap-Chat, 114
Cape Dorset, 45
Cape Freels North, 70
Cardinal, Réjean, 91
caribou, 19, 28, 30, 36, 48
Carrière, Marcel, 6, 227*n*31
carrying capacity, 48, 50
Carvery, Eddie, 235*n*100
Catholicism, 53, 114, 115(f), 116. *See also* churches
CBC North, 51
Central Mortgage and Housing Corporation (CMHC)
—creation of, 10–11, 128
—embraces citizen engagement, 199
—funds given to Halifax for urban renewal, 10, 122, 129
—motivations behind relocation by, 7
—number of urban redevelopment projects undertaken by, 24, 129
—Rudnicki's work for, 189, 200, 201, 202, 204
—Vancouver development projects and: funds given to, 10, 158; property prices paid by Chinese Canadians, 238*n*41; self-evaluation exercise in Strathcona, 194; SPOTA, 180, 190, 191; Strathcona's rehabilitation, 186, 187, 189, 193; Urban Renewal seminar of, 173
centralization, 8, 33, 65, 95. *See also* Fisheries Household Resettlement Program
Centre d'étude en développement régional, 109
ceramics, 45, 46(f), 47
Challenge for Change Program, 82, 184, 202
Chan, Mary, 178
Chan, Shirley: appears before task force on housing, 157, 158, 178; desire for social security, 203; on Egan's appointment to Strathcona Working Committee, 186; importance to SPOTA, 179; photos of, 180(f), 192(f); on power of federal funding, 185; state motivations for relocating, 7; "strategic flirtation" of, 160; on Strathcona as "slum," 6, 157
Chan, Walter, 178
Charlie (Inuit man), 36
Charter of Rights and Freedoms, 145
Chesterfield Inlet, 213*n*22
Chez nous, c'est chez nous (film), 227*n*31
Chinatown (Vancouver): Axworthy on, 184; freeway near, 157; Redevelopment Consultative Committee and, 173; scholars on, 159; SPOTA members from,

179; Strathcona residents' desire to live near, 166–67, 168
Chinatown News, 169
Chinatown Property Owners Association, 168
Chinese Benevolent Association, 166, 167, 180(f)
Chinese Canadian Citizens Association, 167, 169
Chinese Canadians: approach to, 197; community development among, 198; exodus from Strathcona, 174; integration of, 169, 195; numbers slated for relocation, 26; participating in Strathcona rehabilitation program, 188; percentage in Vancouver's East End, 162; pre-SPOTA resistance to redevelopment, 166–69, 173–74, 176; property prices paid by, 168, 238*n*41; on Redevelopment Consultative Committee, 173; second generation's support for redevelopment, 237*n*32; social security of, 203; on SPOTA executive, 160
Chinese Times (newspaper), 178
Chrétien, Jean, 19
Christian missionaries, 19, 35
churches, 52, 103–4, 114, 115(f), 116, 139–40. *See also* Catholicism
citizen engagement and participation: in 1960s protests, 159; approach to, 14; black self-determination and, 155; development as facilitating, 79–80; federal government's model of, 181–85, 190; as goal of development, 18; impact of culture of poverty on, 17; importance to those in development, 198–99; lacking in Africville, 124, 150, 156; lacking in urban development, 25; in Newfoundland, 81; Paul VI on, 116; of poor people generally, 14, 198–99, 210*n*34; Rudnicki on, 203, 204; Vancouver government's model of, 26, 172–75, 176–77, 239*n*66, 240*n*80. *See also* community development; eastern Quebec residents: citizen engagement of; Halifax Human Rights Advisory Committee (HHRAC); Strathcona Property Owners and Tenants Association (SPOTA); Strathcona residents: citizen engagement of
City Below the Hill (Ames), 170
civic culture, 17, 18, 24. *See also* citizen engagement and participation; community development
Civic Unity Association, 173
civil rights movement, 144–45
civil service, 170–71, 181. *See also* urban planners
Clairmont, Donald H., 143, 153
Clarion (newspaper), 145
class, 13, 145, 146, 154, 217*n*101
Clément, Dominique, 145
Clophas, Father, 104–5
CMHC. *See* Central Mortgage and Housing Corporation (CMHC)
Coady, Moses, 53, 54
coercion: approach to, 23; eastern Quebec resettlement program and, 97–98, 99; Newfoundland resettlement program and, 6, 74, 75(f), 76
Cogswell Interchange, 132, 232*n*32
Cold War, 18
Coleman, Charles, 139–40, 149
colonialism and neo-colonialism: applied anthropology as, 38; and creation of conditions justifying relocation, 207; development as, 16, 55; in the North, 33, 35–36, 45, 54, 201
Comité d'aménagement de Sainte-Paule, 110–11
comminterphone, 51, 52(f)
Commission of Conservation (Canada), 126
Commission of Government (Newfoundland), 64, 88
Committee on Works (Halifax), 135, 136, 233*n*49
communications: citizen engagement as strategy of, 173–74, 177; between Inuit and white men, 54
communications technology, 50–51, 52(f), 81, 104–5
community, Canadians' sense of, 18–19, 203–4
Community Chest and Councils of the Greater Vancouver Area, 167–68, 241*n*89
community development: in black communities outside Halifax, 235*n*107; builds capacity among the poor, 16–18; through Challenge for Change, 184; defined, 50; in eastern Quebec, 104, 153;

federal government funding of initiatives for, 183; government and experts' fundamental concern with, 198–99; lacking in Africville, 153–54; in Newfoundland, 22, 79–89, 90, 119, 153; in the North, 50–55, 89, 119, 153, 184; purpose of, 15; role in social security, 203; Rudnicki champions, 202; in Strathcona, 179, 191, 192(f), 195; United Nations definition of, 17–18; in Vancouver, 175–76. *See also* citizen engagement and participation
Community Planning Association of Canada, 141
Compagnie internationale de papier (CIP), 110
Company of Young Canadians, 183
compensation, 135–36, 168, 175. *See also* Africvillers: compensation for
Con, Harry, 179
condominiums, 168
Conseil d'orientation économique du Québec (COEQ), 108
conservation, 126
Constitution Act, 9, 209*n*18
cooperative housing, 158, 168
Co-operative Union of Canada, 54
cooperatives
—in eastern Quebec, 107, 114, 117, 118–19
—in Newfoundland: creation of shipbuilding and producers, 86–87; eastern Quebec and, 92; Extension encourages creation of, 83, 89; failure of, 82, 84; use of radio to encourage, 81
—in the North: as community development, 50, 52–55; create class divisions, 217*n*101; fulfill mandate of Northern Affairs, 20; help politicize Inuit, 196, 200; Newfoundland and, 59, 79, 84, 92; Snowden on, 54–55, 155, 199–200
Copes, Parzival, 61, 62, 77–78
Cornwallis Street Baptist Church, 140, 141
Courville, Serge, 93
Crane, Billy, 85
Crease Clinic, 205
Cross, Max, 186
Crow's Nest Pass Agreement, 9
cultural commuting, 39–40
culture: civic, 17, 18, 24; of eastern Quebec, 101, 103–4; Inuit and, 36–37, 39–40, 41, 42, 44, 215*n*53; of Newfoundlanders, 78–79, 84–85, 86, 88
Cunningham, Frank, 182
Currie, R.D., 89
Curtis, Bill, 179
Curtis, C.A., 128

Dag Hammarskjöld Foundation, 80
Dailey, Lois, 42
Dailey, Robert, 42
Dalhousie University, 143, 152–53
Daly Bay, 49
d'Anjou, Robin, 98
D'Auteuil Lumber Company, 113
Davis, George, 139–40, 149
Davis Island, 73
Deadman's Bay, 70
decay. *See* blight
Decker, Jim, 85, 87
Decks Awash (television program), 81, 87
decolonization, 55
deculturation, 36, 42, 215*n*53
deliberative democracy, 17
democracy: approach to, 18; bureaucratic vs grassroots, 119; citizen participation, empowerment, and, 199; cooperatives as contributing to Northern, 53, 54; and debate over urban renewal, 159, 160. *See also* participatory democracy
demographics, 68, 69, 76, 162, 169
Department of Agriculture (Canada), 7
Department of Citizenship and Immigration (Canada), 201, 202. *See also* Department of Manpower and Immigration (Canada)
Department of Communications (Canada), 51
Department of Community and Social Development (Newfoundland), 20–21, 59, 62, 68–69, 80, 201
Department of Development (Halifax), 135, 142, 143–44, 146
Department of Fisheries (Canada), 7, 10, 68, 76, 80
Department of Fisheries (Newfoundland), 68–69, 75, 88
Department of Health (Canada), 155
Department of Indian Affairs (Canada), 19, 184, 200, 202
Department of Lands and Forests (Quebec), 113, 117, 118

Department of Manpower and Immigration (Canada), 184. *See also* Department of Citizenship and Immigration (Canada)
Department of Municipal Affairs (Quebec), 96
Department of Northern Affairs and National Resources (Canada): community development program of, 50–55; embraces citizen engagement, 199; facilitates movement of Inuit, 38, 41, 213*n*18; handicrafts program of, 44–45, 46(f), 47; hires Rudnicki, 34, 200–1; mandate of, 7–8, 20, 32–33; minister of, 204; need for knowledge about Inuit, 36–37; North Rankin Nickel Mine and, 40, 213*n*22, 214*n*46; paternalism of, 202; R. Williamson's career with, 37–38; rehabilitation centres of, 36, 213*n*25; resource harvesting and marketing program of, 47–50; supports cooperatives, 54–55, 155; types of experts hired by, 19–20
Department of Planning (Vancouver): creation of, 161, 170; on housing policy, 189; replaces Town Planning Commission, 171; seeks guidance on improving Redevelopment Consultative Committee, 172; on SPOTA, 191; Strathcona Rehabilitation Committee reports to, 187. *See also* Sutton Brown, Gerald
Department of Public Welfare (Nova Scotia), 147, 152
Department of Regional Economic Expansion. *See* DREE (Department of Regional Economic Expansion; Canada)
Department of Social Planning (Halifax), 153
Department of Social Planning and Development (Vancouver), 175–76, 179, 186
Department of Transportation (Canada), 38
Department of Welfare (Newfoundland), 65, 219*n*36
Department of Works (Halifax), 135
Desbiens, Jean-Paul, 228*n*56
desegegration. *See* integration
Desmond, Viola, 145
Desperate People (Mowat), 202
Desrosiers, Lawrence, 93
development: approach to, 8–27; beginnings of, 198. *See also* community development; eastern Quebec; Halifax; international development; Newfoundland; North, the; Vancouver
Diefenbaker, John, 33, 34, 145
Diocese of Rimouski, 114–15
Dionne, Hugues, 93
discrimination, 42, 140, 144–45, 169. *See also* racism
Distant Early Warning (DEW) Line, 35, 38
Dominion Bureau of Statistics, 69
Dover, 75(f)
Downtown Halifax Business Commission, 232*n*32
Downtown Waterfront (Halifax), 232*n*37
DREE (Department of Regional Economic Expansion; Canada): as example of growth of Canadian state, 11; minister of, 207; Newfoundland resettlement program and, 10, 68, 70, 72, 77; report on eastern Quebec, 119
Drouin, Ginette, 91
Drouin, Ti-Pierre, 91
Drummond, Kevin, 118
Drydyk, Jay, 119, 199
Dubé, Georges-Henri, 93
Duffy, R. Quinn, 32
Duplessis, Maurice, 108

Earle, Brian, 85
Earle, Fred, 56–57, 58–59, 82, 83–84, 85
East End Survey Area, 162, 163(f), 164, 166, 169. *See also* Vancouver: East End of
eastern Quebec: approach to, 22–23, 93; closure of towns in, 91, 96–98, 109–10, 227*n*22; coerciveness of resettlement program in, 97–98, 99; community development in, 104, 153; economists in, 95, 105; funding for redevelopment in, 10, 22, 95, 227*n*15; growth pole theory in, 96, 116; incomes in, 94, 226*n*10; legibility of, 198; map of, 94(f); motivations for relocation and development within, 22, 92, 94–95; numbers of people relocated in, 22, 98, 117; political culture of rural, 103–4; poverty in, 92, 93–94; rural vs urban planning and, 159; social citizenship in, 125; social security in, 203; sociologists' work in, 104;

success of development initiatives in, 92–93; urban bias in, 119, 122
Eastern Quebec Development Office. *See* Bureau d'aménagement de l'Est du Québec (BAEQ)
eastern Quebec residents
—approach to, 197
—citizen engagement of: Africville and, 124; with BAEQ, 22–23, 98–99, 100–9, 111, 119–20, 199; lack of, 94; Newfoundland, the North, and, 92, 119; portrayed in films, 91; through protests, 93, 109–18, 200
—culture of poverty among, 198
—hope and, 206
—interviews with, 6, 106
—vote on relocation, 97–98, 227*n*27
Economic Council of Canada, 10, 13, 14, 17, 209*n*24
Economic Development Institute, 228*n*33
economic information, Newfoundland's, 68, 69
economic policies, federal, 9, 10–11
economic space, 67
economics, resource, 47, 48
économie et humanisme movement, 100
economists: on growth pole theory, 66–67; work in development generally, 15; work in eastern Quebec, 95, 105; work in Newfoundland, 21, 61, 62, 77–78; work with urban planners, 127
economy: in eastern Quebec, 107, 108; as insufficient for assuring everyone a good life, 11; land values, 163, 194; in Newfoundland, 63–64, 71, 73; in the North, 53–54; role in modernization, 14–15, 199; in Strathcona, 168, 194, 238*n*41. *See also* employment; growth pole theory
education, 62–63, 84, 87, 125
Egan, Maurice, 179, 186
Eisenhower, Dwight, 15
Electors Action Movement, the (TEAM), 191
employment: for Africvillers, 125, 138; community-based job creation programs, 184; for eastern Quebec residents, 94, 95, 100, 104, 107–8, 119; impact on urban housing in Halifax, 128; for Inuit, 44–45, 46(f), 47, 76; for Newfoundlanders, 64, 77; unemployment rates, 11, 61, 94. *See also* fisheries and fishing; forestry; mining
empowerment, 18, 27, 119–20, 190–95, 198, 199. *See also* power
encadrement, 109
enculturation, 215*n*53
England, 52, 63–64
Ennadai Lake, 5–6, 32, 197
equalization payments, 9
Eskimo Point (Arviat), 34–35, 36, 213*n*18, 213*n*25
Esprit-Saint, 109, 111, 112(f)–113(f), 115(f)
Europe, 52
experts: approach to, 7, 11, 23; facilitators of *animation sociale,* 100–1, 102, 120; hired in the North, 19–20; hired by SPOTA, 187, 193; types of, 198; urban renewal as driven by, 25; work in development generally, 15. *See also* anthropologists; economists; lawyers; social workers; sociologists; universities; urban planners
experts, rule of, 18, 172–73
Exploits, 57
Expo 67, 47
expropriation: in Africville, 125, 137, 141–42, 143–44, 147, 152; in other areas of Halifax, 135, 136; in Strathcona, 167, 175; vs relocation in eastern Quebec, 97
Extension Department, Memorial University: as adviser to governments, 20, 21; community development and, 22, 79–80, 81, 83–84, 87–88, 89, 90; embraces citizen engagement, 199; importance in Newfoundland resettlement story, 59

Face of the Arctic (R. Harrington), 30, 31(f)
facilitators of *animation sociale,* 100–1, 102, 120
fairness, 26, 125–26
family allowance, 30, 32
family size, 62
Faris, James C., 78
farming, 100, 104, 107–8, 110
federal government
—activist role in shaping cities, 24
—becomes involved in urban planning, 128
—commitment to tackling urban poverty, 122
—concerns about urban renewal, 177

—in eastern Quebec, 95, 227*n*15
—funds Black United Front, 155, 200
—human rights legislation passed by, 145
—lack of enthusiasm for urban planning, 126
—model of citizen engagement embraced by, 181–85, 190
—in Newfoundland: assessment of Newfoundlanders' level of education, 63; becomes involved in resettlement program, 65; on community development, 80–81; desire for resettlement program to be voluntary, 78; funds resettlement program, 3, 10; funds studies on resettlement program, 76–77; lack of understanding of Newfoundlanders' rural political culture, 79; lack of understanding of scope of resettlement program, 69; loses sight of purpose of resettlement program, 70; relationship with Fogoites, 87–88; typology of places for resettlement, 67–68, 71–72; university advisers to, 20, 21
—in the North, 18, 19, 30–33
—in Strathcona: encourages citizen engagement, 26–27; influence of, 185; role in Strathcona's rehabilitation, 186–87, 189, 193–94; on SPOTA, 190, 193; SPOTA's demands of, 178; SPOTA's influence on, 158
—Three Wise Men of, 114. *See also* ARDA (Agricultural Rehabilitation and Development Administration); *names of specific departments;* social policies and programs
Federal Housing (and Town Planning) Authority, 127
Federal Task Force on Housing and Urban Development, 157, 177–78, 181, 185, 201
Ferguson, James, 15
fermes forestières, 110–11, 113–14, 117, 118
Filion, Pierre, 189
Film Unit, Extension Department of Memorial University, 87
films: Challenge for Change program, 82, 184, 202; as "cool" medium, 86, 89; on eastern Quebec, 91–92, 98, 105, 106–8, 227*n*31; on the North, 40. *See also* Fogo Island: films on
Firestone, Melvin M., 78
fisheries and fishing: in eastern Quebec, 114; in Newfoundland, 59–60, 61–62, 65, 67–68, 72, 84–85; in the North, 49–50
Fisheries Household Resettlement Program: approach to, 20–21; as coercive, 6, 74, 75(f), 76; end of, 222*n*76; funding for, 3, 10; motivations behind, 3, 8, 58, 71, 72, 73, 221*n*69; name changes of, 220*n*39; Newfoundlanders' subversion of, 26, 58, 67, 73–74, 90; numbers of people resettled by, 4, 56, 69, 71; payment to Newfoundlanders through, 65; premised on growth pole theory, 20, 65–67, 71, 72, 77, 96; problems implementing, 68–72; sociologists' assessment of, 76–78, 152; typology of places for resettlement, 67–68, 71–72
Fisherman's Protective Union, 73
fishermen: choose resettlement locations, 70; incomes of, 59, 62; interviews with, 3, 6; state motivations for relocating, 7; use of social programs by, 73. *See also* Newfoundlanders
Flat Island, 57
Fogo (town), 86
Fogo Island: films on, 21–22, 81–88, 105, 106, 202; political culture of, 78; rejection of relocation from, 198
Fogo Island Improvement Committee, 83–84, 86
Fogo Process, 21–22, 82, 88
Fonds de recherche forestières de l'Université Laval (FRUL). *See* FRUL (Fonds de recherche forestières de l'Université Laval)
forestry: community, 110–11, 113–14, 117, 118; eastern Quebec's outdated methods of, 107; Opérations Dignité and, 113–14, 115, 116; in Télé-Club broadcast, 105
Fort Resolution, 38
Fortin, Gérald, 99, 100
Fotheringham, Allan, 157
Foucault, Michel, 18, 90
Fox Island, 57
France, 99
Francois (village), 3, 6, 7, 197
Frank, Andre Gunder, 16
Fraser, Aurèle, 6, 7
FRED (Fund for Rural Economic Development), 10–11

freight rates, 9
Frobisher Bay (Iqaluit), 36, 213*n*25
Front de libération du Québec (FLQ), 113
FRUL (Fonds de recherche forestières de l'Université Laval), 116, 117
Fund for Rural Economic Development (FRED), 10–11

Gagnon, Alain-G., 117–18
Garceau, Raymond, 106–7
Garry Lake, 32, 36, 213*n*18
Gaspé. *See* eastern Quebec
Gaspé-Nord, 96
Gaspé-Sud, 96
Geach, A.D., 169
Gendron, Jean-Marc, 114
Gilmore, Scott, 206–7
Givens, Phil, 24
global South, 16, 33. *See also* international development
Godbout, Jacques, 101, 108
Goldenberg, Carl, 59–60
Good Shepherd Mission, 173
Gottingen Street (Halifax), 135(f)
"Government Game, The" (song), 56
government subsidies, 9
governmentality, 18, 22, 23, 27, 199
governments: approach to, 7; on citizen participation as means of empowerment, 18; international development and domestic relocation policies of, 16; Sauvé on governments' role in addressing poverty, 17. *See also* federal government; *names of specific provincial and municipal governments*
Graham, W.E., 158–59
Grant, D.W., 214*n*45
Grant, Jill L., 130
Grant, Robert, 143–44, 146, 148–49
Great Depression, 9, 93, 126–27
Greater Vancouver Tourism Association, 239*n*66
Grenier, Cécile, 45
Grenier, Claude, 45, 47
Grosses-Roches, 114
growth pole theory, 96, 119, 199. *See also* Fisheries Household Resettlement Program: premised on growth pole theory
Guy, Ray, 58
Guy, Roger, 101, 200, 205
Gwyn, Sandra, 58

Halifax: CMHC funding given to, 10, 122, 129; number of people relocated in, 132, 232*n*31; other areas targeted for redevelopment in, 130–36, 232*n*37; tenants in, 135–36, 169; urban renewal in Vancouver vs, 161, 162; wartime population growth of, 128. *See also* Africville
Halifax government
—Africville subcommittee of, 148–50, 235*n*95
—blamed for Africville's living conditions, 148
—and demolition of Cogswell Interchange, 232*n*32
—HHRAC's influence on, 140–41
—hires G. Stephenson, 122, 129, 130
—hires P. MacDonald, 147
—response to Rose report, 142–43
—response to Stephenson report, 132–33, 152
—shortcomings of resettlement program, 153–54
—special treatment of Africville: Africville's history and, 143–44; costs of redevelopment and, 137; desire to address racism and segregation, 25–26, 125, 133, 135, 146, 152; natural justice and, 234*n*75; Rose's recommendations, 142; social citizenship and, 124, 125, 126, 135
Halifax Human Rights Advisory Committee (HHRAC): conflates housing with social security, 154; creation of, 139; influence on Halifax government, 141; members of, 139–40, 145, 197; moves on from Africville, 153; number of meetings held by, 234*n*58; opposes segregation, 140, 144, 146; presence on Africville subcommittee of Halifax government, 137, 149; vs radical black activists, 155; response to Rose report, 142
Halifax-Dartmouth Labour Council, 139
Hamilton, Alvin, 19
Hamilton, John David, 19
handicrafts, 44–45, 46(f), 47
Harbour Drive (Halifax), 137
Harcourt, Mike, 179
Hardwick, Walter, 176
Harnum, Kenneth, 80

Harrington, Michael, 12, 14
Harrington, Richard, 28, 30, 31, 32
Hart, Robert, 80
Hay River, 44
Heidt, Daniel, 33
Hellyer, Paul, 157, 177–78, 179, 180–81, 184, 201
Henik Lake, 32, 36, 54, 213*n*18
Hermitage, 70
Higgins, Benjamin, 119
Higgins, Bernard, 66
high modernism: in eastern Quebec, 22, 92, 95; of growth pole theory, 66–67; of Le Corbusier, 129; in Newfoundland, 20–21, 58, 73; of Sutton Brown, 161; tenets of, 11
Hin, Siu Gum, 168, 175
Hofmann, Erich, 49
home ownership. *See* land and home ownership
hope, 7, 205–6, 207
House, J.D., 89
housing: of Africvillers after relocation, 153, 154; and blight in Halifax, 130; cooperative, 158, 168; HHRAC's ideas for, 140–41; as income source in Strathcona, 168; photos of Strathcona, 164(f); and rehabilitation of Strathcona, 187, 188(f), 189, 194, 202; Rose on, 142; single elderly tenants in Strathcona, 169; SPOTA's desire to plan, 191, 192(f); urban planning and need for decent, 126–28; Vancouver government's plans for Strathcona, 165–66. *See also* Central Mortgage and Housing Corporation (CMHC); Federal Task Force on Housing and Urban Development; land and home ownership; public housing
Housing Committee (SPOTA), 192
Housing Policy Review Committee (Halifax), 136
Houston, James, 45
Hudson Bay, 33
Hudson's Bay Company, 19, 30, 32, 35
human rights legislation, 145
human rights movement, Nova Scotia, 145
hunting, 48. *See also* caribou

Iceland, 64
identification systems, 30
identity, 4, 58, 206
Iglauer, Edith, 49, 54, 203
Igloolik, 42
Ihalmiut (Inuit woman), 30
Îles-de-la-Madeleine, 17. *See also* eastern Quebec
Illasiak, Alex, 38
Immerwahr, Daniel, 15
incomes: in Africville, 137; in eastern Quebec, 94, 226*n*10; in Halifax, 232*n*30; of Indigenous peoples, 12; in Newfoundland, 59, 61–62; poverty line and, 11; regional inequalities in, 10; in Strathcona, 186
Indian Act, 182
Indigenous peoples: community development among, 184; foreign aid policies and, 16; left out of policy decisions, 182; love for Rudnicki, 204; poverty levels of, 12, 13, 207; recently proposed relocation of, 206, 207; social security of, 202–3; welfare policies for, 201, 202. *See also* Inuit
Industrial Division, Department of Northern Affairs and National Resources, 45, 47–48, 202
industrialization: artists' critique of, 4; cooperatives as reaction to, 52; in eastern Quebec, 99; impact on Africville, 137; modernity and, 199; of Newfoundland, 61–62, 63, 65, 67, 71, 78; in the North, 42; urban planning addresses social costs of, 127, 128
industry. *See* employment
Information Division, BAEQ, 105
infrastructure: in Africville, 121, 122, 137, 138(f), 141, 148; in eastern Quebec, 110; in other areas of Halifax, 132; in Strathcona, 189, 193–94
Institut canadien d'éducation des adultes, 100
Institute of Public Affairs (IPA), Dalhousie University, 143, 152–53
Institute of Social and Economic Research (ISER), Memorial University: as adviser to governments, 20, 21; anthropologists funded by, 78; importance in Newfoundland resettlement story, 59; Newfoundland's social statistics and, 68; studies led by, 76–77; training conference held by, 80

integrated resource development, 118
integration: of Africvillers, 144, 146, 154; of black community outside Africville, 234*n*84; of Chinese Canadians, 169, 195; HHRAC's plans to address discrimination through, 140; Rudnicki on, 202. *See also* segregation
intermediate technologies, 54, 217*n*100
international development, 14–18, 47, 50, 79
Interracial Council, 139
Inuit: adaptation of, 41, 42, 44, 47; approach to, 19–20, 197; community development among, 50–55, 89, 119, 153, 184; culture of poverty among, 198; employment for, 44–45, 46(f), 47, 76 (*see also* mining); hope and, 206; interviews with, 5–6, 34, 35(f), 36, 40–41, 55, 215*n*53; nationalism of, 53; political awareness of, 196, 200; rehabilitation of, 36, 45, 201, 213*n*25; social citizenship as motivation for relocation of, 7–8; starvation among, 28, 30, 31(f), 32–33, 34, 35(f), 36, 201, 202, 213*n*18. *See also* Indigenous peoples
Inuktitut, 51
Inuvik, 213*n*25
Irving, K.C., 113
ISER. *See* Institute of Social and Economic Research (ISER), Memorial University
Isolation Criteria Program, 69–70
Italian Canadians, 173
Itivia, 36, 37, 44
Iverson, Noel, 61, 63, 76–78

Jacob Street (Halifax), 132, 133(f), 136
Jacob Street Redevelopment Area, 132–33, 136, 138, 157–58
JAL (cooperative), 117–18, 119
Jamieson, Don, 80
Jewish Labour Committee, 138
Joe Batt's Arm, 84
Johnson, Lyndon, 12, 13, 15
Joint Planning Committee (Newfoundland), 67, 70, 80
Jones, Burnley "Rocky," 155–56
Jones, Eric, 85
Jones, H. Bond, 136
Juneau, Albert, 104
just society, 115, 182

Keeling, Arn, 215*n*53
Keenleyside, Hugh, 18–19
Keewatin District. *See* North, the
Keewatin Mainland Economic Survey, 48
Kennedy, John F., 15
Kent, Tom, 72
Kierans, Eric, 88
King, Martin Luther, Jr., 140
Kitz, Leonard, 130
Kivalliq region. *See* North, the
Klemek, Christopher, 170
Konrad, Doug, 190
Kouchibouguac National Park, 209*n*21
Krueger, Ralph, 9
Kusserktok (Inuit man), 40

Labrador, 88
Labrecque, Jean-Claude, 91
Lackenbauer, P. Whitney, 33
Laidlaw, Alexander, 54
Laing, Arthur, 204
L'aménagement (newspaper), 104, 105
land and home ownership: by African Nova Scotians, 132; in Africville, 125, 142, 143, 150, 151(t); in Strathcona, 167–68, 186
land values, 163, 194
Langford, Will, 161, 172
language, 41, 51
Latham, Michael, 15
Lau, Jonathan, 179–80, 192
Laugrand, Frédéric, 5
Laval University: advice on community forestry, 110, 114, 116, 117; BAEQ workers from, 22, 95, 101
lawyers: on poverty, 13; work in Halifax, 136, 138–39; work in Strathcona, 167, 179, 238*n*41, 239*n*66
Le Corbusier, 129–30
Le milieu (film), 107
League for Social Reconstruction, 127
Leased Bases Agreement, 65
Lebel, Jean-Claude, 95
Lebret, Louis-Joseph, 99–100, 116
Leckie, Peter, 179
Lee, Bessie, 178, 186
Lee, Jo-Anne, 160, 178, 180, 193
legibility: of Africville, 147, 150, 198; experts' role in creating, 198; as key to statecraft, 30; of Newfoundland, 68, 69, 76, 89–90, 198; Scott on, 235*n*87

Legjuk, Thomas, 39(f)
Lemelin, Pierre, 106
Lemieux, Guy, 81
l'enquête-participation, 99, 116. *See also* eastern Quebec residents: citizen engagement of
Les Capucins, 114
Les insolences du Frère Untel (Desbiens), 228*n*56
Les Jaseries du Père Clophas (radio program), 104–5
Les Méchins, 111, 114
Les smattes (film), 91–92
Lesage, Jean, 33, 95, 108
Leung, Dean, 167–68, 169
Lewis, Oscar, 17
Ley, David, 190, 194
Li, Tania Murray, 18
Liberal Party, 79, 179
Linnell, Marianne, 189
Litt, Paul, 182
Local Initiatives Program (Canada), 184
Locke, Charles, 167, 238*n*41
longliners, 84–85
Low, Colin, 81–82, 83, 85–87, 202
Lower St. Lawrence. *See* eastern Quebec
Lumsden South, 70
Lussier, Louis-Joseph, 116
Lydia (Inuit woman), 36
Lynn Lake, 41

MacDonald, John, 135(f)
MacDonald, Peter: and power of hope, 205; as progressive, 200; work in Africville, 122, 147–49, 150, 152, 153, 198
Mackenzie River, 39
Maclean, Donald, 139, 140, 144, 149
Maclean, Fran, 139, 140
Maclean's, 12, 206
Magill, Dennis, 143, 153
Maitland Street (Halifax), 232*n*37
Making of the English Working Class (Thompson), 6
Malaurie, Jean, 42
Maloney, Aidan, 88
Mandeville, Celine, 38
Manuel, George, 184
Marchand, Jean, 114, 207
marginal and sending communities: in eastern Quebec, 93–94, 96–98, 227*n*22, 227*n*27; in Newfoundland, 69–70, 72, 73–76, 96
Maritime Freight Rates Act, 9
market. *See* economy
Marquise, 65
Marsh, Leonard, 24, 128, 165, 176, 194
Marshall, T.H., 7, 124, 155
Martin, Ferdinand, 119
Marystown, 73
Marzari, Darlene, 179
Matane, 91, 96, 98, 110, 111, 114
Matapédia, 111, 114
Matthews, D. Ralph, 61, 63, 76–78
McCrorie, James N., 11
McKay, Ian, 27, 197
McLean Park, 166, 174, 180
media: on cooperatives, 54; in Halifax, 132; on poverty, 12–13, 206–7; radio, 50–51, 81, 104–5; television, 81, 87, 105, 107. *See also* films; newspapers
Media Unit, Extension Department of Memorial University, 81
Medjuck, Ralph, 136
Memorial University. *See* Extension Department, Memorial University; Institute of Social and Economic Research (ISER), Memorial University
Meren, David, 16
Metra (company), 96–97, 98
mining: closure of North Rankin Nickel Mine, 40, 214*nn*45–46; Inuit culture and, 40, 41, 42, 215*n*53; number of Inuit employed in, 40, 213*n*22, 214*n*46; photos of, 39(f); plan of buildings at North Rankin Nickel Mine, 43(f); R. Williamson's work in, 38, 40–41, 214*n*41; as way of exploiting the North's capacity, 34
Ministry of State for Urban Affairs (Canada), 24
MIT, 15
Mitchell, Margaret, 179
Mitchell, Marybelle, 53, 217*n*101
Mitchell, Timothy, 18, 64, 172
modernism, 170. *See also* high modernism
modernity: of eastern Quebec, 93, 94, 106, 119; of Newfoundland, 62–63, 119, 219*n*22; reflexiveness of, 152
modernization: artists' critique of, 4; development's role in, 14–15, 16; in eastern Quebec, 91, 99, 106–7, 109; and

poor people's sense of belonging, 199; of rural areas generally, 10, 23. *See also* Newfoundland: modernization of
Montreal, 119, 170
Moses, Robert, 170
Mowat, Farley, 3, 4, 30–32, 58, 73, 202
Mulgrave Park, 136
municipal governments: become involved in urban planning, 128; commitment to tackling urban poverty, 122; creation of departments of social planning in, 127; as ineffective at urban planning, 159; in Newfoundland, 88–89; in United States, 172, 239*n*58; urban-reform movement's vision of, 170. *See also names of specific governments*
Munro, John, 155
Muqyunniq, Job, 5–6, 7, 19, 32
Murray, Karen Bridget, 176
music, 56, 227*n*31

National Film Board of Canada (NFB), 40, 82, 106, 184, 202. *See also* Fogo Island: films on
National Housing Act, 128, 129, 158, 169
National Indian Brotherhood, 202
nationalism, 53, 58
Native Council of Canada, 204
natural justice, 144, 147, 148, 234*n*75
NCRC (Northern Coordination and Research Centre), 37, 42
Neale, Stacey, 45, 47
Negro Citizen (newspaper), 145
Neighbourhood Improvement Program (CMHC), 189, 202
Neighbourhood Services Association, 179
Nelson, Jennifer J., 122, 124
Nemtin, Bill, 86
Neville, F.J., 50
New Brunswick, 209*n*21
New Democratic Party (NDP), 139, 235*n*106
New Yorker, 54, 203
Newfoundland: anthropologists in, 68, 78, 86; approach to, 20, 21–22, 23; economists in, 21, 61, 62, 77–78; history of resettlement in, 64–65; legibility of, 68, 69, 76, 89–90, 198; modernity of, 62–63, 119, 219*n*22; modernization of, 58, 66, 70–71, 76, 77–78, 79, 81, 90; motivations for relocation within, 92; population distribution in, 59, 60(f), 61, 63–64, 119; poverty in, 62, 64, 81, 93; social citizenship in, 125; social security in, 63, 71, 73, 203; sociologists in, 21, 61, 76–78, 152; urban bias of development projects in, 119, 122. *See also* Fisheries Household Resettlement Program
Newfoundland Film Project. *See* Fogo Island: films on
Newfoundland government: adapts to changes in resettlement program, 74; community development and, 80, 81; desire for resettlement program to be voluntary, 78; Extension Department's role in making rural areas legible to, 89–90; funds resettlement program, 3; lack of understanding of Newfoundlanders' rural political culture, 79; on Newfoundland's population problem, 59–61, 64; recent resettlement program of, 206; relationship with Fogoites, 87–88; Rudnicki's work for, 201; typology of places for resettlement, 67–68; university advisers to, 20, 21. *See also names of specific departments*
Newfoundlanders: approach to, 197; choose resettlement locations, 70, 71–72, 73–74, 90; and coercion of resettlement, 6, 74, 75(f), 76; culture of poverty among, 198; employment for, 64, 77 (*see also* fisheries and fishing); family size of, 62; Fogo Island films and community development among, 21–22, 79–89, 90, 105, 106, 119, 153; incomes of, 59, 62; non-Fogo Island interviews with, 3, 21, 56–58, 76–77, 88, 206, 207; political culture of rural, 78–79, 86, 88; recent relocation of, 206, 207; state motivations for relocating, 7; subversion of resettlement program by, 21, 58, 67, 73–74, 90. *See also* employment: in Newfoundland
newspapers: in eastern Quebec, 104, 105; in Newfoundland, 64; in Nova Scotia, 145; in Vancouver, 157, 169, 178
NFB. *See* National Film Board of Canada (NFB)
Ng, Wing Chung, 195
Nil en ville (album), 227*n*31

Non-Partisan Association (NPA), 171, 179, 191
North (magazine), 54
North, the, 28–55; anthropologists in, 37–42, 44, 51–52, 76, 205; approach to, 18–20, 23; artists' works on, 28, 30, 31(f), 32, 40, 202; Canadian public's interest in, 18–19, 203–4; community development in, 50–55, 89, 119, 153, 184; handicrafts program in, 44–45, 46(f), 47; legibility of, 198; map of Keewatin, 29(f); motivations for relocation within, 19, 32–33, 92; numbers of Inuit relocated from, 41, 49; rehabilitation of Inuit in, 36, 45, 201, 213*n*25; resource harvesting and marketing program in, 47–50; Rudnicki's legacy in, 200–1; social citizenship in, 125; social workers in, 34, 35(f), 36; trauma experienced by displaced peoples in, 5–6; urban bias of development projects in, 122. *See also* cooperatives: in the North
North End (Halifax), 132, 146
North Rankin Nickel Mine. *See* mining
Northern Cod Adjustment and Rehabilitation Program, 73
Northern Coordination and Research Centre (NCRC). *See* NCRC (Northern Coordination and Research Centre)
Northern Peninsula (Newfoundland), 88
Northern Pilot Project, 51
Noru, Nora, 38
Norway, 63–64
Nova Scotia, 53, 145
Nova Scotia Association for the Advancement of Coloured People, 139, 145
Nova Scotia Civil Liberties and Human Rights Association, 139
Nova Scotia government, 147, 152, 155, 232*n*32
Nova Scotia Human Rights Federation, 139
Nueltin Lake, 5, 32
Nunavut, 53

O'Brien, Allan, 141
Office de développement de l'Est du Québec, 110
Oliver, John, 172
Oliver, W.P., 145, 155
Ommer, Rosemary, 63, 73
Operation Total Involvement of the Neighbourhood (SPOTA), 191
Opérations Dignité, 23, 93, 109–10, 111–18, 119, 200
Opportunities for Youth (Canada), 184
Ordinance No. 50, 135, 137, 233*n*38, 233*n*46
O'Reilly, Kevin, 207
Other America (M. Harrington), 12
Otis, Léonard, 110, 111, 120
outport resettlement. *See* Fisheries Household Resettlement Program

Padleimiut peoples, 28, 30
parochialism, 94, 104, 105
Parsons, Christopher, 132–33
participatory democracy, 26, 79, 81, 89–90, 181–84. *See also* citizen engagement and participation; community development
Paterson, Marcus, 130
Paul VI, Pope, 115–16
Pearson, Lester B., 13
Pelletier, Gérard, 114
People of the Deer (Mowat), 30–31
People of the Rock (film), 40
people power, 160, 182
Perroux, François, 20, 66–67, 96, 100
Phillips, R.A.J., 13, 209*n*24
Picard, Gilles, 104
Pittman, Al, 56, 58
Placentia Bay, 57, 65, 73
planning, social, 127. *See also* urban planners
Plunkett, Thomas J., 239*n*58
policy making, 181–85
political culture, 78–79, 86, 88, 103–4
poor people: challenge of state by, 27; citizen engagement of, 14, 198–99, 210*n*34; civic culture of, 17, 24; Halifax's non-Africville, 146, 154; impact of urban blight on, 127; invisibility of, 12; need to participate in decision making, 16–18, 79–80. *See also* Africvillers; citizen engagement and participation; eastern Quebec residents; Inuit; Newfoundlanders; Strathcona residents
population: demographics, 68, 69, 76, 162, 169; surplus, 48–49, 77–78; of Vancouver, 171
population distribution: in eastern

Quebec, 94, 95, 99, 119; in Newfoundland, 59, 60(f), 61, 63–64, 119; in Vancouver, 194
Populorum Progressio (papal encyclical), 115–16
Port aux Choix, 88
Port Elizabeth, 73–74
Port Huron Statement, 182
Porter, John, 13
poverty: culture of, 17, 94, 198; in eastern Quebec, 92, 93–94; key to eliminating, 205; limitations of rights-based approach in addressing, 126; in Newfoundland, 62, 64, 81, 93; rediscovery of, 11–14, 209*n*24; Rudnicki on, 202; rural, 12, 23; systemic racism and, 155; *Vancouver Redevelopment Study* and, 163; as way for welfare state to extend control, 199. *See also* urban poverty; War on Poverty
power: Africville and, 25, 154; approach to, 7; of civic bureaucracy, 171; disciplinary, 18, 90; displaced Newfoundlanders' lack of, 4; in eastern Quebec, 101, 102, 103; federal government consolidates, 183; hope as, 206; limits of Smallwood's, 71; of the people, 160, 182; poverty and Porter's study of, 13; reinforcement of state, 27, 78, 81, 173, 175, 193, 196, 200; relocation and development as exercise of, 197–98; as seen in Rudnicki's career, 200–3, 204–5; subversion of state, 54, 81, 199–200; of urban planners, 170, 172, 239*n*58. *See also* empowerment
Prime Minister's Office (PMO), 183
Prince Rupert, 87
Privy Council Office, 13–14, 183, 200, 201, 202
Progressive Conservative Party, 79
Progressive reform movement, 170–71
property ownership. *See* land and home ownership
protests, 159. *See also* Opérations Dignité
provincial governments, 122, 128. *See also* *names of specific governments*
psychology, 34, 35(f), 36
public housing: critiques of, 167; and end of urban renewal, 178; in Halifax, 132, 136; in Toronto, 141, 158; in Vancouver, 166, 174, 180
Pushie Commission on the Economic Prospects of Newfoundland and Labrador, 68

Quebec government: activism of, 108; closure of towns by, 91, 96–98, 109–10, 227*n*22; creates BAEQ, 95; desire for resettlement program to be voluntary, 97, 99; funds redevelopment program, 10, 22, 95, 227*n*15; impact of Opérations Dignité on, 113, 116–18, 200; and implementation of BAEQ's plan, 109, 115
Quiet Revolution, 92–93, 95, 108, 118, 228*n*56

race and urban renewal, 124
racism: against Chinese Canadians, 166; creates conditions justifying relocation, 207; environmental, 138(f); HHRAC's plans to combat, 140, 146; home ownership and, 132; integration as not addressing, 154; against Inuit, 44; "Jewish phase" of fight against, 138; P. MacDonald on Africville resettlement and, 147; and special treatment of Africville resettlement, 25–26, 133, 135, 152; systemic, 155. *See also* discrimination
radio, 50–51, 81, 104–5
railway companies, 9
Rankin Inlet: artistic production in, 44–45, 46(f); community development in, 51; Inuit's desire to work in, 41; as overpopulated, 48–49; R. Williamson based in, 37; as segregated community, 42, 43(f); starvation and, 36, 213*n*18
Raymur Place, 166
Raynauld, André, 119
receiving communities, 67–69, 70–72, 74, 219*n*36
Red Harbour, 73–74
Redevelopment Consultative Committee (Vancouver), 26, 172–73, 174–75, 176–77, 189, 239*n*66
Regent Park, 141, 158
regional government (Quebec), 92, 104
regionalization, 8–11
rehabilitation, 36, 45, 201, 202, 213*n*25. *See also* Strathcona: rehabilitation of
relocation, approach to, 4, 5(f), 6–27. *See also* eastern Quebec; Fisheries Household Resettlement Program; Halifax; North, the; Vancouver

renters. *See* tenants
"Report of a Visit to Halifax with Particular Respect to Africville" (Rose), 121
Resettlement Committee (Newfoundland), 67, 69, 70–71, 72, 74, 81
Resettlement Division, Department of Fisheries (Newfoundland), 68–69, 75
Residential Rehabilitation Assistance Program (CMHC), 189, 202
resistance. *See* citizen engagement and participation
resource economics, 47, 48
resource harvesting and marketing program, 47–50
resources, renewable, 34, 47–50. *See also* fisheries and fishing; forestry; mining
Rimouski, 96, 111, 113, 114–15
Rivière-du-Loup, 96
Robb, A. Leslie, 77
Robb, Roberta Edgecombe, 77
Roberts, Dan, 85, 86–87
Robertson, R. Gordon, 20, 33, 53, 214*n*46
Rogers, Malcolm, 57
Rose, Albert: on Africville as issue of rights and welfare, 154; on conservatism, 145–46; criticism of urban renewal, 158; R. Grant and, 144; on segregation, 121, 141; welfare payments and, 153; work in Africville, 122, 141–43, 150
Rosell, Steven, 194–95
Rossiter, W.P., 69–70
Rostow, Walt Whitman, 14, 15, 16
Rowe, William, 59–60, 64
Rowell-Sirois Report, 9
Roy, Gilles, 114, 119
Royal Canadian Mounted Police, 19, 35
Royal Commission on Canada's Economic Prospects, 59
Rudin, Ronald, 209*n*21
Rudnicki, Walter, 34, 35–36, 184, 189, 200–3, 204–5
rural areas: modernization of, 10, 23; poverty line in, 11. *See also* eastern Quebec; Newfoundland; North
rural poverty, 12, 23
rural vs urban development, 159
Russell, Cliff, 206
Rutherford, Paul, 170–71
Rutland, Ted, 124, 125
Sacré-Coeur-Deslandes, 96, 227*n*27
Saint-Jean-Baptiste Society, 108
Saint-Jean-de-Cherbourg, 96
Saint-Octave-de-l'Avenir, 6, 96
Saint-Paulin-Dalibaire, 91, 96, 109, 197
Saint-Thomas-de-Cherbourg, 96, 98, 109
Sainte-Felicité, 114
Sainte-Paule, 109–11, 113–14, 116, 118, 119
Sauvé, Maurice, 17–18
Savoie, Donald, 66
Schumacher, E.F., 217*n*100
Scotia Square, 132
Scott, James C., 11, 147, 235*n*87
Seaview Baptist Church, 139, 234*n*58
Second World War, 32, 126–27, 128, 144
Secretary of State (Canada), 184, 199
sectarianism, 84
segregation: Halifax government's desire to address, 152; as having produced Africville, 141; HHRAC on, 140, 144, 146; history of human rights in Nova Scotia and, 145; as isolation, 125, 140; map of Africville, 123(f); P. MacDonald on, 147–48; in Rankin Inlet, 42, 43(f); Rose on, 121; Steed on, 6, 154. *See also* integration
Seldom, 84, 86
self-determination, 99, 101, 155
self-government, 53, 55, 200
self-sustainability, 33, 49–50
sending communities. *See* marginal and sending communities
settlement pattern. *See* population distribution
Shaw, Alexa, 153, 235*n*106
Shaw, Lloyd, 139, 140, 141, 235*n*106
Shewell, Hugh, 184
Simard, Jean-François, 92–93, 101
Sivertz, Bent, 19
Skeena Terrace, 166, 174
slow violence, 137, 138(f)
slum clearance. *See* urban renewal
Smallwood, Joey: as architect of modernization in Newfoundland, 66; Centralization Program of, 65; on community development, 80; on Fogo Island, 82; letters from would-be resettlers to, 70; limits on power of, 71; Newfoundlanders' subversion and, 67; on Newfoundland's birth rate, 62; on

outport Newfoundland, 21; promotes social citizenship, 8. *See also* Newfoundland government
Snowden, Donald: on Canadians' sense of community, 203–4; cooperatives and, 53, 54–55, 155, 199–200; early career of, 47–48; and power of hope, 205; promotes Northern fisheries, 49; work in Newfoundland, 58–59, 79–80, 81–83, 85–86, 87, 89–90, 202
social citizenship: in Africville, 124, 125, 126, 135, 152; barriers posed by systemic racism to, 155; defined, 7, 124; as motivation for relocation, 7–8; rights revolution and, 145; spatial justice and, 197; in Vancouver, 176
social planning, 127, 175–76
social policies and programs: to address poverty, 13–14; to address regional inequalities, 9–11; in eastern Quebec, 106; family allowance, 30, 32; federal government's increasing focus on, 32; in Newfoundland, 62–63, 73, 219*n*22; in the North, 19, 201; in Vancouver, 176; welfare, 9, 201, 202. *See also* welfare payments
social scientists: approach to, 16; role in making people and places legible, 198; work in development generally, 15; work in eastern Quebec, 95. *See also* social workers; sociologists
social security: Africville definition of, 6; development as part of, 8; as exercise of power, 197; housing as providing, 154; in Newfoundland, 63, 71, 73, 203; in the North, 34; as question of spatial justice, 7, 197; Rudnicki on need for, 202–3; urban bias of, 118–19; as way for welfare state to extend control, 199
social teachings, Catholic, 115–16
social workers, 34, 35(f), 36, 173, 192, 195. *See also* Africville: social workers in
Société d'exploitation des ressources de la Vallée (SERV), 117
sociétés d'exploitation des ressources, 117–18
sociologists: Africville and, 143, 153; on social citizenship, 124; work in eastern Quebec, 104; work in Newfoundland, 21, 61, 76–78, 152; work with urban planners, 127
Soon, Fred, 168
spatial justice, 7, 120, 125, 140, 144, 197
Special Planning Secretariat (SPS), Privy Council, 13–14, 201, 202
Special Senate Committee on Poverty, 14, 210*n*34
Speth, Gus, 206
Spring Garden South (Halifax), 232*n*37
St. Brendan's, 206, 207
St. John's, 88–89
St. John's Telegram, 64
St. Malo, 99
Stanfield, Robert, 145
starvation. *See* Inuit: starvation among
Staveley, Michael, 66
Steed, Leon, 6, 7, 121, 122, 154, 203
Stephenson, Gordon: on Africville as indictment of society, 8, 148; on Africvillers' indigeneity, 143; area studied by, 130, 131(f); background of, 129, 161; hired by Halifax government, 122, 129, 130; humanitarianism of, 163; recommendations of, 126, 132, 133(f), 135, 232*n*31; timeline of plan by, 162
Stevenson, David, 42, 44
Stoney Nation, 204
Story of the Up Top (film), 85
Strathcona: approach to, 25, 26–27, 160; boundaries of, 237*n*28; community development in, 179, 191, 192(f), 195; and end of urban renewal, 178; exodus of Chinese Canadians from, 174; literature on, 159–60; Marsh report on, 165, 176, 194; number of people in, 167; photos of, 164(f); planned phases of development in, 165(f), 166; pre-SPOTA resistance to redevelopment of, 166–69; rehabilitation of, 27, 178, 185–87, 188(f), 189, 190–91, 193–94, 195–96, 202; similarities with Africville, 157–58; social security in, 203. *See also* Vancouver
Strathcona Area Council, 167–68, 169
Strathcona Property Owners and Tenants Association (SPOTA), 178–96; approach to, 166; capacity building by, 185; community development and, 199; creation of, 178; creation of political subjects by, 195–96; empowerment of, 190–95; as experts, 198; federal government's willingness to listen to, 26–27; as fourth

level of government, 158, 192, 193; keys to success of, 179; literature on, 160, 180–81, 189–90, 193; photos of, 180(f); reasons for politicians' interest in, 180–85, 190; roles and responsibilities in rehabilitation project, 186–89, 193–94
Strathcona Rehabilitation Committee (SRC), 26, 27, 187–89, 193, 194
Strathcona residents: citizen engagement of, 25, 26, 157, 166–69, 173–74, 176; compensation for, 168, 175; culture of poverty among, 198; hope and, 206; interviews with, 6, 168. *See also* Chan, Shirley; Strathcona Property Owners and Tenants Association (SPOTA)
Strathcona School, 167, 173
Strathcona Working Committee, 186, 187, 193
Students for a Democratic Society, 182
Subcommittee on Housing and Community Planning (Canada), 128
Suderman, David, 12–13
Suluk, Thomas, 55
sustainable development, 110–11, 113–14, 117, 118
Sutton Brown, Gerald: background of, 161; and federal government's model of citizen engagement, 181; hired by Vancouver government, 170, 171; ignores social concerns in planning, 163; power of, 172, 239*n*58; response to Chinese community's concerns, 169–70, 173–74; on social planning, 175, 179; on Strathcona's rehabilitation, 186; on Town Planning Commission, 177, 240*n*80

Task Force on Housing and Urban Development. *See* Federal Task Force on Housing and Urban Development
task forces and policy making, 181–82
Technical Planning Board (Vancouver), 171
technocrats, 101
Télé-Clubs, 105, 107
television, 81, 87, 105, 107
Témiscouata, 111, 113
tenants: of Africville after resettlement, 153; compensation given to Africville, 150, 151(t); in Halifax, 135–36, 169; in Vancouver, 167, 169, 175, 186
Tennant, Paul, 171
Tennessee Valley Authority, 92
territorial planning, 100
Tétrault, André, 100
thematic apperception test, 34, 35(f)
This Rock within the Sea (Mowat and de Visser), 3, 4
Thompson, E.P., 6
Three Wise Men, 114
Tignish, 87
Tompkins, Jimmy, 53
Toronto, 141
tourism, 169
Town Planning Commission (TPC; Vancouver), 171, 177, 240*n*80
Town Planning Institute of Canada, 126
transportation agreements, 9
Trinité-des-Monts, 111
Trudeau, Pierre: appoints Chrétien, 19; and funding for moderate black organizations, 155; as one of Three Wise Men, 114; on the "right to a good life," 8, 124; supports participatory democracy, 26, 183; task forces increasingly used under, 181; vision of just society, 115, 182
Tungsten, 41
Turner, John, 13
Turner, Nancy, 63

Ukrainian Canadians, 173
unemployment rates, 11, 61, 94
Uniacke Square, 146, 232*n*37
Union des cultivateurs catholiques, 110
United Nations, 14, 16, 17–18, 50, 79
United States: black activism in, 144–45, 154, 155; critics of urban renewal in, 146; international development initiatives of, 15–16; military personnel in Newfoundland, 65; municipal governments, 172, 239*n*58; poverty in, 12, 13–14
universality, 7, 9, 33, 209*n*18
universities: approach to, 16; on citizen participation as means of empowerment, 18; critics of urban renewal in, 158; Snowden's work for, 204; work in development generally, 15; work in Halifax, 129, 141, 143, 152–53; work in Vancouver's East End, 24. *See also* Extension Department, Memorial University; Institute of Social and

Economic Research (ISER), Memorial University; Laval University
University of British Columbia, 24
University of Toronto, 129, 141, 158
Untel, Frère (Brother Anonymous), 104–5, 228*n*56
urban areas, poverty line in, 11. *See also* Halifax; Vancouver
urban bias, 23, 118–19, 122
urban planners: in Halifax, 122, 124; job of, 127; power of, 170, 172; role in making people and places legible, 198; skills of, 171; in Vancouver, 158. *See also* Stephenson, Gordon; Sutton Brown, Gerald
urban planning, 126–28, 159
urban poverty: in Africville, 137, 138(f); CMHC's role in addressing, 10, 128; governments' attempts to alleviate, 23–24, 122; HHRAC and, 146; of Indigenous peoples, 207; integration as not addressing, 154; invisibility of, 12; as question of spatial justice, 120
urban renewal: as act of spatial justice, 125; criticism of, 146, 158, 159, 177, 190, 234*n*83; defined, 128–29, 231*n*18; end of, 178, 186; as expert driven, 25; freeze on, 185; motivations for, 10, 23–24. *See also* Africville; Halifax; Strathcona; Strathcona Property Owners and Tenants Association (SPOTA); Vancouver
Urban Renewal and Public Housing Division (CMHC), 190
Urban Renewal Research Seminar, 158
Urban Renewal seminar (CMHC), 173
Urban Renewal Subcommittee (Vancouver), 240*n*80
urban-reform movement, 170–71
urbanization, 61, 64, 207

Vancouver: areas targeted for redevelopment in, 162, 163(f), 164; CMHC funding given to projects in, 10, 158; community development in, 175–76; East End of, 24, 157–58, 160, 173, 176 (*see also* East End Survey Area); legibility of, 198; numbers of people relocated in, 162, 165–66; social workers in, 173, 192, 195; urban planners' power in, 170; urban renewal in Halifax vs, 161, 162. *See also* Strathcona
Vancouver government: changes in structure of, 171–72, 239*n*58; compensation offered to Strathcona residents by, 168; Graham's work for, 158–59; model of citizen engagement embraced by, 26, 172–75, 176–77, 239*n*66, 240*n*80; obligations under National Housing Act, 169; role in Strathcona's rehabilitation, 27, 186–87, 189, 193–94; on SPOTA, 190–91, 193. *See also names of specific departments;* Sutton Brown, Gerald
Vancouver Redevelopment Study, 161(f), 162, 163–64, 166
Vancouver Sun, 157
Visser, John de, 3, 4
Voice of Women, 139

Wadel, Cato, 78, 87
Wai, Joe, 192
Walker, James W. St. G., 138
Wallerstein, Immanuel, 16
War on Poverty, 12, 13–14, 50, 80, 81, 201
Weaver, Sally M., 182
Webb, Jeff, 76
Wedderburn, H.A.J. "Gus," 139–40, 142, 145, 149, 197
Welfare Division, Department of Northern Affairs and National Resources, 50, 202
welfare payments: to Africvillers, 137, 150, 151(t)–152(t), 153; to Newfoundlanders, 82, 83, 85; to Vancouver residents, 164
welfare policies, 9, 201, 202
welfare state. *See* federal government; *names of specific provincial and municipal governments;* social policies and programs
Wells, Robert, 59–60, 75(f)
Wensley, Gordon, 51–52
Whale Cove, 49
Wherry, Kenneth, 15
Whitaker, Ian, 68
white papers, 88, 90
white people, 35–36, 139, 140, 155
wildlife management, 47–48
Williams Harbour, 206
Williamson, Robert G.: career trajectory of, 37; doctoral research of, 214*n*41; and power of hope, 205; as progressive, 200; work in the North, 38–41, 44, 51–52
Williamson, Tony, 79–80, 87, 88, 89–90
Withers, George, 73

Women's Christian Temperance Union, 241*n*89
Wong, W.P., 167
Wright, Miriam, 58
Yellowknife, 41, 42, 44
Yen, Ng Jung, 168, 175